WITHDRAWN

ENCYCLOPEDIA OF POLITICAL ANARCHY

ENCYCLOPEDIA OF POLITICAL ANARCHY

Kathlyn Gay
and Martin K. Gay

ABC-CLIO

Santa Barbara, California
Denver, Colorado
Oxford, England

Library of Congress Cataloging-in-Publication Data
Gay, Kathlyn.
Encyclopedia of political anarchy / Kathlyn Gay and Martin K. Gay.
p. cm.
Includes bibliographical references.
ISBN 0-87436-982-7 (alk. paper)
1. Anarchists—Biography. 2. Anarchism—Encyclopedias. I. Gay, Martin, 1950– . II. Title.
HX830.G39 1999
320.5'7'0922—dc21
[B] 99-17551
CIP

05 04 03 02 01 00 99 98 10 9 8 7 6 5 4 3 2 1

ABC-CLIO, Inc.
130 Cremona Drive, P.O. Box 1911
Santa Barbara, California 93116-1911

This book is printed on acid-free paper ♾.

Manufactured in the United States of America

CONTENTS

PREFACE

Anarchy is perhaps history's most misunderstood social movement, primarily because adherents oppose authority of any kind; thus they have been stereotyped as people who foster disorder, lawlessness, terrorism, and irrational violence. However, most anarchists are convinced that people can live peacefully and cooperatively; they have searched for ways to develop a society based upon consensus rather than hierarchical structures and the rule of force. Since the eighteenth century, great writers have often sacrificed comfortable lives, positions of high esteem, the love of family and friends, and personal safety to sow the seeds and nurture the growth of an economic, political, and moral construct they believed would lead to a more perfect life for the masses of humanity.

This is a reference book for the curious student and the interested scholar. It is written by two people who, while not anarchist by any standard, became enthralled with the notions and plain old common sense of the philosophy when we wrote a biography of America's most famous anarchist, Emma Goldman. Our intent was to research the subject from the point of view of outsiders in order to answer the most basic questions. Who were the early catalysts of thought and action? Who are the more recent key players in anarchist circles? What are the core terminologies? Is there an anarchist orthodoxy? Is it possible to identify trends and critical events that altered the development of anarchism? What organizations are important in the promulgation of the anarchist ideal? How do recent militia and libertarian movements interface with anarchist traditions? And what about communism? These and other questions then served as the organizing structure for the inquiry, and their answers the de facto criteria for inclusion of various entries.

Our goal is to provide a concise reference resource for others who are fascinated by the possibilities manifested in the actions, the dreams, the writings, and the people who influenced anarchism. The authors hope that readers will be inspired to further their study of this most interesting subject, to read the rationales and the arguments for reinventing our communal lives based on the tenets of liberty, equality, and mutual aid. The comprehensive bibliography points to pertinent texts and resources on anarchism, libertarianism, and leftist and socialist politics as do the references at the end of each entry.

The Encyclopedia of Political Anarchy is the only recent encyclopedic work that has focused solely on anarchism. As such, it should prove to be a useful tool for those seeking information on a wide variety of people and events representing anarchism and anarchists around the globe. Beyond this more common use, the novice seeking a basic overview of the subject and its history might do well to start with *Abrams v. United States,* then proceed along whatever path that might be directed by whimsy or scholarly imperative to eventually reach the final entry, Zeno, who was, as the gods of chaos might have ordained, actually the first anarchist.

Martin K. Gay

INTRODUCTION

"anarchism, n. 1. a. the political theory that all systems of government and law are harmful. Believers in anarchism think that all such systems prevent individuals from reaching their greatest development. b. the practice or support of this belief. 2. terrorism; lawlessness"

—*The World Book Dictionary*

Mention the word "anarchism" to almost any group of individuals, and typically they will know only the secondary definition as presented in the dictionary entry above: chaos, upheaval, terror, murder, and a society run amok because it is not controlled. The relatively small number of persons who call themselves anarchists today are not surprised that the philosophical theories and the substantial body of writings, though well developed and reasoned by virtually any standard, are given short shrift in modern society. Anarchist thought is a threat to the status quo. And that, of course, is the intent.

Anarchism also is such a diverse way of thinking that no simple slogan or political philosophy defines it. "In fact," writes Liz Highleyman for the now-defunct Black Rose anarchist group in Boston, Massachusetts, "if you ask 10 anarchists for their description of anarchism, you are likely to get 10 different answers. Anarchism is more than just a political philosophy; it is a way of life that encompasses political, pragmatic and personal aspects" (Liz A. Highleyman, "An Introduction to Anarchism," 1988, on the internet <http://www.fortunecity.com/boozers/ship/247/intro.htm>).

Anarchist historian Rudolf Rocker explained that

> anarchist ideas are to be found in every period of known history. . . . We encounter them in the Chinese sage, Lao-Tse (*The Course* and *The Right Way*) and in the later Greek philosophers, the Hedonists and Cynics and other advocates of so-called "natural right," and in particular in Zeno who, at the opposite pole from Plato, founded the Stoic school. They found expression in the teaching of the Gnostic, Karpocrates, in Alexandria, and had an unmistakable influence on certain Christian sects of the Middle Ages in France, Germany and Holland, almost all of which fell victims to the most savage persecutions. (Rudolf Rocker, "History of Anarchist Philosophy from Lao-Tse to Kropotkin," on the internet <http://www.geocities.com/Athens/Parthenon/3626/works.html>)

Some early European Christians also practiced a form of anarchy, protesting the oppressive power of the established church and forming a movement known as the Free Spirit during the 1200s and 1300s. These rebels considered the state unjust and evil and declared that individuals should be free of civil laws, answering only to their God and their conscience.

Various groups of Christian dissidents called "pietists," and now sometimes referred to as religious or Christian anarchists, left Germany during the 1700s and 1800s to live in comparative freedom in North America. Anabaptists immigrated from Germany and nearby Moravia (now part of the Czech Republic), Switzerland, and the Netherlands. Among the Anabaptist groups were those who formed the Moravian Church, the Amish (sometimes known as the Plain People because of their plain dress, separation from the rest of the world, and nontechnological way of life), Mennonites, and Hutterites. These German-speaking people opposed government restrictions on individuals, refused to pay taxes, and would not fight in wars. They believed that God directly guided their behavior and religious practices, and they would not submit to any religious authority. As a result, established churches, along with government officials, tried to crush them. They were often imprisoned, publicly flogged, and tortured.

Anarchism as a political theory was first conceived in the writings of William Godwin in response to the oppressive tactics of King George and the Church of England during the war with the American colonies in the eighteenth century. Since that time, anarchism has held that the rights of the individual and innate common sense are the paramount organizational force of a just society. This theory, when taken to its logical conclusion, is a call for a revolutionary change in the way people organize themselves amongst their neighbors.

Traditional hierarchical government structures, the top-down paradigm, strips the common person of his or her individual power and holds him or her in a subordinate role as a pawn of the state. Later anarchist philosophers such as Pierre-Joseph Proudhon, Mikhail Bakunin, and Peter Kropotkin further developed threads of this theory in regard to the way the state and the ruling capitalist powerbrokers act in collusion to institutionalize and codify political and socioeconomic systems that benefit the few at the expense of the many. This situation creates an "unnatural" order, with those in the bottom strata hating those in the top and forcing the small percentage of elites to distrust those who are the basis of their wealth.

During the nineteenth century, totalitarian governments used the "big stick" to keep their citizens in line, and revolutionary actions, often led by anarchist sympathizers, were widespread throughout the world. When the French Revolution, the subsequent Paris Commune of 1871, and various uprisings in other European capitals failed to produce significant changes in conditions for the working class, individual anarchists responded with violent actions. Although these activities over a two-decade period were not coordinated by any central committee, the aggregate incidents have come to be known as the era of propaganda by deed. Anarchism's "greatest moments" came about during the Russian Revolution of 1917, declares professor Paul Avrich. That was the "first occasion when anarchists attempted to put their theories into practice on a broad scale. By means of 'direct action'—expropriation, workers' control, guerrilla warfare, free communes—they endeavoured to build a new society on libertarian lines and to make their stateless vision a reality" (Paul Avrich, ed., *The Anarchists in the Russian Revolution,* Ithaca: Cornell University Press, 1973).

Our modern negative connotations regarding anarchism stem from reports of this time. The image of the bearded, unkempt, wild man tossing a bomb into a street crowded with innocent bystanders does have a basis in historical fact. In the United States, dozens of terrorist incidents were documented in the twenty years between the end of the eighteenth and beginning of the nineteenth centuries. Most of these were initiated by lone men or small groups, frustrated by what they saw as further consolidation of power between capitalists and governments established to keep them in their places. The shooting of Henry Clay Frick of the Homestead Steelworks by Alexander Berkman was typical of these acts. Berkman expected a general uprising to follow in the wake of his symbolic attack against one of the most repressive industrialists of the time. The fact that no civil unrest resulted and Berkman was sent to prison as just another mad anarchist speaks to the reality of the situation: the overwhelming majority of the working class, though poor and abused, accepted its role in society as defined by the state.

In today's society, the working class still accepts the role that the state in alliance with capitalism defines, according to the British-based Anarchist Communist Federation (ACF). The ACF contends that the grip of capitalism (with the support of the state) is so strong and so widespread around the globe that the working class is continually exploited:

> The state is mainly a system of organised violence to maintain the domination of the capitalist ruling class. However, order is best achieved through people's consent, rather than naked force. As a result, the modern state contains elements that are concerned with trying to make us think in certain ways and act as obedient citizens. (Anarchist Communist Federation, *As We See It* (pamphlet), on the internet <http:// burn.ucsd.edu/~acf/ace/aswecit.html>)

Noam Chomsky, perhaps the world's most articulate dissident and radical philosopher alive, observes how the modern democratic state has moved away from the big stick to embrace the "big lie." In the 1992 documentary "Manufacturing Consent" (Necessary Illusions Productions, Canada), Professor Chomsky notes that "propaganda is to democracy what violence is to a dictatorship." Once citizens were allowed to participate in their own governance through the vote, it was not long before the state was compelled to develop mechanisms that created "necessary illusions" with the result being "lives entangled in webs of endless deceit." He explains that manufacturing consent is "a revolution in the practice of democracy . . . a technique of control . . . useful and necessary because the common interests, the general concerns of all the people, elude the public. The public just isn't up to dealing with them. They [general concerns] have to be the domain of . . . a specialized class." His belief is that although it would seem that "indoctrination is inconsistent with democracy," in the real world of the new millennium, "it is the essence."

It is clear to Noam Chomsky that the "myths" about the way our society is organized and the "misunderstandings" regarding radical thought and anarchist philosophy are necessary constructs of a hierarchical power structure made up of corporate interests, a complacent and cooperative government, and an intellectual class that has been duped into perpetuating the status quo. In societies where the Western-style representative system has not been embraced, some would argue that those same myths have been applied to the concept of democracy. Those in power, regardless of how they got there or how they maintain the hierarchy that keeps them there, have an obvious interest in demonizing the enemies.

Anarchists say that Chomsky's notion of indoctrination as the essence of modern democracy does not have to be the case. Regardless of how they identify themselves (libertarian-socialist, anarcho-syndicalist, individualist, anarcha-feminist, anarchist-communist, etc.) or what they believe about the need to own the means of production, destroy the current power structure, or establish cooperative groups, anarchists insist that society must be based on three immutable principles. These are "liberty," "equality," and "mutual aid." Left to their own devices, human beings will seek to live honest lives in harmony and cooperation with those around them. The natural order, if allowed to play out, would bring about free association of like-minded individuals in multitudes of communal groupings small and large. These associations might come and go, expand and contract, as needed, without a hierarchical (oppressive) power structure.

"Liberty is essential for the full flowering of human intelligence, creativity, and dignity," notes a statement on an anarchy website. "To be dominated by another is to be denied the chance to think and act for oneself, which is the only way to grow and develop one's individuality. Domination also stifles innovation and personal responsibility, leading to conformity and mediocrity. Thus the society that maximizes the growth of individuality will necessarily be based on voluntary association, not coercion and authority." ("What Does Anarchism Stand For?" FAQ section A2, on the internet at <http://www.geocities.com/CapitolHill/1931/secA2.html>)

Although many anarchists are idealists, they are not crazed zealots. They are not in favor of a society where "anything goes" and chaos prevails. Would-be assassin Alexander Berkman explained it like this:

> I've heard that anarchists don't believe in organisation. I imagine that you have, but that's an old argument. Any one who tells you that anarchists don't believe in organisation is talking nonsense. Organisation is everything, and everything is organisation. The whole of life is organisation, conscious or unconscious. Every nation, every family, why, even every individual is an organisation or organism. Every part of every living thing is organised in such a manner that the whole works in harmony. Otherwise the different organs could not function properly and life could not exist. ("Alexander Berkman Quotations" on the internet <http://www. spunk.org/library/quotes/ sp000094.txt>)

Anarchists are not all terrorists, though some (such as Christians, capitalists, Jews, policemen, Muslims, etc.) have used terror and violence to make their point. They are not of one mind. They are the original socialists, but they are not necessarily communists. They are the original libertarians, but they are not the Libertarian Party. They are mothers and fathers, sons and daughters. They have remarkably little chance of seeing their ideas gain acceptance in this or any time, but that does not make them any less compelling. In fact, countless individuals attempt to live by anarchist and/or libertarian principles of freedom with responsibility and search for truth in their own way without ever calling themselves anarchists. Just two examples are legendary writers George Seldes and I. F. Stone, who did not accept the "gospel" of any institution—governmental, religious, or otherwise. "Like all great ideas, anarchism is pretty simple when you get down to it—human beings are at their best when they are living free of authority, deciding things among themselves rather than being ordered about" (Harper, vii). This book was not written in defense of anarchist philosophy or to canonize its supporters and outspoken leaders. It was written for the interested reader who is still open enough to see the possibilities that lay behind the desperate actions and heroic sacrifices of a few women and men who believed all people are entitled to a life that could evolve to its fullest potential.

A

Abrams v. United States

The U.S. government's prosecution of Jacob Abrams is considered by some historians to be a flagrant violation of civil rights. Ultimately it led to the important U.S. Supreme Court case of *Abrams v. United States.* Abrams was a member of a Harlem anarchist group of Eastern European Jews who during World War I secretly published antiwar materials. They were opposed to U.S. intervention in Soviet Russia during the spring and summer of 1918, viewing such intervention as a counterrevolutionary maneuver. In their leaflets, they urged American as well as Russian workers to launch a general strike to prevent the Russian Revolution from being crushed. Abrams and his comrades, including his wife, Mary, and the well-known anarchist militant Molly Steimer, were arrested for violating the Espionage Act of 1917, as amended in 1918. Abrams and others were brutally beaten while being transported to or held in prison, and during trial one of the defendants died.

The judge in the Abrams case was openly prejudiced against the defendants and "mocked and humiliated them at every turn" (Bluestein 1983: 7). Their lawyer contended that the Espionage Act was meant to penalize activities that hindered U.S. war efforts against the Germans and that the defendants were not opposing the conflict with Germany but instead the intervention in Russia. Nearly every defense argument was thrown out. Abrams and four others were convicted under the Espionage Act and its amendment, the Sedition Act of 1918, for distributing leaflets that criticized the U.S. military. Three men, including Abrams, were sentenced to 20 years in prison; Mollie Steimer was sentenced to fifteen years. "The barbarity of the sentences for the mere distribution of leaflets shocked liberals and radicals alike. A group of faculty members at the Harvard Law School . . . protested that the defendants had been convicted solely for advocating nonintervention in the affairs of another nation, in short, for exercising the [First Amendment] right of free speech" (Bluestein, 9).

The case was appealed to the U.S. Supreme Court, which upheld the convictions, declaring that each defendant had conspired "when the United States was at war with the Imperial German Government, unlawfully and willfully, by utterance, writing, printing and publication, to urge, incite and advocate curtailment of production of things and products, to-wit, ordnance and ammunition, necessary and essential to the prosecution of the war"(see majority opinion in *Abrams v. United States*).

Justices Oliver Wendell Holmes and Louis Brandeis dissented. In his dissent, Holmes pointed out that the leaflets used to convict did not in any way show intent to hinder U.S. war efforts. He wrote that "sentences of twenty years' imprisonment have been imposed for the publishing of two leaflets that I believe the defendants had as much right to publish as the Government has to publish the Constitution of the United States." Invoking the First Amendment right to free speech, Holmes stated:

> The principle of the right to free speech is always the same. It is only the present danger of immediate evil or an intent to bring it about that warrants Congress in setting a limit to the expression of opinion where

> private rights are not concerned. Congress certainly cannot forbid all effort to change the mind of the country. Now nobody can suppose that the surreptitious publishing of a silly leaflet by an unknown man, without more, would present any immediate danger that its opinions would hinder the success of the government arms or have any appreciable tendency to do so. (U.S. Supreme Court)

Holmes concluded "the defendants were deprived of their rights under the Constitution of the United States." Justice Brandeis concurred with Holmes, and the Holmes-Brandeis dissent marked the beginning of modern theory about First Amendment rights, offering a standard that speech could not be punished unless it presented "a clear and present danger" of imminent harm (American Civil Liberties Union).

References

American Civil Liberties Union, "Briefing Paper Number 10," on the internet <http://www.aclufl.org/ pbp10.htm>.

Avrich, Paul, *Anarchist Portraits* (Princeton: Princeton University Press, 1988).

Bluestein, Abe, ed., *Fighters for Anarchism: Mollie Steimer and Senya Fleshin, a Memorial Volume* (Minneapolis, MN: Libertarian Publications Group, 1983).

U.S. Supreme Court, *Abrams v. United States,* available on the internet at <http://www.bc.edu/cgi-bin/print_hit_bold.cgi/bc_org/avp/cas/comm/free_speech/abrams.html>

Alien and Sedition Acts of 1798

In 1798, the U.S. Congress, dominated by the Federalist Party, passed four separate laws that together became known as the Alien and Sedition Acts of 1798. The legislation was designed to suppress activities and exclude aliens thought to be dangerous to the nation. The acts set the precedent for later legislation that sought to prevent radicals from entering the United States or to expel them altogether.

The Alien and Sedition Acts were passed because the United States was on the verge of war with France, and Federalists believed that the French would achieve victory if dissidents within the United States were able to campaign against U.S. military efforts. The laws were designed to suppress aliens who were thought to be sympathetic to the French cause. For example, the Naturalization Act required aliens to reside in the United States for five to 14 years before they could become citizens, and the Alien Act and Alien Enemies Act allowed the president to deport noncitizens if he considered them a danger to U.S. safety. The Sedition Act forbade anyone to write, print, utter, or publish, or cause anyone to

> knowingly or willingly assist or aid in writing, printing, uttering or publishing any false, scandalous and malicious writing or writings against the government of the United States, or either house of the Congress of the United States, or the President of the United States, with intent to defame the said government, or either house of the said Congress, or the said President, or to bring them, or either of them, into contempt or disrepute; or to excite against them, or either or any of them, the hatred of the good people of the United States, or to excite any unlawful combinations therein, for opposing or resisting any law of the United States, or any act of the President of the United States, done in pursuance of any such law, or of the powers in him vested by the constitution of the United States, or to resist, oppose, or defeat any such law or act, or to aid, encourage or abet any hostile designs of any foreign nation against the United States, their people or government. (U.S. Statutes)

The Sedition Act was vague, enough so that Federalists used it to suppress Republican opponents who criticized the government, thereby violating their First Amendment right of free speech. There were ten convictions under this law—all Republicans—but within two years the Alien and Sedition Acts had expired or were repealed. However, seditious libel was part of U.S. laws for more than 170 years.

As the American Civil Liberties Union (ACLU) has stated,

> Throughout the 19th century and much of the 20th, federal and state sedition, criminal anarchy and criminal conspiracy laws were used repeatedly to suppress expression by slavery abolitionists, religious minorities, early feminists, labor organizers, pacifists and left-wing political radicals. For example, prior to the Civil War every Southern state passed laws limiting speech in an attempt to stifle criticism of slavery. In Virginia, anyone who "by speaking or writing maintains that owners have no right of property in slaves" was subject to a one-year prison sentence. (ACLU)

See also
Antianarchist Laws (United States)

References

"Alien and Sedition Acts," *Britannica Online* <http://www.eb.com:180/cgi-bin/g?DocF=micro/15/47.html>.

American Civil Liberties Union, "Briefing Paper Number 10," on the internet <http://www.aclufl.org/pbp10.htm>.

Preston, William Jr., *Aliens and Dissenters: Federal Suppression of Radicals, 1903–1933,* 2d ed. (Urbana and Chicago: University of Illinois Press, 1994).

The Sedition Act of July 14, 1798, U.S. Statutes at Large, vol. 1, 596–597.

Altgeld, John Peter

See Haymarket Affair; Haymarket Anarchists

American Antigovernment Extremists (1980s, 1990s)

They are known by a variety of names, such as "patriots," "common-law separatists," "freemen," "citizen governments," and dozens of other titles, but they all have one thing in common: They are antigovernment ideologues with a great predilection for violence. Although their antigovernment stance seems similar to the philosophy espoused by anarchists, these groups have little in common with anarchists, who argue for individual freedom and self-government and are convinced that a voluntary, cooperative society can replace a hierarchical order. In contrast, American extremists, who frequently organize and train in military style, are bent on taking over government at the local, state, and national levels. They believe in an authoritarian rule that they themselves establish.

American antigovernment extremists of the 1980s and 1990s are, for the most part, right-wing militants who oppose—often violently—a pluralistic way of life. Many are part of the so-called patriot movement and its armed wing, paramilitary groups or private armies, which are illegal under U.S. law. The patriot movement comprises numerous hate groups such as the Ku Klux Klan, neo-Nazis, the Christian Identity church, and Posse Comitatus.

Militant patriots share a conviction that federal and state officials are conspiring to disarm ordinary Americans in preparation for a "one world order," basing their ideas on the myth of a Jewish conspiracy. That myth, which has been passed down for centuries, stems from a bogus manuscript entitled *The Protocols of the Learned Elders of Zion,* which was written by members of the Russian secret police during the 1890s and is actually a forgery of an earlier publication—a satire on the French dictator Napoleon III. In *The Protocols,* the authors falsely claimed that a Jewish council planned to destroy Christianity and control the world.

Some of the most malicious patriots are members of the Christian Identity church. They follow an openly racist and anti-Semitic ideology, which teaches that Aryans are the chosen people described in the Christian Bible, that people of color are subhuman, and that Jews are descendants of Satan. They say that the promises made to the nation of Israel were meant for the British and the Americans. Calling themselves "true Israelites," they claim that America is their promised land. Using different names for their groups, Christian Identity believers promote paramilitary activities and armed militias to accomplish their mission, which is to destroy people who are not true Israelites.

Since the beginning of the 1990s, militant antigovernment extremists have committed terrorist acts that include arson, bombings, sabotage of railroad lines, bank robberies, physical assaults, and desecrating places of worship. The bombing of the federal building in Oklahoma City in 1995 is the most notorious example of actions by so-called patriots, though evidence of a wider conspiracy in that terrorist act is lacking.

Right-wing extremists have also used another tactic against government institutions. They have created "common law courts," which began with a racist and anti-Semitic group known as Posse Comitatus, a Latin term for "power of the county." Posse advocates believe they have the right to organize local governments and claim to be "sovereign citizens." They contend that their natural and God-given rights exempt them from any legally established federal or state authority in the United States.

Advocates also claim that common law covers only white citizens, or "organic sovereigns" as they are sometimes known. According to Posse interpretation, only the U.S. Constitution and the Bill of Rights are valid; thus, so-called Fourteenth Amendment citizens—blacks and others protected by that amendment—do not have the same inalienable rights guaranteed by the original Constitution and its first ten amendments. As "sovereign citizens," common law advocates set up their own courts and citizen juries that they say have the force of law, even though these courts are not valid in the U.S. legal structure. Since 1994, common law courts have been set up in more than thirty states.

In addition, Posse or common law advocates initiate "paper attacks" against federal and state officials and other enemies. Whereas legitimate liens allow creditors to take property in payment for a debt, common law claims are bogus. Yet they can cause a great deal of frustration, sometimes damaging a person's credit. Some Posse adherents have committed armed robbery and issued bad checks and counterfeit money orders worth millions to support their cause. They use phony checks to pay off loans or they refuse to pay debts, which they say they do not owe, deliberately swindling corporations and public agencies. They insist loans are based on agreements that are not legally binding.

One common law group known as the Montana Freemen came to public attention in 1996, when members were involved in a tense standoff with agents of the Federal Bureau of Investigation (FBI). Several years before this standoff, the Freemen, claiming to be sovereign citizens, set up their own government with their own common law courts, laws, and monetary system. In 1994, the Freemen began stockpiling weapons, food, and other items on a 960-acre wheat and sheep ranch near Jordan, Montana. By the time the FBI surrounded the compound—called Justus Township—in March 1996, others who called themselves Freemen, including women and children, had joined the group. They lived in several buildings and refused to leave land that had been lost to a bank foreclosure. After 81 days, 16 Freemen surrendered to federal agents, ending a potentially explosive situation. Leaders were arrested for conspiracy to impede government function and to prevent a U.S. district judge, a court clerk, and a county sheriff from carrying out their official duties. In addition, the men were charged with threats to kidnap and murder the judge and faced indictments on fraud and other charges.

To counteract such incidents and the multimillion-dollar swindles and bogus liens filed by common law promoters, more than half the states by 1998 had passed or were considering laws to ban common law court activities. In addition, authorities nationwide have made numerous arrests of right-wing terrorists and have broken up alleged plots for bombings and assassinations. Yet those who track antigovernment extremist groups do not expect the violence or terrorist attempts to end, particularly since many extremists believe that a race war will break out in the year 2000.

References

Coates, James, *Armed and Dangerous: The Rise of the Survivalist Right* (New York: Hill and Wang, 1987).

Corcoran, James, *Bitter Harvest: The Birth of Paramilitary Terrorism in the Heartland* (New York: Viking Penguin, 1995).

Dees, Morris, with James Corcoran, *Gathering Storm: America's Militia Threat* (New York: HarperCollins, 1996).

George, John, *Nazis, Communists, Klansmen, and Others on the Fringe: Political Extremism in America* (Buffalo, NY: Prometheus Books, 1992).

Intelligence Report, Issue 90 (Montgomery, AL: Southern Poverty Law Center, Spring 1998).
Stern, Kenneth S., *A Force Upon the Plain: The American Militia Movement and the Politics of Hate* (New York: Simon and Schuster, 1996).

American Labor Reform League

See New England Labor Reform League

Anabaptists

Martin Luther, the German leader of the Protestant Reformation during the 1500s, called Anabaptists enemies of the movement. Since then Anabaptists have been defamed and persecuted for their anarchistic Christian beliefs.

The label *Anabaptists* comes from a German term meaning "rebaptizers," used to deride those who believed that infant baptism was not biblically condoned and that only believers should be baptized. Those who had been baptized in infancy were rebaptized as adults.

As is true today, Anabaptists of the past opposed the use of force to maintain social order and believed that church and state should be separated. These German-speaking people also opposed government restrictions on individuals, refused to pay taxes, and would not fight in wars. Since they believed that God directly guided their behavior and religious practices, they would not submit to any religious authority. As a result, wherever Anabaptists lived, the established church and government officials tried to crush them. Thousands were imprisoned, tortured, and killed. However, Anabaptists were not and are not today of one mind and philosophy. According to anarchist historian James Joll, Anabaptist groups

> included a wide variety of doctrines and temperaments among their adherents. Some were violent revolutionaries, some tranquil and puritanical quietists. Some believed in practical revolutionary action; others preferred . . . to withdraw from this world and its ways and to place their hopes in the next. All of them, however, agreed in denying the necessity of the state. Since the baptized were in direct contact with God, all further intermediaries were unnecessary, indeed evil, since they stood between man and the divine light that was in him and which would direct him how to order his life. (Joll, 24)

During the 1700s and 1800s, Anabaptists emigrated to the United States from Germany and nearby Moravia (now part of the Czech Republic), Switzerland, and the Netherlands. Among the Anabaptist groups were those who formed the Moravian Church, the Amish (sometimes known as the Plain People because of their plain dress, separation from the rest of the world, and nontechnological way of life), Mennonites, and Hutterites.

In the mid-1800s the Hutterian Brethren, or Hutterites, established several communes in what became the states of North and South Dakota, Minnesota, and Montana. But during World War I they were severely mistreated in the United States, and some were imprisoned and brutalized because of their pacifist stance. Consequently, many moved to Canada, where Hutterite colonies survive to this day.

Although some Anabaptists shun modern industrial ways of life, others maintain communication with the world through up-to-date internet websites. One website addresses primarily the Mennonite branch of the Anabaptist movement and invites questions from users. Another is maintained by the Bruderhof, a Christian church group modeled after the earliest Christian church in Jerusalem. According to their website, members try "to live a life that is pleasing to God and of service to all humankind." They state that "for us, this means sharing all property in common, living together in communal settlements, working together to earn our living, and addressing the social problems of today through numerous projects and publications."

See also

Religious Anarchism

References

Bruderhof Home Page, on the internet <http://www1.mhv.net/~Bruderhof/homepage.htm>.

Gay, Kathlyn, *Communes and Cults* (New York: Twenty-First Century Books/Holt, 1997).
Joll, James, *The Anarchists* (Boston: Little, Brown, 1964).

Anarcha-Feminism

The anarchist belief in individual liberty that does not infringe on the rights of another's freedom has attracted many women to anarchism. As anarcha-feminist writer Elaine Leeder states: "The anarchist tradition of direct resistance to authority, the belief in direct action such as strikes, boycotts and other confrontations with those in power, the conviction that humanity is inherently good and society can change for the better are all themes found in the works of anarchist women" (Ehrlich, 1994, 142).

Anarchist women of the past, however, did not necessarily participate in the larger movement of feminists who worked for women's suffrage. Rather, anarchists such as Voltairine de Cleyre, Emma Goldman, Angela Heywood (who with husband Ezra published the anarcha-feminist paper *The Word*), and Helena Born fought for individual liberty. They were avidly opposed to patriarchal and government authority. According to historian Margaret Marsh, the ideology of anarchist-feminists of the 1800s and early 1900s

> insisted that female subordination was rooted in an obsolete system of sexual and familial relationships. Attacking marriage, often urging sexual varietism, insisting on both economic and psychological independence, and sometimes denying maternal responsibility, they argued that personal autonomy was an essential component of sexual equality, and that political and legal rights could not of themselves engender such equality. (Marsh, 5)

Even though anarchism and feminism have been closely linked for decades, the term *anarcha-feminism* stems from the feminist movement of the 1960s. During that time many feminist groups sprang up across the United States, and they were similar to anarchist groups wherever located.

Peggy Kornegger, an anarcha-feminist writer, contends that modern feminists "have been unconscious anarchists in both theory and practice for years." She argues that "we now need to be *consciously* aware of the connections between anarchism and feminism and use that framework for our thoughts and actions." This means transforming patriarchal and authoritarian societies that value such traits as aggressiveness, competitiveness, domination and exploitation to nonauthoritarian societies with such valued characteristics as compassion, cooperation, and sharing (Ehrlich, 1994, 159).

Anarchist feminists "work to end all power relationships," according to Carol Ehrlich, who makes distinctions between radical feminists, social anarchist feminists, and anarchist feminists. She points out that many radical feminists believe that a society led by women would be noncoercive, whereas social anarchists hope to build cooperative communities and redistribute the wealth from the few to the many. But Ehrlich maintains that "neither a workers' state nor a matriarchy will end the oppression of everyone. The goal, then, is not to 'seize' power, as the socialists are fond of urging, but to abolish power" (Ehrlich, 1994).

See also

Born, Helena; de Cleyre, Voltairine; Goldman, Emma; Heywood, Ezra Hervey Hoar

References

Ehrlich, Carol, "Socialism, Anarchism, and Feminism," in Howard J. Ehrlich, ed., *Reinventing Anarchy, Again* (San Francisco: AK Press, 1996).
Kornegger, Peggy, "Anarchism: The Feminist Connection," in Howard J. Ehrlich, ed., *Reinventing Anarchy, Again* (San Francisco: AK Press, 1994).
Leeder, Elaine, "Let Our Mothers Show the Way," in Howard J. Ehrlich, ed., *Reinventing Anarchy, Again* (San Francisco: AK Press, 1996).
Marsh, Margaret S., *Anarchist Women, 1870–1920* (Philadelphia: Temple University Press, 1981).

Anarchism

Anarchism stems from ideas that "are to be found in every period of known history," according to anarchist historian Rudolf Rocker. He explained that anarchism is encountered

> in the Chinese sage, Lao-Tse (*The Course* and *The Right Way*) and in the later Greek

> philosophers, the Hedonists and Cynics and other advocates of so-called "natural right," and in particular in Zeno who, at the opposite pole from Plato, founded the Stoic school. They found expression in the teaching of the Gnostic, Karpocrates, in Alexandria, and had an unmistakable influence on certain Christian sects of the Middle Ages in France, Germany and Holland, almost all of which fell victims to the most savage persecutions. (Rocker)

The term *anarchism* is based on two Greek words: *av,* meaning "absence of," and *apxn,* meaning "authority" or "government." The Greek philosopher Zeno (342–267/270 B.C.) believed that regulating a people's actions was tantamount to restraining their natural tendency to obtain perfection. Zeno declared that the state had no moral right to interfere in or dictate individual life.

William Godwin was the first person to call himself an anarchist and to use the term *anarchism.* During the early 18th century, before Godwin disseminated his ideas, the term *libertarian socialism* carried the same meaning. Today, *anarchism* is usually defined succinctly as the absence of government, or it may describe a political theory that advocates abolishing all forms of government, establishing a society based on voluntary cooperation, and association of free individuals working together to satisfy their needs. Most anarchists and libertarians (who may advocate views similar to anarchism) hold that individuals can organize society from the bottom up rather than be subjected to a hierarchical authority; people can determine what is "right" for themselves. Anarchists declare that domination destroys self-respect by forcing the individual to accept the judgment of others.

Paradoxically, anarchists also say that anarchy cannot exist without controls, which would result in chaos or tyranny. But controls are not rules and regulations set in concrete; they are decisions that reflect the consensus of the people, which in turn brings harmony.

For centuries, however, most people have presumed that they cannot live in a society without government and authority; they equate anarchy and anarchism with disorder, terrorism, and violence. Today the term *anarchism* is often used loosely in the popular media to describe radicals who advocate violence and terrorism. Certainly, some anarchists have been involved in violent acts, but many anarchists—whether known by that label or some other—have consistently argued that anarchism is not synonymous with disorder and crime. Adolph Fischer, one of the Haymarket martyrs (as a result of the 1886 Haymarket affair in Chicago, several anarchists were tried and sentenced to death for inciting a riot that led to the deaths of seven policemen and numerous citizens), pointed out before his execution that the contrary is true. In his view,

> anarchism wants to do away with the now existing social disorder, it aims at the establishment of the real—the natural—order. I think every sensible man ought to conceive, that where ruling is existing on one hand, there must be submission on the other. He who rules is a tyrant, and he who submits is a slave. Logically there can be no other outlet, because submission is the antithesis of rule. Anarchists hold that it is the natural right of every member of the human family to control ourselves. If a centralized power—government—is ruling the mass of people (no matter whether this government "represent the will of the majority of the people" or not) it is enslaving them, and [is] a direct violation of the laws of nature. (Foner, 82)

Many other anarchists before and after Fischer have presented their views about anarchism and its goals. For example, anarchism and socialism have been closely aligned, sometimes being viewed as equivalent. As Rocker noted,

> In common with the founders of socialism, Anarchists demand the abolition of all economic monopolies and the common ownership of the soil and all other means of production, the use of which must be available for all without distinction; for personal and social freedom is conceivable

> only on the basis of equal economic advantages for everybody. Within the socialist movement itself the Anarchists represent the viewpoint that the war against capitalism must be at the same time a war against all institutions of political power, for in history economic exploitation has always gone hand in hand with political and social oppression. The exploitation of man by man and the dominion of man over man are inseparable, and each is the condition of the other. (Rocker)

Although many anarchists today may share ideas with socialists, there is no official dogma or fixed theory that can be defined with simple slogans. Anarchism is continually being defined and redefined, and often there are areas of disagreement, such as whether individual needs should have priority over the needs of the community. Debates also arise over technological advances, with some ecoanarchists advocating a return to a more primitive way of life. Anarcha-feminism focuses on the liberation of women and brings together the ideals of feminism and anarchism.

Other anarchists focus on individualism and self-determination, rejecting traditional personal relationships (such as marriage and family) in favor of voluntary alternatives, such as communal living or homosexual partnerships. Some radical youth groups espouse anarchistic ideals and reject traditional society by creating collectives.

Professor Noam Chomsky, who has written numerous books and essays analyzing anarchism, pointed out in a 1996 interview that

> no one owns the term "anarchism." It is used for a wide range of different currents of thought and action, varying widely. There are many self-styled anarchists who insist, often with great passion, that theirs is the only right way, and that others do not merit the term (and maybe are criminals of one or another sort).... The ratio of such material to constructive work is depressingly high.
>
> Personally, I have no confidence in my own views about the "right way," and am unimpressed with the confident pronouncements of others, including good friends. I feel that far too little is understood to be able to say very much with any confidence. We can try to formulate our long-term visions, our goals, our ideals; and we can (and should) dedicate ourselves to working on issues of human significance. But the gap between the two is often considerable, and I rarely see any way to bridge it except at a very vague and general level. (Lane)

See also

Bakunin, Mikhail A.; Chomsky, Avram Noam; Haymarket Affair; Kropotkin, Peter Alexeyevich; Marx, Karl; Rocker, Rudolf

References

"A.1 What Is Anarchism?" (an anarchist FAQ webpage) on the internet <http://www.geocities.com/CapitolHill/1931>.

"A.2 What Does Anarchism Stand For?" (an anarchist FAQ webpage) on the internet <http://www.geocities.com/CapitolHill/1931>.

Foner, Philip S., ed., *The Autobiographies of the Haymarket Martyrs* (Atlantic Highlands, NJ: Humanities Press, 1969).

Institute for Anarchist Studies, "Why Anarchy?" on the internet <http://www.thecoo.edu/~elusk/oca/anarch.html>.

Keefer, Tom, "Marxism vs. Anarchism," *New Socialist* (March 1996).

Lane, Tom, "Chomsky on Anarchism" (December 23, 1996), on the internet <http://www.worldmedia.com/archive/interviews/9612-anarchism.html>.

Rocker, Rudolf, *Anarchism and Anarcho-Syndicalism*, Chapter 1, London: Freedom Press (1988, orig. publ. as *Anarchosyndicalism* by Martin Secker and Warburg Ltd., 1938).

Anarchist Authors

Despite government repression over the decades, anarchist writers have consistently disseminated views through newspapers, journals, pamphlets, books, and now the internet. Some of the most well-known anarchist writers of the past published their theories in book form.

One important author and forerunner of anarchist thought was Jean-Jacques Rousseau (1712–1778), "who created the climate of ideas in which anarchism was possible" (Joll, 30). Rousseau held that individuals were naturally good but were corrupted by society and the development of agriculture and industry. He argued that even though humans could not return to a natural state they could enter into a voluntary contract for collective sovereignty in which no laws could be made without the consent of the people. Rousseau's views on popular sovereignty had a major impact on French revolutionaries of the 1700s, as well as philosophers of the 1800s, such as the Russians Leo Tolstoy and Peter Kropotkin. He was the progenitor of ideas on education that were put into effect by the Spanish anarchist Francisco Ferrer and others who followed him in the modern school movement of the early 1900s.

Although not philosophers or theorists, numerous authors of the 1900s have written biographies of anarchists or books supporting anarchist movements. Among them are Paul Avrich, who is widely read, and Sam Dolgoff (1902–1994), a New York City anarchist, who wrote and edited such works as *Bakunin on Anarchy* (1972, 1980); *The Anarchist Collectives: Workers Self-Management in the Spanish Revolution, 1936–1939* (1972, 1983); *The Cuban Revolution: A Critical Perspective* (1976); *Fragments: A Memoir* (1986); and *The Relevance of Anarchism to Modern Society* (1977, 1989).

Other authors writing in English on anarchism during the 1900s include Canadian George Woodcock, British anarchist Albert Meltzer, British historian James Joll, American historian James Martin, and, in France, Daniel Guerin (1904–1988) wrote *L'Anarchisme,* which was published in 1965 and later translated into English. Twentieth-century women who have written on anarchism include not only such well-known anarchists as Emma Goldman and Voltairine de Cleyre but also more recent authors such as Wendy McElroy, L. Susan Brown, Janet Biehl, Marie Flemming, Catherine MacKinnon, Margaret Marsh, and Martha Ackelsberg.

During the 1990s, books published in English about little-known anarchists and anarchist movements have included such works as Arif Dirlik's *Anarchism in the Chinese Revolution* (1991); K. Steven Vincent's *Between Marxism and Anarchism: Benoit Malon and French Reformist Socialism* (1992); and Byron K. Marshall's translation of *The Autobiography of Osugi Sakae.*

See also

de Cleyre, Voltairine; Ferrer, Francisco y Guardia; Goldman, Emma; Kropotkin, Peter Alexeyevich; Meltzer, Albert; Modern School Movement; Osugi Sakae; Tolstoy, Count Lev (Leo) Nikolayevich; Woodcock, George

References

Joll, James, *The Anarchists* (Boston: Little, Brown, 1964).

Anarchist Black Cross

The Anarchist Black Cross (ABC) was originally known as the Anarchist Red Cross (ARC), which formed after the 1905 revolution in Russia when the tsarist police initiated countless manhunts for anarchists. Many were arrested and jailed or executed. Some were exiled and lucky enough to find refuge in Western Europe and the United States.

Anarchists in the West "lamented the fate of their comrades languishing in Russian jails or martyred on the gallows or before the firing squad" (Avrich, 113). In 1907, they organized the ARC to organize aid for political prisoners and their families and to defend themselves against political raids. Headquarters were established in New York and London, with branches in major cities in Western Europe and North America.

When the revolutions of 1917 broke out, the organization changed its name to the Black Cross in order to avoid confusion with chapters of the international Red Cross organizing relief in the country. After the Bolsheviks seized power, ABC moved to Germany but continued to aid prisoners of the Bolsheviks, as well as victims of Italian fascism and others. The famous Russian-American anarchists Emma Goldman and Alexander Berkman were among those who raised voices with ABC to protest police harassment of comrades.

During the 1940s, ABC was unable to carry on its activities because of lack of finances. However, by the end of the 1960s ABC had again resumed its work. During the 1980s ABC expanded and today reports that it has organized groups in many different regions of the world. On its website, ABC explains why it exists and the mission it hopes to accomplish:

> We believe that prisons serve no function except to preserve the ruling classes. We also believe that a free society must find alternative, effective ways of dealing with anti-social crime. But a decrease in anti-social crime is only likely to happen (and therefore prison abolition can only be a realistic option) accompanied by a dramatic change in our economic, social, and political systems. . . . We work for a stateless, cooperative/classless society free from privilege or domination based on race or gender. But it's not enough to build the grassroots movements necessary to bring about these changes in society, we must also be able to defend them. The ABC defends those who are captured and persecuted for carrying out acts on behalf of our movements. . . .
>
> The ABC aims to recognize, expose and support the struggles of prisoners in general, and of Political Prisoners and Prisoners of War in particular. . . . To some we send financial or material aid. With others we keep in contact through mail, make visits, provide political literature, and discuss strategy and tactics. We do whatever we can to prevent prisoners becoming isolated from the rest of the movement. . . . We regard prisoners as an active part of our movement and seek to maintain their past and potential contributions by acting as a link back to the continuing struggle. Increased communication between activists both inside and outside prison inspires resistance on both sides of the prison walls.

ABC says that it goes beyond prisoner support work and is committed to resisting the "organized repression of the state" wherever it exists in the world:

> In 1989 we set up an "Emergency Response Network"(ERN) to respond to political raids, crackdowns, death sentences, hunger strikes, torture or killings. . . . An ERN mobilization means ABC groups and others around the world send telegrams and phone calls, organize demonstrations or other actions within 48 hours of the network being alerted. For instance, two Greek anarchist prisoners reported to be held incommunicado and subject to torture were released from solitary confinement and allowed access to lawyers after the ERN's first mobilization brought demonstrations, calls, faxes and telegrams to Greek embassies around the world. The ABC's international network plays the one trump card grassroots movements have in our deck: solidarity. (ABC website)

See also

Berkman, Alexander; Goldman, Emma; Russian Anarchism

References

Anarchist Black Cross, "What Is the Anarchist Black Cross?" on the internet <http://www.au.spunk.anarki.net/texts/groups/anm/sp000132.txt>.

Avrich, Paul, *The Russian Anarchists* (New York: W. W. Norton, 1978).

Anarchist Communist Federation

Calling itself "an organisation of class struggle anarchists," the Anarchist Communist Federation (ACF) is an effort to abolish capitalism and "to create a free and equal society" through a working-class revolution. ACF adherents consider themselves anarchist-communists who view "society as being divided into two main opposing classes: the ruling class which controls all the power and wealth, and the working class which the rulers exploit" (ACF, "Aims and Principles"). ACF declares that rulers "weaken and divide" the working class "by racism, sexism and other forms of oppression, as well as war and environmental destruction. . . . Only the direct action of working class people can defeat these attacks and ultimately overthrow capitalism" (ACF, "Aims and Principles").

One primary aim of the ACF is to completely abolish "wage slavery," but that, they claim, cannot be accomplished through unions because they are part of the capitalist system. As an ACF statement explains:

> Unions . . . have to be accepted by capitalism in order to function and so cannot

> play a part in its overthrow. Trades unions divide the working class (between employed and unemployed, trade and craft, skilled and unskilled, etc.). Even syndicalist unions are constrained by the fundamental nature of unionism. The union has to be able to control its membership in order to make deals with management. Their aim, through negotiation, is to achieve a fairer form of exploitation of the workforce. . . . However, we do not argue for people to leave unions until they are made irrelevant by the revolutionary event. The union is a common point of departure for many workers. Rank and file initiatives may strengthen us in the battle for anarchist communism. What's important is that we organise ourselves collectively, arguing for workers to control struggles themselves.

Real freedom, ACF maintains, can only be accomplished through the active involvement—a revolution—of the working masses. An anarchist communist society must be based on the cooperative efforts of equals who create and shape that society. "In times of upheaval and struggle, people will need to create their own revolutionary organisations. . . . autonomous organisations [that] will be outside the control of political parties," ACF declares.

> As anarchists we organise in all areas of life to try to advance the revolutionary process. We believe a strong anarchist organisation is necessary to help us to this end. Unlike other so-called socialists or communists we do not want power or control for our organisation. We recognise that the revolution can only be carried out directly by the working class. However, the revolution must be preceded by organisations able to convince people of the anarchist communist alternative and method. We participate in struggle as anarchist communists, and organise on a federative basis. We reject sectarianism and work for a united revolutionary anarchist movement. (ACF, "Aims and Principles")

ACF also disseminates its manifesto on its website, which outlines the reasons why ACF views a "crisis of Capitalism" at the end of the 20th century and "offer[s] an optimistic and ultimately an attainable programme for real change." In addition, ACF publishes pamphlets that spell out its views; one explains how anarchist-communists would set up communities after a revolution. Such communities would join with others to voluntarily "create a network of independent yet co-operating organisations" in a system known as a federation. Such "egalitarian structures," ACF argues, would be "accountable and accessible to all" and would probably

> emerge from the workers and community councils which the working class created during the Revolution. We also foresee that a federal structure will emerge globally to coordinate such things as the production and distribution of resources, the making of decisions which concern a number of communities etc. This is the organisational basis for an Anarchist Communist society. Collective decision making leaves no room for governing authorities, and voluntary co-operation will mean that laws and policing can be done away with. Under these new structures, all forms of exchange and money will be abolished and all land and property will be taken into the control of the community. Most of it will be used collectively to provide for the needs of its members. Some may be held by individuals for their personal use—there will be a distinction between 'private property', which exists only prior to the Revolution, and the personal possession and use of resources by the individual for their personal fulfillment—though not at the expense of communal need. No community or individual will be privileged over another in terms of resources. (ACF, "Manifesto")

See also
Anarchist-Communists; Collective

References

The Anarchist Communist Federation, "Aims and Principles," on the internet <http://burn.ucsd.edu/~acf/a&p.html>).

The Anarchist Communist Federation, "As We See It" (pamphlet), on the internet <http://burn.ucsd.edu/~acf/ace/aswecit.html>.

The Anarchist Communist Federation, "Manifesto," on the internet <http://burn.ucsd.edu/~acf/index.html>.

Anarchist Cookbook

Written by William Powell, *Anarchist Cookbook* was originally published in 1971 by Lyle Stuart. Despite its title, the book has nothing to do with socialist philosophy and anarchy, as the chapter titles indicate: chapter 1, "Drugs: From Pot to Hydrangea Leaves"; chapter 2, "Electronics, Sabotage, and Surveillance: From Electronic Bugging Devices to Telephone and Communications Sabotage"; chapter 3, "Natural, Nonlethal, and Lethal Weapons: From Natural Weapons to Defense and Medical Treatment for Gases"; and chapter 4: Explosives and Booby Traps: From How to Make Nitroglycerine to Cacodyal." Almost universally ridiculed in anarchist circles, the concept for the book reportedly was born in an informal meeting at the International Workers of the World (IWW) headquarters in New York City. The author, however, was not an anarchist. His original intent was to publish information about drugs and explosives in poster form throughout the city in order to subvert activities of the Central Intelligence Agency (CIA) and the Federal Bureau of Investigation (FBI). The book is filled with 1960s rhetoric and a great deal of incomplete or dangerously incorrect information.

References

Shirriff, Ken, shirriff@eng.sun.com <http://www.cs.berkeley.edu/~shirriff>.

Anarchist Individualists

See Individualist Anarchists

Anarchist Press

Because anarchists reject the state and most refuse to take part in government, one of the few ways they can attempt to change society is through propaganda, using the press to disseminate ideas. However, most mainstream publications, especially in the United States, have portrayed anarchists as terrorists ready to destroy society. Thus, anarchists have been forced to self-publish their works. Since the 1800s, anarchists around the world have published hundreds of periodicals, including magazines, newspapers, and pamphlets.

Many anarchist publications have lasted only a few months, whereas others continued publishing for many years. Benjamin R. Tucker, for example, promoted individualist anarchism in the United States through his publications *The Radical Review* and *Liberty: Not the Daughter but the Mother of Order* from 1877 to 1901.

One long-lived publication is *Freedom,* published by Freedom Press in London. *Freedom* was founded in 1886, when a British anarchist group, which included the affluent Charlotte Wilson, invited well-known anarchist Peter Kropotkin to come to England after he was released from prison in France. The group began the newspaper and the press, which despite on again–off again operations still exist today.

The world's first daily anarchist newspaper was the *Chicagoer Arbeiter-Zeiting,* which was founded in 1884 by German immigrants who were part of the working-class movement in the United States. They also published a weekly called *Vorbote.* By 1883, five anarchist newspapers were publishing in Chicago, one of which was *The Alarm,* edited by Albert Parsons, a martyr of Chicago's Haymarket affair.

Other American anarchist publications included *Lucifer* (1883–1907), "Devoted to the Emancipation of Women from Sex Slavery." Ezra Heywood was a frequent contributor. *Modern School* was published between 1912 and 1922 by members of the anarchist colony in Stelton, New Jersey. Another anarchist colony in Home, Washington, published several newspapers—*Discontent, The Demonstrator,* and *The Agitator*—between 1898 and 1913. One of the most widely circulated publications was *Mother Earth,* founded in 1906 by the Russian immigrant and well-known anarchist Emma Goldman.

Anarchist publications have been produced in Australia, Canada, China, England, France,

Germany, Great Britain, Italy, Russia, Scotland, Spain, and other countries. Today's periodicals include *Red and Black Revolution* (Ireland), "a magazine of libertarian communism, an anarchist theory and history magazine." It regularly presents an analysis of Irish struggles and campaigns along with news and reports from the international anarchist movement. In keeping with the electronic age, this magazine and others such as *The Anarchives* (Canada), *Black Fist* (Houston, Texas), *Contre Infos* (France), and *Scottish Anarchist* (Scotland) can be found on the internet.

Several sources of anarchist publications are on the internet and include Freedom Press and Spunk Press. The latter acts "as an independent publisher of works converted to, or produced in, electronic format and to spread them as far as possible on the Internet . . . free of charge. The work may not necessarily originate from someone with net access. The major interest of SPUNK PRESS is alternative literature and anarchist material, both old, converted, and newly produced." (Spunk Press)

See also

Freedom Press; Goldman, Emma; Heywood, Ezra Hervey Hoar; Home Colony; Modern School Movement

References

Blatt, Martin Henry, *Free Love and Anarchism: The Biography of Ezra Heywood* (Urbana: University of Illinois Press, 1989).

Spunk Press Library, on the internet <http://black.cat.org.au/spunk/library/pubs/index.html>.

Veysey, Laurence, *The Communal Experience: Anarchist and Mystical Counter-Cultures in America* (New York: Harper and Row, 1973).

Wehling, Jason, "A Brief History of the American Anarchist Press" (March 1993), on the internet <http://www.teleport.com/~jwehling/APressHistory.html>.

Anarchist Red Cross

See Anarchist Black Cross

Anarchist Songs

During the 19th and early 20th centuries, when anarchist activities peaked, songs served as rallying cries, admonishing workers, peasants, and others to join the cause. "The Internationale" was sung in many different languages with variations on the following lyrics:

Arise! ye starvelings, from your slumbers;
Arise! ye criminals of want.
For Reason in revolt now thunders,
And ends at last the age of cant.
Now away with all superstitions.
Servile masses, arise! arise!
We'll change forthwith the old conditions,
And spurn the dust to win the prize.
Then comrades, come rally,
And the last fight let us face.
The Internationale Unites the human race.
We peasants, artisans, and others
Enrolled among the sons of toil,
Let's claim the earth henceforth for
brothers,
Drive the indolent from the soil!
On our flesh too long has fed the raven;
We've too long been the vulture's prey.
But now farewell the spirit craven:
The dawn brings in a brighter day.
Then comrades, come rally,
And the last fight let us face.
The Internationale Unites the human race.
No saviour from on high delivers;
No trust have we in prince or peer.
Our own right hand the chains must
shiver:
Chains of hatred, greed, and fear.
Ere the thieves will out with their booty
And to all give a happier lot,
Each at his forge must do his duty
And strike the iron while it's hot!
Then comrades, come rally,
And the last fight let us face.
The Internationale Unites the human race.

During the Russian Revolution of 1917, activists in the Makhnovists movement—followers of Ukrainian anarchist Nestor Makhno—remembered his army with "La Makhnovshchina":

Makhnovshchina, Makhnovshchina
Your flags are black in the wind
They are black with our pain
They are red with our blood
By the mountains and plains

in the snow and in the wind
across the whole Ukraine
our partisans arise
In the Spring Lenin's treaties
delivered the Ukraine to the Germans
In the Fall the Makhnovshchina
threw them into the wind
Denikin's White army
entered the Ukraine singing
but soon the Makhnovshchina
scattered them in the wind.
Makhnovshchina, Makhnovshchina
black army of our partisans
Who battled in the Ukraine
against the Reds and the Whites
Makhnovshchina, Makhnovshchina
black army of our partisans
who wanted to drive away
all tyrants forever from the Ukraine.

A song from the Spanish Revolution and Civil War (1936–1939) was "Sons of the People," which declared that "injustice cannot go on!" and that "instead of being a slave, it is better to die!" One of the most popular songs associated with the Spanish Revolution and Civil War was "A las Barricadas." A version of the lyrics follows:

Black storms shake the sky
Black clouds blind us
Although death and pain await us
Against the enemy we must go
The most precious good is freedom
And we have to defend it
With courage and faith
The high flag of Revolution
Moving us forward with non-stopping
triumph
To the Barricades
To the Barricades
For the triumph of the Confederation.

A more recent revolutionary song is the "Zapatista Anthem," which came about with the Zapatista uprising in Mexico:

Now we can see the horizon
—Zapatista combatant—
The change will mark
Those who come after us.
CHORUS:
Forward, forward, forward we go
To take part in the struggle ahead
Because our country cries out for
All of the efforts of the Zapatistas
Men, children and women
We will always make the effort
Peasants and workers
All together with the people.

The last chorus of the "Zapatista Anthem" demands an end to exploitation, echoing the views of anarchist movements past and present in their struggles for freedom.

See also
First International; Makhnovists and the Makhnovshchina; Spanish Civil War; Zapatista National Liberation Army

References
"A las Barricadas," translation by Elsa Barreda and Rachael Voland, on the internet <http://flag.blackened.net/revolt/spain/a_las_barricades.html>.
"The Internationale," on the internet <http://flag.blackened.net/revolt/hist_texts/song_international.html>.
"La Makhnovshchina," on the internet <http://flag.blackened.net/revolt/hist_texts/song_makhnovtchina.html>.
"Sons of the People," translation by Dan Clore, on the internet <http://flag.blackened.net/revolt/spain/song_sons_of_people.html>.
"Zapatista Anthem," on the internet <http://flag.blackened.net/revolt/mexico/ezln/anthem.html>.

Anarchist-Communists

Alexander Berkman, in his primer on anarchism (written in 1928, published in 1929), spelled out his views on communist anarchism and why it was the basis for building a society that was free, harmonious, noninvasive, and noncoercive. If a society based on communist anarchism is developed, government would be abolished, he declared. Monopoly and private ownership would be "eliminated as an abridgment of the equal opportunity of all." In Berkman's words, "the meaning of Communist Anarchism is this: the abolition of government, of coercive authority and all its agencies, and joint ownership—which means free and equal participation in the general work and welfare" (Berkman, 195–196).

Although all anarchists agree with the basic principle of abolishing government because it hinders human development, they do not agree on the type of economic system that would assure liberty and self-fulfillment. Many noncommunist anarchists contend that individuals have the right to what they produce and that monopoly is the cause of economic inequality. Once government is abolished, monopolies will disappear too because they exist as a privilege of government. Communist anarchists, in contrast, argue for public ownership of property, which they contend can only come about through social revolution. As Berkman wrote, "Only under Communist conditions could Anarchy prosper, and equal liberty, justice, and well-being be assured to every one without discrimination."

Today, anarchist-communists—sometimes called anarchocommunists, libertarian communists, or communist anarchists—still hold this view and maintain that a libertarian organizational structure is necessary in order to coordinate the struggle against capitalism as well as to expose the authoritarianism of some groups (Leninists in particular) who follow the principles of Karl Marx. The task of anarchist-communists, they state, is to win support among workers for anarchist ideas and methods.

See also

Berkman, Alexander; *Communist Manifesto;* Marx, Karl

References

Berkman, Alexander, *Now and After: The ABC of Communist Anarchism,* New York: Vanguard Press (1929), also published as *What Is Communist Anarchism?* (New York: Dover, 1972).

Anarcho-Capitalism

For many anarchists (of whatever persuasion), anarcho-capitalism is a contradictory term, since "traditional" anarchists oppose capitalism, with its hierarchical structures and economic exploitation supported by the state. Anarcho-capitalists are also opposed to state control, but only because they want to establish a laissez-faire economy. In their view private companies should operate all public services, buildings, and infrastructures. Peter Marshall, in his book on anarchism, explained it this way:

> Anarcho-capitalists are against the State simply because they are capitalists first and foremost. Their critique of the State ultimately rests on a liberal interpretation of liberty as the inviolable rights to and of private property. They are not concerned with the social consequences of capitalism for the weak, powerless and ignorant. Their claim that all would benefit from a free exchange in the market is by no means certain; any unfettered market system would most likely sponsor a reversion to an unequal society with defence associations perpetuating exploitation and privilege. If anything, anarcho-capitalism is merely a free-for-all in which only the rich and cunning would benefit. It is tailor-made for 'rugged individualists' who do not care about the damage to others or to the environment which they leave in their wake. The forces of the market cannot provide genuine conditions for freedom any more than the powers of the State. The victims of both are equally enslaved, alienated and oppressed.

In the United States, the Libertarian Party espouses many anarcho-capitalist views, and writers such as David Friedman, Murray Rothbard, and Ayn Rand have argued for an anarcho-capitalist society based on a completely free market economy. Rand is known in particular for her popular novels *The Fountainhead* and *Atlas Shrugged* and nonfiction works that emphasize 19th-century laissez-faire capitalism. She gained a near-cult following during the 1960s.

See also

Libertarian Party

References

Marshall, Peter, *Demanding the Impossible: A History of Anarchism* (London: HarperCollins, 1992), chap. 36.

Anarcho-Pacifism

See Religious Anarchism

Anarcho-Syndicalism

Anarcho-syndicalism (or syndicalism) stems from revolutionary movements in France, Italy, and Spain during the late 19th and early 20th centuries. *Syndicalism* is a term for radical trade unionism, which sees capitalism and the state as oppressors of working-class people. Anarcho-syndicalists, who were influenced by the philosophies of such men as anarchist Pierre-Joseph Proudhon and socialist Auguste Blanqui, argued that workers must create an industrial union movement in which they themselves (not their leaders) take direct action to accomplish reforms. Strikes at individual factories were just part of the class war anarcho-syndicalists deemed necessary to bring about a general strike that would overthrow and replace the capitalist system with an industrial democracy. A leading figure in the anarcho-syndicalist movement was Rudolf Rocker, who left his native Germany to escape police harassment on several occasions and eventually settled in Crompond, New York, in the 1930s.

Like collectivist and communist anarchists, anarcho-syndicalists insist that a government cannot create an economic order in the interests of the community. Ideally the structure of a syndicalist community would begin with a local *syndicat* of producers. According to *Britannica Online,*

> It would be in touch with other groups through the local *bourse du travail* ("labour exchange"), which would function as a combination of employment and economic planning agency. When all the producers were thus linked together by the *bourse,* its administration—consisting of elected representatives of the members—would be able to estimate the capacities and necessities of the region, could coordinate production, and, being in touch through other *bourses* with the industrial system as a whole, could arrange for the necessary transfer of materials and commodities, inward and outward.

In the United States, the Industrial Workers of the World (IWW), which was formed in 1905, championed syndicalist ideas. Individual proponents or supporters included such well-known activists as William "Big Bill" Haywood, Elizabeth Gurley Flynn, Carlo Tresca, Eugene Debs, Emma Goldman, and Alexander Berkman.

Although IWW membership diminished after World War I, anarcho-syndicalists have, nevertheless, been active since then in the United States and internationally. In 1922, an international conference of syndicalists convened in Berlin, Germany, with representatives from Argentina, Chile, Denmark, Germany, Holland, Italy, Mexico, Norway, Portugal, Sweden, France, and Russia. They founded a syndicalist organization called the International Workingmen's Association (later renamed the International Workers' Association), adopting a set of principles confirming that revolutionary syndicalists (i.e., anarcho-syndicalists) should oppose any economic and social system that monopolizes the means of production. Its principles and goals were amended numerous times during the 1930s, 1950s, and 1970s.

Today, many anarcho-syndicalists hope to build a mass movement of wage earners who use direct action to take over control of the workplace. Anarcho-syndicalists, however, do not espouse the idea that workers should take over society and rule others.

See also

Berkman, Alexander; Debs, Eugene Victor; Flynn, Elizabeth Gurley; Goldman, Emma; Haywood, William Dudley "Big Bill"; Industrial Workers of the World; International Working People's Association; Rocker, Rudolf; Tresca, Carlo

References

Keefer, Tom, "Marxism vs. Anarchism," *New Socialist* (March 1996).

"The Libertarian Thought of Rudolf Rocker," on the internet <http://www.geocities.com/Athens/Parthenon/3626/index.html>.

Rocker, Rudolf, *Anarchism and Anarcho-Syndicalism* (London: Freedom Press, 1988).

"Syndicalism," *Britannica Online* <http://www.eb.com:180/cgi-bin/g?DocF=micro/577/19.html (1998)>.

Andrews, Stephen Pearl (1812–1886)

A staunch abolitionist and the first to systemize a social philosophy regarding economic individualist anarchism, Stephen Pearl Andrews considered himself an "individual sovereign." He was a disciple of the man considered to be America's first anarchist, Josiah Warren. With his book *The Science of Society* (1852) and other writings, Andrews called attention to Warren's individualist ideas.

Born in Templeton, Massachusetts, Andrews was the son of a minister and became interested in social reform, especially abolition, early in life. He was a brilliant scholar and studied law and languages, eventually learning thirty-two languages, writing textbooks on linguistics, and developing an international language called Alwanto, a forerunner of Esparanto.

After the death of his wife, he began to study medicine, primarily because he wanted to participate in the intellectual pursuits of his second wife, a doctor and suffragist. He earned his medical degree from New York Medical College.

For a time Andrews taught in a women's seminary, then in 1839 he began a law practice in Houston, Texas. In Texas, then an independent republic, he became a fearless opponent of slavery, and by 1843 Andrews, his wife, and newborn had to leave the territory because their house was mobbed; they were forced to flee for their lives across the prairie.

Andrews developed a manumission plan, appealing to the federal government to buy slaves and free them, as he himself set out to do. "He immediately went to England to raise money for the purchase of the slaves in the form of a loan from Great Britain to Texas" (Schuster, 106); he was unsuccessful.

Back East, Andrews met Josiah Warren and began writing *The Science of Society* in which he clearly explains what Warren meant by individuality and the law of individual sovereignty: the principle that every person has absolute control over herself or himself but must accept the consequences of actions that harm others. Andrews declared that government

> violates this principle by slavery, commercial restrictions, limitation of free soil, treatment of crime, and finally by the restrictions it places on the marriage and parental relationships of its citizens. Hence he approves free trade, free land, and disapproves of capital punishment, taxation, the army and navy, and nationalism. (Schuster, 109)

In 1851 Andrews helped Warren establish Modern Times in New York (later known as Brentwood), although Andrews never lived in the anarchist community. It was set up without laws, police, or money. Their economy was based on the barter system that Warren had initiated in other communes.

Andrews led a group based on a theory called pantarchy, which rejected conventional marriage, advocated free love relationships, a single standard of morality for both men and women, and communal living. Victoria Woodhull, a well-known feminist, joined the group and espoused its views in a journal, *Woodhull and Claflin's Weekly,* that Andrews helped her start in 1870. Andrews along with Woodhull also supported a U.S. faction of the International Working Men's Association (IWMA), founded in London in 1868 and known as the First International. The IWMA dissolved in 1876, and the Workingmen's Party of the United States was formed; it later reorganized as the Socialist Labor Party.

Although Andrews's ideas were not widely accepted and he did not go out of his way to seek publicity, he continued until his death to espouse his views on the sovereignty of the individual, which to him was an indisputable natural law. He was among a dozen or more Americans remembered as early (i.e., 19th century) individualist anarchists.

See also

First International; Individualist Anarchists; Warren, Josiah; Woodhull, Victoria Claflin

References

Martin, James J., *Men Against the State* (Colorado Springs: Ralph Myles, 1970).

Schuster, Eunice M., *Native American Anarchism: A Study of Left-Wing American Individualism* (Northampton, MA: Smith College, 1932, reprint New York: AMS Press, 1970).

"Woodhull, Victoria," *Britannica Online* <http://www.eb.com:180/cgi-bin/g?DocF=micro/644/13.htm>.

Animal Liberation Front

A loose-knit animal-rights group, the Animal Liberation Front (ALF) frequently and derisively has been called "a bunch of anarchists" and, by its own statement of purpose, "carries out direct action [as advocated by anarchists] against animal abuse in the form of rescuing animals and causing financial loss to animal exploiters." ALF groups believe in individual liberty, including freedom for nonhuman animals, and state they are involved in "a nonviolent campaign." Activists take "all precautions not to harm any animal (human or otherwise). Because [ALF] actions are against the law, activists work anonymously, either in small groups or individually and do not have any centralized organization or coordination" (Animal Liberation Front FAQ).

ALF was founded in Great Britain during the 1970s and became active in North America about 1979. Members have exposed brutal conditions in some research laboratories, and their activities have been the catalyst for needed reforms in animal-protection laws. But for ALF members and some other animal-rights groups, such reforms do not go far enough. Activists want the public to stop exploiting animals and using them as instruments of science and for other inhumane activities.

The clandestine group has claimed responsibility for numerous incidents against North American facilities, including research laboratories, animal-breeding companies that provide animals for research, fur farms, and huge agribusinesses such as factory farms. From late 1995 to mid-1997, for example, ALF-affiliated activists conducted at least 30 raids on farms and ranches raising fur-bearing animals, primarily minks. Thousands of animals were released.

ALF attacks on mink ranches have also occurred with increasing frequency in Sweden, Finland, Austria, and other countries. In Sweden, ALF raids on a fox farm resulted in sanctions against the fur farmer, who had kept animals in cages much smaller than required by law.

Another target for attacks has been horse slaughterhouses. In a communiqué posted on the internet, ALF described its direct action in July 1997 to destroy what it calls a "horse murdering plant" in Redmond, Oregon. According to the communiqué, the team carried in vegan Jello, then

> a number of large holes were drilled into the rear wall of the slaughterhouse office to bypass potential alarms on the doors or windows. Next, the area that housed the refrigeration units was located and again large holes were drilled through the wall at that part of the slaughterhouse. Two teams then poured the Jello into the numerous holes and quickly began to assemble the three electrically-timed incendiary devises that would bring to a screeching halt what countless protests and letter writing campaigns could never stop. While these devises were being assembled some members of the team entered a storage shed/office/construction site . . . and left the remaining 10 gallons or so of jello for dessert. Then two gallons of muriatic acid was poured into the air conditioning vents to taint and destroy any horse flesh that may have survived the fire. Finally, the incendiary devises were set to ignite at exactly the same time. Unfortunately, as the battery was being connected to the device at the refrigeration unit, a spark started that entire area on fire! Fortunately, we had very thorough back-up plans in case anything went wrong and this insured that our departure went quick and smooth. At least $1,000,000 of damage has been done and the entire plant is currently closed and out of operation! (ALF communiqué)

ALF justifies such examples of direct action as helping to prevent one living being from harming or destroying another sentient being.

See also

Anarchism; Direct Action

References

Animal Liberation Front, Cavel-West Communiqué, July 21, 1997.

Animal Liberation Front, Frequently Asked Questions, on the internet <http://www.flashback.se/archive/alf_faq.html>.

Bodovitz, Kathy, "Animal-Rights Group Raids Hayward Rabbitry," San Francisco Chronicle (March 28, 1988).

"Redmond Blaze Destroys Horse-Rendering Company," *The Oregonian* (July 22, 1997).

Reed, Susan, and Sue Carswell, "Animal Passion," *People Weekly* (January 18, 1993).

Wheeler, Tracy, "Activists Release 41 Minks Charged in Vandalism, Breaking and Entering in Medina County," *Beacon Journal* (July 10, 1997).

Zak, Steven, "Ethics and Animals," *The Atlantic,* March 1989.

Antianarchist Laws (United States)

The labor unrest in the United States during the 1880s prompted some federal legislators to seek ways to curb radical activities. Efforts intensified after the 1886 Haymarket affair in Chicago, which resulted in a riot and the subsequent trial and execution of several anarchists for murder. Various immigration laws designed to exclude or deport "dangerous anarchists" were proposed during the 1890s, but none passed. After President William McKinley was killed by the deranged Leon Czolgosz, who claimed ties to anarchists, bills to exclude anarchists from the United States proliferated.

In 1903, the U.S. Congress enacted an immigration law that for the first time prevented the entry of immigrants because of their political ideas and alliances. Called the Immigration Act of 1903, the law prohibited entry into the United States of anyone who advocated a form of social organization other than a government based on law. The act legalized deportation of resident aliens labeled anarchists, and if anarchists were able to come into the country unnoticed, they could be deported if uncovered within three years.

A British anarchist, John Turner, was the first to be deported under the 1903 law. Turner was a prominent labor leader who had been invited by anarchist Emma Goldman to conduct a lecture tour in the United States. The U.S. government wanted to make an example out of Turner and arrested him when he was set to go onstage in New York City. According to a newspaper report, "When the anarchist speaker was put under arrest, his audience was inclined to rescue him by force, and a riot threatened, but Emma Goldman, the Anarchist leader, sprang to the platform and succeeded in controlling her followers" (Drinnon, 93).

Only a small number of avowed anarchists were actually deported under the 1903 law. But in the years that followed immigration authorities, with the help of local police in various districts, attempted to uncover radicals and anarchists. According to William Preston,

> The response was overwhelmingly negative. Twenty-three areas reported no cases at all, and some four districts discovered a handful of anarchists who had lived in the country longer than three years. Along with the exclusion and deportation figures for succeeding years, it was indicative of the small role played by anarchist immigrants in the subversion of American life, and suggested that millions of alien arrivals then as in the nineteenth century were bringing with them and cherishing the basic conservatism of their peasant background. (Preston, 33)

More than a decade after its passage, the 1903 law was strengthened, making it easier for the federal government to deport aliens with radical or anarchistic views. By the time the United States was fully engaged in World War I, Congress had passed the Espionage Act of 1917 and the Sedition Act of 1918, which made it illegal for anyone to use "disloyal, profane, scurrilous, or abusive language" against the U.S. government or the Constitution. Nevertheless, some anarchists spoke out against the war, among them Emma Goldman, who formed the No-Conscription League, which was so successful that within two weeks 8,000 people had declared they would not register for the draft. Goldman asserted that the draft trampled on individual rights, and in one fervent speech she declared, "We, who came from Europe, came here looking to America as the promised land. I came believing that liberty was a fact. And when we today resent war and conscription, it is not that we are foreigners and don't care, it is precisely because we love America and we are opposed to war" (quoted in Falk, 156).

Because of her views, Emma Goldman was arrested and convicted of conspiracy under the

Sedition Act and served two years in prison; in 1919 she was deported to Russia with other anarchists. After the war, other radicals such as leaders, members, and supporters of the Industrial Workers of the World (IWW) were arrested during the infamous Palmer Raids (initiated by Attorney General A. Mitchell Palmer) of conspiracy under the 1917 and 1918 laws.

Other legal efforts to rid the United States of radicals and anarchists took place during the latter half of the 20th century. These have included conspiracy charges against Communist Party members during the 1950s, investigations of groups like the Black Panthers and Students for a Democratic Society during the 1960s and 1970s, arrests of radicals in the sanctuary movement who defied laws in order to provide refuge for endangered illegal aliens during the 1980s, and efforts of Food Not Bombs to feed the homeless (in spite of local laws prohibiting such activities) during the 1990s.

See also

Black Panthers; Czolgosz, Leon; Espionage Act of 1917; Goldman, Emma; Haymarket Affair; New Left; Palmer Raids; Sanctuary Movement (United States); Sedition Act of 1918

References

Drinnon, Richard, *Rebel in Paradise: A Biography of Emma Goldman* (Chicago: University of Chicago Press, 1961).

Falk, Candace Serena, *Love, Anarchy, and Emma Goldman* (New Brunswick, NJ: Rutgers University Press, 1990).

Preston, William Jr., *Aliens and Dissenters: Federal Suppression of Radicals, 1903–1933,* 2d ed. (Urbana and Chicago: University of Illinois Press, 1994).

Antinomianism

The term *antinomianism* stems from a Greek word meaning "against law" and was applied to some early Christians who broke away from the established church. In anarchistic fashion, they rejected manmade codes and believed that they were not bound by moral laws, especially those of the Old Testament and its legalistic dogma. Antinomians followed their own conscience and sense of morality.

During the 16th century, members and clergy of the established church labeled Anabaptists antinomians, and in the 17th century such groups as the Separatists and Ranters were accused of antinomianism. The label was also applied to Anne Hutchinson and other dissenters in colonial America.

See also

Anabaptists; Hutchinson, Anne Marbury; Winstanley, Gerrard

References

"Antinomianism," *Britannica Online* <http://www.eb.com:180/cgi-bin/g?DocF=micro/26/81.html>.

Jacker, Corinne, *The Black Flag of Anarchy: Antistatism in the United States* (New York: Charles Scribner's Sons, 1968).

B

Bakunin, Mikhail A. (1814–1876)

Mikhail Bakunin was "an example of anarchist fervour in action," wrote historian James Joll. Joll also pointed out that Bakunin

> showed how great was the difference in theory and practice between anarchist doctrine and the communism of Marx. . . . Bakunin, too, more than any of his contemporaries, linked the revolutionary movement in Russia with that of the rest of Europe, and derived from it a belief in the virtues of violence for its own sake and a confidence in the technique of terrorism which was to influence many other revolutionaries beside anarchists. (Joll, 84)

Born to an aristocratic Russian family in the province of Tver, Mikhail Bakunin was destined for the privileged life his station should have afforded him. However, while attending the St. Petersburg Artillery School in preparation for an officer's career in the Tsar's military, Bakunin discovered the philosophy of Georg Wilhelm Hegel. There are indications that Bakunin already had shown much empathy for the peasants who lived on or near his family estate, and Hegel's "leftist" approach to life supplied some of the answers to questions of inequality that Bakunin observed on a daily basis. In his twenty-first year, Bakunin renounced the military life and moved to Berlin to pursue philosophy. He soon developed his theory of "revolutionary negation."

Although Hegel's dialectic keyed on the positive outcome of opposing ideas or forces, Bakunin posited that the only way society is changed is through the negative. He believed that annihilation of the old order was always necessary for the liberation of the masses. Revolution, in his view, was essential to negate the authority of the ruling classes and to establish an environment where true freedom might finally prevail.

In succeeding years Bakunin put his ideas into practice, giving speeches designed to incite the masses to action. In France in 1848 he called for Polish independence, which got him expelled from the country. The next year, undeterred, the firebrand made his way to Dresden to take a leadership role in the May insurrection there. He was arrested and condemned to death. Eventually he was extradited to Russia, where he spent eight years in solitary confinement before ending up in Siberian exile for four additional years. This time captivity broke Bakunin's health forever—but not his revolutionary zeal.

In 1861 Bakunin escaped to England by traveling through Japan and the United States. Finding no upheaval or revolutionary hot spots on the European continent, he turned his attention to organizing a secret society in Italy that would work for international revolution. The Fraternity (later the International Alliance of Social Democracy) was started in 1864 as an invisible force to foment unrest among the populace. In 1868 he joined the First International (International Working Men's Association), a loose consortium of radical organizations whose executive committee was dominated by Karl Marx.

Bakunin and Marx rarely saw eye to eye on the means to achieve liberty for the proletariat. Bakunin was convinced that Marx's pseudoscientific analysis of the economic class struggle was proffered only to justify the dictatorship of a new popular bourgeoisie: Marx and his followers. Bakunin held that the only justification for associations and federations among the masses was to facilitate the fall of existing authority. The associations would then naturally disintegrate, to be replaced by the free association of individuals capable, and naturally inclined, to join in temporary cooperatives for the attainment of specific, finite goals. This concept of "collectivism," which stemmed from Pierre-Joseph Proudhon's "mutualism," was more popular among the members of the First International. Collectivism was supported by the Swiss, Belgian, and French committees and was the official policy among the Italians and the Spanish.

Fearing that his power was eroding within the First International, Marx conducted a campaign of slander against his vocal adversary and convinced a committee to expel Bakunin. Eventually vindicated, Bakunin nonetheless took his followers into another competing organization in 1872.

Weary from the Marx intrigue and feeling the effects of his hard time in the Russian prisons, the inspirational voice of revolutionary change retired from the movement in 1874. Two years later he died in Rome. The legacy of Bakunin was most directly seen in the organization of anarcho-syndicalist groups in France and the Spanish revolt during 1936. However, as Noam Chomsky has pointed out, "If one were to seek a single leading idea within the anarchist tradition, it should, I believe be that expressed by Bakunin," who noted:

> I am a fanatic lover of liberty, considering it as the unique condition under which intelligence, dignity and human happiness can develop and grow; not the purely formal liberty conceded, measured out and regulated by the State, an eternal lie which in reality represents nothing more than the privilege of some founded on the slavery of the rest; not the individualistic, egoistic, shabby, and fictitious liberty extolled by . . . schools of bourgeois liberalism, which considers the would-be rights of all men, represented by the State which limits the rights of each—an idea that leads inevitably to the reduction of the rights of each to zero. No, I mean the only kind of liberty that is worthy of the name, liberty that consists in the full development of all the material, intellectual and moral powers that are latent in each person; liberty that recognizes no restrictions other than those determined by the laws of our own individual nature, which cannot properly be regarded as restrictions since these laws are not imposed by any outside legislator beside or above us, but are immanent and inherent, forming the very basis of our material, intellectual and moral being—they do not limit us but are the real and immediate conditions of our freedom. (Chomsky, 374)

See also

Anarcho-Syndicalism; Chomsky, Avram Noam; First International; Marx, Karl; Proudhon, Pierre-Joseph; Spanish Civil War

References

Chomsky, Noam, *For Reasons of State* (New York: Random House/Vintage Books, 1973) also on the internet *Notes on Anarchism* <http://www.worldmedia.com/archive/other/notes-on-anarchism.html>.

Harper, Clifford, *Anarchy: A Graphic Guide* (London: Camden Press, 1987).

Horowitz, Irving L., *The Anarchists* (New York: Dell, 1964).

Joll, James, *The Anarchists* (Boston: Little, Brown, 1964).

Berkman, Alexander (1870–1936)

Russian anarchist Alexander Berkman, affectionately known as Sasha, was a longtime friend of Emma Goldman and a leading figure in the U.S. anarchist movement. He is best known, however, for his bungled attempt in 1892 to assassinate Henry Clay Frick, chairman of the board of Carnegie Steel. Frick had tried to cut the wages of steelworkers at the Carnegie plant in Homestead, Pennsylvania, and workers struck in protest. Frick called in Pinkerton guards to break up the strike in a battle that killed ten workers and three guards, which outraged Berkman. To him, Frick was an oppressor, a tyrant who should be destroyed in order to liberate oppressed people.

The youngest of four children, Berkman was born in Vilna, Russia. His father was a prosperous wholesaler in the shoe industry, and the family was "allowed to move to St. Petersburg, a privilege that was restricted to the upper echelons of Jewish merchants and professionals. Sasha . . . grew up in comfortable surroundings (complete with servants and a summer house near the capital) and attended a classical gymnasium reserved for the privileged elements of society. Yet at a very early age he was astir with dreams of revolt" (Berkman, 1972, Introduction by Paul Avrich, vi).

Although Berkman was a good student, he was rebellious, already influenced as a teen by revolutionary ideas. In early childhood he was deeply affected by the actions of Russian revolutionaries and the assassination of the tsar in 1881. He also idealized his mother's brother, Mark Natanson, known as Uncle Maxim, who was a revolutionary leader and activist with the Socialist Revolutionary Party. Natanson was driven into exile during the Russian Revolution because of his severe criticism of the Bolsheviks.

When Sasha's father died, the family was forced to leave the privileged life and move to Kovno. His mother also died at a relatively early age, and in 1877, when Berkman was sixteen years old, he emigrated to the United States, settling in New York City.

Six months before Berkman's arrival in the United States, the Haymarket martyrs had been tried and executed, an event that stirred controversy for many years and profoundly affected Berkman, prompting him to become an activist in the U.S. anarchist movement. About this time he met Emma Goldman, with whom he lived in a small commune. After several moves they eventually settled in Worcester, Massachusetts. There he planned his dramatic attempt on the life of Frick, an *attentat*—the assassination of a powerful agent of oppression—that broke the back of resistance to the striking workers' demands. It led to Berkman's fourteen-year imprisonment in the Western Penitentiary at Allegheny City.

Despite brutal prison conditions and long periods of solitary confinement, Berkman was able to study and write. He also became a confirmed believer in anarchy, but he no longer accepted that terrorism would change society. When he was released in 1906, Berkman found it difficult to adjust to daily life. Prison had taken a great toll on his emotional well-being, and he became withdrawn and sullen. When he began writing his *Prison Memoirs of an Anarchist* (published in 1912), he also started to recover and gain back his revolutionary spirit. He joined Goldman in organizing anarchist demonstrations and agitating among workers. He also edited Goldman's *Mother Earth,* considered one of the top journals among the anarchist press. In addition, between 1910 and 1911 he helped organize and taught at the libertarian Ferrer Modern School in New York.

In 1917, Berkman and Goldman organized mass rallies to protest the U.S. arms buildup and the conscription of all eligible males into military service. Both were arrested and imprisoned for their activities. Berkman was incarcerated for two years at a federal prison in Atlanta, Georgia; he spent seven months in solitary confinement for protesting beatings of fellow prisoners. He was nearly broken upon release. Yet he and Goldman, who had served a sentence in a federal prison at Jefferson City, Missouri, were reunited and planned a lecture tour to raise funds for lawsuits challenging government raids on anarchists and other activists who were arrested and confined without formal charges. However, the United States was in the midst of the so-called Red Scare and a widespread fear that the effects of the successful 1917 communist revolution in Russia would spread to the United States. By the end of 1919, Berkman, Goldman, and more than 240 other radicals were deported.

Berkman and Goldman were sent to Russia, where they hoped to take part in revolutionary activities. But they soon became disillusioned and deeply anguished by Bolshevik atrocities, including executions of Russian anarchists and the massacre of tens of thousands of protesting workers in what became known as the Kronstadt uprising. In 1925, Berkman's book *The Bolshevik Myth* was published, detailing his shattered illusions and how the Bolshevik dictatorship trampled the masses.

After two years in their homeland, Berkman and Goldman left Russia and went into exile, first in Sweden, then in Germany and France. While in France, Berkman wrote a handbook on anarchism designed for the average reader who knew little or nothing about the philosophy. Originally published in 1929 as *Now and After: The ABC of Communist Anarchism* (reissued in 1972 as *What Is Communist Anarchism?*), the primer clearly spells out Berkman's view that anarchism is "the most rational and practical conception of a social life in freedom and harmony." In the foreword, Berkman wrote: "Government remains strong because people think political authority and legal compulsion necessary. Capitalism will continue as long as such an economic system is considered adequate and just. The weakening of the ideas which support the evil and oppressive present-day conditions means the ultimate breakdown of government and capitalism" (Berkman, 1972: xxi).

Berkman was convinced that communist anarchism would work and that people had to do away with their idea that authoritarianism was necessary. "Life in freedom, in Anarchy, will do more than liberate man merely from his present political and economic bondage. That will be only the first step," he wrote.

> Far greater and more significant will be the *results* of such liberty, its effects upon man's mind, upon his personality. The abolition of the coercive external will, and with it of the fear of authority, will loosen the bonds of moral compulsion no less than of economic and physical. Man's spirit will breathe freely, and that mental emancipation will be the birth of a new culture, of a new humanity. Imperatives and taboos will disappear, and man will begin to be himself, to develop and express his individual tendencies and uniqueness. Instead of "thou shalt not," the public conscience will say "thou mayest, taking full responsibility." That will be a training in human dignity and self-reliance, beginning at home and in school, which will produce a new race with a new attitude to life. (Berkman, 1972: 209)

While working on his handbook, Berkman also helped edit Goldman's life story, which she wrote over a three-year period. Both Berkman and Goldman, who were constantly plagued with financial concerns, hoped the autobiography would sell well and relieve their money worries, but that was not the case. Berkman toiled at a meager living by editing and translating, but he often had to depend on friends for financial aid. He was also in poor health and in agonizing pain because of cancer. Deeply depressed, he committed suicide in 1936.

See also

Anarchist Press; Goldman, Emma; Haymarket Affair; Kronstadt Uprising; Modern School Movement

References

Avrich, Paul, *The Russian Anarchists* (New York: W. W. Norton, 1978).

Berkman, Alexander, *The Bolshevik Myth* (Boulder: Westview Press, 1989).

Berkman, Alexander, *What Is Communist Anarchism?* (New York: Dover, 1972).

Goldman, Emma, *Living My Life,* 2 vols. (New York: Knopf, 1933, reprint New York: Dover, 1970).

Horowitz, Irving L., *The Anarchists* (New York: Dell, 1964).

Berneri, Luigi Camillo (1897–1937)

A popular and controversial figure in the Italian anarchist movement of the 1920s, Luigi Camillo Berneri was a prolific writer. He was influenced by Russian anarchist Peter Kropotkin and, in fact, wrote a pamphlet, *Peter Kropotkin: His Federalist Ideas,* which was first published in 1922 and translated into English during the 1940s. According to one biographer, Berneri contended that only federalism could replace the state, but

> he was not referring to the administrative federalism, imposed from above, that would do no more than create so many small-scale States, but rather to the federalism that comes from social revolution, which would have produced independent communes, freely federated, in which federations of grass-roots councils would have taken over the functions of the bureaucratic State organization. When it came to

> his own country, what Berneri saw as an absurdity was the attempt to govern Italy by a single administration, given the country's great regional diversity. This had led to the rise of a parasitic bureaucracy.
>
> Berneri declared, "In the economic sphere anarchists are possibilists, in the political sphere they are 100% intransigent!" By this he meant that even if the critique of the state and the negation of the principle of authority were aims that could not be dispensed with, the anarchist economic model must remain open and experimental. He personally considered that free rein should be given to individual business and labour and collectivist business and labour. Thus, he condemned collectivization if it were forced, rather than a free choice. This led him to the conclusion that anarchy would not bring about a society of absolute harmony, but one of tolerance. (Toni)

Born in Lodi, in northern Italy's Lombardy region, Camillo was the son of a self-educated civil official and a primary school teacher. He became a member of the Italian Socialist Youth Federation, and in 1912 he attended a conference that the federation held in Reggio Emilia, where he lived at the time. In 1914, he wrote his first article, entitled "The Lies of the Old Testament," which attacked the clergy. Not long afterward, Berneri became an anarchist and married a sixteen-year-old anarchist, Giovanna Caleffi. The couple's eldest daughter, Marie Berneri, became a well-known anarchist in her own right.

When Berneri was drafted to serve in the military, he agitated against the war, which led to his imprisonment. Released after the war, he joined veteran anarchist Errico Malatesta in Florence to work on the anarchist daily *Umanita Nova*. But when the former socialist-turned-fascist Benito Mussolini became dictator, the newspaper and other radical publications were suppressed.

Because of fascist persecution, Berneri was forced to leave Florence and move to Umbria, where he taught in a teacher's training school. He continued his political propaganda, however, and along with his wife and daughters was soon expelled from Italy, taking refuge in France. But he was also "expelled from France as a 'dangerous anarchist,' and then proceeded to be kicked out of Belgium, the Netherlands, Luxembourg, Germany and Spain. At that point, unable to be expelled into any other country, he could legally reside in France" (Toni).

While living in Paris during the 1930s, he wrote numerous articles published in European and North American journals and tried to convert Italian exiles living in France to anarchism. "In this period his daughter married the English anarchist Vernon Richards, who subsequently wrote a text on [Errico] Malatesta and took part in the Spanish Civil War" (Toni).

When the Spanish Civil War erupted in 1936, Berneri went to Spain along with other Italian anarchists. He was at the Aragón front for a time, but because of vision and hearing problems he was sent to Barcelona, where he tried to warn people about a fascist takeover through the prestigious Italian-language revolutionary anarchist paper *Guerra di Classe.*

In 1937, the communists, who had great political influence and encouraged the totalitarian trend of the Spanish government, engaged in bitter fights with anarchists in Barcelona. In May of that year Berneri was gunned down in the street by communists.

See also

Berneri, Marie Louise; Kropotkin, Peter Alexeyevich; Malatesta, Errico; Spanish Civil War

References

"Anarchism: ANARCHISM AS A MOVEMENT: Anarchism in Spain." *Britannica Online* <http://www.eb.com:180/cgi-bin/g?DocF=macro/5007/8/6.html>.

Toni, trans. by David Short, "Luigi Camillo Berneri—Biography of the Italian Anarchist," on the internet <http://flag.blackened.net/revolt/spain/berneri.html>.

Berneri, Marie Louise (1918–1949)

The elder daughter of Italian anarchists Camillo and Giovanna Berneri, Marie Louise Berneri was born in Arezzo, Italy. In 1926, after her father agitated against dictator Benito

Mussolini, she and her family were deported to France. She used the French version of her name, Maria Luisa, and during the 1930s studied at the Sorbonne University, where she became involved in the anarchist movement.

When her father went to Spain to fight in the Spanish Civil War, Marie was able to visit him once in Barcelona. She returned there after her father was murdered by communists. But she soon moved to Great Britain and worked for the anarchist paper *Freedom.* She also helped found *War Commentary,* an antiwar publication. She and three other editors were arrested and convicted of "incitement to disaffection." However, "she was acquitted on a legal technicality . . . and when her three comrades were imprisoned she took on the main responsibility for maintaining the paper into the postwar period. After her death in 1949 from a viral infection, several of her works were published posthumously by Freedom Press" (*Freedom Press*).

See also

Berneri, Luigi Camillo; Freedom Press; Italian Anarchism

References

"Marie Louise Berneri Biography," *Freedom Press* (1986), on the internet <http://www.pitzer.edu/~dward/Anarchist_Archives/bright/berneri/berneribio.html>.

Berrigan, Philip (1924–)

Former Roman Catholic priest Philip Berrigan has never been called an anarchist, but he has practiced the type of civil disobedience that religious anarchists have exercised over the centuries. One judge called him "a moral giant, the conscience of a generation." Since the 1960s, Berrigan, as a peace activist, has advocated disarmament and has frequently called himself "a criminal for peace." His older brother, Father Daniel Berrigan, a Jesuit priest and poet who has long ministered to cancer and AIDS patients, has often joined him in protests.

Born in Minnesota, Philip Berrigan grew up in a poor family. Even though his father, Thomas Berrigan, possessed many skills, he often worked at jobs that went nowhere. Still, he managed to somehow feed, clothe, and house his wife and their family of six boys through various odd jobs; their mother cared for the family by washing the clothes (sometimes in nearby streams), preparing meals, shopping, mending, and caring for the children, in short, leading the life of a frontier woman.

According to numerous reports, Thomas Berrigan was tyrannical, ruthless, violent in his moods, and impossible to please, expecting precise obedience to his demands. He also preached to his children that if they disobeyed they would be punished by the wrath of God. In contrast, Berrigan's mother, Freda, was instrumental in establishing a way to endure through nonviolence and nonconfrontation.

In 1927 the family moved to Syracuse, New York, and Philip Berrigan followed in the footsteps of his brother, receiving an education in Catholic elementary and secondary schools, then entering Jesuit school, an order that requires strict obedience to church doctrine. Although Philip Berrigan became a Jesuit priest, he left the priesthood and married Elizabeth (Liz) McAlister, a former nun. The couple has three children, the last born in 1981, and all have been activists within the peace movement.

During the 1960s, Philip and Daniel were outspoken critics of the Vietnam War. They came into national prominence in 1968 when they and seven others went to Catonsville, Maryland, where the group, which became known as the Catonsville Nine, burned some 600 draft cards in a parking lot. After the fire was started they waited for the police to arrive. The Catonsville event marked a turning point in the growing antiwar movement, which prior to that time had been less confrontational—more in the nature of carrying protest signs. Now, civil disobedience was being encouraged by the antiwar leadership. Because of their actions, Philip and Daniel were imprisoned for two years.

In 1973, Philip Berrigan and Liz McAlister founded Jonah House, a community home in a low-income neighborhood in Baltimore, Maryland. Their purpose was to bear witness to their beliefs and to establish a community of like-minded people (the Jonah House "family") dedicated to nuclear disarmament and nonviolent resistance. In 1995, the group built a two-story house on the edge of a Catholic cemetery, land that the church allowed the Jonah House to use in exchange for maintenance work on part of the cemetery.

Since its founding the adults and children in the family have lived a life of voluntary poverty. "The adults work a few days a week as house painters to make a sustainable living. They also grow vegetables, work with the poor, engage in local and national peacemaking efforts, and spend at least four nights a week reading scripture, praying, holding meetings and planning nonviolent actions" (Dorsey).

Berrigan and McAlister also are part of Plowshares, an activist organization that believes in the biblical injunction to beat swords (in this case nuclear armaments) into plowshares. Their first action took place in 1980 in King of Prussia, Pennsylvania, where they damaged two unarmed warheads at a General Electric nuclear facility. Since that first action, Berrigan and McAlister have taken part in numerous confrontational antiwar protests. The two agreed early in their marriage that in order for one parent to be with their children they would never take part in protests that would bring about simultaneous jail terms.

In early 1997, Philip Berrigan joined several other Plowshare activists at the Bath Iron Works in Portland, Maine, where they pounded and damaged the launch tubes of an Aegis destroyer and poured their own blood over the ship. The group was arrested on conspiracy charges, and Berrigan began serving a two-year prison sentence in October 1997. Then in 1998, he was visited by Mairead Corrigan Maguire, who was awarded the Nobel Peace Prize in 1976 for her attempt (along with Betty Williams) to bring peace to Northern Ireland. Afterward she staged a nonviolent sit-in in support of Berrigan. She was arrested and soon released, and Berrigan was punished by prison officials. Because Berrigan did not alert the prison that Maguire was planning a protest, a disciplinary committee denied any visitors for a year. This type of punishment has usually been applied to a prisoner trying to smuggle drugs. As the *Boston Globe* pointed out in an editorial: "Berrigan and others who commit acts of civil disobedience know that they risk spending time in prison. But punishing him for someone else's support is excessive in a country that values free expression and protects political dissent" (*Boston Globe,* April 2, 1998). Many anarchists of various persuasions echo such words.

References

Buckley, Stephen, "Berrigan Released While Appealing Contempt Term," *The Washington Post* (March 28, 1992).

"A Crime Against Philip Berrigan," Editorial, *Boston Globe* (April 2, 1998).

Lockwood, Lee, "Still Radical After All These Years," *Mother Jones* (September/October 1993).

McNulty, Timothy, "Jail Time Still Doesn't Deter Philip Berrigan," *Chicago Tribune,* June 20, 1994.

Polner, Murray, *Disarmed and Dangerous: The Radical Lives and Times of Daniel and Philip Berrigan* (Boulder: Westview Press, 1997).

Wackerman, Daniel T., "Mind's Eye" (interview), *America* (March 18, 1995).

Black Flag

When Ukranian anarchist Nestor Makhno led rebels in their fight against numerous armies during the Russian Revolution of 1917, he or one of his commanders carried the black flag, long a symbol of anarchist groups. However, anarchists have also carried a red flag, as philosopher Peter Kropotkin indicated in his description of a march of workers in Bern, Switzerland, organized by anarchists in defiance of the Swiss government (Kropotkin, 397). In addition, anarchists have used the circle-*A* symbol to represent their cause. On some occasions all three symbols have been displayed to show revolt against the state.

No one is sure where the black flag originated, but anarchist historians speculate Louise Michel carried it for the first time during a workers' demonstration in Paris, France. In the United States, the black flag was first displayed by August Spies, one of the most defiant of the Haymarket anarchists, tried and executed in 1887. According to historian Paul Avrich, the black flag symbolized hunger, misery, and death (Avrich, 144). Others have suggested that the flag expressed workers' bitterness and anger. In his book *Reinventing Anarchy,* Howard Ehrlich declares that anarchists hoist the black flag because it

> is the negation of all flags. It is the negation of nationhood which puts the human race against itself and denies the unity of all humankind. Black is a mood of anger and outrage at all the hideous crimes against humanity perpetrated in the name of allegiance to one state or another. It is anger and outrage at the insult to human intelligence implied in the pretenses, hypocrisies, and cheap chicaneries of governments.
>
> Black is also a color of mourning; the black flag which cancels out the nation also mourns its victims the countless millions murdered in wars, external and internal, to the greater glory and stability of some bloody state. It mourns for those whose labor is robbed (taxed) to pay for the slaughter and oppression of other human beings. It mourns not only the death of the body but the crippling of the spirit under authoritarian and hierarchic systems; it mourns the millions of brain cells blacked out with never a chance to light up the world. It is a color of inconsolable grief. (Quoted in Wehling)

References

Avrich, Paul, *The Haymarket Tragedy* (Princeton: Princeton University Press, 1984).

Dorsey, Gary. "Jonah House Under Seige." Convicts of Strong Conviction." *Christian Century,* April 15, 1998.

Ehrlich, Howard J., ed., *Reinventing Anarchy: What Are Anarchists Thinking These Days?* (London: Routledge and K. Paul, 1979).

Kropotkin, Peter, *Memoirs of a Revolutionist* (Boston: Houghton Mifflin, 1899).

Wehling, Jason, "Anarchism and the History of the Black Flag" (July 14, 1995), on the internet <http://www.teleport.com/~jwehling/BlackFlag.html>.

Black Panthers

The radical Black Panther Party (BPP), originally called the Black Panther Party for Self-Defense, was part of the revolutionary freedom struggle and antiwar movement during the 1960s and early 1970s. Though not labeled as anarchist, the BPP created controversy through its antigovernment views and violent tactics. Many people considered the group to be one of urban terrorists. But even though the BPP espoused violence at times, it also carried out food giveaway programs and voter registration drives and set up medical clinics in black communities. At its peak, the BPP had branches in 48 U.S. cities. In addition, the BPP inspired other groups to organize and agitate against the established order, such as Mexican American "Chicano" groups; the Chinese Red Guard; the Puerto Rican Young Lords; and even the Gray Panthers, who addressed abuse of the elderly. Around the world in Africa, Asia, Europe, and South America, BPP support groups began to form.

The BPP was founded in 1966 in a poverty program office in Oakland, California. Cofounders Huey P. Newton, who became minister of defense, and chairman Bobby Seale created a ten-point program of empowerment. It included the power to determine the destiny of black and oppressed communities; a call for full employment, decent housing, and education; "an end to the robbery by the capitalists of our black and oppressed communities"; and an "end to police brutality and murder of black people, other people of color, all oppressed people inside the United States" (Black Panther Party Platform and Program).

In 1967, BPP joined forces with the Student Nonviolent Coordinating Committee (SNCC), which had been founded in 1960 and had taken part in numerous nonviolent civil rights efforts but had begun to support black power militantly. Stokely Carmichael, long associated with SNCC, wrote in 1966:

> For too many years, black Americans marched and had their heads broken and got shot. They were saying to the country, "Look, you guys are supposed to be nice guys and we are only going to do what we are supposed to do—why do you beat us up, why don't you give us what we ask, why don't you straighten yourselves out?" After years of this, we are at almost the same point—because we demonstrated

> from a position of weakness. We cannot be expected any longer to march and have our heads broken in order to say to whites: come on you're nice guys. For you are not nice guys. We have found out. (Quoted in Barbour, 63–64)

Stokely Carmichael was appointed prime minister of BPP and began to link the Black Panther Party's "ideological struggle with struggles in the third world." Carmichael

> redefined his call for "Black Power" into an appeal for pan-Africanism. Huey Newton contributed the idea of "intercommunalism" and asserted that imperialism had reached such a degree that sovereign borders were no longer relevant and that oppressed nations no longer existed; only oppressed communities within and outside artificial political borders existed. Members of the BPP used this concept as a rallying cry for an international coalition of oppressed peoples to fight against American and western imperialism.
>
> At the same time, the BPP in particular attempted to make the Marxist literature of third world revolutionaries relevant to the struggle in the United States. . . . As members sought solidarity with third world struggles for independence, they exported a unique brand of American black nationalism that was evident in the goals and objectives of foreign revolutionary groups. In addition, they inspired fear in unfriendly governments that American black nationalists would ignite flames in Europe, Asia, Africa, Latin America, and the Caribbean. The BPP also tied black liberation to an international struggle for freedom and independence and pledged leadership and unity with oppressed peoples of the world. Representatives of SNCC and BPP abroad pledged revolutionary solidarity with all groups engaged in the struggle against imperialism, racism, capitalism, and fascism. (Williams)

Throughout the late 1960s and into the 1970s BPP was constantly in conflict with the police. In 1967, BPP began publishing its newspaper, using the label "pig" for police and bigots; in October of that year Newton was critically wounded in a predawn shootout with Oakland police. He was arrested and charged with the murder of an Oakland police officer. On the first day of his trial, nearly 3,000 protestors marched to the Alameda County Courthouse, staging one of the first of many "Free Huey" rallies. Newton was found guilty of manslaughter and sentenced to state prison, but he appealed and his sentence was reversed. He was retried twice, both efforts ending in mistrials. Newton eventually earned a doctorate at the University of California at Santa Cruz. He had a problem with drug abuse and was killed by a drug dealer in 1989.

In 1968, *Soul on Ice* by BPP Minister of Information Eldridge Cleaver was published, and the autobiography soon became a national best-seller. It was written while Cleaver was in Folsom Prison, where he served nine years for rape; he was released due to the efforts of his lawyer, Beverly Axelrod.

The following year, BPP Chairman Bobby Seale was tried along with seven others in Chicago. In the infamous Chicago Eight trial, as it was called, Seale was accused of crossing state lines to incite rioting at the 1968 Democratic National Convention. He so disrupted the trial that the federal judge ordered Seale gagged and shackled to a metal folding chair and eventually tried him separately.

By 1969, BPP was plagued with internal bickering and began to split into two factions—one led by Newton, the other by Cleaver. The two sides were involved in a shootout that left two members dead. Also that year, police raided an apartment in Chicago and killed two BPP members, Fred Hampton and Mark Clark.

Federal government officials infiltrated BPP meetings to prevent the group from forging links with revolutionaries in other parts of the world. Some members such as Cleaver and Newton had fled the United States to find refuge in Cuba and Algeria. The Federal Bureau of Investigation (FBI) under J. Edgar Hoover launched a campaign against the BPP, using bogus letters and documents, illegal wiretaps, informants, and other secret means in a counterintelligence operation called "Cointelpro." The operation was designed to discredit civil rights and antiwar efforts by whatever means possible, which led to an investigation of the FBI by the U.S. Senate Intelligence Committee that eased, but did not stop entirely, the harassment.

By the end of the 1970s, the Black Panthers had lost most of its leaders, and members had drifted away. Although the revolutionary group died out, the lessons and history of the party are now being disseminated through the Dr. Huey P. Newton Foundation under the direction of cofounder David Hilliard, former BPP chief of staff.

References

Barbour, Bloyd B., ed., *The Black Power Revolt* (Toronto: Collier-Macmillan, 1968).

Black Panther Party Platform and Program (October 1966), on the internet <http://cs.oberlin.edu/students/pjaques/bpp-program.html>

Burdman, Pamela, "Political Revival—Black Panther Philosophy Coming Back into Vogue," *San Francisco Chronicle* (August 29, 1994).

Williams, Yohuru, "American Exported Black Nationalism," *Negro History Bulletin* (July-September 1997).

Blanqui, Louis Auguste (1805–1881)

A French philosopher and activist, Louis Auguste Blanqui was well known in Europe's radical circles during the 19th century. At the center of the revolutionary uprisings in France between 1827 and 1870, Blanqui spent half his life in prison because of his dedication to the cause of workers. He held that an elite minority must lead the workers in a revolt against factory owners and the state. Once successful, this group would establish a temporary dictatorship. Blanqui reasoned that this was the most efficient mechanism for implementing the necessary transformation to a just society. His views predated and likely inspired the actions of Vladimir Ilich Lenin and the Soviet communists when they overthrew the tsar in Russia in the 1900s. Blanqui's efforts also have inspired numerous followers (the Blanquists) and other anarchists, who played a critical role in the European workers' movement well after his death.

Blanqui was born at a time when Napoleon Bonaparte was in power and gaining ever more territory, finally controlling a vast empire that stretched from France to the Russian borders. Blanqui's father was an administrator in Napoleon's empire and as a result amassed a modest fortune, but that was lost when Napoleon was forced into exile in 1814. Yet the Blanqui family managed to maintain a middle-class standard of living, and Auguste and his older brother, Adolphe, were well educated. Adolphe, in fact, became a respected economics scholar, and Auguste "carried off all the prizes in school, showing equal proficiency in the ancient classics, composition, history, and mathematics" (Nomad, 22).

When Blanqui was ten years old, the Bourbon dynasty was again restored and France was ruled by Louis XVII, who died in 1824. His brother, Charles X, inherited the throne.

Even before the rule of Charles X, secret reform groups made up primarily of the educated middle class were organizing and attempting to find ways to overthrow the monarchy. In 1821, one reform group known as the Chabonniers planned an uprising, but many members were arrested. At the age of 17, Blanqui witnessed the execution of four group members, who became "martyrs for the cause of French democracy." Their execution had a profound effect on Blanqui, who even in his old age visited their graves (Nomad, 23).

Blanqui joined the French Carbonari, another rebel group, in 1924 when he was 19, and from then on he was involved in numerous revolutionary activities against the policies of Charles X, who abolished freedom of the press and restricted individual liberties. At the same time, Blanqui earned a living as a tutor or teacher in a private school and while in his twenties as a reporter for a daily newspaper. He took part in the many demonstrations and riots that broke out in Paris in 1830. Workers, students, and many middle-class citizens who adamantly opposed Charles X set up barricades in Paris streets, and when government troops were sent to repel them, the rioters threw flower pots, furniture, washtubs, shovels, and other implements at the soldiers, who refused to fire on the people and joined their cause. The Bourbon dynasty was overthrown in a few days, but middle-class leaders set up a constitutional monarchy and crowned Louis Philip as king.

When the king rejected continual demands for social and economic reforms, discontent grew among the millions of unemployed workers, radical intellectuals, and socialists calling for a governmental structure in which the people owned businesses and property in common. Blanqui joined a radical society called Amis du Peuple (Friends of the People), which published articles calling for another revolution. Fifteen militants in the group, including Blanqui, were indicted for their activities. All were acquitted except Blanqui, who made a violent speech against the wealthy and was imprisoned for one year on charges of disturbing the peace.

After his release from prison, Blanqui joined another radical organization, the Society of the Families, in 1835. Most members of the clandestine group owned rifles, and they set up a secret laboratory to manufacture gunpowder for their weapons. In 1836, authorities discovered the laboratory and arrested Blanqui and the other leaders. Although they were sentenced to two years in prison, they were released after eight months. Blanqui was not allowed to live in Paris, however, and was forced to move to a small town nearby, where he and his wife lived for at least a year in relative contentment.

During his time outside Paris, Blanqui developed a new revolutionary group, which took part in a 1839 uprising against the government in Paris. He was sentenced to nine years in prison for his part in the insurgency. His wife died within a year, and his health steadily deteriorated. By 1844 he was so ill that prison authorities pardoned him. He remained in a hospital for most of the next two years and was eventually banished to another small town, where he stayed until he received news in February 1848 that the monarchy had once more been overthrown. But the new constitutional government under Louis Napoleon, nephew of Napoleon Bonaparte, as president did not last long. In 1851, Napoleon established a dictatorship.

Blanqui, who had returned to Paris in 1848, continued his agitation and participation in uprisings. He was imprisoned again from 1861 to 1865, then was able to escape to neighboring Belgium. But he secretly returned to Paris to meet with newly formed Blanquist groups of students and dissenting workers. In 1868, he wrote *Instruction Pour Une Prise D'Armes,* a manual on urban guerrilla warfare tactics.

In 1870, Blanqui returned to Paris again and openly protested the French government's military defeat and eventual surrender of Louis Napoleon to Germany in the Franco-Prussian War. Some Blanquists did take part in the establishment of the Third Republic that arose at that time, but Blanqui was convinced that the new government was not adequately prepared to defend the country. He and other Blanquists took part in two attempted revolts in 1870 and 1871 in order to gain power for themselves. Once more Blanqui was arrested, but the following day the Paris Commune insurrection took place. A council of radicals, the Paris Commune included not only Blanqui's followers but also those of the anarchist Pierre-Joseph Proudhon. It took over the capital and set up its own government, hoping to create a confederation of communes or communities within France. Blanqui was elected president even though he was in prison, but he was never released to lead the Paris Commune; it collapsed weeks later. Nevertheless, Blanqui became an important symbol of the movement.

After Blanqui was released from his final imprisonment, he took part in political activities and ran for office as a reform candidate. He was no longer hounded by the government, which was now more tolerant of opposition views. Although Blanqui was not elected to a government office, he spent the last 18 months of his life delivering political speeches, advocating the overthrow of the monarchy and restraints on the power of the church. He died of a stroke on January 1, 1881.

See also

Paris Commune of 1871; Proudhon, Pierre-Joseph

References

Bernstein, Samuel, *Auguste Blanqui and the Art of Insurrection* (Woodstock: Beekman Publishers, 1971).

"Blanqui,(Louis Auguste)" *Britannica Online* <http://www.eb.com:180/cgi-bin/g?DocF=micro/72/77.html>.

Nomad, Max, *Apostles of Revolution* (New York: Collier Books, 1961).

Bluestein, Abraham (1909–1997)

Abraham Bluestein grew up in a home in which anarchism was a common topic of discussion; books on anarchism by such writers as Peter Kropotkin filled the house. During his lifetime Bluestein sought to live by anarchist principles and was actively involved in numerous anarchist activities, including a trip to Spain to take part in the revolution there (1936–1939).

Born in Philadelphia, Abraham—or Abe, as he was usually called—was the son of immigrants, Mendel and Esther Bluestein, who had been involved in the revolutionary movement in Russia. When Mendel Bluestein killed a tsarist soldier, he and Esther had to flee; they made their way to the United States, where they helped organize the International Ladies Garment Workers Union (ILGWU).

After Abe completed third grade in public school, his parents enrolled him in the private, radical modern school of Stelton, New Jersey, one of several so-called free schools based on principles established by Francisco Ferrer y Guardia in Spain during the early 1900s. Bluestein attended the Stelton school until his high school years, then enrolled in public high school in New Brunswick, New Jersey; he later graduated from City College of New York and became a teacher. While in college he joined a prominent anarchist group known as the Vanguard Group.

At 21 Bluestein met his lifelong love and partner, Selma Cohen, who became a fine artist and, because of Bluestein's influence, an activist in the anarchist movement. During the Spanish Civil War they traveled as a team to Spain to support the Spanish Loyalists (or Republicans). Loyalists opposed the military uprising of General Francisco Franco and included members of the anarcho-syndicalist trade union Confederación Nacional del Trabajo (CNT) and the socialist federation Unión General Trabajadores (UGT), as well as various communist, socialist, and republican groups. Bluestein was a reporter for the Canadian Broadcasting Company and worked as an information officer for CNT. He "made radio broadcasts for the anarchist movement, stationed for the most part in Barcelona and Catalonia." After returning to the United States, Bluestein and Cohen "settled down to family life, eventually moving to Croton, New York, where they raised three boys and one girl." Cohen, along with raising her family, continued her art career and held numerous one-woman shows (A-Infos News Service).

Before and during World War II, Bluestein, a pacifist, could not support the war effort; he thus became alienated from anarchist groups that supported the fight against fascism. Following the war, he worked as a reporter for the *Jewish Daily Forward* and the *American Labor Union* and also worked with the Libertarian Book Club. Among his edited works is *Fighters for Anarchism: Mollie Steimer and Senya Fleshin,* a memorial volume published in 1983. For a time, he also worked with union-affiliated organizations such as the United Housing Foundation.

Bluestein's friends included such well-known anarchists as Emma Goldman and Rudolf Rocker. Although he was not active in the movement during his later years, he supported trade unions and cooperatives until his death at age 88.

See also

Goldman, Emma; Modern School Movement; Rocker, Rudolf; Spanish Civil War; Stelton School and Colony

References

A-Infos News Service, "Obit: Abraham (Abe) Bluestein," January 2, 1998, on the internet <http://www.ainfos.ca>.

Avrich, Paul, *Anarchist Voices: An Oral History of Anarchism in America* (Princeton: Princeton University Press, 1995).

Dewitt, Rebecca, "Abe Bluestein: An Anarchist Life," *Perspectives on Anarchist Theory* (Newsletter Institute for Anarchist Studies, Spring 1998).

Thomas, Robert McG. Jr., "Abraham Bluestein, 88, Dies: An Advocate of Anarchy," *New York Times* (December 14, 1997).

Bookchin, Murray (1921–)

Murray Bookchin is known for numerous published works and attempts to bring together ideas from two historic periods, "the era of traditional proletarian socialism and anarchism, with its working-class insurrections and struggles against classical fascism, and the postwar era of growing corporate capitalism, environmental decay, statist politics, and the technocratic mentality" (Biehl).

Bookchin was born in New York City, but his family roots were across the Atlantic, as his parents were involved in the Russian Revolution. The stamp of radical thinking and revolutionary action was there from the beginning. He was a member of the communist youth movement during the 1930s, and although he was too young to take part in actual fighting during the Spanish Civil War (which took the lives of two brothers), he participated through support and organizational activities.

Bookchin eventually lost his zeal for the communist approach, even quitting the Trotskyists when their actions seemed far from egalitarian. He found a philosophical home within the libertarian socialist communities of German exiles in New York and New Jersey. However, this did not occur until after an introduction to libertarianism as part of the American labor movement in the Congress of Industrial Organizations (CIO) during the early 1940s and after he returned from duty in the army during World War II. At that time he was intricately involved with the politics and actions of the United Auto Workers (UAW).

During the 1960s, Bookchin was a part of the countercultural and New Left movements. His trailblazing ideas on social ecology were spelled out in his first American book, *Our Synthetic Environment,* a most important contribution to anarchist thought that linked environmental degradation to historic hierarchical social constructs like patriarchies. The book appeared in the United States in 1962, six months before Rachel Carson's better known work *Silent Spring.* His publications in Germany during the 1950s and 1960s moved that nation to examine its own ecological role in the world.

In Europe and North America, Bookchin's pioneering work on the environment spurred the development of international environmental organizations and movements. Nevertheless, he has been an avid critic of so-called deep ecology as practiced by some ecoanarchists, referring to the movement as "silliness." In a 1992 article posted on the internet, he states that

> after dealing with deep ecologists in North America for quite a few years, I have reluctantly come to the conclusion that . . . [many adherents] are motivated in their allegiances by theological rather than rational impulses. There is no reasoned argument, I suspect, that will shake a belief-system of this kind—hence I will leave discussion of the issues involved to others who still have the energy to deal with mindless dogmas.
>
> . . . One wonders whether deep ecology's biocentric maxim that all living beings can be equitable with one another in terms of their "intrinsic worth" would have had any meaning during the long eras of organic evolution before human beings emerged. The entire conceptual framework of deep ecology is entirely a product of human agency—a fact that imparts to the human species a unique status in the natural world. All ethical systems (including those that can be grounded in biotic evolution) are formulated by human beings in distinctly cultural situations. Remove human agency from the scene, and there is not the least evidence that animals exhibit behaviour that can be regarded as discursive, meaningful, or moral. When Elisée Reclus, the anarchist geographer, tells us that pussycats are . . . "natural anarchists," or worse, that "there is not a human sentiment which on occasion they [i.e., cats] do not understand or share. . . ." Reclus is writing ethological and ecological nonsense. That anarchist writers celebrate the author of such an anthropomorphic absurdity as "ecological" is regrettable to say the least. To the extent that "intrinsic worth" is something more than merely an agreeable intuition in modern ecological thought, it is an "attribute" that human beings formulate in their minds and a "right" that they may decide to confer on animals and other creatures. It does not exist apart from the operations of the human mind or humanity's social values. (Bookchin, 1992)

He has also advocated the incorporation of "libertarian municipalism" ideals for an alternative, decentralized economy. By establishing a confederation of municipal and local entities, he believes, society can avoid the centralized economies and political structures that are key elements of capitalism and even Marxist and syndicalist paradigms.

According to his longtime companion, Janet Biehl, since the late 1970s Bookchin

> has been an important stimulus in the developing Green movements throughout the world, and he has written many works dealing with the nature and future of Green politics. One of his most important demands in recent decades has been for a "new politics," or what he calls libertarian municipalism, a politics based upon the recovery of direct-democratic popular assemblies on municipal, neighborhood, and town levels. To avoid the danger of civic parochialism, he has advanced a civic confederalism, by which a decentralized society confederates in opposition to the centralized nation-state.
>
> He has also advanced the demand for a municipalized economy, in opposition to the present corporate capitalist system of ownership and management, to the nationalized economy promulgated by Marxian socialists, and to the workers' ownership and self-management of industry advocated by syndicalists. These ideas have been widely discussed in Green movements in North America and Europe. (Biehl)

Murray Bookchin's published works include: *The Philosophy of Social Ecology: Our Synthetic Environment* (Alfred A. Knopf, 1962); *Crisis in Our Cities* (Prentice Hall, 1965); *Post-Scarcity Anarchism* (Ramparts Books, 1971); *The Limits of the City* (Harper and Row, 1974); *The Spanish Anarchists* (Harper and Row, 1977); *Toward an Ecological Society* (Black Rose Books, 1981); *The Ecology of Freedom* (Cheshire Books, 1982). With his companion, Janet Biehl, and others he has published the theoretical newsletter *Green Perspectives.* Among his most recent works are *The Third Revolution Reenchanting Humanity* and *The Politics of Cosmology.*

See also

Anarcho-Syndicalism; Ecoanarchists; Social Ecology

References

Biehl, Janet, "Murray Bookchin" (1994), on the internet <http://www.pitzer.edu/~dward/Anarchis/Archives/bookchin/bio1.html>.

Bookchin, Murray, "Deep Ecology, Anarcho-Syndicalism and the Future of Anarchist Thought" (1992), on the internet <//http://www.lglobal.com/TAO/Freedom/book2.html>.

Bookchin, Murray, *Post-Scarcity Anarchism* (Berkeley, CA: Rampart Books, 1971).

Born, Helena (1860–1901)

A member of a Boston, Massachusetts, anarchist group, Helena Born had been an activist in labor, socialist, and feminist movements in England during the late 1800s. In 1890, she emigrated to the United States and attempted to live according to feminist and anarchist principles. Helena Born was the only child of wealthy parents, who sent her to a girl's academy for her education but "refused to allow her to attend a university or train for a profession." Her father provided her with ample income for her livelihood (Marsh, 25).

Raised in Bristol, she was expected to be a "proper woman," but she became active in a feminist organization while in her twenties. She and a friend, Miriam Daniell, became involved in the British socialist movement and settled into a working-class neighborhood in Bristol, where she became secretary of the Bristol Gas Workers and General Laborers Union. When workers struck in 1889, Born gave speeches, collected funds, and picketed. She also tried to organize seamstresses in Bristol but failed. After that she and Daniell left for the United States.

Although she had been politically active in her homeland, she did not get involved in U.S. politics. Instead she declared that labor organizing and similar activities were secondary to learning to know oneself and trying to live by a certain set of principles. For Born, a dedicated feminist, those principles were in line with American anarchist ideas.

> [Born] wanted to live her life not circumscribed by her gender. Instead of articulating a feminist principle, she planned a life of feminist practice. Anarchism provided a theoretical rationale for goals she had already espoused. She gave up her private income and became a typesetter, but this did not entirely satisfy her desire to separate herself from a political and social system of which she did not approve. In 1893, therefore, she and Daniell moved to a rural commune in California, where they built a house and hoped to settle permanently. (Marsh, 27)

Born was unable to realize her dream, however. Not only was her home destroyed, but her friend died in 1894; she returned to Boston, where her lover, William Bailie, lived. Although Bailie was married, Born did not hide her relationship with him. The couple operated a small restaurant together.

Until she died in 1901, Born acted "on the belief that her most useful contribution to political activism was her continuing refusal to cooperate with a system that she found repressive and confining. Her life and work demonstrated a consistency which marked her as one of the most successful of the anarchist women" of her time (Marsh, 28).

References

Marsh, Margaret S., *Anarchist Women, 1870–1920* (Philadelphia: Temple University Press, 1981).

C

Chinese Anarchism

Although the tendency toward utopian anarchistic ideas existed in China long before the 20th century, anarchism had widespread influence on Chinese politics and culture during the first three decades of the 1900s. Roots of the anarchist movement were in Tokyo and Paris, where Chinese intellectuals were sent to study, particularly between 1906 and 1907. During that period two Chinese societies "devoted to the propagation of anarchism, one in Paris, the other in Tokyo" were formed (Dirlik, 44).

Despite government repression in Japan, radicals such as Kotoku Shusui, who had read Russian anarchist Peter Kropotkin's theories and advocated an anarchist revolution across Asia, were espousing social change in both Japan and China. "Kotoku deliberately sought out the Chinese students and was the featured speaker at the first meeting of the Chinese Society for the Study of Socialism" founded in 1907 (Zarrow, 54). Kotoku argued that anarchism rather than socialism was a practical way to bring about social change, because

> it would abolish capitalists and the state to enable the workers to plan for their own welfare. Socialism might make land and wealth public but would end by handing them over to government. Government is not necessary; it is historically contingent: the result of a minority using coercion and then making laws. This can benefit only the haves. Moreover, people are not by nature violent but rather enjoy peace and security. It is government that obstructs the development of human nature. (Zarrow, 54)

The Chinese Society in Tokyo lasted only a few years, as government suppression forced anarchists to flee the country. However, in Paris the World Society, established in 1906, served over the next four decades "as a conduit between European and Chinese anarchism and as a source for anarchist ideas, as well as a recruiting ground for the movement" (Chang and Dirlik, 17). Chinese radicals in Paris were influenced not only by Kropotkin, who was a friend of anarchist publisher and editor Jean Grave in France, but also by the French anarchist-geographer Elisée Reclus. Both Kropotkin and Reclus espoused anarcho-communism as first set forth by Russian anarchist Mikhail Bakunin.

Paris was the center of Chinese student radicalism, which was led by four men: Wu Zhihui, Li Shizeng, Zhang Jingjiang, and Chu Minyi. They supported the Chinese revolutionary Sun Yat-Sen, who in 1905 organized the Revolutionary Alliance in Japan and, after the revolution erupted in China in 1911, transformed the alliance into the federated political party known as the Guomindang (Zarrow, 59). The involvement of these anarchist leaders with a political party—a contradiction of anarchist antigovernment principles and their vow to overthrow the state—created great controversy over the next decade, eventually leading to a split among Chinese anarchists. But those who cooperated with or took leadership roles in the Guomindang justified their actions as necessary to bring about social revolution.

Anarchist journals were published in Paris and read by Chinese students worldwide. The ideas the publications disseminated were widely discussed by intellectuals in China, who considered anarchism the most progressive of political views. Most young Chinese anarchists were against tradition and authority of all types—religious, political, familial, militaristic, and social. They also denounced Confucian morality and the oppression of women, strongly supporting women's liberation and anarcho-feminism.

Chinese anarchists held firm beliefs in the efficacy of science and humanist theories to solve social problems, and some advocated revolution and violence as means to attain their goals, since the state had to be destroyed in order to bring about human freedom. Yet as in other countries, anarchists in China ranged from revolutionary terrorists, "who found in anarchism justification for their activities, to Buddhist monks, who discovered in the anarchist message of love something akin to Buddhist ideals, to esthetes, who perceived beauty in the anarchist ideal of a beautiful society" (Dirlik, 84).

Anarchism reached its peak in popularity in China during the 1920s. After the Chinese Communist Party was formed in 1921 (including some anarchists as members), anarchism began to lose ground to communism—or more specifically the communism as espoused by the Bolsheviks led by Vladimir Ilich Lenin, who gained power and took control of the Russian government, creating a proletarian dictatorship. At first, like radicals in other countries, Chinese anarchists supported the Bolshevik takeover, but they became disenchanted upon learning of the Bolsheviks' brutal suppression of anarchists.

Chinese communists and anarchists competed for followers, but anarchism began to die out as a movement. "By the 1930s it was evident that most Chinese believed the state to be necessary to carry out the social revolution and to resist imperialism. But the small group of intellectuals who discovered and reinvented anarchism just after the turn of the century made their point, too: the highest human goal is to combine liberty and equality" (Zarrow, 258).

See also

Bakunin, Mikhail A.; French Anarchism; Kotoku Shusui; Kropotkin, Peter Alexeyevich

References

Chan, Ming K., and Arif Dirlik, *Schools Into Fields and Factories: Anarchists, the Guomindang, and the National Labor University in Shanghai, 1927–1932* (Durham and London: Duke University Press, 1991).

Dirlik, Arif, *Anarchism in the Chinese Revolution* (Berkeley: University of California Press, 1991).

Scalapino, Robert A., and G. T. Yu, "The Chinese Anarchist Movement," Berkeley Center for Chinese Studies, on the internet <http://www.pitzer.edu/~dward/Anarchist_Archives/worldwidemovements/scalapino.html>.

Zarrow, Peter, *Anarchism and Chinese Political Culture* (New York: Columbia University Press, 1990).

Chomsky, Avram Noam (1928–)

Noam Chomsky was born to Zev Chomsky and Elsie Simonofsky in Philadelphia in 1928, fifteen years after his father left Russia to avoid service in the tsar's army. The family honored education and the intellectual pursuits, and both of his parents taught in the religious school of the Mikveh Israel congregation. Dr. Chomsky eventually took the principal position at this school.

Young Noam was sent to a progressive school before age two. He stayed there until he was twelve, at which time he matriculated to a public, college-oriented high school in the city. Although he never understood he was a good student because of the emphasis his first school put on creativity and individual learning, it soon became obvious that Chomsky was an exceptional scholar. His "first two years of college [at the University of Pennsylvania] were pretty much an extension of high school, except in one respect," he said in an interview. "I entered with a great deal of enthusiasm and expectation that all sorts of fascinating prospects would open up, but these did not survive long." After two years, he was ready to put aside his formal schooling to pursue his own areas of interest. "This was 1947," he noted, "and I had just turned eighteen. I was deeply interested, as I had been for some years, in radical politics with an anarchist or left-wing (anti-Leninist) Marxist flavor, and even more deeply involved in Zionist affairs and activities" (in Peck, 6–7).

He considered a trip to a kibbutz in Israel to pursue his interest in politics and the possibilities of Arab-Jewish cooperation (as opposed to the Zionist antidemocratic movement that was very popular at the time). However, before he could leave the influence of Penn completely, he met Zellig Harris, a leading linguist who founded the first department of linguistics in the United States and a charismatic scholar with broad interests. Chomsky began taking graduate courses under Harris. He would eventually receive a bachelor's and master's degree from the university, concentrating on philosophy, linguistics, and logic. His doctorate was conveyed in 1955, even though he had almost no formal contact with the university after the initial years.

"Morphophonemics of Modern Hebrew" was Chomsky's B.A. honors thesis. This most original and controversial work was the basis for the groundbreaking analysis of language that would, in and of itself, assure the scholar a place in history. Therein, as well as in his doctoral thesis ("Transformational Analysis") and the seminal 1957 work *Syntactic Structures,* he defined a new form of linguistic analysis called transformational-generative grammar. By 1955 he was teaching linguistics at the Massachusetts Institute of Technology (MIT); he holds a professorship at that institution to this day. Chomsky's work in this area was widely accepted and changed the study of linguistics in the second half of the 20th century. His theory that humans have an innate ability to understand the hidden structures of language has had its detractors, however, as with his views on politics and the prevailing social structure.

Chomsky rarely takes the safe path in regard to politics. He has always been fearlessly unflinching in his critique of power structures both internationally and within the United States. He first came to prominence on this front with his outspoken writings and commentary against the U.S. position in the Vietnam War. In his 1970 book, *At War with Asia,* he was highly critical of the U.S. role, and wherever he could find an audience he gave speeches raising questions almost no one else was yet asking.

Chomsky calls himself a libertarian socialist, but his views readily live alongside prominent anarchist thinkers like Mikhail Bakunin and Rudolf Rocker. He ascribes to the latter's declaration that "the problem that is set for our time is that of freeing man from the curse of economic exploitation and political and social enslavement" (Chomsky, 1973, 371). His special contribution to anarchist thought in the modern era must be his analysis of the comparable evils engendered by dictatorial and democratic governments alike. Always willing to focus the spotlight on hypocrisy, he chastises his and other governments and the institutions that maintain the "necessary illusions" of liberty and individual freedom, the vital elements in the props of modern capitalistic governance. Business, the press, and the intellectual elite are Chomsky's favorite targets, yet the scholar is no negative complainer. As James Peck notes in closing his introduction in *The Chomsky Reader,*

> Chomsky is not a cynical man. Nor is he disillusioned. To become disillusioned is to have been illusioned and this Chomsky is not. There is a deep affirmation in these writings which cuts through the bleakness, a certain nobility of humanity is reaffirmed. This comes not just from the struggles of a single mind refusing to bend to a myriad of ideological pressures in our time, but from the way Chomsky's willingness to stand so outside prevailing beliefs makes him so central to a reaffirmation of a concern with human freedom and dignity, with creativity, and with the commitment to seek their multiple manifestations. (Peck, 6)

Speaking for himself in a 1995 interview, Chomsky noted that his views have not changed much since his youth.

> I think it only makes sense to seek out and identify structures of authority, hierarchy, and domination in every aspect of life, and to challenge them; unless a justification for them can be given, they are illegitimate, and should be dismantled, to increase the scope of human freedom. That includes political power, ownership and management,

> relations among men and women, parents and children, our control over the fate of future generations (the basic moral imperative behind the environmental movement, in my view), and much else. Naturally this means a challenge to the huge institutions of coercion and control: the state, the unaccountable private tyrannies that control most of the domestic and international economy, and so on. But not only these. That is what I have always understood to be the essence of anarchism: the conviction that the burden of proof has to be placed on authority, and that it should be dismantled if that burden cannot be met. (Chomsky interview)

Noam Chomsky has published more than seventy books and 1,000 articles on psychology, politics, cognitive science, philosophy, and linguistics.

See also

Bakunin, Mikhail A.; Rocker, Rudolf

References

Barsky, Robert F., *Noam Chomsky: A Life of Dissent* (Cambridge: MIT Press, 1998).

Chomsky, Noam, "Anarchism, Marxism and Hope for the Future," Interview, first published in *Red & Black Revolution,* No 2 (1996), on the internet <http://www.geocities.com/CapitolHill/2419/index.html">.

Chomsky, Noam, *For Reasons of State* (New York: Random House/Vintage Books, 1973) also on the internet *Notes on Anarchism* <http://www.worldmedia.com/archive/other/notes-on-anarchism.html>.

Peck, James, *The Chomsky Reader* (New York: Pantheon Books, 1987).

Collective

The term *collective* most often refers to the concept of "collective bargaining," whereby a group of workers—like today's modern labor unions—joins together to negotiate with managers and business owners to improve conditions in the workplace. Prior to the mid-19th century, workers' rights to freely associate and organize in a collective to increase power and achieve positive change were limited at best. In most countries—as well as many areas in the United States—such activity was illegal.

When men and women had the courage to meet in public, protest conditions, and defiantly strike against employers, the results could be tragic. The bombing and riots in Chicago's Haymarket Square in 1886 were the result of police reaction to a collective strike against the McCormick Harvesting Machine Company in support of an eight-hour workday.

Today, *collective* is often used in connection with communes or communistic communities that work together for the common good. A collective may also be a cooperative, such as the farm collectives instituted by Joseph Stalin in the Soviet Union. During the 1930s nearly all of the agricultural production in the Soviet Union was collectivized—taken over by the government—although members of collectives could own small plots of land and animals. Voluntary agricultural collectives have been highly successful in Israel. And during the 1950s and 1960s, numerous agricultural collectives were established by radical groups in the United States. A few have survived to this day.

To some anarchist groups, *collective* can be defined more broadly. As an example, the Heatwave Communist-Anarchist Federation, a group out of Dallas, Texas, relies on the collective, describing it on its website as

> the type of organization that is the most democratic and where the members are the most equal. Basically, a collective is a group of individuals that talk to each other face-to-face and try and reach a common goal based on what each member will contribute. In a collective, each member should contribute to discussion and action, this depends on a person . . . that has ideas and desires and wants to see if others want them as well. . . . Be tolerant of others so that they will be tolerant of you in return and always try and reach a common understanding.

See also

Communism; Haymarket Affair

References

Heatwave Communist-Anarchist Federation home page <http://flag.blackened.net/heatwave/collective.html>.

Communism

The social and economic system known as *communism* has been interpreted in numerous ways over the centuries, but basically it refers to a system in which all real property and the means of production are held in common by all members of a society rather than by individuals. Ancient Greeks developed ideals for communistic societies that influenced many philosophers thousands of years later, including William Godwin (1756–1836), whose philosophical principles eventually became known as anarchism. According to historian Mark Holloway,

> the earliest communistic society of which we have any record is that of the Essenes, who flourished in Palestinian Syria some time before the birth of Christ. These men, about 4,000 strong, were scattered in various towns and villages, and did not live in separate communal settlements, yet they kept to a most rigid communism of property, and to a meticulously strict set of religious observances. A league of virtuous celibates, they depended for the increase of their numbers upon the adoption of children. . . . We know little of the origins of these grave silent brethren . . . but it is possible that they had connections with the Pythagorean and Orphic religions. (Holloway, 26)

Some early Christian communities were also communistic, and common ownership of land was part of the doctrine of religious communities such as the Roman Catholic Trappists—priests, brothers, and sisters of the Order of Cistercians of the Strict Observance, as it is formally known, founded in 1098 in Citeaux, France. Hundreds of years later they transported their ideas to the United States.

Between the 1500s and the 1800s, various communistic groups came to the forefront, including the Anabaptists of Germany and the Diggers led by Gerrard Winstanley in England. When industrialization took hold in Europe, communism became part of the philosophies of idealists who denounced the evils of private property and attempted to launch communistic settlements.

Anarchists and revolutionists, who took part in the widespread uprisings in Europe in 1848, hoped to overthrow established governments and set up a universal society with property in common. Communism and socialism were espoused, and the terms were often used synonymously. However, communists were inclined to abolish all private property, whereas socialists emphasized state ownership of all means of production. Although anarchists at this time usually referred to themselves as socialists and agreed that all private property should be abolished, they also advocated the overthrow of the state—that is, all forms of government.

In 1848, the *Communist Manifesto* by Karl Marx and Friedrich Engels appeared, articulating the communist ideal known as "scientific socialism" (as opposed to utopian theories). Since that time, Marx and his theories have generated great controversy, and modern communism is more often associated with the dictatorial Bolsheviks who established the Communist Party and the Union of Soviet Socialist Republics (USSR) during the Russian Revolution of 1917. The Bolsheviks established a system based on the rule of a single party—the Communist Party—and collective ownership of all means of production. With the collapse of the USSR in 1991, this form of communism has been widely discredited except in some Asian countries (China in particular) and Cuba.

Most communistic groups in the United States were not founded on Communist Party principles or those articulated in the *Communist Manifesto* of 1848 and practiced in Eastern Europe and China. American communistic groups, for the most part, were opposed to revolution as a method for reform and instead hoped to set up a form of communism that led to an ideal society.

Religious communistic communities were common in the United States from the late 1700s through the 1800s. Communism was practiced in some cases to establish societies similar to the early Christians, who tried to live by the principles of communion, sharing, and caring for one another. They held property in common, and production was divided equally among members of the community. Other types of communistic communities were established in the United States, particularly with the huge influx of European immigrants during the 1800s. Some immigrants were fleeing religious persecution and were searching for an ideal lifestyle—a utopia.

Some communities were set up as models for reform. People believed that individualism could not effectively deal with the growing societal problems brought on by industrialization and deep divisions between property owners and workers. So they based their communities on ideals that could be applied on a small scale—usually with groups ranging from a little more than 100 to perhaps several thousand people. A variety of anarchists communes in the United States were set up on this basis.

See also

Anabaptists; Collective; *Communist Manifesto;* Diggers; Godwin, William; Marx, Karl; Winstanley, Gerrard

References

Gay, Kathlyn, *Communes and Cults* (New York: Twenty-First Century Books/Holt, 1997).

Holloway, Mark, *Heavens on Earth: Utopian Communities in America, 1680–1880,* 2d ed.(New York: Dover, 1966).

Nordhoff, Charles, *The Communistic Societies of the United States: From Personal Observations* (New York: Harper and Brothers, 1875, reprint New York: Dover, 1966).

Communist Manifesto

Originally published in German in 1848, the *Manifest Der Kommunistischen* (Manifesto of the Communist Party) is a pamphlet by Karl Marx and Friedrich Engels that was written to delineate the tenets of the newly formed Communist League, a secret propaganda society of European workingmen. This most important and famous of socialism's documents celebrated its 150th anniversary in 1998, and from the earliest days of its distribution it served to define a philosophy and a movement that would alter the course of history. The introduction opens thus:

> A spectre is haunting Europe—the spectre of Communism. All the Powers of old Europe have entered into a holy alliance to exorcise this spectre: Pope and Tsar, Metternich and Guizot, French Radicals and German police-spies.
>
> Where is the party in opposition that has not been decried as Communistic by its opponents in power? Where the Opposition that has not hurled back the branding reproach of Communism, against the more advanced opposition parties, as well as against its reactionary adversaries?
>
> Two things result from this fact.
>
> I. Communism is already acknowledged by all European Powers to be itself a Power.
>
> II. It is high time that Communists should openly, in the face of the whole world, publish their views, their aims, their tendencies, and meet this nursery tale of the Spectre of Communism with a Manifesto of the party itself. To this end, Communists of various nationalities have assembled in London, and sketched the following Manifesto, to be published in the English, French, German, Italian, Flemish and Danish languages.

The work was an explanation of human social history—from feudal times to the industrial revolution of the mid-19th century—from Marx's "scientific socialist" point of view. He maintained that all social interaction to that point was a result of class struggle and a natural conflict that arises when humans attempt to eke a living out of the earth. He believed that all socialism before the Marx-Engels theory was "utopian socialism" based on an untenable ideal.

The *Communist Manifesto* had very little effect on the 1848 revolutions in Europe, and neither Marx nor Engels held much sway within the emerging labor union movement for nearly two decades. But Marx's time came in 1864, when the First International (International Working Men's Association) evolved from a gathering of workers, anarchists, socialists, and political philosophers in London. Marx's faction dominated this organization, and his manifesto became a blueprint for the spread of Marxist ideals and associations across the continent, becoming "one of the great classics of history" (Nomad, 96).

See also
First International; Marx, Karl; Revolutions of 1848

References
Nomad, Max, *Apostles of Revolution* (New York: Collier Books, 1961).
Riazanov, David, and Joshua Kunitz, trans., *Karl Marx and Frederick Engels: An Introduction to Their Lives and Work,* first published 1927, Monthly Review Press (1973), on the internet <http://www.marx.org/Riazanov/Archive/1927-Marx>.
"Socialism: MARX AND THE RISE OF SOCIAL DEMOCRACY: The First International," *Britannica Online* <http://www.eb.com:180/cgi-bin/g?DocF=macro/5007/6/5.html>.

Confederación Nacional del Trabajo

Founded in 1911, the Confederación National del Trabajo (CNT) was a Spanish federation of workers' and peasants' unions. Dominated by anarchists, CNT's goal was "the overthrow of capitalism and the state and the establishment of an anarchist-communist society. This they believed could only be done by the workers and peasants seizing the means of production in order to produce and distribute goods and services in the interests of the community" (Harper).

The CNT grew rapidly, creating strongholds in Catalonia (especially Barcelona), Aragón, and Andalusia, where insurrectionist movements had been common since the 1860s. "In Barcelona and the other cities of Catalonia the federalist, anarchist tradition had been unbroken since the time of the First International" in 1864 (Joll, 239). By 1919, the membership of CNT totaled 700,000. In 1936, there were 1.6 million members and more than 2 million during the Spanish Civil War.

> The structure of the CNT was non-hierarchical and consisted of a federation of many unions—*syndicatos.* Each union was made up of workers grouped each in their own particular trade. Such unions joined together in local or district federations which in turn were grouped into regions. The CNT itself was formed out of these regional federations. Regular union assemblies elected delegates to all organisations . . . there were no permanent bureaucrats or paid officials, and all union activity was done after work hours. The national federation was directly responsible to the regions and so on down to the base the assemblies of workers and peasants. (Harper)

At first CNT backed the Russian Revolution of October 1917, hoping a workers' international would develop, but leaders soon became disillusioned with the dictatorship of the proletariats and broke their ties with the Bolsheviks. Between 1917 and 1923, however, CNT staged strikes across Spain, and during that period militant protests "brought government in Spain almost to a stop . . . each act of violence by one side brought its reprisals from the other" (Joll, 242).

When Primo de Rivera became dictator of Spain in 1923, CNT was declared illegal, and it had to operate in secret. "Anarchist periodicals were largely banned; anarchist and syndicalist offices were closed and over 200 leading militants were arrested" (Joll, 244–245). Although some of the federations remained intact, anarchist militants founded a new organization, the Federación Anarquista Ibérica (FAI) or the Anarchist Federation of Iberia. FAI was also a clandestine organization, made up of "young, fanatical revolutionaries who were determined to restore the anarchist movement to a course of uncompromising opposition to the existing order, and to put an end to the flirtations with the republican politicians of which they suspected some of the CNT leaders" (Joll, 244–245).

At the start of the Spanish Revolution and Civil War in 1936, CNT and FAI came out in the open. Leaders urged workers to prepare for a general strike and to arm themselves in order to resist fascists and communists who supported Gen. Francisco Franco and the military takeover of the government. During the first year of the revolution, workers and peasants, encouraged by CNT and FAI, were able to appropriate land and factories in hundreds of villages in Andalusia, Catalonia, and Levante. They set up communes and formed democratic militias. When George Orwell, the now famous novelist who fought during the revolution, visited Barcelona he found that "unions had simply taken over the factories, sometimes keeping the old managers as technical advisers; public services were run by the workers themselves; the small shopkeepers, the barbers and the bakers were organized in syndicates" (quoted in Joll, 256).

A lesser-known observer reported in 1937 that he found CNT to be the

> most vital of the working-class organisations in Spain. That was evident on all sides. The large industries were clearly, in the main, in the hands of the CNT—railways, road, engineering, textiles, electricity, building, agriculture. . . . I was impressed by the outward signs of the power of the CNT. At Barcelona it has taken over . . . a monumental building, comparable with the vast structure which is the headquarters of the London Passenger Transport Board at St. James' Park. At Valencia the CNT occupies the palace of a Marquis of the old regime. Both headquarters are hives of well-organised activities—secretarial, transport, defence, propaganda, organisation, publication, international departments, etc. And these are only the co-ordinating headquarters. Scattered about both cities one saw large buildings occupied by the various Unions—building workers, electrical workers, transport workers, federated in the CNT. (Brockway)

This observer also expressed his admiration for the CNT membership's "full participation in the war against the Fascists . . . the literature and posters issued to stimulate the workers to give their all in the struggle against Franco" (Brockway).

However, CNT collectives did not last long, primarily because the revolution was undermined by German and Italian fascists who sent money and arms to support Franco and his army. Although Russia sent aid to the anarchists, it was "on condition that the tiny Spanish Communist Party be given government positions and the popular militias be 're-organised.' The communists refused arms to the CNT militias at the front and began disarming the Barcelona workers; attacks on anarchists were stepped up" (Harper). In one such attack Italian anarchist Camillo Berneri, who had smuggled arms to anarchists, was killed by communists with machine guns.

The Barcelona collectives were soon taken over by the central government, which was increasingly influenced by communists. From mid 1937 until the end of the war in 1939, CNT and FAI were weakened and members were demoralized as leaders made one compromise after another with the government. An example was Federica Montseny, "the one true intellectual" among those who cooperated with the government; she became the minister of health, but it was a painful decision. Coming from a family of anarchists and antiauthoritarians, her position with the government created a personal dilemma. As she noted:

> For us who had struggled constantly against the state, who had always said that the state could achieve absolutely nothing, that the words Government and Authority meant the negation of any possibility of liberty for individuals and peoples, our incorporation as an organization and as individuals into a government project meant either an act of historical audacity of fundamental importance or a theoretical and tactical correction of a whole structure and a whole chapter of history. . . . What reservations, what doubts, what inner anguish I had personally to overcome before accepting this task! . . . It was simply a breach with all my work, with all my life, with all my past. (quoted in Joll, 265–266)

Many historians contend some anarchists were mistaken to work within the government of Barcelona. Others, however, see their cooperation as a necessity of the time, for otherwise CNT and other anarchists were destined to lose everything. In effect, that was the outcome. Eventually Franco was victorious and became dictator, dooming most Spanish anarchists to death or imprisonment; some were able to escape into exile.

See also
Anarcho-Syndicalism; Berneri, Luigi Camillo; Collective; Orwell, George; Spanish Anarchism; Spanish Civil War

References

"Anarchism: ANARCHISM AS A MOVEMENT: Anarchism in Spain." *Britannica Online* <http://www.eb.com:180/cgi-bin/g?DocF=macro/5007/8/6.html>.

Brockway, Fenner, "The CNT as I Saw It" (July 19, 1937), on the internet <http://au.spunk.org/library/places/spain/sp000068.txt>.

Harper, Clifford, "Spain's Revolutionary Anarchist Movement," from *Anarchy: A Graphic Guide,* on the internet <http://flag.blackened.net/liberty/spain rev.html>.

Joll, James, *The Anarchists* (Boston: Little, Brown, 1964).

Kaplan, Temma, *Anarchists of Andalusia, 1868–1903* (Princeton: Princeton University Press, 1977).

Wetzel, Tom, "Workers Power and the Spanish Revolution," on the internet <http://www.uncanny.net/~wsa/spain.html>.

Contemporary Anarchism

Although the anarchist movement of the late 1800s and early 1900s declined considerably after the Spanish Civil War (1936–1939) and World War II, anarchism continued to develop in various parts of the world. During the postwar period, radicals often espoused Marxist ideals and considered themselves communists. Nevertheless, by the 1960s

> anarchism reemerged as a significant force. The Communist party was identified with bureaucratic inertia and dogmatism, with rigid adherence to an outworn ideology at the moment that a new generation of students sought alternatives to the military-industrial complex that was widely identified with the war to stamp out communism in Vietnam. The student revolt of the 1960s stretched from Berkeley to Paris to Amsterdam, from Tokyo to Mexico City. (Sonn, 101)

In the United States, anarchist ideas had been reflected in the direct action tactics and civil disobedience, such as bus boycotts and sit-ins, of the civil rights movement of the 1950s. During the 1960s and 1970s, the anarchist demands for individual freedom and rejection of authority were demonstrated by such groups as the Black Panthers and Students for a Democratic Society. Protests (some of them violent), back-to-nature movements, communal living, consciousness-raising groups, the underground press, guerrilla theater, and many other anti-establishment activities were part of anarchist-like events in the United States. "The new utopians rejected the work ethic, the hierarchies of corporation and university, the patriarchal nuclear family, and rampant consumerism as much as they protested against class- and race-based oppression" (Sonn, 102).

In other parts of the world, the anarchist spirit was manifest in such direct action as the student revolts in France in May 1968, when university students at the Sorbonne University began to protest overcrowded facilities, lack of access to teachers, and inflexible rules and regulations established by university officials. When police were called in, a major confrontation erupted. Students built barricades and occupied the Sorbonne University, creating a commune reminiscent of the Paris Commune of 1871. Factory workers joined the fray with strike after strike, paralyzing France for two weeks until the government initiated labor and political reforms.

Although many other manifestations of contemporary anarchist ideas emerged during the 1960s and 1970s, only small groups of anarchists worldwide have continued to try to live by anarchist principles. These include activists in such groups as Food Not Bombs, which in spite of government repression takes direct action to provide free food for the poor and homeless; women's groups who call themselves anarcho-feminists; and individuals who adhere to the social ecology theories of Murray Bookchin, who argues that the principles of anarchy (such as eliminating hierarchical structures) are needed to save the planet from total destruction by humans.

However, libertarian socialist Noam Chomsky saw a shift in anarchist ideology during the 1980s and 1990s:

> In the Anglo-American sphere, anarchism is being divested of its social ideal by an

emphasis on personal autonomy, an emphasis that is draining it of its historic vitality. A Stirnerite individualism—marked by an advocacy of lifestyle changes, the cultivation of behavioral idiosyncrasies and even an embrace of outright mysticism—has become increasingly prominent. This personalistic "lifestyle anarchism" is steadily eroding the socialistic core of anarchist concepts of freedom.

Let me stress that in the British and American social tradition, autonomy and freedom are not equivalent terms. By insisting on the need to eliminate personal domination, autonomy focuses on the individual as the formative component and locus of society. By contrast, freedom, despite its looser usages, denotes the absence of domination in society, of which the individual is part. This contrast becomes very important when individualist anarchists equate collectivism as such with the tyranny of the community over its members. (Chomsky interview)

A variety of anarchist philosophers, writers, and historians expressed their views during the latter half of the 20th century. Their ideas appear not only in printed form but also on ever-increasing websites maintained throughout the world. Although a worldwide anarchist revolution is not likely at present, many who call themselves anarchists continue to question institutions, authorities, and a social structure that emphasizes the dominance of one human over another. Forging a revolutionary movement inspired by anarchist ideas, wrote Sam Dolgoff, "is a task of staggering proportions. But therein lies the true relevance of anarchism."

See also

Anarcha-Feminism; Anarchist Authors; Black Panthers; Bookchin, Murray; Chomsky, Avram Noam; Food Not Bombs; Individualist Anarchists; May 1968; Social Ecology; Stirner, Max

References

"Anarchism: CONTEMPORARY CURRENTS," *Britannica Online* <http://www.eb.com:180/cgi-bin/g?DocF=macro/5007/8/8.html>.

Chomsky, Noam, "Anarchism, Marxism and Hope for the Future," Interview, first published in *Red & Black Revolution,* No. 2 (1996), on the internet <http://www.geocities.com/CapitolHill/2419/index.html">.

De Leon, David, *The American as Anarchist: Reflections on Indigenous Radicalism* (Baltimore: Johns Hopkins University Press, 1978).

Dolgoff, Sam, *The Relevance of Anarchism to Modern Society* (Minneapolis: Soil of Liberty, 1977).

Perlin, Terry M., ed., *Contemporary Anarchism* (New Brunswick, NJ: Transaction Books, 1979).

Sonn, Richard, *Anarchism* (New York: Twayne/Macmillan, 1992), chap. 5, "Contemporary Anarchism."

Cooperative

The modern cooperative movement—and the type of economic organization often referred to as the *cooperative* in anarchist and socialist literature—was based on the concept of living for the common good. Whether the intent is to achieve a cooperative ("co-op" in the United States) system for agriculture, purchase of equipment or services, electric power, banking, housing, consumer goods, or any combination of the above, the organization is owned and operated by members for their own benefit. Membership is almost always open, and decisions are made by direct representation of that membership. If a profit is created in a retail-type cooperative, proceeds are usually divided among members. Oftentimes, some money is set aside for education and communal projects as decided by the membership in a general meeting.

The cooperative movement spread throughout Europe during the 19th century, especially among working-class communities in England and Scotland. Many cooperatives used variations of the bylaws established by the Rochdale Society of Equitable Pioneers founded in 1844 in England. Numerous cooperatives were also established in France, Germany, Norway, the Netherlands, Denmark, Finland, and the United States.

In the United States, various cooperatives formed in the 1800s. Some were religious communes. Others were socialist or communistic experiments ranging

from those that cooperated on a very limited scale, like a colony that might build

> together an irrigation system, to a comprehensive communism that abandoned all private holdings. In whatever manifestation the common life was considered superior. The model colony might be small, but it was expandable, exportable, and repeatable. . . . It was seldom revolutionary in the Marxist sense. Instead, it leaned in the direction of perfectionism, the belief espoused by [John Humphrey] Noyes that man and societies are malleable and, in the near future, perfectable. (Hine, 201)

Noyes's colony, the Oneida Community in Upstate New York, was founded in 1848, one of hundreds of cooperative colonies established during the 1800s and early 1900s. Other examples include Robert Owen's New Harmony in Indiana, Fourierist communities in Wisconsin and other states, and colonies in the West designed by labor unionists and socialists.

The largest and most famous of the cooperative experiments occurred during the Soviet era when the Union of Soviet Socialist Republics (USSR) and the Eastern European countries within its sphere of influence used marketing and purchasing cooperatives to leverage their power in world markets. The farm cooperatives under the Soviet system grouped all agricultural land together, eliminating private property, so that it could be worked in common. When harvest time came, income was distributed according to the amount of work contributed to the production.

See also

Communism; Fourierism; Noyes, John Humphrey; Owen, Robert; Socialism

References

"Cooperative" *Britannica Online* <http://www.eb.com:180/cgi-bin/g?DocF=micro/143/40.html>.

Hine, Robert V., *Community on the American Frontier: Separate but Not Alone* (Norman: University of Oklahoma Press, 1980).

Cuban Anarchism

In Cuba, anarchist ideas and the labor movement developed side-by-side during the mid-19th century. "They grew so closely together that it is impossible to trace the history of one without the other," according to anarchist historian Sam Dolgoff. "The forerunners and organizers of the Cuban labor movement were the Spanish anarcho-syndicalist exiles who in the 1880s came to Cuba. It was they who gave the Cuban labor movement its distinct social revolutionary orientation" (Dolgoff, 37).

Cuban workers adapted economic theories that originally stemmed from Pierre-Joseph Proudhon and his ideas on mutualism. Cuba's first mutualist (Proudhonian) society was founded in 1857, but Proudhon's concepts did not take root until the mid-1860s, when they were described in the libertarian press and voluntary associations of tobacco workers, typesetters, and other wage earners were organized.

Another important influence on Cuban anarchists was Mikhail Bakunin, who devoted years to making the social democratic movement anarchist and international and demanded abolition of the state, which eventually created conflict with followers of Karl Marx. Even though he died in 1876, Bakunin's revolutionary approach inspired class consciousness, and anarchists stressed anarcho-syndicalist ideas among Cuban workers.

Anarchist Enrique Roig San Martín was primarily responsible for spreading anarcho-syndicalist ideas through his weekly *El Productor* (The Producer), founded in 1886. Using his newspaper, San Martín organized the Cuban proletariat and also numerous strikes and helped create the Workers' Alliance, patterned after Bakunin's concepts.

> This Workers' Alliance was strongly supported in two tobacco industry locations in the United States, Tampa and Key West. In 1887 the first Federation of Tobacco Workers was organized in Havana . . . and it embraced almost all the workers in that industry. Tampa and Key West followed. . . .
> In 1889 a general strike was declared in Key West which ended with the triumph of the workers in the first days of 1890. (Fernandez)

Cuban exiles, anarchists, and other supporters of Cuban independence were also preparing for a struggle against their colonial ruler, imperial Spain. Since the 1700s, there had been frequent uprisings against the Spanish government and owners of sugar plantations who had long suppressed workers—slaves and freemen alike. A rebellion called the Ten Years War (1868–1878) occurred, whereby enslaved Africans and indigenous people, free Cubans of African descent, and former Spanish citizens attempted to throw off Spanish rule. The conflict ended with the Spanish army ruthlessly reasserting control over the colony.

Although the Spanish government tried to stem political and social unrest, resistance was never really broken. Some Cubans fled to the United States and began to plan for a war of independence. Tampa, West Tampa, and Ybor City, Florida, became strongholds of activists, including numerous anarchists. But there was conflict among liberation leaders, some of whom did not trust Afro-Cubans, as they were called. At the same time, black revolutionists questioned whether participation would earn them social justice. And workers were concerned about what capitalists planned for an independent Cuba. It took the skills and persuasive powers of a man known as the father or apostle of the independence movement, José Martí, to bring all the factions together. A Cuban native, writer, and lecturer, Martí had been deported from Cuba and settled in New York City, where he formed the Cuban Revolutionary Party. When he arrived in Florida, he

> spoke persuasively about the need to resolve just grievances of workers and to build an independent Cuba where no one would suffer exploitation. On the question of racism, he was forthright and unequivocal: "For me the one who promotes hatred in Cuba or who tries to take advantage of that which exists is a criminal, and he who tries to suffocate the legitimate aspirations of a good and prudent race is also a criminal." (Greenbaum, 4–5)

When civil war broke out in Cuba in 1895, Martí joined the rebels in their fight, as did many anarchists. Martí died in the war, which did not end until the United States intervened and defeated Spain in the Spanish-American War. During this time, anarchists in exile and in Cuba supported the struggle by raising funds and campaigning in the United States and Europe. In the words of historian Dolgoff:

> Anarchist participation . . . was based upon the following considerations: For the exploited, oppressed masses, bourgeois independence was of secondary importance. For them, abolition of colonial despotism also signified the end of their age-long servitude, and with it, the inauguration of a new era of economic equality, social justice and personal freedom. The people's struggle for independence simultaneously took on a social-revolutionary character. Anarchist propaganda . . . encouraged the masses to turn the struggle for political independence into the struggle for the Social Revolution. (Dolgoff, 41)

Anarchist activity continued in Cuba after the end of the Spanish-American War, and Cuba became an independent republic. During the first two decades of the 1900s anarchists participated in numerous strikes called by workers in the tobacco, sugar, construction, maritime, and other industries. Anarchists also organized worker and agrarian cooperatives.

When the Russian Revolution erupted, many Cuban anarchists believed that a just and free society would soon be established worldwide. They supported the Bolsheviks until they learned through writings of various anarchist exiles, such as Alexander Berkman and Peter Kropotkin, about the communists' dictatorial abuses. Anarchists then joined and supported other class struggles, including labor campaigns for higher wages and shorter workdays and against the high cost of living. Despite efforts by the government to suppress radicals, they formed the "National Labour Confederation of Cuba, Confederación Nacional Obrera de Cuba (CNOC), an umbrella organisation of all the unions, fraternal associations, guilds, brotherhoods and mutual aid associations in Cuba: 128 collectives and more than 200,000 workers were represented by 160 delegates" (Fernandez). However, when dictator General Gerardo Machado became president, he brutally repressed CNOC, which later was taken over by the communists working with the government. The Federación de Grupos Anarquistas de Cuba (FGAC) or Federation of Cuban Anarchist Groups exposed the communists and supported a general strike initiated by anarchists within the railway and streetcar unions.

The Machado government was brought down by an insurrection in 1933, and Carlos Manuel de Céspedes became president of Cuba. Within three weeks he was overthrown by a "sergeants' revolt" organized by Fulgencio Batista, who made himself a colonel and commander in chief of the army. As de facto president, Batista ruled through various appointees between 1933 and 1944. Batista's administration enacted some reforms, but when he ran for election in 1944 he was defeated. In 1952 he regained power by spending huge sums of money to influence the election and by organizing support in the military and government and among business and industrial leaders. Batista won the election, and between 1952 and 1959, with the help of the Communist Party, he maintained a dictatorship that terrorized, jailed, killed, and deported enemies. Anarchists and other rebels organized to oppose Batista and finally brought down his regime. Among the rebels were Fidel Castro and the Argentine revolutionary Ernesto Che Guevara. Castro returned to Cuba from Mexico, where he had gone to prepare for a guerrilla war against Batista's government.

After Batista was overthrown he fled the country, and Castro took over. Within a year, he began suppressing anarchists and the anarchist press. The Castro dictatorship was able to reduce anarcho-syndicalists "to a mere handful of dedicated militants" (Dolgoff, 61).

See also

Bakunin, Mikhail A.; Berkman, Alexander; Kropotkin, Peter Alexeyevich; Martí, José; Marx, Karl; Mutualism; Proudhon, Pierre-Joseph; Russian Anarchism

References

Dolgoff, Sam, *The Cuban Revolution: A Critical Perspective* (Montreal: Black Rose Books, 1976).

Fernandez, Frank, *Cuba—the Anarchists and Liberty* (London: ASP, 1989).

Greenbaum, Susan, *Afro-Cubans in Ybor City: A Centennial History* (Tampa: University of South Florida, 1986).

Czolgosz, Leon (1873–1901)

Leon Czolgosz, whose parents were Polish immigrants living in Detroit, Michigan, was 28 years old when he shot and fatally wounded U.S. President William McKinley on September 6, 1901, while the president was attending the Pan-American Exposition in Buffalo, New York. After McKinley died eight days later, authorities tried to link Czolgosz with anarchist Emma Goldman, claiming that she and other anarchists had conspired with Czolgosz to assassinate the president. A few weeks earlier, Czolgosz, using the name Nieman, had been introduced to Goldman while she visited friends in Chicago, and he expressed a desire to meet anarchists, but Czolgosz and Goldman never met again. Nevertheless, newspapers widely reported that anarchists had plotted McKinley's murder; according to one historian,

> the excited emotions of the country found vent in demanding reprisals against all anarchists everywhere. The deed had the menace and the insolence of conspiracy. A hunt for his [Czolgosz's] accomplices was pressed in Cleveland, Chicago, Detroit, and other industrial centers. Hundreds of anarchist sympathizers were questioned, and some were arrested and detained. Second only to Czolgosz in popular odium was Emma Goldman, whom he had spoken of with admiration to the police. She was generally supposed to have instigated his crime, and there was high satisfaction when she was tracked down and arrested in Chicago. (Leech, 597–598)

After her arrest, Goldman was interviewed in jail by a reporter for *The New York Times.* She told the reporter that Czolgosz

> planned the deed unaided and entirely alone. There is no Anarchist ring which would help him. There may be Anarchists who would murder, but there are also men in every walk of life who sometimes feel the impulse to kill. I do not know surely, but I think Czolgosz was one of those downtrodden men who see all the misery which the rich inflict upon the poor, who

> think of it, who brood over it, and then, in despair, resolve to strike a blow, as they think, for the good of their fellow-men. But that is not Anarchy. (Quoted in Wexler, 106)

There was never any evidence that Goldman had conspired with anyone to assassinate the president. Czolgosz confessed to the murder and during hours of questioning by police repeatedly told officers that "she [Goldman] didn't tell me to do it" (quoted in Drinnon, 70). After fifteen days in jail, where she lost a tooth because of a policeman's blow, Goldman was released. Less than two months after his arrest Czolgosz was executed.

See also
Goldman, Emma

References

Drinnon, Richard, *Rebel in Paradise: A Biography of Emma Goldman* (Chicago: University of Chicago Press, 1961).

Goldman, Emma, *Living My Life,* 2 vols. (New York: Knopf, 1933, reprint New York: Dover, 1970).

Leech, Margaret, *In the Days of McKinley* (New York: Harper and Brothers, 1959).

Wexler, Alice, *Emma Goldman: An Intimate Life* (New York: Pantheon, 1984).

D

Darrow, Clarence (1857–1938)

To anarchists during the early 1900s Clarence Darrow was known as the famous trial lawyer who defended William "Big Bill" Haywood, leader of the radical Industrial Workers of the World, and numerous other anarcho-syndicalists and labor organizers such as socialist Eugene Debs. But Darrow's fame in the United States stems primarily from his defense of a young teacher, John T. Scopes, who taught the theory of evolution in defiance of a Tennessee law. Darrow went up against William Jennings Bryan, and the trial became a passionate confrontation between two men whose arguments stemmed from totally different points of view. Darrow was a lifelong agnostic, Bryan devoutly religious. Darrow changed his client's plea to guilty at the eleventh hour of trial, anticipating the appeal. The case then went to the Supreme Court of Tennessee, where it was dismissed on a technicality. Much later, laws prohibiting the teaching of evolution were ruled unconstitutional.

Before the Scopes trial, one of Darrow's most famous cases was that of Nathan Leopold and Richard Leob, who had murdered a fourteen-year-old boy. The public was horrified by the calculation of the two; they had killed for the thrill alone. The boys had never been mistreated; they had, in fact, been given every advantage. When Darrow helped Leopold and Leob escape the death penalty, the public was outraged.

Darrow's view of the criminal mind had been shaped by a pamphlet written by John Peter Altgeld, who later became governor of Illinois and pardoned three anarchists falsely convicted of inciting a riot in Chicago. In the pamphlet, Altgeld rejected the prevailing attitude that crime was due to a criminal's innate sinfulness. Instead, he argued, personality and environment had an effect on criminal behavior. As Altgeld became more involved in politics and was appointed a judge, he and Darrow met and developed a lifelong friendship.

Darrow was also profoundly influenced by his parents, who taught their seven children to be critical thinkers. His father, Amirus, had attended seminary but lost his faith upon graduation; he became a cabinet maker and eventually a coffin maker to support his large family. Darrow's mother, Emily, was an advocate of women's rights and kept up her knowledge of current events until her death, when Clarence was 14.

The fifth child, Darrow learned debate from two of his older siblings, Edward and Mary, who took him on Friday nights to a literary society. He completed one year at Allegheny College, his father's alma mater. He then taught for three years, until his family convinced him to enroll at the University of Michigan. Amirus, Edward, and Mary believed he would make a good lawyer, and they offered to pay for his education. Darrow completed one year there before becoming a lawyer's apprentice.

His legal career, which began in small Ohio towns, did not really take off until he moved to Chicago, where he practiced law for the city's legal department and with the Chicago and North Western Railway Company before concentrating on labor cases. He became involved in trying to free the Haymarket Eight, who had been convicted of killing police and others in a bombing at a workers' rally at Haymarket

Square in 1886. Three of the men's sentences were commuted to life, one committed suicide, and the other four were hanged.

For 17 years, Darrow took cases defending unions and workers' rights to strike. He championed the cause of coal miners, who labored under extremely hazardous conditions for little pay. In 1906, he defended labor leader Bill Haywood and others, who were tried for the murder of a former governor of Idaho; they were found innocent.

The last labor case Darrow took on was the defense of brothers Joseph and James McNamara, socialists accused of dynamiting the *Los Angeles Times* building in October 1910. Twenty-one people died in the explosion. During the early 1900s, union organizers often planted explosives at job sites where company owners refused to allow workers to organize. Darrow was strongly opposed to such violence to settle labor disputes, but he agreed to defend the McNamaras. Darrow persuaded them to plead guilty and accept a pretrial sentencing agreement, hoping to avoid a jury trial he was sure would end in conviction and the death penalty for his clients. The plea bargain outraged labor leaders, who never again hired him for major cases.

Not long afterward, Darrow was accused of attempting to use an intermediary on his staff to bribe a juror into voting for the McNamaras' acquittal. Darrow was tried in 1912 on bribery charges; at the end of his long trial Darrow presented a nearly two-hour summation in his own defense, declaring in part:

> I am tried here because I have given a large part of my life and my services to the cause of the poor and the weak, and because I am in the way of the interests. These interests would stop my voice—and they have hired many vipers to help them do it. They would stop my voice—my voice, which from the time I was a prattling babe my father and mother taught me to raise for justice and freedom, and in the cause of the weak and the poor. (Cowan 1993)

The jury acquitted Darrow, but his reputation was in shambles. He returned to Chicago and never again argued another labor case, but he rebuilt his private practice. Until the end of World War I, he defended people who refused to serve in the military and those who were communists or socialists. Then he focused on criminal law. In the 1920s, the Leopold and Leob trial and the Scopes trial brought Darrow back into the public eye.

When Darrow died in 1938 at 80, his former law partner, Judge William Holly, delivered a eulogy that included text from Darrow's funeral address for his mentor, Altgeld. Holly praised Darrow's "life of kindness, of charity, of infinite pity to the outcast and the weak. . . . A truer, greater, kindlier soul has never lived and died; and the fierce bitterness and hatred that sought to destroy this great, grand soul had but one cause—the fact that he really loved his fellow man" (Cowan, 1993: 445).

See also

Anarcho-Syndicalism; Debs, Eugene Victor; Haymarket Affair; Haywood, William Dudley "Big Bill"; Industrial Workers of the World

References

Cowan, Geoffrey, *The People v. Clarence Darrow: The Bribery Trial of America's Greatest Lawyer* (New York: Times Books/Random House, 1993).

Darrow, Clarence, *The Story of My Life* (New York: Charles Scribner's Sons, 1932).

Gay, Kathlyn, and Martin K. Gay, *Heroes of Conscience* (Santa Barbara, CA: ABC-CLIO, 1996).

Straub, Deborah Gillan, ed., *Contemporary Heroes and Heroines, Book II* (Detroit: Gale Research, 1992).

Tierney, Kevin, *Darrow: A Biography* (New York: Thomas Y. Crowell, 1979).

Day, Dorothy (1897–1980)

Dorothy Day has been called one of the most famous American religious anarchists, a Christian social activist, a saint, a strong pacifist, a tireless worker for labor and the poor, and "a lifelong agitator for peaceful but revolutionary change" (Coy). Day cofounded the Catholic Worker movement, launched in 1932, and its newspaper, *Catholic Worker,* which beginning in 1933 spread information about the movement's efforts to help the urban poor and to establish communal farms.

Born in Brooklyn, New York, Dorothy was the third of five children of John and Grace

(Satterlee) Day, who moved their family to Oakland, California. After the San Francisco earthquake of 1906, the Days moved to Chicago, where Dorothy learned firsthand about the effects of unemployment. Her father was out of a job for a time but eventually found work with a Chicago newspaper. As a result, the family was able to move into a comfortable home on Chicago's north side.

In Chicago, Dorothy Day began reading books by authors who stressed the need for social reforms. Upton Sinclair's novel *The Jungle,* for example, prompted Dorothy to see for herself what Chicago's poor neighborhoods were like, the beginning of her commitment to advocacy for the masses and the working class and her opposition to capitalism.

In 1914, Day received a scholarship to the University of Illinois–Urbana, but she dropped out after two years, intending to become a writer. She moved to New York City and went to work as a reporter for *The Call,* a socialist daily, and joined the Industrial Workers of the World (IWW), a radical union that advocated overthrow of the capitalist system. She later worked for two other publications, *The Masses* and *The Liberator,* writing articles not only about the labor movement but also about women's rights issues. In 1917, Day was arrested along with other women for picketing the White House and demanding women's suffrage. She was one of 40 women sentenced to 30 days in a brutal penitentiary. The women protested with a hunger strike; a presidential order finally freed them.

Because of her strong antiwar beliefs, Day decided in 1918 to do more than write about pacifism. She became a nurse's trainee at King's County Hospital in Brooklyn. More than a year later she left, traveling to Europe then returning to the United States. From the early 1920s on she worked at various reporting jobs in Chicago, New Orleans, and New York City; she also wrote an autobiographical novel, *The Eleventh Virgin,* which centered on her love affair with a fellow journalist (an abortion had left her deeply longing for a child).

In 1925, Day met anarchist Forster Batterham, botanist and atheist, with whom she lived in a common law marriage for about four years. The couple's daughter, Tamar Theresa, was born in 1927, but Batterham had not wanted the child, declaring the world too violent for raising children. The relationship between Day and Batterham became strained, primarily because Day began developing strong religious convictions. When Day joined the Catholic Church in 1927, the couple separated.

Although Day was still strongly opposed to the capitalist system, she tried to find ways to mesh her religious faith and radical views. For a time, she worked for the Catholic publication *Commonweal,* but in 1932 she met Peter Maurin, a Franciscan priest and French immigrant who had lived in Canada. Maurin had developed a philosophy that combined the ideals of a communal society (communism) with Catholicism, and Day readily accepted his ideas. Together they launched the Catholic Worker movement, which included not only the *Catholic Worker* publication but also the St. Joseph's House of Hospitality in New York City. Numerous other hospitality houses were established in other U.S. cities, as were communal farms across the United States. These houses and farms provided refuge for the poor and homeless.

During World War II, the Catholic Worker movement emphasized pacifism; after the war, the focus was disarmament and antinuclear protests. Day was also involved in antiwar protests during the Vietnam era. She and many others in the movement were often jailed for acts of civil disobedience. Throughout the decades, Day continued to write, publishing numerous articles and six books, including her popular autobiography *The Long Loneliness* (1952).

For more than 50 years, Dorothy Day and other Catholic Workers advocated for social justice and against a government and laws that forced people to wage war. Today the Catholic Worker movement still has devoted followers. During the Dorothy Day Centennial celebrated in 1997, a Catholic Worker, Rosalie Riegle, noted that since its beginning this lay community of women and men has been

> dedicated to living the social dimension of the Gospel in a radical way by serving the

poor, struggling for social and economic justice, and working for peace. Co-founder Peter Maurin's three-point program called for informed social criticism, houses of hospitality, and communal farms where the unemployed could learn a skill. To this, Day added the unyielding pacifism which first attracted my interest. When I was introduced to Day and the Catholic Worker at the height of the Vietnam War, I was impressed with the Worker commitment to nonviolence and its insistence on a personalist response to political problems. When I began to meet individual Catholic Workers, I learned of Day's hundreds of friendships and of her very human weaknesses—a craving for coffee, a sometime abruptness in conclusion, a leadership style that caused friends to refer to her as "the abbess." I came to know someone more human and approachable. (Riegle)

See also

Religious Anarchism

References

Coy, Patrick G., "Wondering at Her Simplicity," editorial, *Fellowship Magazine,* November 1997, on the internet <http://www.nonviolence.org/for/fellowship/fel1197–05.htm>.

Day, Dorothy, *The Long Loneliness* (Chicago: Saint Thomas More Press, 1993).

Ellsberg, Robert, ed., *Dorothy Day: Selected Writings* (Maryknoll, NY: Orbis, 1992).

Gay, Kathlyn, and Martin Gay, "Dorothy Day," *Heroes of Conscience* (Santa Barbara, CA: ABC-CLIO, 1996).

Riegle, Rosalie G., "Mystery and Myth: Dorothy Day, the Catholic Worker, and the Peace Movement," *Fellowship Magazine,* November 1997, on the internet <http://www.nonviolence.org/for/fellowship/fel1197–11.htm>.

de Cleyre, Voltairine (1866–1912)

In the view of biographer Paul Avrich, Voltairine de Cleyre was "a brief comet in the anarchist firmament." Emma Goldman called her America's "most gifted and brilliant anarchist woman," even though Goldman and de Cleyre often disagreed on many matters. De Cleyre, who was in poor health most of her adult life, died young, but she played a prominent role in the libertarian movement between 1887 and 1912. She was a poet and essayist, producing a large amount of work that appeared in such magazines as *Liberty, Free Society,* and *Mother Earth.* Yet very little has been written about her until recent years, and much of her writing is not well known due to its publication in obscure journals.

Born in the small town of Leslie, Michigan, Voltairine was the youngest of three daughters of Hector Auguste and Harriet de Claire, as they spelled their name. (Voltairine later used the spelling de Cleyre.) Auguste named his daughter Voltairine for Voltaire, the pen name of a 1700s author who championed individual liberty and wrote against organized religion. The de Claires separated when Voltairine was of preschool age, and she and her sister lived with their mother in St. Johns, Michigan, surviving on Harriet's meager earnings as a seamstress. The eldest sister had drowned while swimming. When Voltairine was 12, her mother sent her to live with her father in Port Huron, because, as Margaret Marsh noted in her book on anarchist women, "Harriet had lost control over her wild, free, intellectually precocious, and impulsive younger daughter" (Marsh, 125).

Auguste de Claire claimed to be a free thinker, espousing separation of church and state and the belief that religious matters should be left to individual conscience and reasoning. But he gave up his free-thought views and returned to the Catholic Church, as he had been reared. He insisted that Voltairine become a nun and sent her to a convent in Ontario, Canada. Hating the repression and strict discipline in the convent, she ran away, but her father forced her to return. She continued to rebel, but her time at the convent developed in her "a love of order and a powerful belief in the necessity of self control. For the rest of her life these aspects of her emotional makeup conflicted strongly with the passionate, nearly irrational urge for untrammeled liberty" (Marsh, 127).

After graduation from the Catholic academy, Voltairine lived for a time in Michigan with relatives. She left in 1887 to become a free-thought lecturer, which brought her into contact with radical groups throughout the Midwest and East. She at first espoused the individualist anarchism of Benjamin Tucker, but she was most deeply influenced by her friend and lover, Dyer D. Lum, a married man with children. Lum was a mutualist and a longtime union organizer. Both he and de Cleyre hoped to unite the varied anarchist factions, which proved to be impossible. Lum, who suffered from depression like de Cleyre, committed suicide in 1893.

De Cleyre also made several attempts to end her life, and not long after the assassination of President McKinley by an alleged anarchist, one of de Cleyre's students attempted to kill her. She survived gunshot wounds and continued to write and lecture. De Cleyre also had a lengthy relationship with James Elliott, a carpenter active in the free-thought movement. The two lived together for a time until de Cleyre became pregnant, which embittered her. She did not want to have a child and after her son, Harry, was born, she left him with Elliott. She shut out Harry from her life without discernible regret or serious reflection, according to Marsh.

During the late 1880s and 1890s, de Cleyre developed and articulated her anarchist-feminist ideas. She denounced marriage and male domination, demanding freedom for women to control their own lives through economic independence. She called for every woman to ask herself, "Why am I the slave of Man? Why is my brain said not to be equal of his brain? Why is my work not paid equally with his? Why must my body be controlled by my husband? Why may he take my children away from me? Will them away while yet unborn? Let every woman ask" (McElroy). She provided answers to these questions in her essay "Sex Slavery," writing that the reasons were "ultimately reducible to a single principle—the authoritarian supreme power GOD-idea, and its two instruments—the Church—that is, the priests—and the State—that is, the legislators. . . . These two things, the mind domination of the Church and the body domination of the State, are the causes of Sex Slavery" (McElroy).

As with other anarchists, her creed included the belief that all forms of authority should be replaced by self-control, although she had only vague ideas as to how this would be accomplished. As she developed her concepts she lectured in the United States and Europe and wrote hundreds of essays and poems. One essay that has been republished numerous times is "Anarchism and American Traditions," which relates anarchist ideas to the American Revolution, except that in the article de Cleyre rejects any form of government even if minimal, as the American revolutionaries envisioned.

Near the end of her life in 1911, de Cleyre took up the cause of the Mexican Revolution, believing that the Mexican revolutionaries might establish an anarchist society. But she never learned the outcome of the insurrection, which prompted at least two decades of armed conflict. De Cleyre became ill from complications following surgery and died in 1912 at the age of 45.

See also

Anarcha-Feminism; Direct Action; Goldman, Emma; Tucker, Benjamin R.

References

Avrich, Paul, *An American Anarchist: The Life of Voltairine de Cleyre* (Princeton: Princeton University Press, 1978).

Avrich, Paul, *Anarchist Voices: An Oral History of Anarchism in America* (Princeton: Princeton University Press, 1995).

de Cleyre, Voltairine, *The Selected Works of Voltairine de Cleyre* (New York: Mother Earth, 1914).

Marsh, Margaret S., *Anarchist Women, 1870–1920* (Philadelphia: Temple University Press, 1981).

McElroy, Wendy, "Anarchy and Feminism," no date, on the internet <http://alumni.umbc.edu/~akoont1/tmh/voltair.html>.

Presley, Sharon, "Voltairine de Cleyre," *The Storm!* (Winter 1979).

Silverman, Henry, ed., *American Radical Thought: The Libertarian Tradition* (Lexington, MA: D. C. Heath, 1970).

De Leon, Daniel (1852–1914)

An American Marxist and one of the foremost theorists of socialism, Daniel De Leon joined such labor organizers as William "Big Bill" Haywood, Eugene Debs, Mary "Mother" Jones, and Lucy Parsons at the founding convention of the Industrial Workers of the World (IWW) in Chicago in 1905. The IWW goal was to form "One Big Union," and its Preamble called for workers to "come together on the political as well as the industrial field." A 1908 amendment deleted any reference to political organization, which caused a split. De Leon lead a splinter group that established headquarters in Detroit, Michigan, and was known as Detroit IWW or the "yellow" IWW. The other main faction, the "red" IWW, was based in Chicago and advocated free speech and direct action to accomplish its goals. In 1915, De Leon's faction renamed itself the Workers International Industrial Union (WIIU), but the group lasted only ten years, folding in 1925.

When the IWW first formed in Chicago, De Leon was espousing his view that American unions should be involved in politics, a theory now called "socialist industrial unionism." He claimed, "Industrial Unionism is the Socialist Republic in the making; and, the goal once reached, the Industrial Union is the Socialist Republic in operation. Accordingly, the Industrial Union is at once the battering ram with which to pound down the fortress of Capitalism, and the successor of the capitalist social structure itself" (De Leon, 1913).

De Leon was born on the island of Curaçao but spent much of his adult life in New York City, where he lectured on constitutional and international law at Columbia University. At that time, he had not yet adopted Marxist ideas, but he was an outspoken radical, which prompted the university to fire him in 1889. That year he joined the Socialist Labor Party (SLP) and in 1891, when the party's newspaper, *The People,* was established, De Leon became its editor, a position he held for the rest of his life. He also edited SLP's *The Daily People.* His editorials spelled out the socialist philosophy that he developed, which one historian described as a complete change in the structure of government, abandoning the use of geographical constituencies (towns, counties, provinces, etc.). The local and national economic congresses would consist of delegates elected by the workers in the various occupational functions—manufacturing, transportation, agriculture, education, health, recreation, and so on. This "industrial form of government," which would replace the political form, would have only economic responsibilities. Thus, De Leon, like Marx, agreed partially with anarchists, insofar as saying that a truly classless society must also be stateless and have no coercive power distinct from and ruling over the populace.

De Leon's philosophy differed from most anarchists and anarcho-syndicalists in insisting that the working class can abolish the state only by first capturing control of the offices of political government (i.e., the coercive and geographically based form of government) in order to dismantle it. Therefore, the working class requires organization on the political field. The ballot, he said, "raises the labor movement above the category of a conspiracy." However, the ballot is considered purely "destructive," in that it seeks to attain control of the state only for the purpose of dismantling it. The sole "constructive" power of the working class is considered to be the industrial union. (Lepore)

De Leon continued to promote his ideas on industrial unionism through WIIU, but the group had little impact. After De Leon died in 1914, WIIU soon disappeared.

See also

Debs, Eugene Victor; Haywood, William Dudley "Big Bill"; Industrial Workers of the World; Jones, Mary "Mother"; Parsons, Lucy

References

De Leon, Daniel, "Industrial Unionism, *The Daily People* (January 20, 1913).

Lepore, Mike, "A Short Review of the Life and Work of Daniel De Leon," on the internet <http://www.marx.org/deleon/bio.htm>.

Werstein, Irving, *Pie in the Sky, an American Struggle: The Wobblies and Their Times* (New York: Delacorte, 1969).

Debs, Eugene Victor (1855–1926)

Eugene Victor Debs spent his adult life trying to better the conditions of American workers, particularly railroad workers, and advocating on behalf of socialism. Although he never called himself an anarchist, he helped organize the radical Industrial Workers of the World (IWW) in 1905 and consistently took part in the struggle between workers and capitalists. He also headed the Social Democratic Party, formed in 1898, which eventually became part of the Socialist Party of America. Debs ran five times as the Socialist candidate for U.S. president.

Eugene Debs was the third child of six children born to Marguerite Bettrich Debs and Jean Daniel Debs, who emigrated from Europe in 1849 and settled in Terre Haute, Indiana, where Daniel Debs eventually established a grocery store. Eugene attended elementary and high school but, bored, dropped out when he was 14 years old. Yet always eager to learn, he continued his education under his father's excellent tutelage, studying French and German classics.

His religious education was limited to one visit to St. Joseph's Cathedral, where, he once recalled, the priest delivered an address on hell. The sermon was filled with threats of terrible horrors that would be visited on "all who did not accept the interpretation of Christianity as given by the priest"; Debs left "with a rich and royal hatred of the priest as a person, and a loathing for the church as an institution" (Ginger, 10). He vowed never to return because he believed the church should preach Christ's love rather than fear of retribution.

During the 1870s, Debs worked for the Terre Haute and Indianapolis Railway as a fireman, but at his mother's urging he left the dangerous job and became a billing clerk for a wholesale grocer. He maintained ties with the railroad, however, joining the Brotherhood of Locomotive Firemen; at the age of 20 he was elected secretary of the local lodge.

In 1885 he married Kate Metzel. Their marriage was childless, and Kate Debs spent many lonely days while her husband worked for the union or was on the political trail. Debs got into politics in the latter part of the 1880s, winning the office of city clerk, then a term as a state legislator. But rather than run for reelection he became assistant editor and eventually editor of *Locomotive Firemen's Magazine* and was actively involved with not only the magazine but also in organizing the American Railway Union (ARU), which began in 1893 and quickly grew from a few thousand to tens of thousands of members by 1894. That same year, the union was almost destroyed by the notorious Pullman strike against drastic wage cuts, layoffs, and poor working conditions at the Pullman Palace Car Company. Although Debs was against the strike, he supported ARU members when they voted to boycott trains with Pullman cars attached; as a result, rail traffic between Chicago and points west ceased. A federal court issued an injunction to stop the strike; Debs ignored it and was arrested and indicted for conspiracy to interfere with interstate commerce. President Grover Cleveland sent federal troops to Illinois to smash the strike.

The criminal charges were dropped against Debs, but he served six months in jail for contempt of court, which changed his life. He began to ponder the significance of the failed strike and determined that the class struggle between big business and labor could only be resolved through socialism. When he was released from jail, he delivered a speech on personal liberty and how powerful corporations threatened the liberties of American workers.

By the end of the 19th century, Debs had transformed what was left of the ARU into a socialist political party, which in 1901 became the Socialist Party of America. He spent the last 25 years of his life speaking and writing about his socialist views and the labor movement, becoming the Socialist Party's perennial candidate for president.

Before the United States entered World War I, Debs delivered numerous antiwar speeches castigating the "master class" for advocating a war in which the "subject class" had to do battle. In a speech in Canton, Ohio, he declared:

> The master class has had all to gain and nothing to lose, while the subject class has had nothing to gain and all to lose—including their lives. . . . The working class who fight all the battles, the working class who make the supreme sacrifices, the working class who freely shed their blood and furnish the corpses, have never yet had a voice in either declaring war or making peace. It is the ruling class that invariably does both. (Debs, 425)

Although President Woodrow Wilson had promised to keep the United States out of

World War I, after war was declared, Wilson's administration, the press, and many religious and educational institutions treated antiwar activists harshly. Many, like Debs, were charged with violating the Espionage Act of 1917. Debs was convicted but during his trial he declared "I am prepared for the sentence. . . . Years ago I recognized my kinship with all living beings, and I made up my mind that I was not one bit better than the meanest of earth. I said then, and I say now, that while there is a lawyer class, I am in it; while there is a criminal element, I am of it; while there is a soul in prison, I am not free" (Debs, 437).

Debs received a ten-year sentence, and while in jail he once more ran for president. In the 1920 election he received nearly 1 million votes. Debs was pardoned by President William Harding in 1921 and released on Christmas Day. Upon his release, he continued supporting socialist and labor causes. Even though his health was failing, he wrote *Walls and Bars,* addressing prison conditions and the need for reforms. When he died of a heart attack in October 1926, he was mourned by hundreds of thousands, the wealthy and famous as well as the common folk he championed.

See also

Espionage Act of 1917; Industrial Workers of the World; Socialism; Socialist Party of America/Socialist Party USA

References

Currie, Harold W., *Eugene V. Debs* (Boston: Twayne Publishers, 1976).

Debs, Eugene, *Writings and Speeches of Eugene V. Debs* (New York: Hermitage Press, 1948).

Ginger, Ray, *The Bending Cross: A Biography of Eugene Victor Debs* (New Brunswick, NJ: Rutgers University Press, 1949).

Whitman, Alden, ed., *American Reformers* (New York: H. W. Wilson, 1985).

Dellinger, David (1915–)

Known for leading rallies of young peace activists, anarchists, and other New Left dissidents during the 1960s, David Dellinger was still speaking out about radical pacifism and the need for a social revolution in 1996 at age 80. Dellinger also became notorious as a draft resister during World War II and since then has been arrested time and again for actions on behalf of peace and in civil rights protests.

Born to conservative parents who traced their ancestry to prerevolutionary America, Dellinger was not raised to be a radical. The Dellingers, who made their home in Boston, Massachusetts, were well educated, affluent, and very much part of the established order. As a child, David respected his father's ability to get along with everyone with whom he had contact, and he considered him to be one of the most loving persons he knew. But he eventually came to oppose his father's more conservative views, especially the intolerance he showed for members of other groups in society like anarchists, atheists, labor leaders, and the like.

As a youngster, David was deeply affected by the trial and execution of Italian-born anarchists Nicola Sacco, a shoemaker, and Bartolomeo Vanzetti, a fish peddler. Many believe the two men were wrongly convicted of murder because of their ancestry and anarchist beliefs. When Sacco and Vanzetti were arrested, David was only five years old, but by the time of their deaths he was 12 and had come to see them as victims of a repressive government and a bigoted social structure. He learned that his father had spoken intimately with the governor and could have asked for mercy for the men, but when he did not, David became increasingly disillusioned about people of high social class—including his father—who would not speak out for justice.

Dellinger enrolled at Yale University when he was 17 years old and soon became an activist. Among his many activities was an effort to start a union to improve conditions for nonacademic employees of the university. When Dellinger showed interest in helping this cause, the dean warned him not to get involved because the communists would try to recruit him at one of the organizing meetings. Nevertheless, Dellinger decided to take part and discovered that Christian radicals (similar to religious anarchists of the past) were leading the effort. Their strong love ethic and commitment to nonviolent action influenced Dellinger greatly. He equated their efforts to the objectives and teachings of Mohandas

Gandhi, the Indian leader who was very much in the news during this time.

In an effort to further his own practical education, the young collegian would often dress in his poorest clothes and take to the streets near the university. It was the height of the Great Depression, and he learned firsthand what life was like for the homeless, hungry, and desperate. He was often befriended by people who were learning to survive on nothing. These were not slackers and drunks, as he had been told by his peers, but ordinary citizens caught in changes to what Dellinger concluded was an inhumane capitalist system. He often stood in breadlines, spent nights in shelters, rode freight trains, and visited "hobo" villages in his quest to understand what was happening to people. From such experiences he became committed to live according to principles of love and solidarity rather than by competitiveness.

Dellinger graduated from Yale magna cum laude in 1936, then attended Yale Divinity School and the Union Theological Seminary in New York City. In 1940 he acted upon his principles (similar to the way anarchists of earlier times took direct action) by refusing to register for the draft. As a divinity student he was exempt from the draft, but he was required by law to register. He was promised the directorship of a conscientious objector camp if he would follow that legally acceptable path. He determined, however, that to do so was to work in complicity with a system that had little moral accountability. He was sentenced to a year and a day for breaking the law. While in solitary confinement in a Danbury, Connecticut, prison he came close to death yet remained steadfast in his convictions.

Dellinger married soon after his release and started the Peoples Peace Now Committee in 1943. That group led a demonstration in the nation's capital protesting the continued bombing in Germany. He was arrested weeks later when the federal government cited him for refusing to take his Selective Service physical. He received a two-year sentence. And so the pattern was set.

Through his writings (which include six books, among them *Revolutionary Non-Violence; More Power Than We Know: The People's Movement Toward Democracy;* and his autobiography, *From Yale to Jail: The Life of a Moral Dissenter*) and personal leadership, Dellinger's life has become a model for ethical activism. During the 1960s, he was on the frontlines of the struggle for racial equality and justice in the northern urban centers, in prisons, and in the dangerous days of the southern freedom marches. His commitment to nonviolence and pacifism made him a leader of the antiwar protests against government conduct during the Vietnam War. He even went to North Vietnam and negotiated with the government for the release of American prisoners of war.

One of Dellinger's most publicized actions was a 1968 address to 50,000 peace demonstrators in Chicago for the Democratic National Convention. Demonstrators had gathered outside the convention hotel, and police moved in to disperse the crowd. The brutality that followed was seen by millions of Americans on the evening news, and the federal government arrested the top leadership of the antiwar movement in its wake. Bobby Seale, Tom Hayden, Rennie Davis, Abbie Hoffman, Jerry Rubin, Lee Weiner, John Froines, and David Dellinger were charged with conspiracy and crossing state lines to incite a riot.

The trial of the Chicago Eight (later called the Chicago Seven when Bobby Seale's case was separated) became a circus in the courtroom of Judge Julius Hoffman. After more than four months, Dellinger and four codefendants were convicted (Dellinger was also convicted of contempt of court). Eventually, all of the convictions were overturned, except for Dellinger's contempt of court charge.

In 1996, Dellinger once more made plans for a protest outside the Democratic National Convention. Weeks before the event, he traveled to Chicago to address a group protesting inequities in the U.S. criminal justice system. Just a month earlier, he had been arrested in Washington, D.C., because of a demonstration on behalf of "political prisoners." Summing up Dellinger's life, a minister who had been jailed with him during the 1940s described him as "the most resolute practitioner of nonviolent action that I know . . . a gentle spirit, but absolutely firm in his convictions" (Griffin).

See also
Gandhi, Mohandas "Mahatma" Karamchand; Religious Anarchism; Sacco, Nicola, and Bartolomeo Vanzetti

References

Dellinger, David, *From Yale to Jail: The Life of a Moral Dissenter* (New York: Pantheon Books, 1993).
Farber, David, *Chicago '68* (Chicago: University of Chicago Press, 1988).
Griffin, Jean Latz, "Dellinger Protests Even If Whole World's Not Watching," *Chicago Tribune* (June 24, 1996).

Dick, James and Nellie

See Stelton School and Colony

Dielo Trouda (Workers' Cause)

In 1925, Russian and Ukrainian anarchists—particularly Nestor Makhno and Piotr Arshinov—who had taken part in the Russian Revolution were in exile in France. There they launched a bimonthly called *Dielo Trouda* (Workers' Cause). The following year the group published an organizational platform, which called for the formation of the General Union of Anarchists and began with an acknowledgment that

> in spite of the strength and incontestably positive character of libertarian ideas, and . . . the forthrightness and integrity of anarchist positions in the facing up to the social revolution, and finally the heroism and innumerable sacrifices borne by the anarchists in the struggle for libertarian communism, the anarchist movement remains weak . . . and has appeared, very often, in the history of working class struggles as a small event, an episode, and not an important factor.
>
> This contradiction between the positive and incontestable substance of libertarian ideas, and the miserable state in which the anarchist movement vegetates, has its explanation in a number of causes, of which the most important, the principal, is the absence of organisational principles and practices in the anarchist movement. In all countries, the anarchist movement is represented by several local organisations advocating contradictory theories and practices, having no perspectives for the future, nor of a continuity in militant work, and habitually disappearing, hardly leaving the slightest trace behind them. Taken as a whole, such a state of revolutionary anarchism can only be described as 'chronic general disorganisation' . . . [which] has shaken it for dozens of years.
>
> It is nevertheless beyond doubt that this disorganisation derives from some defects of theory: notably from a false interpretation of the principle of individuality in anarchism: this theory being too often confused with the absence of all responsibility. The lovers of assertion of "self," solely with a view to personal pleasure, obstinately cling to the chaotic state of the anarchist movement, and refer in its defence to the immutable principles of anarchism and its teachers. But the immutable principles and teachers have shown exactly the opposite.
>
> Dispersion and scattering are ruinous: a close-knit union is a sign of life and development. This lax of social struggle applies as much to classes as to organisations. Anarchism is not a beautiful utopia, nor an abstract philosophical idea, it is a social movement of the labouring masses. For this reason it must gather its forces in one organisation, constantly agitating, as demanded by reality and the strategy of class struggle. ("Organisational Platform of the Libertarian Communists")

The platform shows how Russian anarchists were unable to counteract the influence of the Bolsheviks and other political groups among workers and sets up a guide for a more effective anarchist movement. In conclusion, the platform declares that

> the General Union of Anarchists has a concrete and determined goal. In the name of the success of the social revolution it must above all attract and absorb the most revolutionary and strongly criti-

cal elements among the workers and peasants.

Extolling the social revolution, and further, being an antiauthoritarian organisation which aspires to the abolition of class society, the General Union of Anarchists depends equally on the two fundamental classes of society: the workers and the peasants. It lays equal stress on the work of emancipating these two classes. As regards the workers trade unions and revolutionary organisations in the towns, the General Union of Anarchists will have to devote all its efforts to becoming their pioneer and their theoretical guide.

It adopts the same tasks with regard to the exploited peasant masses. As bases playing the same role as the revolutionary workers' trade unions, the Union strives to realise a network of revolutionary peasant economic organisations, furthermore, a specific peasants' union, founded on anti-authoritarian principles.

Born out of the mass of the labour people, the General Union must take part in all the manifestations of their life, bringing to them on every occasion the spirit of organisation, perseverance and offensive. Only in this way can it fulfil its task, its theoretical and historical mission in the social revolution of labour, and become the organised vanguard of their emancipating process. ("Organisational Platform of the Libertarian Communists")

Prominent international anarchists, such as Voline, Sébastien Faure, Molly Steimer and Senya Fleshin, Alexander Berkman, and Errico Malatesta, attacked the platform. In one response, Voline, Steimer, and others declared:

We do not believe that the anarchists should lead the masses; we believe that our role is to assist the masses only when they need such assistance. This is how we see our position: the anarchists are part of the membership in the economic and social organizations. They act and build as part of the whole. An immense field of action is opened to them for ideological, social and creative activity without assuming a position of superiority over the masses. Above all they must fulfill their ideological and ethical influence in a free and natural manner.

The anarchists and their specific organizations (groups, federations, confederations) can only offer ideological assistance, but not in the role of leaders. The slightest suggestion of direction, of superiority, of leadership of the masses and development inevitably implies that the masses must accept direction, must submit to it; this, in turn, gives the leaders a sense of being privileged like dictators, of becoming separated from the masses.

In other words, the principles of power come into play. This is in contradiction not only with the central ideas of anarchism, but also our conception of the social revolution. The revolution must be the free creation of the masses, not controlled by ideological or political groups. (Quoted in Bluestein, 53)

Despite criticism, the *Dielo Trouda* group held an international congress near Paris in 1927 and proposed that participants recognize the need for the General Union of Anarchists and a program to effectively bring about a revolution. Although the platform did not have an international impact, some anarchist groups contend it has relevance today. As the Workers Solidarity Movement points out, "The basic ideas of 'The Platform' are still in advance of the prevailing ideas in the anarchist movement internationally. Anarchists seek to change the world for the better, [and the platform offers] some of the tools we need for that task" (MacSimoin).

See also

Berkman, Alexander; Eikhenbaum, V. M. (Voline); Faure, Auguste Louis Sébastien; Makhno, Nestor Ivanovich; Malatesta, Errico; Russian Anarchism; Steimer, Mollie, and Simon Fleshin; Workers Solidarity Movement

References

Bluestein, Abe, ed., *Fighters for Anarchism: Mollie Steimer and Senya Fleshin, a Memorial Volume* (Minneapolis, MN: Libertarian Publications Group, 1983).

Dielo Trouda, "Organisational Platform of the Libertarian Communists" (1926), first Irish edition published by the Workers Solidarity Movement 1989, on the internet <http://flag.blackened.net/revolt/platform>.

MacSimoin, Alan, Preface to the "Organisational Platform of the Libertarian Communists" (1926), first Irish edition published by the Workers Solidarity Movement 1989, on the internet <http://flag.blackened.net/revolt/platform>.

Diggers

Led by Gerrard Winstanley and William Everard between 1649 and 1650, the Diggers were a group of poor farmers in England. The Diggers were similar to but more radical than the Levellers, a reform group that called for an end to nobility and demanded voting rights for all Englishmen. Calling themselves the True Levellers, the Diggers declared that the very poor should be able to cultivate unclaimed land to grow food. They not only expressed demands; in anarchist fashion they also acted upon them, creating agrarian communes on property that was not claimed or enclosed.

In April 1649, about 20 men gathered at St. George's Hill, Surrey, to protest the use of commonland for grazing animals belonging to the rich and royals. The farmers began to cultivate this common area, arguing through Winstanley and others that the result of the civil wars had been the death of Charles I and that the land should be made available to the very poor for cultivation in order to alleviate the extremely high costs of food. When the numbers of Diggers more than doubled in a year, the commonwealth government and local landowners (who also claimed the land) became alarmed. Even though they foreswore the use of force, the government under Oliver Cromwell continually harassed and attacked members of the commune. According to one story, the group was given their name because every morning after an attack the farmers had to dig plots to bury their dead. By 1650 the colony no longer existed.

More than 300 years later, in the 1960s, an anarchist group of artists, musicians, and actors, many of whom had come together as members of the guerilla theater company known as the San Francisco Mime Troop, honored the Winstanley brigade by adopting the "Digger" name. Noting that writing and performing plays was an inadequate vehicle for actualizing real social change, this dedicated group experimented in ethical living at their anarchic West Coast Digger commune. They worked to attain "absolute freedom" by establishing free housing, free food, and free medical clinics in the Haight-Ashbury district.

See also
Winstanley, Gerrard

References

Coyote, Peter, *Sleeping Where I Fall* (Washington: Counterpoint Press, 1998).

"Digger," *Britannica Online* <http://www.eb.com:180/cgi-bin/g?DocF=micro/170/34.html>.

Interview with Peter Coyote on "Fresh Air," WHYY Radio (National Public Radio), Philadelphia, April 28, 1998.

Roberts, John Morris, *History of the World* (New York and Oxford: Oxford University Press, 1993).

Sutherland, Donald R., "The Religion of Gerrard Winstanley and Digger Communism," on the internet <http://viva.lib.virginia.edu/journals/EH/EH33/suther33.htm>.

Direct Action

German anarchist Rudolf Rocker, who emigrated to the United States in 1933, defined *direct action* as immediate warfare against economic and political oppressors. Such action has included the strike, the boycott, and "sabotage in all its countless forms; antimilitarist propaganda, and in particularly critical cases, . . . armed resistance of the people for the protection of life and liberty" (Rocker, 66).

Voltairine de Cleyre, who played a prominent role in the libertarian movement between 1887 and 1912, wrote,

> Every person who ever had a plan to do anything, and went and did it, or who laid his plan before others, and won their co-operation to do it with him, without going to external authorities to please do the thing for them, was a direct actionist. All co-operative experiments are essentially direct action.
>
> Every person who ever in his life had a difference with anyone to settle, and went

> straight to the other persons involved to settle it, either by a peaceable plan or otherwise, was a direct actionist. (de Cleyre)

One of the earliest attempts at direct action occurred in England in 1649. In her book on antistatism in the United States, Corinne Jacker explained that Gerrard Winstanley, a clergyman, declared that "authority corrupts; by authority, Winstanley meant all forms of power, including the domestic authority of a husband over his wife or of a father over his son. All men were entitled to equal liberty, he said. Private property, because it was a kind of authority, was evil. The only way to get justice and equality was for the people to rise up and seize the land." But Winstanley advocated that people take over only vacant land that was not part of a lord's estate. He and 20 or 30 of his followers did just that in 1649, inciting the wrath of the king and lords. Winstanley and his group surrendered to the king's troops in 1650 (Jacker, 15–16).

Revolutions, such as the American Revolution (1775–1781), the French Revolution of the 1800s, and the Russian Revolution of 1917 have been the result of direct action by individuals and cooperative groups. Many religious anarchists and pacifists have used direct action—nonviolent resistance and civil disobedience—when refusing to serve in wars. Other religious anarchists have used acts of civil disobedience to bring about changes in unjust practices. One of the best known proponents of civil disobedience is Mohandas Gandhi, who helped gain India's independence from Great Britain.

Countless maneuvers by workers during the 18th and 19th centuries have also been forms of direct action. In the words of the Industrial Workers of the World (IWW),

> Direct action means industrial action directly by, for, and of the workers themselves, without the treacherous aid of labor misleaders or scheming politicians. A strike that is initiated, controlled, and settled by the workers directly affected is direct action. . . . Direct action is industrial democracy. . . . The worker on the job shall tell the boss when and where he shall work, how long and for what wages and under what conditions. (IWW)

Other than walking off the job, other types of direct action by labor include sit-down strikes, or staying on the job but refusing to work. Direct actions also include slowdowns and the tactic of strictly observing work regulations (e.g., postal workers following a rule to weigh every piece of mail to check proper postage). IWW recommends that workers, especially those in service industries, be overly solicitous to customers and undercharge for services, creating financial problems for businesses.

During the 1960s, so-called New Left groups in the United States often engaged in anarchistic direct action in attempts to bring about societal changes. Environmental groups such as Earth First! and other ecoanarchists and animal rights organizations such as the Animal Liberation Front have also used direct action in attempts to further their causes.

See also

Animal Liberation Front; de Cleyre, Voltairine; Earth First!; Ecoanarchists; Gandhi, Mohandas "Mahatma" Karamchand; Industrial Workers of the World; Religious Anarchism; Rocker, Rudolf; Winstanley, Gerrard

References

de Cleyre, Voltairine, "Direct Action," on the internet <http://www.spunk.org/library/writers/decleyre/sp001334.htm.

Rocker, Rudolf, *Anarchism and Anarcho-Syndicalism* (London: Freedom Press, 1988, orig. publ. as *Anarchosyndicalism* by Martin Secker and Warburg Ltd., 1938).

"What Is Direct Action?" Industrial Workers of the World, on the internet <http://iww.org/labor/direct_action/s0.html>.

Dolgoff, Sam

See Anarchist Authors

Durruti (or Durutti), Buenaventura (1896–1936)

One of the major Spanish anarchists and a legendary militia army leader at the beginning of the Spanish Civil War (1936–1939), Buenaventura Durruti was called "the very soul of the Spanish revolution" (Kern, 206). He was born in Leon, a mountainous area in north-central Spain, a place with little anarchist activity. However, early on Durruti learned about the brutality of government and became interested in anarchist ideas.

The second of nine boys, Durruti quit school when he was 14 to follow his father's footsteps. His father was a railway mechanic in Leon and called himself a libertarian socialist. The young Durruti began work with the railroad as a trainee mechanic, and in 1917 he was working in the rail yard when the Union General de Trabajadores (UGT) called an official strike of the Northern Railway Workers. According to biographer Peter Newell,

> Durruti took an active and prominent part in the strike which, after the government had refused to accept the terms agreed between the employers and the Union, became a general strike throughout the area. The general strike . . . was crushed in three days. The Spanish Government brought in the Army, which behaved with extreme barbarity. They killed 70 and wounded over 500 workers. Moreover, the authorities also jailed 2,000 of the strikers. . . . Durruti managed to escape, but had to flee abroad to France. The brutality of the Spanish State had a profound and lasting effect on the young Durruti. (Newell)

Durruti remained in Paris until 1920, when he returned to Spain and soon met a local anarchist group in San Sebastian. He joined the recently formed Confederación Nacional del Trabajo (CNT), a syndicalist union controlled by anarchists and based on the idea of one big union as established by the Industrial Workers of the World (IWW) in America.

Durruti soon went to Barcelona, capital of Catalonia and one of the few industrial centers in Spain at the time. Since the early 1900s, thousands of new workers had crammed into Barcelona; competition for jobs was fierce, prompting employers to cut wages. For two decades there had been labor unrest with some rioting, and the government ruthlessly suppressed the anarchist movement, jailing or executing many syndicalists.

In 1919 seven workers in a large electric plant were fired because of their political activities, and the CNT called a strike (in support of the dismissed workers as well as for a wage increase). Although the strike was legal and peaceful, government officials arrested and jailed CNT leaders and declared martial law. This prompted a general strike throughout Barcelona and other areas, with thousands of workers—including miners, stevedores, bakers, and construction workers—walking off the job. Many were arrested and jailed.

Faced with such repression, Durruti and an anarchist friend, Francisco Ascaso, a bakery worker, determined that they had to meet "violence with violence, assassination with assassination." By 1923 dictator Primo de Rivera was in power, and Durruti and his friend were forced to leave Spain, fleeing to South America, where they wandered from country to country trying to find refuge. At the same time, they took part in numerous anarchist activities, organizing workers, robbing banks to obtain funds for their exploits, and staying just ahead of pursuing police.

In 1924 the two returned to Europe, settling for a time in Paris, where they met exiled anarchists such as Nestor Makhno, the Ukrainian who made a great impact on Durruti and Ascaso. Makhno's ideas for a militia army later inspired Durruti at the beginning of the Spanish Civil War to form his own militia.

While in France Durruti and Ascaso and a third comrade, Gregorio Jover, attempted but failed to assassinate King Alfonso XII of Spain, who was visiting Paris in July 1926. They were jailed for months pending trial, and anarchists staged massive protests. As the case dragged on, with arguments surfacing between factions in France, "publicity spotlighted Buenaventura Durruti and made him into a romantic, mysterious, and almost idealistic revolutionary. It was as if Europeans longed for the simpler days of primitive rebels. . . . Spanish anarchism emerged from the shadows as a major political movement." In 1928, the French government "washed its hands of the whole affair" and deported Durruti, Ascaso, and Jover to Belgium (Kern, 72–73). They did not return to Spain until 1931, after the dictatorship of Primo de Rivera ended and the monarchy fell.

Although a republic was formed, CNT and the Federación Anarquista Ibérica (FAI), founded in 1927 by various anarchist groups throughout Spain, were openly antigovernment and called for nothing less than a social revolution. Between 1931 and 1936, there were numerous anarchist uprisings, but none succeeded. In early January 1932, for example, Durruti and FAI organized a revolt of miners in Catalonia, which suffered rising unemployment. "Arms were secured, gunmen and militants arrived from Barcelona, and . . . the entire district FAI organization, proclaiming libertarian communism, seized mines and government buildings." Libertarian communists believed that the working class should take over and manage the economy and refashion it according to social justice. Five villages "were heavily defended by the anarchists, and for five days Durruti and his followers withstood government attempts to restore order." Government troops, however, were able to put down the insurrection. "Durruti and Ascaso were arrested and transported to the prison ship *Buenos Aires*" (Kern, 109–111). Along with more than 100 other anarchists, they were deported to Spanish Guinea and then to Spanish Rio de Oro in Morocco. However, they were soon released and returned to Spain, where Durruti lived a relatively settled life for a few years with his wife and young daughter. But he was constantly hounded by police. The government also called on General Francisco Franco to put down outbursts of anarchist and worker opposition.

When the Spanish Civil War erupted in 1936 with a military revolt led by General Franco, CNT, FAI, and other radicals formed militias and held the major cities of Madrid, Barcelona, and Valencia as well as most of the eastern part of Spain, where numerous collectives were formed in industries and agriculture. "From July 1936 until May 1937 the anarcho-syndicalists worked to prosecute the war and simultaneously to realize their long-held dreams of social revolution" (Sonn, 1992: 88).

Durruti led a militia army in the Aragon region, patterning his actions after Nestor Makhno's guerrilla anarchists in Russia. Writes historian Robert Kern:

> Under Durruti the militia army quickly became embued with anarchist principles. Rank had only minimal importance. All units elected their officers. . . . Representatives elected to the Council of Workers and Soldiers wielded the real power. Each unit elected one man to present its wishes to the army at large. The council thrashed out most of the militia plans, even down to where and when to advance, what units to use, and how to administer liberated territory. (Kern, 161)

Less than a year after the Spanish Civil War began, it became an international conflict. Spanish nationalists received aid from Nazi Germany, which sent bombers and weapons, and from fascist Italy, which sent ground forces. On the opposite side, International Brigades made up of volunteers from Europe and the United States went to Spain to fight fascism, and the Soviet Union sent advisers and weapons to support the Spanish republicans. The Spanish Civil War became an ideological struggle between freedom (democracy) and tyranny (fascism).

Near the end of 1936, Franco's armies converged on Madrid and a battle began

> between a well-equipped army supported by German and Italian bombers on one side, and an ill-armed mass of urban workers on the other. In this situation of desperate crisis, Durruti decided to move 4,000 members of his Column from Aragon across the country to help relieve Madrid. His arrival had a tremendous effect on the besieged workers of the city. It saved Madrid, at least for a while. But on November 20th, just as he was getting out of a car, a stray bullet hit him in the back of the head, and he died immediately. On

November 22nd his body was brought back to Barcelona, accompanied by a number of his closest comrades. It lay in state until the following morning. Thousands filed past the open coffin. (Newell)

See also

Anarcho-Syndicalism; Confederación Nacional del Trabajo; Industrial Workers of the World; Libertarian Socialism; Makhno, Nestor Ivanovich; Spanish Civil War

References

Joll, James, *The Anarchists* (Boston: Little, Brown, 1964).

Kern, Robert W., *Red Years/Black Years: A Political History of Spanish Anarchism, 1910–1937* (Philadelphia: Institute for the Study of Human Issues, 1978).

Newell, Peter E., "Fighting the Revolution," pamphlet (London: Freedom Press, 1971).

E

Earth First!

The environmental movement Earth First! (EF!) is included in the "ecoanarchist" category by some theorists. Others reject the group, even though EF!ers generally are motivated by anarchist philosophy and take direct action approaches to protect the natural environment and draw public attention to ecological crises. Murray Bookchin, a noted scholar on the relationship between anarchists and ecologists, has called the group "ecofascists" and "macho mountain men." Bookchin has been especially critical of EF! leaders Dave Foreman and Edward Abbey, who during the 1980s espoused a back-to-the-Stone Age philosophy and viewed people as a pox on the planet.

Earth First! began about 1980, with Foreman, Abbey, and several other men rejecting the mainstream environmental movement with the slogan "no compromise in defense of Mother Earth." Based on an ideology known as deep ecology—which advocates preserving Earth regardless of the consequences to humans—EF! leaders and followers used tactics described in Abbey's 1975 novel *The Monkey Wrench Gang.* Their activities included "monkeywrenching" (vandalizing) machinery and confrontational protests to prevent major industries from destroying natural areas. EF! concentrated especially on logging industries in the Pacific Northwest and used obstructive measures such as ramming huge steel spikes into trees, thereby making them unharvestable. But the spikes were also a hazard to humans, as some loggers were injured when saws hit steel.

By early 1990 a faction of northern California EF!ers under the leadership of the late Judy Bari (a union organizer who died of cancer in 1997 at the age of 47), began to pull away from the original group. Foreman left the movement and is now on the board of the Sierra Club, a mainstream environmental group he had assailed in earlier years. Bari publicly denounced tree-spiking and declared that there would be no monkeywrenching during a campaign to save California redwood trees. She also tried to forge an alliance with labor groups.

In May 1990, after a planning meeting for Redwood Summer, patterned after the voter registration drives in Mississippi during several summers in the 1960s, Bari's car was bombed. She was nearly killed, and friend Darryl Cherney was severely injured. The Federal Bureau of Investigation (FBI) charged Bari and Cherney with deliberately setting the bomb. Although evidence clearly showed the bomb exploded under Bari's car seat, she was arrested in the hospital; Cherney was held in jail for five days. The charges were eventually dropped, but the FBI continued investigations, and Bari and Cherney filed a civil rights lawsuit in 1991 against the agency, which says, in Cherney's words,

> that the FBI and the Oakland police violated our rights of freedom of speech and freedom of assembly by falsely arresting us and continuing to call us suspects in order to stymie the organization of Redwood Summer. There are also habeas corpus violations: we are charging them with arresting us when they knew we were innocent of the bombing. We were arrested and held without being charged with any crime. In

> addition, to the lawsuit, we also have opened a Congressional investigation of the FBI's handling of this case. The Congressional investigation is being conducted by Don Edwards of the House Judiciary committee. He is the same one who exposed Cointelpro actions against the Black Panthers and later against AIM (American Indian Movement) and CISPES (Committee in Solidarity with the People of El Salvador). At this point it is limited to this particular case, but we'd like him to take a broader look at FBI behavior. (Rizzo)

There also have been attempts to link Earth First! with convicted Unabomber Theodore Kaczynski. Just two days after Kaczynski was arrested in 1996, Peter Jennings on ABC's *World News Tonight* introduced a story claiming the accused had a "connection to a radical environmental group." Film footage from the 1980s gave the impression that EF!ers were attacking loggers, but they actually were trying to protect biologist Peter Galvin, whom loggers were dragging along the ground by the hair. Numerous other news programs have tried to tie Kaczynski with Earth First! and its philosophy, but there is no proof of any association.

Since the early 1990s, the EF! collective has practiced nonviolent civil disobedience in struggles such as attempting to prevent destruction of some of America's last remaining old growth forest in the Warner Creek area of Oregon's Willamette National Forest. In 1996 Earth First! joined Cascadia Forest Defenders and set up the Cascadia Free State, which many in the group called an anarchist community. The ecoanarchists built barricades of logs and cement and dug deep trenches to prevent the U.S. Forest Service from logging old growth trees. Similar activities have taken place in the ancient redwoods in the Headwaters in Humboldt County, California. A fall 1996 protest in that area included religious leaders and celebrities as well as environmental activists among more than 2,000 protesters; about 900 people were arrested for trespassing on land owned by Pacific Lumber Company, which also owns the redwood grove. The protesters were soon released.

See also
Ecoanarchists

References

Barnum, Alex, "Thousands Take a Stand to Protect Headwaters," *San Francisco Chronicle* (September 16, 1996).

Cockburn, Alexander, "Judi Passes," *The Nation* (March 24, 1997).

Heider, Ulrike, *Anarchism: Left, Right, and Green* (San Francisco: City Lights Books, 1994).

Rizzo, Lori, "No Compromise." (Interview with Earth First! activist Darryl Cherney) in *The Shadow* on the internet <http://www.connix.com/~Larry/Cherney.htm>

Sonn, Richard D., *Anarchism* (New York: Twayne/Macmillan, 1992).

Thompson, Clay A., "America's Other Politics—Enviros Create a Free State in National Forest," *Pacific News Service,* July 31, 1996.

Ecoanarchists

Since the 1960s and 1970s, when the environmental movement became widespread in the United States and other industrialized countries, groups calling themselves ecoanarchists have espoused a variety of theories that emphasize the social nature of ecological problems. Basically, most ecoanarchists contend that ecological destruction is the result of authoritarian social structures, such as capitalism, that place profitmaking and consumption above ecological protection. A webpage of frequently asked questions about anarchy points out that

> unless we resolve the underlying contradictions within society, which stem from domination, hierarchy and a capitalist economy, ecological disruption will continue and grow, putting our Earth in increasing danger. We need to resist the system and create new values based on quality, not quantity. We must return the human factor to our alienated society before we alienate ourselves completely off the planet. (Anarchist FAQ webpage, sec. E)

Although he did not use the term *ecoanarchist,* the renowned anarchist philosopher Peter Kropotkin (1842–1921) developed the concept that species were interconnected with each other and with their environment and that the major factor in evolution is not competition, as some claim, but rather cooperation. To bring about cooperation, ecoanarchists emphasize the need to replace the typical capitalist corporation and its pyramid structure with socially owned and worker-managed firms. Producer cooperatives would not expand as rapidly as corporations (which depend on technological and worker growth to obtain profits for those at the top of the pyramid) and thus would not contribute to the destruction of ecological systems.

Ecoanarchists insist that along with cooperatives, direct democracy is essential to prevent ecological crises because people at the grassroots level are "more likely to favour stringent environmental safeguards than the large, polluting special interests that now dominate the 'representative' system of government." Such a transformation, though, would "amount to a political revolution," which would not be possible unless there is "mass psychological transformation . . . a deconditioning from the master/slave attitudes absorbed from the current system." Without such a change, a new ruling elite would simply replace the old (Anarchists FAQ webpage, sec. E).

Ecoanarchists, according to one writer on the subject, can basically be divided into two camps: social ecologists and ecocommunalists. They have commonalities:

> Both seek to abolish the modern nation State and confer maximum political and economic autonomy on decentralized local communities. Second, both argue not only that anarchism is the political philosophy that is most compatible with an ecological perspective but also that anarchism is grounded in, or otherwise draws its inspiration from, ecology." They also "oppose all forms of social domination . . . [and] in varying degrees and for varying reasons, the domination of the nonhuman world. (Eckersley)

Despite similarities, ecoanarchist theories are diverse. One philosophy is embodied in the Green political movement, or the social ecology movement, as defined primarily by Murray Bookchin, cofounder of the Institute for Social Ecology. Social ecologists maintain that every individual in a society should be able to directly participate in social policymaking, which means that social hierarchies and domination have to be eliminated. Bookchin emphasizes the social nature of ecological problems and argues that humankind's domination of nature is a result of autocratic concepts within humanity itself. He contends that humans should be stewards of Earth and take an active role in the evolution of the planet. (Eckersley)

In a 1991 article in *The Progressive,* Bookchin decried

> certain trends in the ecology movement—trends that seem to be riding on an overwhelming tide of religious revivalism and mysticism. I refer not to the large number of highly motivated, well-intentioned, and often radical environmentalists who are making earnest efforts to arrest the ecological crisis, but rather to exotic tendencies that espouse deep ecology, biocentrism, Gaian consciousness, and eco-theology, to cite the main cults that celebrate a quasi-religious "reverence" for "Nature" with what is often a simultaneous denigration of human beings and their traits.

Some ecocommunalists are part of the mysticism trend that Bookchin describes. Earth First! is a prime example. Earth First!ers, who call themselves Ecommunards, have issued a manifesto stating they "merge the libertarian and anarchistic traditions with the deep ecological paradigms, in order to fight the greed of contemporary society and to build a new, based on Liberty, Ecology & Humanity" (Ecommunard Manifesto). Such ecocommunalists apply direct action techniques.

Earth First! became well known for monkeywrenching (i.e., vandalizing machinery that contributes to the destruction of ecological habitats). The monkey wrench is considered "the symbolic weapon of choice, the wilderness warrior's tomahawk, for it was not a club or gun aimed at human beings, but a tool meant to take apart other tools—the perfect symbol for those defending genetic diversity and wilderness against the machinery of industrial society" (One Earth, One Chance). During the 1980s, EF! members took part in dramatic public protests such as vandalizing machinery, cutting fences, and ramming spikes into trees to prevent lumbering in ancient forests. Some of the monkeywrenching tactics (which sometimes injured innocent people) as well as the back-to-the-Stone Age and racist views of some devotees caused a breach in the group. By 1990 a new faction had formed, practicing nonviolent civil disobedience in struggles to block government officials and business owners from destroying ecological habitats.

See also

Bookchin, Murray; Earth First!; Kropotkin, Peter Alexeyevich; Social Ecology

References

"An Anarchist FAQ Webpage," on the internet <http://www.geocities.com/CapitolHill/1931/index.html>.

Bookchin, Murray, "The Dismal Science," *The Progressive* (December 1991).

Eckersley, Robyn, "Ecoanarchism: The Non-Marxist Visionaries," on the internet <http://user.hk.linkage.net/~greenpow/essays/ecoanarch.htm>.

Ecommunard Manifesto, on the internet <http://www.geocities.com/RainForest/4544/manifest.htm>.

Heider, Ulrike, *Anarchism: Left, Right, and Green* (San Francisco: City Lights Books, 1994).

Hughes, James, "Democratic Socialism and Green Politics," on the internet <http://www.dsausa.org/rl/ESR/JDSEco.html>.

One Earth, One Chance, "An Introduction to Monkeywrenching" on the internet <http://www.geocities.com/RainForest/4544/mwinfo.htm>.

Sonn, Richard D., *Anarchism* (New York: Twayne/Macmillan, 1992).

Thompson, A. Clay, "America's Other Politics—Enviros Create a Free State in National Forest," Pacific News Service, July 31, 1996.

Eikhenbaum, V. M. "Voline" (1882–1945)

Known by the pseudonym Voline, Vsevolod Mikhailovich Eikhenbaum was a prominent Russian anarchist, a prolific writer and lecturer, and comrade of celebrated Ukrainian anarchist Nestor Makhno. Voline played major roles during the revolutions in Russia in 1905 and 1917 and wrote "the most impressive anarchist-inspired history of the Russian Revolution, which has been translated into many languages" (Avrich, 1988: 125).

Eikhenbaum was born into an intellectual Jewish family that lived in south-central Russia near the city of Voronezh. He and his brother, Boris, who became a distinguished literary critic, were educated by tutors and learned to speak and write French and German fluently. After attending the gymnasium, Voline enrolled in St. Petersburg University, where he intended to study law. But he soon became involved in revolutionary activities, abandoned his studies, and joined the Socialist Revolutionary Party. According to Mollie Steimer, he "organized workers and peasant clubs, and gave them all his time and energy. He developed libraries, organized schools and created a special program of adult education. . . . One of his outstanding activities was direct, personal propaganda. He gave hundreds of lectures, edited periodicals, published hundreds of leaflets" (quoted in Bluestein, 71).

In 1905 Voline was actively involved in the Russian revolutionary movement and revolt, which was soon put down. He was imprisoned; because of the intervention of his family he was exiled to Siberia. But he managed to escape to France, where "he reached the conclusion that the State could never give freedom and well-being to the people. He declared himself an anarchist" (Bluestein, 72). He quit the Socialist Revolutionary Party and devoted the rest of his life to anarchism.

While in France, Voline met Sébastian Faure; the pair later collaborated on an anarchist encyclopedia. He became an antiwar activist, and when World War I broke out he spoke out against it, and authorities sought to imprison him. With the help of friends, however, he was able to flee to the United States in early 1916, leaving his wife and children in France. In New York City, Voline joined the anarcho-syndicalist Union of Russian Workers of the United States and Canada and became a staff member of its journal *Golos Truda* (Voice of Labor). He also lectured in U.S. and Canadian cities.

When the February 1917 revolution erupted in Russia, Voline was determined to return to his homeland. With the help of the Anarchist Red Cross (later called the Anarchist Black Cross), he and other staff members of *Golos Truda* went to Petrograd, where they continued to publish their anarcho-syndicalist weekly. Voline became its editor, establishing it "as the most influential anarcho-syndicalist journal of the Russian Revolution" (Avrich, 1988: 128). When the Petrograd Union of Anarcho-Syndicalist Propaganda was formed in June 1917, its founding declaration was published in *Golos Truda*. The declaration's conclusion pointed out that

> the Anarcho-Syndicalists do not form a separate political party because they believe that the liberation of the working masses must be the task only of workers' and peasants' non-party organizations. They enter all such organizations and spread propaganda about their philosophy and their ideal of a stateless commune, which in essence merely represents the deepening and systematization of the beliefs and methods of struggle put forward by the working masses themselves. Adopting the position that the basic purpose of any social upheaval must be economic reconstruction, the Anarcho-Syndicalists will apply their energies above all to work in those mass economic organizations which must carry out the reorganization of production and consumption on completely new lines. (Avrich, 1973: 72)

After the Bolsheviks gained power, Voline became sharply critical of their dictatorial leadership as well as their agreement to cede land and industry to Germany in exchange for ending the warfare. Voline issued a manifesto in *Golos Truda* calling for the masses to fight against the Austro-German invasion of the Ukraine. He insisted he had to march with the people and left the newspaper to go to the front. Not long afterward, however, some of his comrades asked him to leave the front and guide the Nabat (the Confederation of Anarchist Organisations), which sought to unify various anarchist factions. Voline also edited the confederation's newspaper.

The Bolsheviks, meanwhile, had begun to harass and suppress anarchist groups and by mid-1919 intensified persecutions. At this time, Voline joined the Ukrainian guerrilla band led by the legendary Nestor Makhno. At the end of 1919, he became ill with typhus; bedridden, he was arrested by the Bolsheviks and imprisoned. He was released in late 1920 after anarchists staged protests but was jailed once again in 1921, along with comrade Gregori Maximoff, who was part of the *Golos Truda* group. Voline and others staged a hunger strike, leading to intervention by European syndicalists, at the time attending a congress of the Red Trade Union International (usually referred to as Profintern). The syndicalists negotiated with Bolshevik leader Vladimir Lenin to gain freedom for Voline and his comrades, all of whom were later banished from Russia.

In 1922 Voline went to Berlin, where "Rudolf Rocker and other prominent German anarchists helped him and his family get settled." Voline, his wife, and five children lived in a small attic, staying in Berlin for about two years. Faure then invited Voline to Paris to work on the anarchist encyclopedia. In addition, during the next twelve years, Voline "contributed to a range of anarchist periodicals" published in Paris, Berlin, and the United States (Avrich, 1988: 130–131).

When the Spanish Civil War broke out in 1936, the anarcho-syndicalist trade union Confederación Nacional del Trabajo (CNT) asked Voline to edit its Paris-based journal. But when CNT supported the loyalist government, Voline resigned. Shortly thereafter his wife died.

During World War II, Voline was consistently against what he saw as a capitalist war. He was subjected to police harassment, and he could find no work. In dire poverty and without a home, he spent much of his time in the library writing a history of the Russian Revolution, *The Unknown Revolution,* completed in 1941.

When the Nazis invaded France, Voline had to move from one hiding place to another. His friends and comrades, Molly Steimer and Senya Fleshin, urged him to leave the country and move to Mexico with them. But he refused to seek refuge. Somehow he survived the Nazis but died of tuberculosis in 1945. "His body was cremated and the ashes buried in the Pére-Lachaise Cemetery, close to the grave of Nestor Makhno, who had succumbed to the same disease eleven years before. The old comrades were thus reunited in death, their remains resting by those of the martyrs of the Paris Commune" of 1871 (Avrich, 1988: 134).

See also

Anarchist Black Cross; Anarcho-Syndicalism; Faure, Auguste Louis Sébastien; Maximoff, Gregori Petrovich; Paris Commune of 1871; Rocker, Rudolf; Spanish Civil War; Steimer, Mollie, and Simon Fleshin

References

Avrich, Paul, *Anarchist Portraits* (Princeton: Princeton University Press, 1988).

Avrich, Paul, *The Russian Anarchists* (New York: W. W. Norton, 1978).

Avrich, Paul, ed., *The Anarchists in the Russian Revolution* (Ithaca: Cornell University Press, 1973).

Bluestein, Abe, ed., *Fighters for Anarchism: Mollie Steimer and Senya Fleshin, a Memorial Volume* (Minneapolis, MN: Libertarian Publications Group, 1983).

Engel, George

See Haymarket Affair

Espionage Act of 1917

Considered by some to be a veiled attack on civil liberties, the Espionage Act of 1917 was passed by the U.S. Congress to prevent opposition to U.S. efforts in World War I. The Espionage Act provided for heavy penalties against those who urged resistance to federal laws, refused to do military service, or obstructed the draft.

The law was used against many radical and anarchist groups as well as members of the Industrial Workers of the World (IWW), which struck for an eight-hour workday and better wages. The Wobblies, as they were called, also spoke out against what they called a "rich man's war" and declared they would not fight for any cause except freedom for workers. Many were arrested for conspiracy and intimidation during labor disputes.

Some IWW leaders were jailed and fined. One of the arrested leaders, William Haywood, sentenced along with 14 others to 20 years in prison, jumped bail and fled to Russia. More than 30 other Wobblies received ten-year prison sentences. Fines totaling \$2.25 million were imposed on the Wobblies. By the following year, Congress had passed the Sedition Act of 1918, which, combined with the 1917 law, further enabled federal authorities to censor citizens who opposed the war.

See also

Haywood, William Dudley "Big Bill"; Industrial Workers of the World; Sedition Act of 1918

F

Faure, Auguste Louis Sébastien (1858–1942)

Called an "original libertarian," Sébastien Faure was a leading member of the anarchist movement in France at a time when the terms *libertarian* and *anarchist* were used interchangeably. Faure did not present original ideas, but he was a highly effective propagandist and an important contributor to the anarchist press.

Born into a middle-class Catholic family in Saint-Etienne (near Lyon in central France), Faure was well educated and intended to become a priest. After his father's death he went into the insurance business, then served in the military. Following military service he married, moving to Bordeaux.

As a young adult Faure left the church and became a socialist, but by 1888 he had come under the influence of Peter Kropotkin and other anarchists. Breaking away from socialism, he joined the French anarchist movement and settled in Paris. The rest of his life was dedicated to writing and speaking on behalf of anarchism, lecturing throughout France. He divorced but in later years reconciled with his wife.

For a time, Faure was a close friend of Louise Michel, prominent anarchist, poet, and member of the Paris Commune of 1871, a short-lived revolutionary government established by workers. In 1895, when Michel began writing for an anti-Semitic and hate-mongering newspaper, Faure publicly criticized his friend, as did other anarchists. Their criticism became intense during the so-called Dreyfus affair (1894–1906). Michel hesitated to speak out against the anti-Semitic persecution of Captain Alfred Dreyfus, convicted of being a spy (Dreyfus was later vindicated). She said "anarchists had no business defending a bourgeois career military officer," which so provoked Faure that he declared Michel "was allowing herself to be used by people who were really sinister militarists and nationalists and no longer revolutionaries" (Varias, 71).

Faure wrote for and edited several anarchist newspapers, among them *Le Libertaire* (The Libertarian), a weekly that he cofounded with Michel, and wrote numerous articles, pamphlets, and books. His most ambitious project was the *Encyclopedie Anarchiste,* written in collaboration with Russian anarchist Vsevolod Eikhenbaum (Voline). A moderate opponent of World War I, Faure issued the manifesto *Vers la Paix* (Toward Peace) and

> produced a general left-wing weekly from April 1916 to December 1917. After the war he revived *Le Libertaire,* which continued from 1919 until 1939. In 1921 he led the reaction in the French anarchist movement against the growing Communist dictatorship in the Soviet Union. In January 1922 he began *La Revue Anarchiste* (*Anarchist Review*), the leading monthly magazine of the French anarchist movement between the world wars. In the late 1920s he . . . advocated what he called an "Anarchist Synthesis" in which individualism, libertarian communism and anarcho-syndicalism could co-exist. In 1927 he led a secession from the national Union Anarchiste, and in 1928 he helped to found the Association des Federalistes Anarchistes and to begin its paper, *La Voix Libertaire* (*Libertarian Voice*), which lasted from 1928 until

1939. He was reconciled with the national organisation and *Le Libertaire* in 1934. During the 1930s he took part in the peace movement as a prominent member of the International League of Fighters for Peace. In 1940 he took refuge from the war in Royan (near Bordeaux), where he died in 1942. ("Sébastien Faure")

See also
Anarchist Press; Eikhenbaum, V. M. (Voline); Michel, Louise

References
"Sébastien Faure—An Original Libertarian," in *The Raven,* on the internet <http://flag.blackened.net/liberty/faure.html>.
Varias, Alexander, *Paris and the Anarchists: Aesthetes and Subversives During the Fin de Siècle* (New York: St. Martin's Press, 1996).

Federation des Bourses du Travail
See Pelloutier, Fernand

Ferm, Alexis (1870–1971), and Elizabeth (1857–1944)

During the early 1900s, Alexis and Elizabeth Ferm operated several "free" or modern schools, including one at the anarchist colony in Stelton, New Jersey. Before arriving at Stelton, the Ferms had founded their own schools in New York, where they met Russian-born Emma Goldman and other anarchists who were part of the Ferrer Association, founded in 1910 and named for Spanish anarchist and modern school advocate Francisco Ferrer. Goldman was especially impressed with the Ferms, writing in her autobiography:

> The Ferms were the first Americans I met whose ideas on education were akin to mine; but while I merely advocated the need of a new approach to the child, the Ferms translated their ideas into practice. In the Playhouse, as their school was called, the children of the neighbourhood were bound by neither rules nor textbooks. They were free to go or come and to learn from observation and experience. I knew no one else who so well understood child psychology as Elizabeth and who was so capable of bringing out the best in the young. She and Alexis considered themselves single-taxers, but in reality they were anarchists in their views and lives. It was a great treat to visit their home, which was also the school, and to witness the beautiful relationship that existed between them and the children. (Goldman)

Some members of the Ferrer Association left New York in 1914 and established a colony and modern school in Stelton, New Jersey, about 30 miles from the city. The Ferms went to Stelton in 1920 to be coprincipals of the school, saving it from near disintegration. For about five years before the Ferms' arrival the school was in chaos. "Children were given practically no discipline, in part because certain members of the staff really believed in such an extreme policy, but also as a result of the simple state of confusion that prevailed." There had been frequent changes in principals and teachers, which "had a highly unsettling effect." In the boardinghouse where the children lived, conditions became so "wildly uncontrolled that caretakers would usually resign after a few weeks" (Veysey, 134).

When the Ferms arrived at Stelton, Elizabeth was soon recognized as the most dominant of the pair. Known as "Aunty," Elizabeth had married Alexis after the death of her estranged husband, Martin Battle, who had insisted that his wife be submissive. Elizabeth, however, "refused to accept his authority. When [Martin] kept her locked at home all day one Sunday, she threatened him with a hatchet until he opened the door to let her out. Soon after this she left him" (Veysey, 136).

Elizabeth Battle earned a living for a time giving piano lessons; after completing a training course in education during the 1890s she took charge of a kindergarten in Brooklyn. She met Alexis Ferm about this time; they married in 1898, soon after Martin Battle died. Alexis was 13 years younger than Elizabeth and considered a "doer," someone who liked to do handyman work. Apparently, he recognized Elizabeth's gifts as an educator and "began taking only those jobs which would leave much of his time free to assist her in her educational work. Of course, since he had long been interested in the field of education, he managed in this way to fulfill his own desires. Though never in danger of losing his own dignity, he nonetheless became his wife's willing disciple" (Veysey, 137).

In schools established by the Ferms, children were encouraged to voluntarily take part in a great variety of creative activities, such as basket making, carpentry, printing, gardening, dancing, and sports. As educators, the Ferms believed children should be allowed to grow in natural ways, rather like plants, but shielded from outside interference so that they could develop their talents. They also encouraged children to be self-reliant and to learn how to cope with dangers by experiencing them—such as learning the danger of a hot stove by touching it and getting burned.

When the Ferms arrived at Stelton, a new school building was being completed; the couple organized the interior into four workshop areas for crafts and manual training, a space for a kindergarten, and a library for studying academic subjects. "This program led to a remarkable creative flowering among the children, who produced, among other things, the *Voice of the Children,* which they wrote, illustrated and printed entirely themselves" (Perrone). Some of the parents, however, became disenchanted with the Ferms' approach to education. They wanted more emphasis on academics—reading, for example—and attention given to the proletarian struggle. But the Ferms refused to change their methods; in 1925 they left the school.

During the 1930s coprincipals James and Nellie Dick, who had replaced the Ferms, left Stelton to start their own school, and the Ferms were persuaded to return. But the school was undergoing financial hardship. Because of the Great Depression, many parents lost their jobs and could not afford to keep their children in the school. The school remained open until 1953 with only 15 students enrolled. Elizabeth Ferm had died nearly a decade before, in 1944, and Alexis Ferm retired four years later. He died in 1971.

See also

Goldman, Emma; Modern School Movement; Stelton School and Colony

References

Goldman, Emma, *Living My Life,* vol. 1, chap. 26, on the internet <http://www.pitzer.edu/~dward/Anarchist_Archives/goldman/living/living1_26.html>.

Perrone, Fernanda, "History of the Modern School of Stelton," Special Collections and University Archives, Rutgers University Libraries, on the internet <http://www.libraries.rutgers.edu/rulib/spcol/modern.htm>.

Veysey, Laurence, *The Communal Experience: Anarchist and Mystical Communities in Twentieth-Century America* (Chicago: University of Chicago Press, 1978).

Ferrer Association

See Modern School Movement

Ferrer, Francisco y Guardia (1859–1909)

Calling himself a "philosophical anarchist," Francisco Ferrer y Guardia established a number of private progressive schools in Spain beginning in 1901 with his first school, Escuela Moderna, in Barcelona. He believed that education should be free of church and state authority, and his network of schools was an alternative to the church-controlled education system operated by clerics who emphasized rote instruction in Catholicism and used brutal discipline. According to anarchist writer Murray Bookchin,

> these clerics openly inveighed against any political group, scientific theory, or cultural tendency which displeased the church. Coeducation, tolerated in the countryside only for want of school space, was rigorously prohibited in the cities.
>
> To this bleak establishment Ferrer proposed a program and method of instruction that the clerics could regard only as "diabolical." He planned to establish a curriculum based on the natural sciences and moral rationalism, freed of all religious dogma and political bias. Although students were to receive systematic instruction, there were to be no prizes for scholarship,

> no marks or examinations, indeed no atmosphere of competition, coercion, or humiliation. The classes, in Ferrer's words, were to be guided by the "principle of solidarity and equality." During a period when "wayward" students in clerical schools were required to drop to their knees in a penitent fashion and then be beaten, the teachers in the Escuela Moderna were forewarned that they must "refrain from any moral or material punishment under penalty of being disqualified permanently." Instruction was to rely exclusively on the spontaneous desire of students to acquire knowledge and permit them to learn at their own pace. The purpose of the school was to promote in the students "a stern hostility to prejudice," to create "solid minds, capable of forming their own rational convictions on every subject." (Bookchin)

Born into a devout Catholic family in Alella near Barcelona, Spain, Ferrer was raised in the traditional manner. His father owned a vineyard and provided a moderate income for his family. According to Bookchin, Ferrer showed no signs of rebellion "until he was sent off to work in a Barcelona firm at the age of fifteen. The owner, a militant anticleric, apparently exercised a great influence on his young employee. In any case, by the time Ferrer had reached twenty he had declared himself a Republican, an anticleric, and joined the Freemasons, the traditional haven for liberal thought and political conspiracy in Spain" (Bookchin).

As a young man, Ferrer worked with Spanish exile Manuel Ruiz Zorrilla, a radical Republican, living in Paris. Ferrer carried messages to army officers whom Zorrilla hoped would stage a Republican coup. Ferrer also helped smuggle political refugees from Spain to France. However, he soon quit his political activities to devote his time to education. At the time,

> nearly 70 percent of the Spanish population was illiterate. Teachers were grossly underpaid, and rural schools (where there were any) were often little more than shacks in which barefooted, ill-nourished children were given only the most rudimentary instruction. . . . Although Spain had a universal education law, the majority of schools were run by clerics who used brutal teaching methods and emphasized rote instruction in Catholic dogma. These clerics openly inveighed against any political group, scientific theory, or cultural tendency which displeased the church. Coeducation, tolerated in the countryside only for want of school space, was rigorously prohibited in the cities. (Bookchin)

Ferrer's first school began with 30 students, a number that doubled within ten months. During the next few years at least fifty modern schools were set up in Spain; Ferrer also published booklets on science and culture that were distributed to peasants and workers who had never been exposed to the world outside their villages. The Catholic clergy became increasingly agitated by Ferrer's activities and the growth of his progressive schools, but the Church was unable to restrict Ferrer's work until a Spanish workers' protest erupted into a rebellion known as the Tragic Week. Numerous churches and convents were desecrated or burned, and Spanish authorities accused Ferrer of inciting an insurrection. During his trial no evidence connected Ferrer to the rebellion, yet he was convicted and executed. Before the firing squad he maintained his innocence, calling out "Long live the Escuela Moderna!" In her autobiography, Emma Goldman memorialized Ferrer with these words: "The consciousness that his executioners represented a dying age, and that his was the living truth, sustained him in the last heroic moments" (Goldman).

Although Ferrer was not well known outside groups of anarchists and free-thinkers, his execution prompted cries of protest throughout the world. His followers, particularly those in the United States, established the Ferrer Association in 1910 and opened modern schools in New York and New Jersey.

See also

Bookchin, Murray; Goldman, Emma; Modern School Movement

References

Bookchin, Murray, "Francisco Ferrer's Modern School," on the internet <http://flag.blackened.net/revolt/spain/ferrer.html>.

Goldman, Emma, *Anarchism and Other Essays* (New York: Dover, 1969, reprint of 1910 ed.).

McCabe, Joseph, "Francisco Ferrer y Guardia" (1913), on the internet <http://www.geocities.com/Athens/Acropolis/5422/ferrer1.html>.

Fielden, Samuel

See Haymarket Anarchists

First International

The International Working Men's Association (IWMA), briefly known as the International and then the First International, was formed in London in 1864 and held its first congress in Geneva, Switzerland, in 1866. The aim of IWMA was to unify workers of the world according to the principles of the *Communist Manifesto* by Karl Marx and associate Friedrich Engels. Marx was not part of the group that organized IWMA, but he was later elected to its general council and soon became its leader.

IWMA was dominated by mutualists—that is, followers of Pierre-Joseph Proudhon and Robert Owen—and numerous European anarchists joined. In 1868 anarcho-communists such as Mikhail Bakunin and his followers became members and often were in conflict with mutualist ideas.

In 1872 IWMA moved its headquarters from Europe to New York, losing many European members as a result. Its U.S. membership grew, however. By 1876 it was known as the Working Men's Party of the United States; a year later it became the Socialistic Labor Party; in 1890 the name was changed once more to the Socialist Labor Party.

Followers of Bakunin split in 1872. Anarchists decided to form their own international, named the Chicago Black International (CBI) for its black flag. (When a communist international met it was known as a Red International.) But it was ten years before CBI met, primarily because of members' "personal and theoretical opposition to any kind of central authority and their essential belief in small, autonomous local units." CBI failed, and anarchists tried to rejoin socialists and "to gain some sort of authority within the Socialist Second International, but they were ejected from the London Congress of 1896 and never again tried to join the socialists" (Jacker, 92–93).

See also

Bakunin, Mikhail A.; *Communist Manifesto;* Marx, Karl; Owen, Robert; Proudhon, Pierre-Joseph; Socialism

References

"International, FIRST," *Britannica Online* <http://www.eb.com:180/cgi-bin/g?DocF=micro/292/29.html>.

Jacker, Corinne, *The Black Flag of Anarchy: Antistatism in the United States* (New York: Charles Scribner's Sons, 1968).

Fischer, Adolph

See Haymarket Affair

Flynn, Elizabeth Gurley (1890–1964)

Elizabeth Gurley Flynn was known as the "rebel girl" after the song composed by labor leader and martyr Joe Hill, who wrote to her just before he was executed, asking her to "be sure to locate a few more Rebel Girls like yourself, because they are needed and needed badly." A strong feminist and syndicalist, Flynn was not an anarchist as such, but she spent much of her life working for an industrial union movement based on anarchist ideas and advocating direct action to bring about labor reforms. She inspired hundreds of thousands of workers to organize and strike for better pay and working conditions, which were appalling at the time. Workers in eastern textile mills, for example, earned about $6 for 56 hours of labor per week in poorly ventilated, unsanitary, and unsafe factories. In mines, lumber camps, and other industries, workers suffered even greater hazards for little pay.

Born in Concord, New Hampshire, to Thomas and Annie Gurley Flynn, Elizabeth wrote that she came from Irish ancestors who were immigrants and revolutionists. In fact, her great-grandfather was known as Rebel Paddy, and for generations many Flynn relatives rebelled against British rule over the Irish.

While Elizabeth was growing up, her family moved several times, first to Cleveland, Ohio, then back to various New England towns; they finally settled in South Bronx, New York. As a teenager Elizabeth was exposed to political ideas through family discussions as well as meetings conducted by American socialists and anarchists like Emma Goldman and Alexander Berkman. Elizabeth was also influenced by such books as Edward Bellamy's *Looking Backward,* a novel describing an imaginary Utopia based on socialist principles, and Mary Wollstonecraft's *Vindication of the Rights of Women.*

In high school, Flynn joined the debate society and became an excellent public speaker. Her first political speech was given in 1906, when she was 16, before the Harlem Socialist Club. She soon mounted the soapbox at street corners to speak to crowds about socialist ideas and the evils of capitalism. Her first arrest (along with her father) occurred for "speaking without a permit" and "blocking traffic" on Broadway in New York City.

Flynn became associated with the Industrial Workers of the World (IWW), a militant, working-class union, about a year after it was founded in 1906. She was a popular and passionate orator, and at the request of IWW and other unions she traveled to numerous cities and towns in the West and Midwest to speak to workers, urging them to organize.

During a speaking trip out West she met Jack Jones, an ore miner and labor organizer. They were married in January 1908, Elizabeth not quite 18. Their son, Fred, was born in 1910. By the next year, however, the marriage failed; leaving her son in the care of her mother, Flynn continued her agitation for better working conditions. She led workers in actions such as the famed 1912 Lawrence textile mill strike in Massachusetts and the Patterson strike the following year in New Jersey.

Throughout her years as a labor advocate, Flynn, like other organizers and strikers, faced police brutality and trumped-up charges that led to arrests and imprisonment—and more brutal treatment. She was arrested numerous times for "disturbing the peace" or "obstructing the highway," or the more serious "inciting to riot" and "conspiracy," charges often brought against labor organizers by authorities.

During the Lawrence strike, Flynn met Carlo Tresca, an anarcho-syndicalist and political refugee from Italy. They eventually became comrades and lovers, working together in the efforts to defend anarchists Sacco and Vanzetti, who were indicted on circumstantial evidence for the robbery and murder of shoe company employees.

In 1920 Flynn helped found the American Civil Liberties Union, and later in the decade she applied for membership in the Communist Party, becoming an active member. When anticommunist hysteria swept the United States in the 1950s, Flynn was targeted and arrested under the Smith Act, which made it a felony to teach or advocate the overthrow of the U.S. government or to belong to a group with such intentions. She was convicted and served 28 months at the federal women's reformatory in Alderson, West Virginia. After her release, she defended others hounded and charged during U.S. Senator Joseph McCarthy's notorious campaign to find "reds" everywhere. She still maintained her membership in the Communist Party and was elected national chair in 1961.

Flynn's book about her prison life, *The Alderson Story: My Life as a Political Prisoner,* was published in 1963; she planned to write a second autobiographical volume. She left the United States in 1964 to find seclusion in Moscow and to write. She died in September of that year at the age of 74 without completing her book.

See also

Berkman, Alexander; Goldman, Emma; Haywood, William Dudley "Big Bill"; Hill, Joe (Joel Emmanuel Häägland); Industrial Workers of the World; Lawrence Textile Mill Strike; Sacco, Nicola, and Bartolomeo Vanzetti; Tresca, Carlo

References

American Civil Liberties Union, Corliss Lamont, ed., *The Trial of Elizabeth Gurley Flynn* (New York: Horizon Press, 1968).

Camp, Helen C., *Iron in Her Soul: Elizabeth Gurley Flynn and the American Left* (Pullman: Washington State University Press, 1995).

Flynn, Elizabeth Gurley, "Memories of the IWW," Web edition of transcript by Eugene W. Plawiuk, on the internet <http://www.geocities.com/CapitolHill/5202/rebelgirl.html> (1997).
Flynn, Elizabeth Gurley, *The Rebel Girl: An Autobiography; My First Life (1906–1926)*, originally published by Masses and Mainstream as *I Speak My Own Piece: Autobiography of "The Rebel Girl,"* reprint New York: International Publishers (1973).

Food Not Bombs

An outgrowth of the U.S. antiwar and antinuclear movements, Food Not Bombs (FNB) started as street theater, according to Keith McHenry, who along with a small collective of pacifists founded the group during the 1980s. Living and working cooperatively in a shared economy in Cambridge, Massachusetts, FNB adherents, technically not anarchists, are committed to using nonviolent direct action in order to solve social problems such as poverty and homelessness. They hope to create a "world free from domination, coercion and violence" (FNB flyer). FNB, with national headquarters in San Francisco, California, believes that homelessness in the United States is an outrage given the huge amounts of money spent on defense while millions of people live in poverty.

This all-volunteer organization has no formal leaders, is dedicated to nonviolence, and strives to include everyone in its decisionmaking process. A loose network of FNB groups distributes free vegetarian food to the hungry in dozens of cities across the United States, Canada, and Europe. FNB collects fresh foods from produce warehouses and grocery stores. The food would otherwise be thrown out because its appearance diminishes its salability; however the food is still safe and useful. Prepared the same day it is collected, the food is often served to homeless people on city streets, to poor people in neighborhoods, and at demonstrations protesting the military-industrial complex.

Along with sharing free food, FNB groups have staged hundreds of events over the years to not only call attention to the plight of the hungry and homeless but also to highlight the power and control of multinational corporations and to protest police brutality. Police have frequently arrested FNB demonstrators. Founder Keith McHenry has been arrested hundreds of times, beaten by police (which has sometimes resulted in hospitalization), and jailed—most often in San Francisco, where the city administration, in an effort to keep the homeless out of downtown and public areas, has outlawed food handouts. In a 1997 encounter with police, McHenry was attempting to deliver food to a protest demonstration called the Beggar's Banquet outside the U.S. Conference of Mayors meeting in San Francisco. According to a San Francisco Liberation Radio report,

> After placing Keith in handcuffs, some of the officers repeatedly banged his head into the front end of his truck, while others executed a series of pain-compliance holds, all the while telling him to "calm down." As Keith was already in handcuffs, and had offered no resistance anyway, the violent measures taken against him seem designed for no other purpose other than punitive. (Edmondson)

Numerous members of Food Not Bombs in California and other states have also been arrested and jailed or issued tickets for trying to share food. Amnesty International has considered adopting jailed FNB members as "prisoners of conscience." Despite police and government harassment, FNB continues to work for social change, often combining efforts with such groups as Earth First! and the Anarchist Black Cross's Homes Not Jails.

See also

Direct Action; Earth First!

References

"Cook for Peace," Food Not Bombs flyer, on the internet <http://home.earthlink.net/~foodnotbombs/flyer2.html>.
Edmondson, Richard, "Food Not Bombs Co-Founder Keith McHenry Beaten, Arrested," San Francisco Liberation Radio (June 1997).
Vogl, Marc, "Killer Cops and Hungry Folks: A Chat with Keith McHenry," Bay Area CitySearch7, San Francisco: Politics Feature, ABC channel 7 (February 19, 1997), on the internet <http://www.citysearch7.com/E/V/SFOCA/0010/51/34>.

Foreman, Dave

See Earth First!

Fourierism

Fourierism is based on the ideas of Charles Fourier of France (1772–1837), one of the first social philosophers to advocate a restructuring of society into communal groups, which he called "phalanges" or "phalanxes." His ideas, along with those of fellow Frenchman Henri de Saint-Simon and Englishman Robert Owen established a philosophical base for the social theory known as socialism. Fourier's concepts also foreshadowed the development of anarchist principles as well as the theories of Karl Marx and Friedrich Engels.

Fourier hated the social evils associated with industrialization and believed that all classes of people should work together cooperatively. He claimed that God's true plan for a harmonious universe depended upon "the law of Attraction" and the gratification of passions. In Fourier's view, the passions not only brought pleasure but also led to "spontaneous association of human beings for the purposes of work" (Holloway, 142). The cooperative, he argued, was a more natural ordering of individuals and would lead to a more equitable distribution of the group's aggregate output and a happier existence for members. Phalange members would exchange roles with anyone taking a hierarchical power position for extended periods.

Fourier's elaborate plan for communal living filled volumes. He believed his theories would spread and be applied around the world. Although some historians have called Fourier's view of Utopia more like a fairy tale than a practical theory, several attempts were made in France to establish phalanxes. Not long after Fourier died in 1837, one of his disciples, Albert Brisbane, brought Fourierism to the United States.

Brisbane adopted the most workable aspects of Fourierism and described them in the 1840 book *Social Destiny of Man*. Brisbane's interpretation of Fourierism impressed Horace Greeley, who at the time was editor of *New Yorker* magazine and later editor of the *New York Tribune*. Greeley, in fact, became an enthusiastic supporter of Fourierism and provided space in the *Tribune* for a regular column, Fourieristic Associations and Phalanxes. During the early 1840s, the fanfare over Fourierism was so prolific that the doctrines became very popular in the United States. As one historian has noted:

> Associations and Conventions of Associationists began to spring up everywhere, but especially in the northeastern states, where a particularly sharp economic crisis had recently caused much unemployment. The anti-slavery movements also helped the growth of Fourierism; for as the former movement gathered momentum it began to include as one of its aims the abolition of wage-slavery as well as chattel-slavery. (Holloway, 105)

Between 1840 and 1860 more than 40 other phalanxes began in midwestern states and Texas. All failed, usually within a year or two, although a few managed to survive for periods ranging from five to 12 years. Most did not have a unifying force to hold them together, and often there were not enough farmers to provide the food needed for survival (Hine, 209–210).

See also

Owen, Robert; Socialism

References

Gay, Kathlyn, *Communes and Cults* (New York: Twenty-First Century Books/Holt, 1997).

Hine, Robert V., *Community on the American Frontier: Separate but Not Alone* (Norman: University of Oklahoma Press, 1980).

Holloway, Mark, *Heavens on Earth: Utopian Communities in America, 1680–1880,* 2d ed. (New York: Dover, 1966).

Free Spirit Movement

The Free Spirit movement began around 1200 in Paris when intellectuals protested the extraordinary power the church held over the common people. The main organizer of this first quasianarchist political groundswell was William Aurifex, who was quickly executed, along with his core followers, after they openly mocked monks and priests. Nevertheless, Free Spirit ideas spread, and key centers of protest and unrest grew within the trading capitals of Europe.

The concept that "just rewards" could be achieved on Earth, and not delayed until heaven, was widely accepted among merchants and artisans. "Hedgerow priests" traveled the roads delivering this radical gospel to the disenfranchised and the poor wherever they could be found. The church struck at such heresy, excommunicating and executing those considered insubordinate or guilty of free thought.

Among the persecuted was Marguerite Porete, author of the widely distributed book *Mirror of Simple Souls,* in which she dared to put Free Spirit ideas about equality, individuality, and sexual pleasure to the printed page. Her views were linked to "the Beguines, groups of religious women who did not live in cloister or follow a recognized rule of life" (*Britannica*). As a result, Porete was burned at the stake in 1310.

The movement's most notable achievement occurred at the end of the 14th century when peasants, under the leadership of Wat Tyler, rose up in England. Known as Wat Tyler's Rebellion or the English Peasants' Revolt of 1381, the uprising was one of numerous such rebellions in Europe during the 14th and 15th centuries caused by widespread economic problems resulting from the Hundred Years War between England and France. In addition, plagues and diseases such as smallpox and typhus killed millions, and there were great dislocations of masses of people. The roots of the English Peasants' Revolt

> lay in the ways in which landlords had increased their demands under the spur of necessity and in the new demands of royal tax collectors. Combined with famine, plague and war they made an always miserable existence intolerable. "We are made men in the likeness of Christ, but you treat us like savage beasts," was the complaint of English peasants who rebelled in 1831. (Roberts, 413)

During the rebellion, a people's army gathered and ransacked manor houses and estates as the rebels moved toward London. Sympathetic people inside the city gates helped the peasants enter and take over the prisons, releasing the prisoners. At first, the government agreed to the peasants' demands to abolish serfdom, to lower rents, and to eliminate restrictions on wages. But the king quickly regained control when Tyler was killed by the mayor of London and the rebels were hunted down.

References

"Christianity: ASPECTS OF THE CHRISTIAN RELIGION: Christian mysticism: HISTORY OF CHRISTIAN MYSTICISM: Western Catholic Christianity," *Britannica Online* <http://www.eb.com:180/cgi-bin/g?DocF=macro/5001/28/172.html>.

Roberts, John Morris, *History of the World* (New York and Oxford: Oxford University Press, 1993).

Freedom Press

Founded in 1886 and financed largely by Charlotte Wilson of Great Britain, Freedom Press has long published the newspaper *Freedom.* The first periodical arose from the British socialist movement of the early 1800s and numerous overlapping publications. Although anarchists were involved in many groups and periodicals, there was no separate anarchist group or publication.

In 1884 Charlotte Wilson, a socialist writer and speaker, began advocating anarchism and in 1886, with other British anarchists and famed anarchist philosopher Peter Kropotkin, began *Freedom.* It was described as a journal of anarchist socialism. Then, in 1889, it was called a journal of anarchist communism, representing the mainstream tradition of anarchism by giving a voice to differing views. Freedom Press concentrated on publishing the journal, but it also produced pamphlets, booklets, and books by British and foreign writers, including not only Kropotkin but also Errico Malatesta, Emma Goldman, Alexander Berkman, Pierre-Joseph Proudhon, and Mikhail Bakunin.

For years *Freedom* was the main English-language anarchist newspaper in Great Britain. However, after World War I, publication of the newspaper stopped and was not resumed until the outbreak of the Spanish Civil War in 1936. It helped revive the anarchist movement in Britain, Spain, and the rest of the world.

With the beginning of World War II, Freedom Press began *War Commentary,* another anarchist newspaper, and also opened a bookshop. *War Commentary* advocated radical pacifism, and Freedom Press became involved in subversive activity and circulated antimilitaristic material. As a result, the press was raided; three editors were imprisoned as the war closed in Europe. After the war ended in the Pacific, the periodical, published monthly, once again was named *Freedom.* To this day, Freedom Press in London publishes the paper, as well as the anarchist quarterly *Raven* and many anarchist books and pamphlets. The press also operates an anarchist bookshop and distributes publications from some North American anarchist publishers.

See also

Anarchist Press; Bakunin, Mikhail A.; Berkman, Alexander; Goldman, Emma; Kropotkin, Peter Alexeyevich; Malatesta, Errico; Proudhon, Pierre-Joseph

References

"The History of Freedom Press," on the internet <http://au.spunk.org/texts/pubs/freedom/raven/sp000616>.

Freemen

See American Antigovernment Extremists

French Anarchism

Revolutionary uprisings were common in France beginning with the French Revolution in 1789 (which had an impact on the rest of Europe as well as North America) until the Paris Commune of 1871. The French Revolution launched the beginning and spreading of egalitarian ideas throughout Europe and helped to partially break down the old social order of monarchies and the many privileges of the nobility and clergy.

The anarchist movement in France, however, was more complex than those in Spain and Italy, where impoverished peasants revolted. Notes historian Alexander Varias:

> French syndicalism offered the most vivid example of a mass movement revolving around anarchism. Exponents of this controversial union movement loosely modeled their ideas on anarchism and endeavored to organize urban workers, not in hopes of negotiating with capitalist leaders to achieve reforms, but of destroying the system. Nevertheless, they were disappointed as the numbers of participants did not approach those found in Spain. Generally speaking, French anarchism was less of a mass movement and more likely to attract intellectuals or isolated individuals who could be receptive to popular rhetoric. (Varias, 7)

Charles Fourier (1772–1837) was one of the first social philosophers in France to advocate a kind of utopian socialism, a restructuring of society into communal groups, which he called "phalanges" or "phalanxes." His ideas, along with those of Louis Auguste Blanqui (1805–1881), foreshadowed the development of anarchist principles as well as the theories of Karl Marx and Friedrich Engels espoused in the *Communist Manifesto.* Blanqui, however, was much more the rebel than was Fourier, spending half his life in prison because of his direct action against authority of all kinds.

Pierre-Joseph Proudhon was another important anarchist philosopher, providing ideas that spurred the anarchist movement. In 1840 he posed the question, "What is property?" and answered, "Property is theft." He became a "relentless critic of the whole of existing society" (Joll 61–62). During 1848–1849, when revolutions swept Europe, Proudhon developed his libertarian theories and ideas on mutualism, influencing many socialists and anarchists as well as such well-known artists as Gustave Courbet, who became a disciple and longtime friend. He

> called for a fundamental restructuring of moral, social, and economic relations . . . implored workers to isolate themselves from the debilitating egoism of the wealthy . . . insisted that they form their own organizations and rely on their own

> efforts. Advocating a reform of property that would eliminate "idlers," who lived off the labor of others, he wanted to return control and direction of the economy to the hands of workers. This was to be achieved not through strikes or revolution, but through working-class associative/mutualist action. (Vincent, 10)

Proudhon's followers injected his ideas into the First International, which originated as the International Working Men's Association in 1864 with the aim of uniting workers of the world according to the principles of the *Communist Manifesto.* French socialists and anarchists attended its first congress in Geneva, Switzerland, in 1866. There was hope that the International would help oppressed workers combat the established social and economic systems. Yet there was little if any change in the oppression and exploitation workers suffered under successive governments, from the regime of Napoleon Bonaparte, who abolished the republic and made himself emperor in 1804, to the monarchy of 1815–1848, the Second Republic (1848–1852), and the Second Empire of Napoleon III (1852–1870). In 1870 the French were defeated in the Franco-Prussian War, and Napoleon was captured. By January 1871 all French resistance was crushed. This led to widespread discontent and set the stage for the Paris Commune established a few months later.

With the support of anarchists and other radicals, Parisians who opposed the national government set up a communal government and elected a council or central committee. The council claimed that Paris was sovereign and called for other communes, or communities, to be set up throughout France. The Paris Commune lasted only 71 days and was brutally put down, leaving thousands dead and forcing others to flee for their lives. But the Paris Commune had a major impact on France for years. During the next three decades many communards in exile and those able to reenter France wrote and spoke about their experiences. Some who had never before espoused anarchism began to do so, whereas others blamed the Paris Commune's authoritarian structure for its failure.

From the 1880s to the early 1900s, many French anarchists came into the public spotlight. Among them was Emile Pouget, a radical journalist who, with Louise Michel, led an 1883 demonstration protesting worker exploitation. "Pouget attempted for five years to raise the level of workers' resentment and anger by printing works filled with violent rhetoric. He carried out this task largely through the adoption of workers' slang and illustrated caricature. In his use of the latter, Pouget was the first anarchist journalist to employ artists" (Varias, 31).

Others who were publicly prominent included Jean Grave, anarchist-editor of *La Révolte;* anarchist and acclaimed geographer Elisée Reclus, who taught that the truth of anarchism would be found through scientific investigation; and painters Camille Pissarro and Paul Signac, who often depicted working-class people and industrial landscapes.

French anarchism faded somewhat during the first half of the 20th century. In fact, many political writers wrote off anarchism as a lost cause. But during the 1960s, not only in France but also other parts of Europe as well as North America, anarchistic direct action became more common. One of the most dramatic events was the student insurrection at the Sorbonne University, accompanied by worker strikes during May and June 1968, now known simply as "May 1968."

See also

Blanqui, Louis Auguste; *Communist Manifesto;* Direct Action; First International; Marx, Karl; May 1968; Michel, Louise; Paris Commune of 1871; Proudhon, Pierre-Joseph

References

"Anarchism: ANARCHIST THINKERS: French anarchist thought," *Britannica Online* <http://www.eb.com:180/cgi-bin/g?DocF=macro/5007/8/2.html>.

Joll, James, *The Anarchists* (Boston: Little, Brown, 1964).

Sonn, Richard D., *Anarchism and Cultural Politics in Fin de Siècle* (Lincoln: University of Nebraska Press, 1989).

Varias, Alexander, *Paris and the Anarchists: Aesthetes and Subversives During the Fin de Siècle* (New York: St. Martin's Press, 1996).

Vincent, K. Steven, *Between Marxism and Anarchism: Benoit Malon and French Reformist Socialism* (Berkeley: University of California Press, 1992).

Frente Zapatista de Liberación Nacional

The recently constituted Frente Zapatista de Liberación Nacional (FZLN) or Zapatista Front of National Liberation is a "civil and nonviolent organization, independent and democratic, Mexican and national, which struggles for democracy, liberty, and justice in Mexico. It is a new political force that forms a part of a broad opposition movement" (FZLN webpage). This grassroots group has been formed in response to the "Declarations of the Lacandona Jungle" by Subcomandante Marcos of the Zapatista Army of National Liberation.

Professing to be a force for "democracy at all levels," the group is attempting to become an alternative, nonauthoritarian leader in the effort to create a new constitution for Mexico, a country rife with political corruption, the result of long domination by the ruling Institutional Revolutionary Party. The FZLN says it has no desire to hold public office or to control the government.

See also

Zapatista National Liberation Army

References

"Frente Zapatista de Liberación Nacional," on the internet <http://www.peak.org/~joshua/fzln> (no date).

Hernandez, Oscar, "Two Years After Someone in Mexico Finally Said 'That's Enough,'" on the internet <http://www.physics.mcgill.ca/~oscarh/RSM/96twoyearhistory.html (1996).

"Zapatistas in Cyberspace: A Guide to Analysis and Information," an Accion Zapatista Report, on the internet <http://www.eco.utexas.edu/faculty/Cleaver/zapsincyber.html> (no date).

G

Galleani, Luigi (1861–1931)

A staunch advocate of "propaganda by deed" and a powerful orator, Luigi Galleani inspired thousands of workers, from construction laborers to miners to tailors, and "breathed life into the Italian anarchist movement" in the United States during the first two decades of the 20th century (Avrich, 1988: 167). Among Galleani's followers were Nicola Sacco and Bartolomeo Vanzetti, working-class anarchists who were convicted and executed for armed robbery and murder in the United States.

Galleani was born in Vercelli, near Turin, and attended the University of Turin, where he studied law. But he never practiced law. Instead, he embraced anarchism and "became an outspoken militant whose hatred of capitalism and government would burn with undiminished intensity for the rest of his life" (Avrich, 1988: 167).

Because of his radical views, Galleani was threatened with arrest; he escaped to France but was banished for taking part in a May Day celebration. He found refuge in Switzerland but was expelled from that country when he organized a celebration for the martyrs of the Haymarket affair. Returning to Italy, Galleani was soon arrested, convicted of conspiracy, and imprisoned.

In 1900 Galleani escaped from prison, eventually making his way to the United States, settling in Paterson, New Jersey, in 1901, just a month after President William McKinley was shot by the deranged Leon Czolgosz, who many thought was an anarchist. Galleani had been in the United States less than a year when he took on the cause of workers striking against the Paterson silk mill, urging them in fiery speeches to stage a general strike and help overthrow capitalism. During the strike Galleani was shot; he was later indicted for inciting a riot. He escaped to Canada but returned to the United States to live clandestinely under an assumed name in Barre, Vermont, shielded by anarchist friends.

In Barre, Galleani began publishing *Cronaca Sovversiva,* considered "one of the most important and ably edited periodicals in the history of the anarchist movement. Its influence, reaching far beyond the confines of the United States, could be felt wherever Italian radicals congregated, from Europe and North Africa to South America and Australia" (Avrich 1988, 168). Galleani produced hundreds of articles and essays for his periodical, and many of them were collected and published in book form. One book—*The End of Anarchism?*—was a series of articles written in response to former anarchist Saverio Merlino, who had predicted the end of anarchism. In that work, Galleani argued for communist anarchism and against socialism, "preaching a militant form of anarchism that advocated the overthrow of capitalism and government by violent means, dynamite and assassination not excluded" (Avrich 1988, 169). An English translation of the book was published in 1982.

Galleani and his followers opposed World War I because, in their view, the only war worth fighting was a war to overthrow capitalism. Throughout the hostilities Galleani used the slogan "Against the War, Against the Peace. For the Revolution!" (Avrich 1991, 58). When the United States entered the conflict, Galleani was harassed and arrested for obstructing the war effort. In 1919 he and other radicals were deported; Galleani went to Italy, leaving his wife and five children in the United States.

Before and after the war, numerous Galleanists were involved in acts of terrorism, including a plot to bomb government officials and others working directly or indirectly to repress anarchists and workers. None of the targets was hurt, but the bombings helped fuel the so-called Red Scare, which was exploited by Attorney General A. Mitchell Palmer, who ordered raids on and arrests of radicals across the United States, actions considered to be unconstitutional.

In Italy Galleani continued publishing *Cronaca Sovversiva* and agitating for the anarchist cause. He was imprisoned twice between 1922 and 1926 and then banished from the mainland. When he was allowed to return in 1930, he was in poor health. He died the following year in the village of Caprigliola.

See also

Italian Anarchism; May Day; Palmer Raids; Sacco, Nicola, and Bartolomeo Vanzetti

References

Avrich, Paul, *Anarchist Portraits* (Princeton: Princeton University Press, 1988).

Avrich, Paul, *Sacco and Vanzetti: The Anarchist Background* (Princeton: Princeton University Press, 1991).

"Italian Anarchists," on the internet <http://www.radio4all.org/anarchy/galleani.html>.

Gandhi, Mohandas "Mahatma" Karamchand (1869–1948)

Many religious anarchists throughout the years have looked to Mohandas Gandhi as the prime example of a person who defied the state and the brutalities of authorities by practicing passive resistance. According to a biographer, people worldwide believed "that when Gandhi fell by the assassin's three bullets the conscience of mankind had been left without a spokesman. . . . No one who survived him had faced mighty adversaries at home and abroad with the weapons of kindness, honesty, humility, and nonviolence, and, with these alone, won so many victories" (Fischer, 8).

Born in Porbandar, a town in what was then a semi-independent coastal state in western India, Mohandas was the youngest of four children of Karamchand and Putlibai Gandhi, the fourth wife of Karamchand. In his autobiography Gandhi described his father as "a lover of his clan, truthful, brave, and generous, but short-tempered," a man "who had no education save that of experience" and little religious training other than "religious culture" that came from frequent visits to Hindu temples. Gandhi's memory of his mother was "that of saintliness." She was devoutly religious, an adherent of Jainism, a Hindu sect based on the concepts of nonviolence, vegetarianism, and caring for the poor (Gandhi, 3–4).

Gandhi's well-to-do family was of the commercial caste known as the Bania. India's ancient caste system (probably originating 3,500 years ago) was rigidly in force, dividing people socially and economically and creating a group at the bottom known as pariahs—"untouchables"—or outcastes of society. Gandhi's efforts later in life contributed to the passage of laws that banned untouchability.

When Gandhi was 13, his parents, in traditional fashion, arranged for his marriage to Kasturbai, a girl of the same age. Eventually the couple had four children. But after his marriage, Gandhi completed high school and followed another custom: tutoring his wife, who had no formal schooling, a task that Gandhi admitted he conducted in an authoritative manner. When he graduated he went to England to study law, leaving his wife and son behind and ignoring caste leaders who declared him an outcaste because they believed he would compromise his religion by eating meat and drinking alcohol, which were forbidden.

Earning his law degree in 1891, Gandhi returned to India to practice in Bombay. But his practice was not successful, and in 1893 he accepted an offer to work as a legal adviser for a large trading firm with offices in South Africa, then under British control. His wife and children joined him in 1896.

Not long after his arrival in South Africa, Gandhi faced discrimination and abuse from whites because of his skin color, and he quickly learned that other Indians suffered ill treatment as well. For two decades—until 1914—Gandhi worked for Indian rights in

South Africa, publishing a newspaper, promoting civil disobedience, and organizing strikes among mine workers. Because of his activism against the British, he was often arrested. But he also sided with the British when he felt it was the just thing to do—for example, working for the ambulance corps during the Boer War (1899–1902) when Dutch farmers in South Africa fought the British. "I felt that, if I demanded rights as a British citizen, it was also my duty, as such, to participate in the defence of the British Empire. I held then that India could achieve her complete emancipation only within and through the British Empire"(Gandhi, 214).

Gandhi's experiences in South Africa shaped his philosophy of life, his spiritual vision, and quest for truth based on *ahimsa* or "nonviolence" and the principles of *satyagraha,* meaning "truth-force" or "love-force," a characteristic of the soul, thus "soul-force" as it was known. Biographer Fischer explained, "Satyagraha is peaceful. If words fail to convince the adversary, perhaps purity, humility, and honesty will. The opponent must be . . . weaned, not crushed; converted, not annihilated. . . . Satyagraha is just the opposite of the policy of an eye-for-an-eye-for-an-eye which ends in making everybody blind" (Fischer, 77).

Based on this philosophy, Gandhi lived and dressed simply, followed a vegetarian diet, and removed himself as much as possible from the materialistic way of life. He believed that "modern civilization" was a threat to

> man's true nature by inculcating false wants generated by the capacity for excessive consumption; and furthermore, through the unequal distribution of wealth and the factory system of production, inevitably led to competition and violence between man and his fellows. It was truly the reign of the devil and unrighteousness, as opposed to the reign of truth and morality: it had the West in its grip and through Western influence threatened to strangle the life out of India. (Brown, 88)

In 1914, just as World War I began, Gandhi and his family returned to India by way of England. When he again settled in his homeland in January 1915, he felt that India should uphold Britain in the war and recruited for the British Army, despite his principles of nonviolence and the protests of friends and villagers. He reasoned that India enjoyed the protection of England and thus should support the empire. He also hoped that India would eventually enjoy a partnership with Britain like Australia, Canada, and New Zealand.

Nevertheless, Gandhi soon became the leader of the Indian nationalist movement and involved in organizing labor. The British passed the Rowlatt Act in 1919 to deal with conspiracies against the government, a law that suspended safeguards for individual liberties and provided for quick trials and punishments with no appeals. Gandhi's response was to lead a nationwide *hartal,* or "suspension of economic activity," to demonstrate against British authorities, an idea that "united vast multitudes in common action; it gave the people a sense of power. They loved Gandhi for it. The *hartal* paralyzed economic life; the dead cities and towns were tangible proof that Indians could be effective" (Fischer, 177).

But the British retaliated. In one incident in the Punjab, 10,000–20,000 people gathered inside a walled garden to celebrate the Hindu New Year's Day in the holy city of Amristar, and British troops were sent to disperse the crowd. There was only one way out of the garden, and people were unable to move out quickly and orderly. The troops fired on the crowd, killing nearly 400 people. Following the Amristar Massacre, as it became known, Gandhi became even more determined to lead a nonviolent campaign for national status. He soon launched the Indian National Congress, based on noncooperation with the British.

Living with followers in *ashrams,* communal groups following common spiritual principles, Gandhi dedicated his life and work to Indian independence from the British. He also concentrated on the social problem of untouchability. Even though he often spoke against rejection of a whole group of people, he became even more opposed to the practice during the 1920s as he traveled widely through India and saw the grinding poverty and terrible degradation it caused. One of his strategies to end the outcaste status was personal example, eating with untouchables and treating them as equals with other *ashram* members. He also denounced the inequities in the total caste system and the subordination of women. When advocating any social and political reforms, he exhorted his followers to practice nonviolent civil disobedience.

One of the best known acts of civil disobedience was a protest in 1930 against the Salt Acts, which made it illegal to possess salt that was not purchased from the government. Gandhi led a 200-mile march to the sea, where he and his followers evaporated seawater to make salt. The British reacted with brutal repression, and Gandhi was arrested and jailed—as he was often in the years that followed.

Whether in or out of jail, Gandhi continued his nonviolent disobedience campaigns during World War II, often fasting to call attention to British injustices and reprisals. Great Britain finally granted India independence in 1947 but partitioned the land into two nations—Pakistan, a predominantly Muslim state, and India, with its Hindu majority—which was not what Gandhi had envisaged. He adamantly opposed partition and consistently advocated peaceful coexistence of all peoples regardless of religious or political affiliations.

As Hindus and Muslims went to their respective new nations, riots broke out, and hundreds of thousands were killed or injured. To restore peace between religious groups Gandhi began a fast on January 13, 1948, which ended in five days after religious leaders agreed to stop fighting. Just 12 days later, he was shot by a Hindu fanatic who feared Gandhi's advocacy for a single nation and tolerance for all people. He died on January 30. Jawaharlal Nehru, who was a Gandhi supporter and had often been imprisoned because of his leadership role in the nationalist movement, became the first prime minister of India.

See also
Religious Anarchism

References

Ashe, Geoffrey, *Gandhi* (New York: Stein and Day, 1968).

Brown, Judith M., *Gandhi: Prisoner of Hope* (New Haven: Yale University Press, 1989).

Fischer, Louis, *Gandhi: His Life and Message for the World* (New York: Signet Key Book, 1954).

Fischer, Louis, *The Life of Mahatma Gandhi* (New York: Harper and Brothers, 1950).

Gandhi, Mohandas K., Mahadev Desai, trans., *An Autobiography: The Story of My Experiments with Truth* (Boston: Beacon Press, 1957).

Green, Martin, *Gandhi: Voice of a New Age Revolution* (New York: Continuum, 1993).

Green, Martin, ed., *Gandhi in India: In His Own Words* (London: University Press of New England, 1987).

Rolland, Romain, *Mahatma Gandhi: The Man Who Became One with the Universal Being* (New York: The Century Co., 1924).

German Anarchism

Among the earliest German anarchists were peasants who took part in a revolt during the 1500s. Many peasants were followers of Martin Luther, a German monk who called for reforms in the Catholic Church and whose beliefs led to the Protestant Reformation. Peasants accepted Luther's doctrine that individuals could interpret the Bible in their own way and choose their own religious leaders. They also demanded an end to serfdom and feudal rent payments, and in 1525 they rose in armed revolt throughout Germany, killing noble landlords and looting and burning property.

The 14th century was also the time when Christian Anabaptists (or Rebaptizers) rebelled against the Lutheran and Roman Catholic Churches. Anabaptists were so named because they were against infant baptism, which was the established religious practice, and believed in adult baptism as a public confession of faith; that act was punishable by death. Anabaptists also believed that church and state should be separated, opposed government restrictions on individuals, and refused to pay taxes. Since they believed that God directly guided their behavior and religious practices, they would not submit to any religious authority.

In 1535 Anabaptists took over the city of Munster in the state of Westphalia, then under the rule of a Lutheran bishop. Anabaptists forced Lutherans and Catholics to leave and burned property, tax, and other records in contempt of established laws and authority. A communal society was established, but it lasted only a few months. After fierce fighting, Anabaptist leaders were captured, tortured, and executed.

Most Anabaptists of the 14th and 15th centuries, however, decried violence and were pacifists. Yet wherever Anabaptists lived, established church and government officials tried to crush them. Thousands were imprisoned, tortured, and killed. During the 1700s and 1800s German Anabaptists emigrated to the United States, seeking freedom from civilian and church authority.

Yet many other Germans who came to the United States were anarchists of a secular nature, and a large number had taken part in the 1848–1849 revolutions that swept Europe. Among them were followers of Karl Marx, who along with Friedrich Engels is credited with founding "scientific socialism": ideal communism in which the working class rules. When branches of the First International, which was dominated by Marx's ideas, were established in the United States during the late 1860s, Germans made up most of the original membership.

Johann Most became one of the most well known German anarchists in the United States, and in 1882 he established the anarchist weekly *Freiheit,* which he had previously published in Britain. Most was a pamphleteer who advocated revolutionary action and destruction of capitalism. In 1883 he led a movement of communist anarchists who formed a federation known as the International Working People's Association (IWPA). Members held a convention in Pittsburgh, Pennsylvania, issuing a manifesto calling for the working class to liberate itself from economic bondage.

A Chicago group of IWPA members soon formed and included German anarchists who would participate in the 1886 Haymarket affair and later be executed. One of the Germans was August Spies, editor of *Arbeiter-Zeitung,* an anarchist daily. The other executed Germans were Adolph Fischer, a typographer for the daily, and George Engel, an active member of IWPA. Two of the three anarchists pardoned by Illinois Governor John Peter Altgeld were Germans Michael Schwab and Oscar Neebe.

After the executions of the Haymarket martyrs, as they were called, some German anarchists in the United States continued for a time to follow the teachings of Johann Most. However, when one of his disciples, Russian Alexander Berkman, tried to kill steel plant manager Henry Clay Frick in Homestead, Pennsylvania, Most denounced the deed, shocking Russian anarchist Emma Goldman, one of Most's early followers.

Although German anarchists in the United States became less influential during the early 1900s, they continued to write and speak out. One of the most widely read German anarchists was (and still is) Rudolf Rocker (1873–1958), who advocated that workers take direct action (strikes, boycotts, etc.) to overcome their economic and political oppressors. In his view, voting and participation in government had a poisonous effect on the labor movement because parliamentary politics deluded people into thinking that they would be helped by those who dominated them.

See also

Anabaptists; Anarchist-Communists; Haymarket Affair; Haymarket Anarchists; International Working People's Association; Marx, Karl; Most, Johann; Pittsburgh Manifesto; Revolutions of 1848; Spies, August

References

O'Connor, Richard, *The German-Americans: An Informal History* (Boston: Little, Brown, 1968).

Rocker, Rudolf, *Anarchism and Anarcho-Syndicalism* (London: Freedom Press, 1988, orig. publ. as *Anarchosyndicalism* by Martin Secker and Warburg Ltd., 1938).

Godwin, William (1756–1836)

William Godwin is regarded by most scholars as the first writer to develop a coherent set of philosophical principles describing what would become known as anarchism. By the time 19th-century progressive activists, leftists, and labor organizers eventually popularized these tenets, however, his work was almost totally forgotten. He was mentioned in passing by Pierre-Joseph Proudhon and others, but only Peter Kropotkin seemed to understand the important foundation laid by this influential thinker.

Godwin was raised in North Cambridgeshire, when England was dominated by a corrupt gentry and powerful crown. Early training followed his father and grandfather, both ministers in the Dissenters tradition. That group, typically pious and religious, had broken from the Church of England the previous century, rejecting its most basic elements. Though not officially banned by the state, followers were not allowed to hold public office, and their offsprings' births could not be recorded. Dissenters remained a fiercely independent lot nonetheless.

Young William was educated by some of the best in the Dissenter ministry and in schools where a liberal social consciousness and freedom of thought were held paramount. He intended to lead a life among the clergy, but attempts to find employment were largely unsuccessful. His diverse studies and the influences of such political philosophers as John Locke and Jean-Jacques Rousseau were not the sort of background most rural parishes were looking for in their spiritual leader.

In the academies, Godwin had learned that the mind at birth is a blank slate that develops from individual experiences, and he came to believe that reasoning was the crucial process that translated experience into knowledge and wisdom. He cited education and social conditioning as the key to character transformation. As revolution raged in the American colonies across the Atlantic and as the English monarchy did what it could to maintain power over its dissident masses, Godwin reasoned that the most basic problem with society was government itself. He moved to London in 1783 and took up writing as a career. He continued to develop a philosophy based on the preeminence of the individual. As he noted, "There is but one power to which I can yield a heart-felt obedience, the decision of my own understanding, the dictate of my own conscience" (quoted in Woodcock, 41). He believed that if individuals were left to their own devices, they would naturally develop societies based on equality and the voluntary exchange of wealth.

With the news accounts of the French Revolution, Godwin actually believed that liberty might be achieved on the continent, and he subsequently wrote his greatest work, *Enquiry Concerning Political Justice and Its Influence on General Virtue and Happiness.* His book was published in 1793, just weeks after Thomas Paine was forced to flee England under threat of death for authoring *The Rights of Man.*

There was some real danger that Godwin's work, outlining the economic and political structures of an ideal society without government, might prompt the government to brand him a traitor, as it did Paine. Luckily for the writer, the book cost three guineas: too expensive to facilitate broad distribution, or so the government assumed. In reality, *Political Justice* was sold at about half the cover price and purchased by clubs so that it could be read aloud to members at meetings throughout the country. Copies were distributed in Scotland and Ireland, and Godwin was famous almost overnight. The revolutionary ideas of this unassuming man struck a chord with a populace weary of conditions that held them powerless and in eternal poverty and unhappiness.

In 1796 Godwin renewed a friendship with and eventually married Mary Wollstonecraft, credited as the first major feminist writer. Godwin had decried the institution of marriage as one of society's worst monopolies yet agreed to marry the pregnant Wollstonecraft to protect her from the type of scorn she had received upon the birth of her first child, likewise out of wedlock. In answering critics—who took delight in the seeming inconsistency between action and opinion—Godwin held that individual happiness was more important than any political point. After a happy but brief life together, his wife died while giving birth to their daughter, Mary. Mary Godwin would go on to marry poet Percy Bysshe Shelley, who came to the Godwin home on a pilgrimage to meet the great philosopher of freedom and justice.

William Godwin's fortunes peaked during the years after publication of *Political Justice,* but as revolutionary fervor died out in France and England he fell from favor. He ended his life in poverty. For decades his legacy fell from the consciousness of the world he had tried to perfect.

See also
Paine, Thomas; Shelley, Percy Bysshe; Wollstonecraft, Mary

References

Clark, J. P., *The Philosophical Anarchism of William Godwin* (Princeton: Princeton University Press, 1977).

Harper, Clifford, *Anarchy: A Graphic Guide* (London: Camden Press, 1987).

Marshall, Peter, ed., *The Anarchist Writings of William Godwin* (London: Freedom Press, 1986).

Ward, Dana, "William Godwin: An Intellectual History," on the internet <http://www.pitzer.edu/~dward/Anarchist_Archives/godwin/godwincom.html>.

Woodcock, George, *Anarchism: A History of Libertarian Ideas and Movements* (Cleveland: World Publishing Company, 1962, reprint New York: New American Library, 1974).

Goldman, Emma (1869–1940)

In the early 1900s the United States press labeled Emma Goldman "Red Emma" and portrayed her as the most dangerous woman in the country. Emma Goldman was, however, a spellbinding speaker and passionate, prolific writer. In exposing the way the state exploited citizens, she became an enemy of the U.S. government and monopolistic business interests that held sway over it. In her view, people should live free and unfettered by governments that could compel them to wage war, work under inhuman conditions, and ignore natural proclivities to pursue truth and beauty.

Goldman's philosophy of anarchism grew from the harsh discrimination that all Jews experienced in her native tsarist Russia. Later she developed her views in the United States under the tutelage of Johann Most and other radicals of the European anarcho-syndicalist and social revolutionary movements. That philosophy coalesced into an activist cause after the executions following the Haymarket riots in 1886. Goldman and many others believed the men were tried and convicted in a kangaroo court to deter the efforts of social protesters. She became determined to make the cause of the Haymarket martyrs her own.

Goldman pursued her goal for almost 50 years, lecturing worldwide, writing books and articles, and publishing the magazine *Mother Earth.* She subscribed to the theories of Michael Bakunin and other anarchist writers who saw the industrial-based economy and the modern state as the successor to the tsars, kings, and despots who kept the common people in Europe in virtual slavery. For her, the ancient communities of individuals and families that gathered to meet their own needs was the appropriate structure for human existence. As she wrote: "Human society then was not a State but an association; a voluntary association for mutual protection and benefit. . . . Political government and the State were a much later development, growing out of the desire of the stronger to take advantage of the weaker, of the few against the many" (Schulman 1972, 89–90).

Emma Goldman believed it was her mission to help humankind throw off the yoke of oppressive government—any form of government or oppression. After a botched attempt early during her activist career to aid her lover, Alexander Berkman, in the assassination of industrialist Henry Clay Frick, whom they blamed for oppressing workers, she repudiated violence as a means to achieve her ends. From that time on, words were her weapons. Her controversial statements attacking social institutions were reported by newspapers in every city where she appeared, and the popular media vilified and demonized her for her outspoken attacks against injustice. Goldman became the most visible anarchist in the United States.

On September 6, 1901, newspapers nationwide carried banner headlines reporting that President William McKinley had been shot. Accompanying stories related how the accused assassin, Leon Czolgosz, had been inspired to act after hearing a speech by Goldman days before. Arrested later in Chicago, she was held in jail for 15 days. Police questioned her intensely for hours at a stretch. She even lost a tooth when one of the men smashed her in the mouth with his fist.

Although Goldman had been introduced to Czolgosz by an associate, there was no evidence that she collaborated with him. The chief of police was convinced of her innocence, and he ordered her released. The publicity, however, forever linked the assassination to anarchism and Emma Goldman.

During national speaking tours Goldman was in danger from individuals and vigilantes who blamed her for the president's death. In one instance, a mob attacked and captured her manager, Ben Reitman, who was tarred and feathered before being driven out of town. The police did little to protect Reitman or Goldman. Often the police would attempt to ban her appearances on the pretense she was out to provoke violence, lawlessness, and revolution. But as she wrote in her autobiography, she "welcomed the difficulties. They helped to rekindle my fighting spirit and to convince me that those in power never learn to what extent persecution is the leaven of revolutionary zeal" (Goldman 1970, 331).

Goldman was arrested many times for defying police orders, which she knew violated the right to free speech guaranteed by the First Amendment of the U.S. Constitution. However, she found many ways to circumvent the obstacles and to speak out for workers' rights, birth control, open education, and women's rights. She also opposed U.S. involvement in World War I in Europe and the draft that was eventually instituted to fight it.

In June 1917 the U.S. government seized an opportunity to finally silence Emma Goldman, arresting her and Berkman for conspiring to oppose the draft. The marshal who came to her offices had no warrant and no legal authority to confiscate papers that were taken from her. In short order, Goldman was convicted and sentenced to prison.

The federal government went even further. The immigration department had been investigating Goldman's U.S. citizenship, based on a marriage to a naturalized citizen in Rochester, New York, years before. Immigration authorities voided her former husband's citizenship status, which made her an illegal alien too. Now she could be charged under the recently passed Anarchist Exclusion Act, which barred known anarchist aliens from entering the United States and sanctioned deportation of those already in the country. The U.S. government deported Goldman, Berkman, and 247 aliens who it labeled anarchists.

Goldman and Berkman went to Russia, where at first they championed the 1917 revolution, but they soon became disillusioned with the Bolsheviks and their brutal treatment of workers. In fact, Goldman became highly critical of Vladimir Lenin, the "father" of the revolution. In her view, Lenin had sacrificed both the country and the revolution to the centralized State. Goldman wrote:

> Lenin was the most pliable politician in history. He could be an ultra-revolutionary, a compromiser and conservative at the same time. When like a mighty wave the cry swept over Russia "All power to the Soviets!" Lenin swam with the tide. When the peasants took possession of the land and the workers of the factories, Lenin not only approved of those direct methods but went further. He issued the famous motto, "Rob the robbers," a slogan which served to confuse the minds of the people and caused untold injury to revolutionary idealism. Never before did any real revolutionist interpret social expropriation as the transfer of wealth from one set of individuals to another. Yet that was exactly what Lenin's slogan meant. The indiscriminate and irresponsible raids, the accumulation of the wealth of the former bourgeoisie by the new Soviet bureaucracy, the chicanery practised toward those whose only crime was their former status, were all the results of Lenin's "Rob the robbers" policy. The whole subsequent history of the revolution is a kaleidoscope of Lenin's compromises and betrayal of his own slogans. (Quoted in Schulman, 314)

Goldman left Russia and during the next two decades lived in exile in England, France, and Spain, never ceasing to write and speak out for anarchist ideals. Until her death, she consistently and publicly questioned and condemned the role of government in the individual's life.

See also

Bakunin, Mikhail A.; Berkman, Alexander; Czolgosz, Leon; Haymarket Affair; Most, Johann

References

Chalberg, John, *Emma Goldman: American Individualist* (New York: HarperCollins, 1991).

Drinnon, Richard, *Rebel in Paradise: A Biography of Emma Goldman* (Chicago: University of Chicago Press, 1961).
Falk, Candace Serena, *Love, Anarchy, and Emma Goldman* (New Brunswick, NJ: Rutgers University Press, 1990).
Gay, Kathlyn, and Martin K. Gay, *Heroes of Conscience* (Santa Barbara, CA: ABC-CLIO, 1996).
Goldman, Emma, *Anarchism and Other Essays* (New York: Dover, 1969, reprint of 1910 ed.).
Goldman, Emma, *Living My Life,* 2 vols. (New York: Knopf, 1933, reprint New York: Dover, 1970).
Shulman, Alix, ed., *Red Emma Speaks: Selected Writings and Speeches by Emma Goldman* (New York: Random House, 1972).
Solomon, Martha, *Emma Goldman* (Boston: Twayne, Macmillan, 1987).

Goodman, Paul (1911–1972)

One of the most influential social critics in the United States, Paul Goodman gained his reputation from his 1960 book *Growing Up Absurd: Problems of Youth in the Organized Culture.* During the 1960s, he supported many New Left causes and was an early opponent of the Vietnam War. Many of his stories, poems, and essays condemn conformity in organized society and education. Goodman had no use for centralized authority and in effect was an individualist anarchist. However, in his last book, *New Reformation* (1970), he identified himself as a "conservative anarchist" in the tradition of Thomas Jefferson. He also wrote on other topics, such as city planning; *Communitas* (1947) is a classic written in collaboration with his brother, Percival. Following some psychoanalytic therapy he wrote *Gestalt Therapy* (1951) and began to practice therapy on his own.

Born in New York City, Paul Goodman was the fourth child of American-born German-Jewish parents. Goodman's father, who failed in business, left the family, and relatives cared for Paul while his mother worked. Educated in the New York public schools as well as in Hebrew school, Goodman attended City College of New York between 1927 and 1931 and earned his doctorate at the University of Chicago in 1954.

During the 1940s Goodman traveled, taught, and actively pursued a bisexual lifestyle. He was fired from one teaching position because of his homosexual behavior, but he never made a secret of his relationships—whether with men or women. For several years he lived with Virginia Miller; the couple's daughter, Susan, was born in 1939. In 1945 he began a relationship with Sally Duchsten; their son, Mathew Ready, was born in 1946.

World War II led Goodman to anarchism. He avoided the draft and was revolted by the "cultural and social conditions of wartime, which he saw as ugly." He was apparently influenced by anarcho-pacifists, and in 1945 some of his first anarchist essays appeared in libertarian magazines (Widmer, 38). Although Goodman wrote about architecture, city planning, education, linguistics, literature, politics, and psychology, he argued that he did not write about many subjects but rather concentrated on the here and now and on people in their humanmade environment. He insisted that society should adapt to individual needs, not the reverse.

Besides *Growing Up Absurd,* Goodman published ten other major books between 1959 and 1970, among them *The Empire City, The Society I Live in Is Mine, Community of Scholars, Compulsory Mis-Education,* and *New Reformation.* During the turbulent 1960s he taught at several colleges and universities. He died of a heart attack in 1972.

See also
Individualist Anarchists; New Left

References

Knapp, Gregory, "The State Is the Great Forgetter: Rexroth and Goodman as Antecedents of Cultural Ecology, Political Ecology, and the New Cultural Geography," paper presented at the 93rd Annual Meeting of the Association of American Geographers (April 2, 1997).
Stoehr, Taylor, "Growing Up Absurd—Again: Rereading Paul Goodman in the Nineties," *Dissent* (Fall 1990).
Stoehr, Taylor, ed., *Crazy Hope and Finite Experience: Final Essays of Paul Goodman* (San Francisco: Jossey-Bass, 1994).
Widmer, Kingsley, *Paul Goodman* (Boston: Twayne Publishers, 1980).

Grave, Jean

See French Anarchism

Greene, William Bradford (1819–1878)

A mutualist and anarchist writer, William Bradford Greene was greatly influenced by Pierre-Joseph Proudhon's ideas, as is clearly shown in two of his books, *Mutual Banking* and *Socialistic, Mutualistic, and Financial Fragments.* Like Proudhon, Greene believed that mutualism would replace the political system. In his view, "Mutualism operates, by its very nature, to render political government, founded on arbitrary force, superfluous, that is, it operates to the decentralization of the political power, and to the transformation of the State, by substituting self-government instead of government *ab extra.*" Greene contended that "we are all mutually dependent, morally, intellectually, and physically upon each other. What we possess, we owe partly to our own faculties, but mainly to the educational and material aid received by us from our parents, friends, neighbors, and other members of society" (quoted in Schuster, 132).

Born in Haverhill, Massachusetts, William Greene was the son of Nathaniel Greene, editor of *Boston Statesman.* William was educated at West Point. He became interested in economic and social reforms, and around 1842 he enrolled at Harvard Divinity School. After graduation he served for several years as a Unitarian minister in West Brookfield, Massachusetts. He spent much of that time writing, publishing *Mutual Banking* in 1850. Greene proposed in his writings that society be reformed with the establishment of a federal Bank of Exchange. To reach this goal, Greene "presented petitions to the Senate and House of Representatives of Massachusetts, requesting the formation of such a bank, in 1850–1851, and in 1873. . . . The character of this economic order would be *federative* and *non-authoritarian,* an order in which the individual would be sovereign in his own sphere, but at the same time responsible to society" (Schuster, 131).

Although Greene's philosophy was similar to that of Josiah Warren, called the first American anarchist, the two apparently did not know each other. Greene was instead "an independent disciple of Proudhon and attempted to inject into the labor movement the practical solutions of Proudhon." He also worked with individualist anarchists in the United States who were active in the labor reform movement, such as Benjamin Tucker, Lysander Spooner, and Ezra Heywood (Schuster, 134).

Greene, however, did not spend his entire adult life in America. From 1853 to 1861, Greene, along with his father, resided in Paris. When the U.S. Civil War broke out Greene was commissioned but resigned from the military in 1862 to dedicate himself to labor reform. Greene served as vice president of the New England Labor Reform League and as president of the Massachusetts Labor Union. "He was also active in the French-speaking Working People's International Association" and the First International of 1872 (Schuster, 130). Greene then moved to England, living there until his death in 1878.

See also

First International; Heywood, Ezra Hervey Hoar; Individualist Anarchists; Mutualism; Proudhon, Pierre-Joseph; Spooner, Lysander; Tucker, Benjamin R.; Warren, Josiah

References

Schuster, Eunice M., *Native American Anarchism: A Study of Left-Wing American Individualism* (Northampton, MA: Smith College, 1932, reprint New York: AMS Press, 1970).

Guerin, Daniel

See Anarchist Authors

Guevara, Ernesto "Che" (1928–1967)

Ernesto Guevara Lynch de la Serna of Argentina, better known by his nickname "Che" (meaning "friend"), has been called an icon of the 1960s and a hero of the Cuban revolution. He has also been vilified by many Cuban exiles. A legendary figure worldwide, his death in 1967 at the hands of Bolivian soldiers—reportedly trained and equipped by U.S. officers from the Green Berets and Central Intelligence Agency (CIA)—has been controversial and added to the Che myth.

Born in Rosario, Argentina, Che was the

first child of an aristocratic family. His father, an architect, had suffered some financial problems but still maintained a comfortable lifestyle. When Ernesto was two, he developed asthma, which plagued him throughout life. The family moved often in attempts to find a healthier climate for their son. Because of the frequent moves and asthma attacks, Che was unable to regularly attend school, but his brothers and sisters brought him lessons to complete. He was also an avid reader; among the books he studied were those by Karl Marx and Friedrich Engels, whose ideas influenced the youth. During his youth, however, he seemed to show little interest in the political rise of Juan and Eva Perón and their control over Argentina.

Although Che practically educated himself during his early years, he did enroll in high school and was able to continue advanced studies. In 1953, he earned a medical degree. Before completing his academic courses, however, he traveled by bicycle and on foot throughout Latin America, visiting remote jungle villages and learning whatever he could about tropical diseases.

When he became a doctor, Che went to Guatemala to work with impoverished Indians. He arrived in the country not long after Jacobo Arbenz Guzmán had been elected president and had nationalized large landholdings, including the United Fruit Company, a major U.S. firm that had great economic and political influence. Guevara was enthusiastic about this "socialist experiment." But while he was in Guatemala, an invasion force, backed by the United States, ended the nationalization process and brought down the revolutionary government. In Guevara's view, Guatemala "succumbed before the cold, premeditated aggression of the USA, hidden behind a smokescreen of continental propaganda. Its apparent leader was the Secretary of State, John Foster Dulles, who by a strange coincidence was also the lawyer for a stockholder in the United Fruit Company" (quoted in Ortiz, 37).

Guevara went to Mexico feeling "defeated, united in my pain to all the Guatemalans, hoping, seeking a way to recreate a future for that bleeding land." In Mexico, he met Fidel Castro, who was "seeking neutral territory on which to prepare his men" for a major attack against Cuban dictator Fulgencio Batista. Already there had been an assault on the Moncada barracks in Santiago de Cuba. The new recruits, including a number of anarchists, trained at a ranch in Mexico and became part of "the 26th of July Movement (named for a date marking the 1953 attack on the Moncada barracks)." As Guevara noted, "A very hard task was beginning for those in charge of training these people under necessary conditions of secrecy in Mexico. They were fighting against the Mexican government, against American FBI agents, and also against Batista's spies; they were fighting against these three forces which in one way and another joined together, money and personal sellouts playing a large role" (quoted in Ortiz, 37).

In 1956 Che and 80 others sailed for Cuba on the *Granma*. Years later, Castro recalled that the "trip was very hard" for Che, because "he could not even provide himself with the medicine he needed and throughout the trip he suffered from a severe attack of asthma, with nothing to alleviate it, but also without ever complaining" (quoted in Ortiz, 14).

Although Che started out as the doctor for the group, he soon became a *comandante,* leading revolutionaries into battle and eventually helping to bring down Batista. For years after the revolution, Che was part of the Cuban government, but between 1963 and 1964 Guevara's industrialization plan for Cuba brought about economic decline, and he lost political power. Guevara also hoped to bring about revolutions in other parts of Latin America and in Africa. In a 1965 letter to Fidel Castro, he wrote:

> I feel that I have fulfilled the part of my duty that tied me to the Cuban revolution in its territory, and I say good-by to you, the comrades, your people, who are already mine. I formally renounce my positions in the national leadership of the party, my post as minister, my rank of major, and my Cuban citizenship. Nothing legal binds me to Cuba. The only ties are of another nature; those which cannot be

> broken as appointments can. . . . Other nations of the world call for my modest efforts." (Quoted in Ortiz, 284)

Guevara left his wife and children, who he felt would be well cared for by the state, and attempted to bring about a revolution in the Belgian Congo, which was a failure. He then went to Bolivia, where he thought revolutionary ideology would take root due to the extreme poverty among the peasants. Che also expected the revolution to spread quickly from a Bolivian base if his guerrillas were successful. Beginning in 1967, the guerrillas fought Bolivian soldiers for three months, with only one casualty compared to 30 Bolivian deaths. By fall 1967 U.S. CIA agents and the Green Berets (special forces) were deeply involved in efforts to aid the Bolivians (Rodriguez, 184).

In October 1967 Che was captured by Bolivian soldiers and executed. His body was buried in a secret, unmarked grave along with several other revolutionaries. Thirty years later, however, the bodies were unearthed, and Che's remains were sent to Cuba, where Castro and other officials held a ceremony to honor Guevara. Che was reburied in Santa Clara, Cuba.

The reburial and several recent biographies have inspired and revitalized the hero worship of Che Guevara. But the Anarchist Communist Federation (ACF) magazine *Organize!* denounced Guevara as a "jaded Stalinist" who proved to be the most authoritarian and brutal of the guerrilla leaders. In fact, Che set about transforming volunteer bands of guerrillas into a classic army, with strict discipline and hierarchy. ACF concluded that despite the mythology and cult that have grown up around Che Guevara, his own words and "actions reveal him to be no friend of the working masses, whether they be workers or peasants" ("Myths and Legends").

See also

Anarchist Communist Federation; Cuban Anarchism; Marx, Karl

References

Evans, Paola, Kim Healey, Peter Kornbluh, Ramon Cruz, and Hannah Elinson, "The Death of Che Guevara: A Chronology," on the internet <http://www.geocities.com/Hollywood/8702/che.html>.

"Myths and Legends—Che Guevara," on the internet <http://www.spunk.org/texts/groups/acf/sp001768.html>.

Rodriguez, Felix I., *Shadow Warrior* (New York: Simon and Schuster, 1989).

Ryan, Henry Butterfield, *The Fall of Guevara* (New York: Oxford University Press, 1997).

H

Haymarket Affair

The events that led to a riot just north of Chicago's Haymarket Square on May 4, 1886, actually began months—even years—before. During the 1880s, tens of thousands of industrial workers across the United States organized and struck for an eight-hour workday. The average workday at the time was a little more than ten hours, with the workweek being 60–65 hours. Strikes were so frequent that the period became known as the Great Upheaval.

At first many anarchists did not support the movement for an eight-hour workday, primarily because they viewed it as a compromise: They wanted to abolish the wage system entirely. However, by 1886 anarchists' position changed as leaders began to see the movement as part of the overall class struggle against domination. In cities like Chicago, Milwaukee, and New York, anarchists began to step up efforts to organize and agitate for the shorter workday. Chicago became the major center of the eight-hour movement, and militant trade unionists such as Albert Parsons and August Spies espoused direct action, including force and violence, to attain working-class goals.

Workers at the McCormick Harvester Machine Company outside Chicago staged a strike in February 1886, and the walkout continued for weeks. By May 1 half the McCormick workforce was on strike, agitating for the eight-hour day. McCormick hired nonunion laborers to replace those who walked off the job, and on May 3 striking workers joined others at a mass meeting about a block from the McCormick plant. August Spies addressed the strikers, urging them to stick together. While he was speaking, McCormick strikebreakers left the factory, and strikers demonstrated. When police came to break up the protest, they attacked the strikers without warning, clubbing and shooting. One worker was killed and several others were severely injured.

Spies was outraged over the police brutality and the following day published a pamphlet urging workingmen to arm themselves as protection against their "thieving masters." He and other anarchists called for a protest meeting on the evening of May 4 at Haymarket Square in Chicago. Because the crowd was not as large as anticipated, the meeting place was moved to a nearby alleyway where Spies and other speakers used a wagon as a platform. After several speeches, a threatening storm interrupted the meeting, and people began to leave. Police arrived and demanded that the meeting end at once. Seconds later a bomb was thrown amid the police. One policeman was killed and dozens more were injured (six more policemen later died as a result of their injuries). Police immediately began to fire on the crowd, killing and wounding an undetermined number of civilians.

After the melee, Chicago was in a state of hysteria. The press, clergy, politicians, mainstream unions, and many others condemned anarchists, socialists, and communists, accusing them of murdering the policemen and being a menace to society. They called for justice and revenge, which in their view meant the same thing. Such reactions were typical across the United States and many parts of Europe as word of the bombing spread.

Chicago police attempted to find those they held responsible for the killings. Without search warrants police ransacked homes, offices, meeting halls, and other places where anarchists might gather. As suspects were rounded up, some people were beaten and tortured; others were bribed to act as witnesses for the state. Thirty-one people were indicted for the bombing and for conspiring to commit murder. Eight men eventually stood trial on those charges: George Engel, Samuel Fielden, Adolph Fischer, Louis Lingg, Oscar Neebe, Albert Parsons, August Spies, and Michael Schwab.

The state offered no proof that the Haymarket Eight, as they became known, were responsible for the bombing and police deaths. But before and throughout the trial, the intentions of the judge, jury, and state's attorney were clear. Jurors publicly stated their prejudice against the defendants, and at the end of the trial State's Attorney Julius S. Grinnell told jurors that anarchy was on trial and the defendants were "indicted because they were leaders. They are no more guilty than the thousands who follow them. Gentlemen of the jury: convict these men, make examples of them, hang them and you save our institutions and our society" (Foner 1969, 8).

All of the men were convicted; seven were sentenced to die by hanging, and the eighth, Oscar Neebe, was sentenced to a 15-year prison term. The case was appealed, but the Illinois Supreme Court sustained the verdicts; the U.S. Supreme Court declined to hear the case. A campaign for clemency began, and thousands of Americans as well as European supporters wrote letters, signed petitions, staged protest meetings, and personally pleaded with Illinois Governor Richard Ogelsby to pardon the condemned men. Ogelsby did commute the sentences of Fielden and Schwab to life imprisonment, but the others were condemned to death. Lingg committed suicide the night before he was to be hanged. Engel, Fischer, Parsons, and Spies were executed by hanging on November 11, 1887.

Hundreds of thousands mourned the hanged men, who quickly became known as the Haymarket martyrs. In 1893 a memorial in their honor was placed in Waldheim Cemetery in Chicago, where the men were buried. That year, Illinois Governor John Peter Altgeld pardoned the three survivors, saying they were innocent of the crime for which they had been convicted. As historian Henry David concluded:

> A biased jury, a prejudiced judge, perjured evidence, an extraordinary and indefensible theory of conspiracy, and the temper of Chicago led to the conviction. The evidence never proved their guilt. Nor can the conclusion that the bomb was probably thrown by a member of the social-revolutionary movement affect this statement. . . . If the eight men were guilty . . . because they had urged the use of force, then [newspaper publisher] William Randolph Hearst should have been tried as an accessory to the murder of McKinley because he wrote, in an editorial attacking the President, that "if bad institutions and bad men can be got rid of only by killing, then the killing must be done" (David, 541).

See also

Haymarket Anarchists; Haywood, William Dudley "Big Bill"; Industrial Workers of the World; Lingg, Louis; Parsons, Albert; Spies, August

References

Avrich, Paul, *The Haymarket Tragedy* (Princeton: Princeton University Press, 1984).

David, Henry, *The History of the Haymarket Affair* (New York: Russell and Russell, 1936).

de Cleyre, Voltairine, *The First Mayday: The Haymarket Speeches, 1895–1910* (Over-the-Water, Sanday, Orkney, UK: Cienfuegos Press, New York: Libertarian Book Club, 1980).

Foner, Philip Sheldon, ed., *The Autobiographies of the Haymarket Martyrs* (Atlantic Highlands, NJ: Humanities Press, 1969).

Preston, William Jr., *Aliens and Dissenters: Federal Suppression of Radicals, 1903–1993,* 2d ed. (Urbana and Chicago: University of Illinois Press, 1994).

Roediger, Dave, and Franklin Rosemont, eds., *Haymarket Scrapbook* (Chicago: Charles H. Kerr, 1986).

Haymarket Anarchists

The Haymarket events of 1886 in Chicago resulted in the arrest of eight anarchists who were charged with the murder of several policemen. The policemen were killed by a bomb thrown by an unknown person following a striking workers' meeting featuring speeches from anarchist writers and union organizers. Despite public protests and calls for amnesty, the anarchists were convicted in a trial that some consider to be a low point in the history of American justice. Four anarchists were hanged: George Engel, Adolph Fischer, Albert Parsons, and August Spies. Hours before his scheduled execution, Louis Lingg committed suicide. Out of eight anarchists, three were spared. The sentences of Samuel Fielden and Michael Schwab were commuted to life imprisonment, and Oscar Neebe received a 15-year prison sentence. Fielden, Schwab, and Neebe were eventually pardoned by Illinois Governor John Peter Altgeld. Thus became the Haymarket martyrs.

When they were executed in 1887, Altgeld was a judge in Cook County Circuit Court and had no authority to grant pardons. In 1892 he was elected governor of Illinois, and after he took office in 1893 he received a petition with 60,000 names urging clemency for the jailed anarchists. By this time many legal experts were condemning the trial and the court; famed attorney Clarence Darrow also wrote to his friend Altgeld, urging him to pardon the remaining defendants. Altgeld began studying the court records. Although he had never publicly presented his views on the Haymarket convictions, he issued pardons for Fielden, Schwab, and Neebe on June 26, 1893; the next day he released his reasons for freeing the men.

Based on the records of jurors' statements, Altgeld found that the defendants had to accept a panel that was prejudiced against them. In one instance a juror was not only "bitterly prejudiced" but "also was related to one of the [police]men who was killed and for that reason he felt more strongly against the defendants than he otherwise might, yet he was held to be competent." In addition, Altgeld wrote, "the State has never discovered who it was that threw the bomb that killed the policemen" and the evidence showed that

> the bomb was, in all probability, thrown by someone seeking revenge; that a course had been pursued by authorities which would naturally cause this; that for a number of years prior to the Haymarket affair there had been labor troubles, and in several cases a number of laboring people, guilty of no offense, had been shot down in cold blood by Pinkerton men [hired guards], and none of the murderers were brought to justice. The evidence taken at coroner's inquests and presented here, shows that in at least two cases men were fired on and killed when they were running away, and there was consequently no occasion to shoot, yet nobody was punished; that in Chicago there had been a number of strikes in which some of the police not only took sides against the men, but without any authority of law invaded and broke up peaceable meetings, and in scores of cases brutally clubbed people who were guilty of no offense whatever. (Altgeld, 33–36)

Altgeld further found there was no real case against Schwab or Fielden, who was charged with firing a revolver into the crowd; there were "serious doubts" that Fielden ever had a gun during the meeting or ever owned one. Furthermore, even if Fielden had "given pernicious criminal advice to large masses to commit violence, whether orally, in speeches, or in print, it must be shown that persons committing the violence had read or heard the advice; for, until he had heard or read it, he did not receive, and if he never received advice, it cannot be said that he acted on it" (Altgeld, 54).

As for the final defendant, Altgeld wrote, "the State's Attorney said he did not think he had a case against Neebe, and that he wanted to dismiss him, but was dissuaded from doing so by his associate attorneys, who feared that such a step might influence the jury in favor of the other defendants." Altgeld wrote that he "examined all of the evidence against Neebe with care, and it utterly fails to prove even the shadow of a case against him. Some of the other defendants were guilty of using seditious language, but even this cannot be said of Neebe" (Altgeld, 54–57). Despite the stirring nature of Altgeld's written pardon, he was heavily criticized and never again sought public office.

See also
Darrow, Clarence; Haymarket Affair; Parsons, Albert; Spies, August

References
Altgeld, John P., *Reasons for Pardoning The Haymarket Anarchists* (Chicago: Charles H. Kerr Publishing, 1986, orig. publ. in 1893).
Foner, Philip Sheldon, ed., *The Autobiographies of the Haymarket Martyrs* (Atlantic Highlands, NJ: Humanities Press, 1969).

Haymarket Riot

See Haymarket Affair

Haywood, William Dudley "Big Bill" (1869–1928)

"Big Bill" Haywood became famous for his leadership of the Industrial Workers of the World (IWW), commonly known as the Wobblies, a syndicalist movement founded in 1905. Like other syndicalists of the time, however, the Wobblies were not committed to anarchism but did believe in using direct action to attain their goals (Bookchin). In his autobiography, published a year after his death, Haywood recalled that he opened the first IWW meeting by using a board as a gavel, announcing:

> This is the Continental Congress of the working-class. We are here to confederate the workers of this country into a working-class movement that shall have for its purpose the emancipation of the working-class from the slave bondage of capitalism. . . . The aims and objects of this organization shall be to put the working-class in possession of the economic power, the means of life, in control of the machinery of production and distribution, without regard to the capitalist masters.

Haywood shared the speakers' platform with Socialist Party leader Eugene Debs and 75-year-old labor organizer Mary "Mother" Jones.

Haywood was born in Salt Lake City, Utah, and went to work as a miner at the age of 15. He soon began what would be a long history of radical politics and labor organizing. In 1900 he became secretary-treasurer of the Western Federation of Miners and within five years was leading the new labor activist consortium, IWW.

Not long after the IWW was founded Haywood was arrested and charged with the attempted murder of a former Idaho governor. The trial and a subsequent acquittal turned the spotlight on the socialist organizer. He took advantage of his notoriety during a five-year national speaking tour through 1913 to support IWW causes and local strike actions.

By 1917 Haywood found himself once again behind bars, charged with sedition. Because of their opposition to fighting World War I, Wobblies were common targets of the government. While out on bail in 1921, Haywood fled the country for Russia, much to the distress of his friends and supporters. There he became affiliated with the Red Trade International. He was embraced by the new revolutionary government of Vladimir Lenin, and he accepted a position as an administrator. He spent the rest of his life in the Soviet Union.

See also
Anarcho-Syndicalism; Direct Action; Industrial Workers of the World

References
Bookchin, Murray, "The Ghost of Anarcho-Syndicalism," on the internet <http://www.tao.ca/~ise/library/b_ghost.html>, 1992).
Brissenden, Paul F., *The IWW: A Study of American Syndicalism* (New York: Columbia University Press, 1919).
Dubofsky, Melvyn, *We Shall Be All: A History of the Industrial Workers of the World* (New York: Quadrangle Books, 1969).
Flynn, Elizabeth Gurley, "Memories of the IWW," Web edition of transcript by Eugene W. Plawiuk, on the internet <http://www.geocities.com/CapitolHill/5202/rebelgirl.html> (1997).
"Haywood, William D(udley)," *Britannica Online* <http://www.eb.com:180/cgi-bin/g?DocF=micro/263/30.html> (1997).

Heywood, Ezra Hervey Hoar (1829–1893)

According to biographer Martin Henry Blatt, Ezra Heywood was "an individualist anarchist

. . . an active participant in the abolitionist, labor reform, and free-love movements in nineteenth-century America." Like most American reformers of the 1850s, Heywood "envisioned a decentralized social order regulated only by rational self-control and voluntary cooperation of individuals," although few called themselves anarchists. Heywood attempted to live the Jeffersonian ideal of self-reliant individuals. He declared that anarchism was an American product, "a new assertion of the ideas of self-rule and self-support" that Jefferson put into the Declaration of Independence, which states that all people are endowed with the inalienable rights of life, liberty, and the pursuit of happiness. In his arguments for women's suffrage and a woman's right to make decisions regarding her own body, Heywood often invoked the idea that "inalienable rights" belonged to women as well as men. Over a period of two decades, he was repeatedly jailed for his views about women's reproductive rights—or the "Woman Question" as it was called—and his ideas on free love expressed in numerous publications.

Born in Westminster, Massachusetts, to Ezra and Dorcas Hoar, Ezra Hervey was the sixth of nine children. A few years after Ezra's birth, the Hoars moved to a farm near Princeton, Massachusetts. As the children grew older, most of them stayed on to work the farm, which was essential after Ezra's father died in 1845. A few years later, Ezra's older brother, Samuel, who had left to establish a successful shoe and boot business, petitioned the state to have the family name changed to Heywood. Samuel feared that the name Hoar on his business sign would be read "whore." Dorcas Hoar and others in the family, including Ezra, objected, but the name change became legal.

Although most of Ezra Heywood's life was spent denouncing church authority, he converted to evangelical Protestantism during his early adult years. He decided to become a minister and borrowed money from brother Samuel to pay for six years of study at Brown University in Providence, Rhode Island. However, at the university Ezra was deeply influenced by two radical feminists and abolitionists, Phebe Jackson and Ann Whitney. Whitney convinced him that marriage was a from of slavery for women. Jackson and Whitney encouraged Heywood to attend antislavery meetings, and he became an avid abolitionist. Like many in the North, he especially condemned the federal Fugitive Slave Law, which required that runaway slaves be returned to their owners.

Heywood left the church in 1858 "to save his soul," as his biographer put it, and became a full-time abolitionist, following the leadership of the famed William Lloyd Garrison, who believed that slavery was a sin that must be eradicated by direct nonviolent action. During 1859–1864 Heywood delivered hundreds of lectures under the auspices of the Anti-Slavery Society, and he often condemned clerics for not speaking out against slavery. However, Heywood's belief in nonresistance faded, as it did for many northern abolitionists, just before the Civil War. Most declared that the Union cause justified armed conflict. But as the war progressed, Heywood began to question and then denounce all killing as wrong, sinful, and barbarous.

Despite his objections to the oppressiveness of marriage, Heywood married abolitionist Angela Tilton in 1865. He said he felt forced to give in to the institution of marriage just as he had to accept government taxation. Both Angela and Ezra, however, were committed to free-love ideas, advocating freedom in personal relationships and demanding that women have the right to control their own bodies, especially being able to choose whether or not to have sex or to procreate.

The Heywoods also worked together on antislavery, labor reform, and other social issues. Before his marriage, Heywood met Josiah Warren, who had founded several anarchist colonies. Warren introduced Heywood to individualist anarchist ideas about self-rule and labor reform. Heywood's labor reform concepts were based on Warren's theory that people were entitled to set the price for their own labor and the goods they produced. In Warren's system, which could only work in small communities, workers exchanged their labor by bartering—an hour's carpentry work for an hour's service from a retail merchant, for example. Heywood believed, however, that the capitalist system could work if monopolies were eliminated and the laws of supply and demand were allowed to operate freely.

Ezra Heywood was incensed by the terrible conditions, long hours, and small pay that most workers had to endure. He became deeply involved in the labor reform movement and helped organize the New England Labor Reform League in 1869 and the American Labor Reform League in 1871. The following year he began his own newspaper, *The Word,* publishing articles by anarchists, labor reformers, and advocates for women's rights. He also founded the Cooperative Publishing Company to publish his own materials and those of other anarchists and reformers.

Among Heywood's numerous publications was a pamphlet titled "Cupid's Yokes," which among its arguments declared that marriage destroyed individual freedom and denied women the right of self-rule. This pamphlet and other materials on free-love concepts provoked Anthony Comstock, a religious fanatic obsessed with the idea that people were being corrupted by pornography and sexually explicit articles. Comstock lobbied Congress to pass what became known as the Comstock Act of 1873. The law, which violated free-speech rights yet was not overturned until 1930, banned obscene materials, including information on birth-control devices, from the mails. Postal authorities were allowed to determine what was or was not obscene. Comstock aggressively hounded Heywood and was responsible for having Heywood arrested five times on various obscenity charges. Heywood was convicted twice and served prison terms, the last from 1890 to 1892. While imprisoned, he became ill, suffering from what was probably tuberculosis. A year after his release from prison, Heywood died from a recurrence of the disease.

See also

Anarchist Press; Hutchinson, Anne Marbury; Individualist Anarchists; Religious Anarchism; Warren, Josiah

References

Blatt, Martin Henry, *Free Love and Anarchism: The Biography of Ezra Heywood* (Urbana: University of Illinois Press, 1989).

Martin, James J., *Men Against the State* (Colorado Springs: Ralph Myles, 1970).

Schuster, Eunice M., *Native American Anarchism: A Study of Left-Wing American Individualism* (Northampton, MA: Smith College, 1932, reprint New York: AMS Press, 1970).

Hill, Joe (Joel Emmanuel Hääglund) (1879–1915)

Known as the songwriter for the Industrial Workers of the World (IWW) or Wobblies, Joe Hill became a folk hero and martyr to labor's cause. Born in Jevla, Sweden, as Joel Emmanuel Hääglund, apparently in 1879 (several different birth dates are recorded), Joel emigrated to the United States about 1901 or 1902 and changed his name to Joe Hillstrom, later shortened to Joe Hill.

During the next ten years, Hill was a wanderer and itinerant worker, finding jobs wherever he could—on farms, in mines, in construction, and at sea. As he drifted from job to job, he wrote poems and songs put to tunes of popular music and hymns. Little else is known about his early life in the United States, except that he joined IWW about 1910 and began agitating for the union and participating in strikes. He continued to write songs that were picked up by workers and adopted by IWW as its own. Some of the most popular tunes included "Casey Jones," "The Union Scab," and "Rebel Girl," which was named for labor organizer Elizabeth Gurley Flynn.

In 1914 Joe Hill was in Utah, where he got jobs with construction crews and in the copper mines, but he was unemployed when he was accused of killing a grocer and his son in a Salt Lake City robbery. Although there was no direct evidence that he had committed the crime, the state of Utah and the general public were eager to find him guilty, primarily because they learned he was connected to the Wobblies (and thus considered a dangerous anarchist). "Even before his case came to trial, Joe Hill had been convicted in the court of public hysteria," historian Melvyn Dubofsky wrote, adding that in Hill's case "many of the basic principles of due process" were violated:

> From the time of his arrest until the trial began, Hill lacked legal assistance. Police and press created a hostile environment which reduced the already minimal prospects for a fair trial. Later the trial judge reportedly favored the prosecution and hampered the defense. No witness ever absolutely identified Hill as the murderer; no motive was ever introduced to account for the crime; no bullet could be found to link Hill to the killer allegedly wounded in the grocery; and no gun could be located to connect Hill with the murder of either the grocer or his son. Yet on June 26, 1914, a jury found Joe Hill guilty, and on July 8 a judge sentenced him to death. (Dubofsky, 310)

Hill's conviction brought a storm of protest from all over the world, and the IWW and many sympathizers launched a campaign on his behalf. Thousands wrote to Utah's governor, requesting a pardon for Hill. President Woodrow Wilson asked the governor for a new trial, and even the Swedish government tried to intervene. But after more than a year of public protests, Joe Hill's life was not spared. He was executed by firing squad on November 19, 1915. The evening before, he had written to IWW leader Big Bill Haywood, telling him: "Don't waste any time in mourning. Organize." Those words became the motto and rallying cry for the IWW. Hill also became a martyr and legendary character in labor history. Countless stories and a play titled "The Man Who Never Died" were written about him, and his songs, published in *Little Red Song Book,* are still popular with many IWW members today.

See also

Flynn, Elizabeth Gurley; Industrial Workers of the World

References

Camp, Helen C., *Iron in Her Soul: Elizabeth Gurley Flynn and the American Left* (Pullman: Washington State University Press, 1995).

Dubofsky, Melvyn, *We Shall Be All: A History of the Industrial Workers of the World* (New York: Quadrangle Books, 1969).

Flynn, Elizabeth Gurley, *The Rebel Girl: An Autobiography, My First Life, 1906–1926* (orig. publ. by Masses and Mainstream as *I Speak My Own Piece: Autobiography of "The Rebel Girl,"* reprint New York: International Publishers, 1973).

Foner, Philip Sheldon, *The Case of Joe Hill* (New York: International Publishers, 1965).

Foner, Philip Sheldon, ed., *The Letters of Joe Hill* (New York: Oak Publishers, 1965).

Werstein, Irving, *Pie in the Sky, an American Struggle: The Wobblies and Their Times* (New York: Delacorte, 1969).

Home Colony

Referring to Home Colony, one of several communitarian experiments set up in Washington State during the late 1800s, historian Charles LeWarne asked whether it was a "nest of anarchy or haven of individualism." One of those colonies, called Equality after a novel by Edward Bellamy, was a socialist community along Puget Sound, established in 1897 but lasting only until 1903.

Home began because of the failure of another communal experiment called Glennis near Tacoma, Washington. Glennis became so restrictive that there were numerous disputes, and the colony soon dissolved. Three former residents of Glennis found another site for a colony on Von Geldern Cove and with their families established Home in 1896. The founders stressed individualism and distrusted, even despised, authority of any kind. "Considering rules and laws an interference and distrusting government generally, the founders avoided formal organization for almost two years. But practical needs prevailed, and the Mutual Home Association (MHA) was effected in January 1898" (LeWarne, 171).

Members of the association, who paid a dollar to join, could buy one or two acres of land from MHA, which in turn used the money to purchase additional land. "Houses and other improvements were considered personal property that could be sold or bequeathed, but the land itself was retained by the association and could never be sold, mortgaged, or disposed of" (LeWarne, 172). Although colonists owned land in common, they emphasized individuality and personal liberties. A number of professed anarchists settled at Home, and one of the most famous anarchists of the time, Emma Goldman, visited for an extensive period in 1898.

For a time Home existed with little interference from neighboring communities, even though critics sometimes condemned members' radicalism and individualistic lifestyles. However, widespread concern was growing throughout the United States that anarchists were bent on committing terrorist acts, such as Alexander Berkman's attempt to kill industrialist Henry Clay Frick. In 1901, when Leon Czolgosz, who called himself an anarchist, shot President William McKinley at the Pan-American Exposition in Buffalo, New York, people in Washington became suspicious of Home colonists, although Czolgosz had never been part of the group and was not known by most anarchists nationwide. When the president died eight days later, groups of "patriots" and federal officials harassed the colony. Newspapers, the clergy, and lawmakers demanded that the colonists be driven out of the state.

Eventually the threats against Home and its members subsided, and the colony continued until 1921. Then it became the victim of internal strife, disorganization, and idealism that could not be practically applied, and so the colony disbanded.

See also

Berkman, Alexander; Goldman, Emma

References

Hine, Robert V., *Community on the American Frontier: Separate but Not Alone* (Norman: University of Oklahoma Press, 1980).

LeWarne, Charles Pierce, *Utopias on Puget Sound, 1885–1915* (Seattle: University of Washington Press, 1975).

Hutchinson, Anne Marbury (1591–1643)

Anne Hutchinson was among the early Christian anarchists who emigrated from Europe to the Massachusetts Bay Colony during the 1630s. Christian anarchists were similar to individualist anarchists, believing in the right of individuals to determine their own lives. They did not recognize civil authority, formal religious laws, and doctrines of any church. However, unlike individualist anarchists, Christian anarchists believed in a personal religion and spiritual connections with God through the Holy Spirit.

Hutchinson was born in the small town of Alford in Lincolnshire, England. She was the third child of Bridget (Dryden) and Francis Marbury, who eventually had a family of 15 children, several of whom died in infancy. Anne grew up during a time of religious challenges to the Church of England, established in 1534 by King Henry VIII, who had broken with the Roman Catholic Church. During the late 16th century, the church was under the rule of Queen Elizabeth I; she demanded absolute conformity with the church's doctrines. However, reformers, particularly Puritans, believed that the church needed to purify itself and move even further from Catholic ceremonies and its hierarchy. Although Mary's father had never openly claimed to be a member of a reform group, he was jailed three times for his outspoken criticism of the church and for demanding better education and training for the clergy.

In 1605, the Marburys moved to London, where Mary's father was appointed minister of St. Martin's church. He died in 1611, leaving a substantial inheritance to each of his children. Mary's brothers used their inheritance to obtain an education, but Mary, in spite of her intellectual abilities, was not allowed to attend school. At the time, females were banned from formal schooling and required to remain at home until a suitable guardian in the form of a husband could be found. The following year Mary married a wealthy Alford businessman, William Hutchinson, whom she had known since childhood. In 1634, the couple and their family emigrated to Boston in the Massachusetts Bay Colony, following John Cotton, a minister they both admired. The Hutchinsons attended the First Church of Boston, where Cotton officiated (Schuster, 19–20).

Although Mary Hutchinson at first complied with Puritan doctrines and practices, she began to question the theocracy, the legalistic religion, that Puritans had established in the colony. From the time she was a small child she had been schooled by her father in biblical teachings and the concept of religious freedom. She argued that godliness did not come about by conforming with strict religious laws. Rather, she insisted that the Holy Spirit had to dwell within a person to guide him or her to true godliness and salvation. Hutchinson discussed her views with other dissenters in meetings she held in her home (Schuster, 21).

Hutchinson gained numerous followers, and also the support of her brother-in-law, the Reverend John Wheelwright, who had arrived in Boston in 1636. The dissident faction of the Boston church, including Hutchinson, attempted to have Wheelwright installed along with Cotton as a teacher. Wheelwright was denied the position and he set up his own church, preaching against law because it destroys the spirit.

For his heresy, Wheelwright was banished from the Massachusetts colony in 1637. That same year, Hutchinson was tried and found guilty of sedition, and the colony passed the Alien Act of 1637, which, like later laws devised to suppress radicals, banned the entry of immigrants who were assumed to have extremist views. The 1637 act was specifically designed to restrain Hutchinson's friends and relatives, who on their arrival in Boston "were given only a four month dispensation to remain, at the end of which time they were . . . forced to leave the Commonwealth" (Schuster, 25).

In 1638 Hutchinson was excommunicated from the Boston church, accused of being evil and a dangerous messenger of Satan. She and her family were expelled from the colony and with a small band of followers settled in what is now Portsmouth, Rhode Island. Even in this settlement that fostered religious freedom, the Hutchinsons were harassed by Massachusetts officials, particularly by her bitter adversary, Governor John Winthrop. The Hutchinsons and their supporters also became involved in controversies with other settlers, some of whom wanted to join the Massachusetts Bay Colony. After her husband died in 1642, Hutchinson feared that she and her children would be harmed, and so she moved her family to a small Dutch settlement that is now Pelham Bay, outside New York City. A war between the Dutch and Native Americans in the area erupted in fall 1643, and during the fighting Anne and all but one of her children were massacred (Grolier).

See also

Alien and Sedition Acts of 1798; Espionage Act of 1917; Individualist Anarchists; Religious Anarchism; Sedition Act of 1918

References

"Anne Marbury Hutchinson," *Grolier Electronic Publishing* (1996).

Ilgenfritz, Elizabeth, *Anne Hutchinson* (New York: Chelsea House, 1991).

Schuster, Eunice M., *Native American Anarchism: A Study of Left-Wing American Individualism* (Northampton, MA: Smith College, 1932, reprint New York: AMS Press, 1970).

Williams, Selma R., *Divine Rebel: The Life of Anne Marbury Hutchinson* (New York: Holt, Rinehart, and Winston, 1981).

Huxley, Aldous Leonard (1894–1963)

The famous social critic and satiric novelist Aldous Leonard Huxley was born into a family of intellectual elites who were members of the British ruling class. His father was biographer Leonard Huxley, and his grandfather was the noted biologist Thomas Henry Huxley.

Huxley's eyesight was impacted early when he contracted *keratitis punctata* (near blindness) while at Eton, but he was able to read with difficulty and to continue his education at Oxford University, graduating with honors in 1916, the same year he published his first book. Three years later he married Maria Nys; Matthew, their only child, was born in 1920. During the 1920s, the family traveled, living in England and also Italy and visiting India and the United States. In the late 1930s they settled in California.

Huxley's earliest writings show a remarkable disdain for modern English social customs and intellectual pretensions. *Crome Yellow, Antic Hay, Barren Leaves,* and *Point Counter Point* (all written between 1921 and 1928) established the young man as a major author. But it was the publication of *Brave New World* in 1932 that brought him world fame as a biting political satirist. This classic work, which has often been compared to George Orwell's novel *1984* about a tyrannical world, foresaw a negative Utopia built on social caste–determined opportunities and strict monitoring and control of individuals' movements and thinking. Huxley himself compared his work with Orwell's novel by pointing out:

> the future dictatorship of my imaginary world was a good deal less brutal than the future dictatorship brilliantly portrayed by Orwell. . . . The society described in *1984* is a society controlled almost exclusively by punishment and the fear of punishment. In the imaginary world of my own fable punishment is infrequent and generally mild. The nearly perfect control exercised by the government is achieved by systematic reinforcement of desirable behavior, by many kinds of nearly non-violent manipulation, both physical and psychological, and by genetic standardization. (Huxley 1958: 4–5)

Though not written from a strictly anarchist perspective, *Brave New World* can be classified as social libertarian monograph. In the foreword to the 1946 edition of the work, Huxley does nod to the anarchist forbears when he states his belief that the only way to avoid the shortcomings of modern political society is through a "Kropotkinesque and cooperative" decentralization of the power structure. In that same source, his thinking predates Noam Chomsky's ideas about the modern state's need to "manufacture consent." Huxley writes:

> There is, of course, no reason why the new totalitarianisms should resemble the old. Government by clubs and firing squads, by artificial famine, mass imprisonment and mass deportation, is not merely inhumane (nobody cares much about that nowadays); it is demonstrably inefficient and, in an age of advanced technology, inefficiency is the sin against the Holy Ghost. A really efficient totalitarian state would be one in which the all-powerful executive of political bosses and their army of managers control a population of slaves who do not have to be coerced, because they love their servitude. To make them love it is the task assigned, in present-day totalitarian states, to ministries of propaganda, newspaper editors, and school teachers.

Later, in *Brave New World Revisited* (1958), Huxley continues the anarchist theme, penning ideas that could have been written decades before by Pierre-Joseph Proudhon, Max Stirner, or Mikhail Bakunin. He advocated the free association of individuals and noted that "organization is indispensable; for liberty arises and has meaning only within a self-regulating community of freely cooperating individuals" (Huxley 1958: 23) His book covers real-life problems, such as overpopulation, overorganization, brainwashing, and other psychological manipulation techniques—tools that a government can use to deprive people of freedom, an abuse that Huxley adamantly denounced.

Huxley went on to explore mysticism and the Hindu tradition as possible alternative answers to the problems inherent in organizing human societies, and he even experimented with psychedelics during the 1950s. His was a great, fertile mind, and his literary contributions on all his subjects will continue to influence.

See also

Bakunin, Mikhail A.; Chomsky, Avram Noam; Orwell, George; Proudhon, Pierre-Joseph; Stirner, Max

References

Bedford, Sybille, *Aldous Huxley: A Biography* (New York: Knopf, 1974).

Huxley, Aldous, *Brave New World* (New York and London: Harper, 1946).

Huxley, Aldous, *Brave New World Revisited* (New York: Harper and Row, 1958).

"Huxley, Aldous (Leonard)" *Britannica Online* <http://www.eb.com:180/cgi-bin/g?DocF=micro/283/12.html>.

Woodcock, George, *Dawn and the Darkest Hour: A Study of Aldous Huxley* (New York: Viking Press, 1972).

I

Individualist Anarchists

Individualist anarchists follow a form of anarchism that is primarily an antistatist view developed in the United States. Early during the nation's history, people such as religious anarchist Anne Hutchinson of the mid-1600s taught a type of individualist anarchism—antinomianism—that rejected humanmade laws, opposed the dogmatic moral codes of any church, and accepted only the law of God revealed through the Holy Spirit. Before and during the American Revolution, many rebels espoused individualist anarchist ideas, although they were not necessarily known as anarchists. Among the most outspoken was Thomas Paine, whose pamphlet "Common Sense" helped motivate colonists to overthrow British rule.

Other individualists in the United States "were concerned with the freedom of the individual, who would live with other free persons in a voluntary nongovernment association, which would be formed through individual self-interest for economic and social convenience" (Jacker, 10). Some who championed this view included Josiah Warren, William Bradford Greene, Lysander Spooner, and Benjamin R. Tucker.

See also

Greene, William Bradford; Heywood, Ezra Hervey Hoar; Hutchinson, Anne Marbury; Noyes, John Humphrey; Paine, Thomas; Religious Anarchism; Spooner, Lysander; Tucker, Benjamin R.; Warren, Josiah

References

Jacker, Corinne, *The Black Flag of Anarchy: Antistatism in the United States* (New York: Charles Scribner's Sons, 1968).

Lockwood, George B., *The New Harmony Movement* (New York: D. Appleton, 1905).

Nordhoff, Charles, *The Communistic Societies of the United States: From Personal Observations* (New York: Harper and Brothers, 1875, reprint New York: Dover, 1966).

Schuster, Eunice M., *Native American Anarchism: A Study of Left-Wing American Individualism* (Northampton, MA: Smith College, 1932, reprint New York: AMS Press, 1970).

Woodcock, George, *Anarchism: A History of Libertarian Ideas and Movements* (Cleveland: World Publishing Company, 1962, reprint New York: New American Library, 1974).

Industrial Workers of the World (IWW)

The preamble to the constitution of the Industrial Workers of the World (IWW), commonly known as the Wobblies, begins thus:

> The working class and the employing class have nothing in common. There can be no peace so long as hunger and want are found among millions of the working people and the few, who make up the employing class, have all the good things of life. Between these two classes a struggle must go on until the workers of the world organize as a class, take possession of the means of production, abolish the wage system, and live in harmony with the Earth.

Formed in 1905, IWW hoped to create one big union composed of both skilled and unskilled workers, women as well as men, and workers from all racial backgrounds. The labor organization stemmed from the syndicalist movement of the late 1800s, which aimed to overthrow capitalism and the wage system through anarchist tactics of direct action—strikes, boycotts, and industrial sabotage. However, IWW was never controlled by anarchists, and during its formative years in the United States it was led by such socialists as Eugene Debs and Big Bill Haywood. Daniel De Leon, a Marxist, and laborer-songwriter Joe Hill, along with other radicals, also played major roles in IWW's beginnings.

IWW grew out of bitter and often violent labor disputes during the late 1800s, particularly the brutal conflicts between miners and capitalists in the Rocky Mountain West. Many miners were members of the Western Federation of Miners (WFM) and its closely allied Western Labor Union, which later became the American Labor Union (ALU). According to labor historian Melvyn Dubofsky,

> from 1894 to 1904 Western miners literally waged armed war with their capitalist adversaries. Miners' unions sometimes purchased and stocked rifles and ammunition, drilled in military fashion and prepared if all else failed to achieve their objectives with rifle, torch, and dynamite stick. . . . mine operators proved equally martial, and usually less compromising. . . . Businessmen also stored arms and ammunition . . . and paid private armies to defend their properties when public authorities refused to provide such protection. (quoted in Dubofsky 1969: 37)

In 1904 WFM initiated conferences of various labor unions, including ALU, to establish a union that would represent the unorganized and exploited working class, which had been ignored by the American Federation of Labor (AFL), a union of skilled craftsmen. By June 1905 the Continental Congress of the Working Class convened in Chicago with more than 200 delegates; the chair of the congress, Big Bill Haywood, declared they would "confederate the workers of this country into a working class movement that shall have for its purpose the emancipation of the working class from the slave bondage of capitalism" (Dubofsky 1969, 81). Haywood proclaimed that the main purpose was to put workers in control of production and distribution of goods, in short to develop a labor union the equivalent of the Socialist Party. From this congress the Industrial Workers of the World was born.

Socialist Eugene Debs, a spokesman for the labor movement, was one of the leaders of the newly organized IWW. But Debs and Socialist Labor Party leader Daniel De Leon left the IWW in 1908, primarily because the union did not adhere to the idea that political action was an important part of the working-class struggle against the capitalist system. In 1915 De Leon formed a splinter group in Detroit, which was also called the IWW but soon changed its name to the Workers International Industrial Union. The union dispersed in 1925.

Meanwhile, the Chicago IWW continued to function, and from 1909 to about 1913 it was involved in numerous free-speech controversies, winning the right to speak out on the class struggle and taking direct action to attain goals. Wobblies also took part in strikes, supporting textile mill workers in Lawrence, Massachusetts, in 1912 and in Paterson, New Jersey, in 1913. These strikes were also encouraged by such well-known labor organizers as Elizabeth Gurley Flynn and anarchists Carlo Tresca, Emma Goldman, and Alexander Berkman, who were active for a time in IWW activities. But organizers as well as workers often were subjected to violence and repressed by police, federal troops, and vigilantes. Flynn, Tresca, Goldman, and Berkman were among the many IWW supporters jailed for their efforts. Other activists were subjected to brutal beatings by vigilantes with blackjacks and other implements, clubbings and bayoneting by police, barbaric treatment by jail guards, and mass attacks (sometimes on entire families) by militia.

Before and during U.S. involvement in World War I, Wobblies were against efforts to support what they considered to be an imperialistic and capitalistic war. Some IWW leaders encouraged strikes, which many American citizens and authorities believed were meant to sabotage the war effort. Although not all IWW members dared to openly espouse antiwar propaganda, those who did prompted vigilante action. In one incident, IWW organizer Frank Little was abducted, tortured, and lynched by vigilantes in Butte, Montana; authorities did nothing to apprehend the murderers. Another well-known case was that of IWW songwriter Joe Hill, who was arrested and convicted on circumstantial evidence of murder charges; after his execution, he became a martyr to the cause.

IWW began to disintegrate after the war, and some leaders joined the Communist Party during the 1920s, but the organization itself remained intact, albeit without power. During the 1930s and after World War II, numerous IWW members joined such unions as the AFL and the Congress of Industrial Organizations (CIO)—later the AFL-CIO. As a result of the U.S. hysteria over "reds" during the Cold War, the IWW was listed as a subversive organization. Since World War II, the IWW has held conventions and continued to publish *Industrial Worker.* It maintains an informative site on the world wide web.

See also

Anarcho-Syndicalism; Flynn, Elizabeth Gurley; Haywood, William Dudley "Big Bill"; Hill, Joe (Joel Emmanuel Hääglund)

References

Brissenden, Paul F., *The IWW: A Study of American Syndicalism* (New York: Columbia University Press, 1919).

Dubofsky, Melvyn, *We Shall Be All: A History of the Industrial Workers of the World* (New York: Quadrangle Books, 1969).

Flynn, Elizabeth Gurley, "Memories of the IWW," Web edition of transcript by Eugene W. Plawiuk, on the internet <http://www.geocities.com/CapitolHill/5202/rebelgirl.html> (1997).

Gambs, John S., *The Decline of the IWW* (New York: Columbia University Press, 1932).

Preston, William Jr., *Aliens and Dissenters: Federal Suppression of Radicals 1903–1933,* 2d ed. (Urbana and Chicago: University of Illinois Press, 1994).

"What Is the IWW?" on the internet <http://www.iww.org> (no date).

Institute for Anarchist Studies

Founded in 1996, the Institute for Anarchist Studies (IAS) was established "to fight for radical, antiauthoritarian scholarship" because of the "current scarcity of serious, politically committed scholarship on social contradictions and the possibilities of social transformation," writes Chuck Morse in the IAS newsletter. He adds, "We believe it is necessary and possible to revitalize this type of theoretical work, and that this requires the construction of politically engaged organizations dedicated to this purpose" (Morse).

According to an IAS statement on its website:

> The goals and means of anarchism have matured over time, guided by the need to refine this anti-authoritarian principle into a coherent theory and politics of social freedom. The primary concern of classical anarchists such as Michael Bakunin and Peter Kropotkin was opposition to the state and capitalism. They proclaimed that these political and economic hierarchies are not permanent features of existence but rather impediments to the full realization of human freedom. This was complemented by an ideal of directly democratic, self-managed communities and a reconstructive politics of spontaneity and decentralization. (Institute of Anarchist Studies)

To carry out its purpose, the IAS provides grants to writers working on themes relevant to anarchism. The institute, for example, "might support studies of the general dynamics of domination, the history of anarchism, and/or the relationship between art and utopian politics." However, the IAS does not support newsletters, magazines, organizations, and demonstrations.

References

Institute for Anarchist Studies, "Why Anarchy?" on the internet <http://www.empireone.net/~ias/Default.htm>.

Morse, Chuck, "Some Comments on the IAS," *Perspectives on Anarchist Theory* (Spring 1997), on the internet <http://home.newyorknet.net/ias/comments.htm>.

Institute for Social Ecology

See Social Ecology

International Workers' Association

The International Workers' Association (IWA) unites revolutionary unionist groups around the world. It was formed at the 1922 Berlin Congress of Revolutionary Unionist Organizations. Delegates from nine countries representing more than one million workers attended.

Today, groups and unions in more than a dozen countries, from the Anarcho-Syndicalist Group in Melbourne, Australia, to the Workers Solidarity Alliance in the United States, are affiliated with IWA. Affiliates pledge to accept IWA's Declaration of Principles and Goals, which were first adopted in 1922 and amended and reaffirmed during the 1930s, 1950s, and 1970s.

IWA principles and goals are based on revolutionary unionism, transforming society to abolish "the present political and economic regimes and to establish libertarian communism." One primary aim is

> to unite all workers in combative economic organizations, that fight to free themselves from the double yoke of capital and the state. Its goal is the reorganization of social life on the basis of libertarian communism via the revolutionary action of the working class. Since only the economic organizations of the proletariat are capable of achieving this objective, revolutionary unionism addresses itself to workers in their capacity as producers, creators of social wealth, to take root and develop amongst them, in opposition to the modern workers' parties, which it declares are incapable of the economic reorganization of society. (IWA "Principles")

Spelling out its principles, the IWA declares that "revolutionary unionism is the staunch enemy of all social and economic monopoly"; one goal is to abolish "all state functions in the life of society." They would be replaced by "economic communities and administrative organs run by the workers in the fields and factories, forming a system of free councils without subordination to any authority or political party, bar none." In addition, along with abolishing "a property owning caste, must come the disappearance of central ruling caste; and that no form of statism, however camouflaged, can ever be an instrument for human liberation, but that on the contrary, it will always be the creator of new monopolies and new privileges" (IWA "Principles").

The function of IWA and revolutionary unionism is "to carry on the day-to-day revolutionary struggle for the economic, social and intellectual advancement of the working class within the limits of present-day society, and to educate the masses so that they will be ready to independently manage the processes of production and distribution when the time comes to take possession of all the elements of social life" (IWA "Principles").

See also

Anarcho-Syndicalism; Communism; Workers Solidarity Movement

References

"Principles, Goals, and Statutes of the IWA," on the internet <http://www.uncanny.net/~wsa/iwaprinciple.html>.

International Working Men's Association

See First International

International Working People's Association

The International Working People's Association (IWPA) was a militant and revolutionary labor organization founded in 1883. It was based primarily on the ideas of German anarchist Johann Most. Among its founding members were activists August Spies and Albert Parsons, two Haymarket martyrs. At the time IWPA was formed, the socialist movement in the United States was split into various factions, some leaning toward anarchistic individualism and others toward syndicalism. IWPA was designed to bring all antiauthoritarian groups under one umbrella organization and to unite workers.

In October 1883 the IWPA convention was held in Pittsburgh, Pennsylvania, where delegates issued a document known as the Pittsburgh Manifesto. The proclamation advocated the overthrow of capitalism and outlined ways society could be reconstructed with workers managing their own affairs. Although affiliated groups were organized in numerous industrial cities of the Midwest, the militant IWPA was crushed by local, state, and federal authorities; by 1888 it was no longer active.

See also

Haymarket Affair; Most, Johann; Parsons, Albert; Pittsburgh Manifesto; Spies, August

References

David, Henry, *The History of the Haymarket Affair* (New York: Russell and Russell, 1936).

Foner, Philip Sheldon, ed., *The Autobiographies of the Haymarket Martyrs* (Atlantic Highlands, NJ: Humanities Press, 1969).

Irish Anarchism

See Workers Solidarity Movement

Isaak, Abe (1856–1937), and Maria (Mary) (1861–1934)

Abe and Maria (Mary) Isaak were pacifist Mennonites who married and lived in a Mennonite community near Odessa, Ukraine. They moved to Odessa proper, where Abe worked in a bookstore and became interested in antitsarist revolutionary literature. He soon became active in anarchist activities and was threatened with imprisonment. He escaped the country, sailing to Rio de Janeiro. In 1889 he went to the United States, where his wife and three children joined him in New York.

The couple moved to Portland, Oregon, found jobs, and started an anarchist newspaper in 1895 called *The Firebrand*. They purchased a farm outside Portland; for two years they cultivated the farm, produced their own food, and continued their publishing venture. The newspaper carried controversial articles on radical feminism, advocating free love and the emancipation of women. But such positions were attacked by anarchists like Lucy Parsons, who was more concerned about "wage slavery" and living conditions. She declared in an article for *The Firebrand* that "the first issue to be settled . . . is woman's economical dependence which makes her enslavement to man possible" (Ashbaugh, 202).

In 1897 Abe and two editors were arrested because the newspaper had printed a Walt Whitman poem titled "A Woman Waits for Me," which authorities declared was "obscene" and illegally sent through the mail. When Abe was released from prison, the family moved to San Francisco and again began publishing their paper under the title *Free Society*. In 1900 the family moved to Chicago, where it continued the newspaper and often hosted visiting anarchists and radicals.

In 1901 President William McKinley was shot, lingering near death for days. During that time police tried to link the Isaaks to Leon Czolgosz, later convicted of the president's assassination. Several months earlier Emma Goldman had stayed with the Isaaks, and a man who identified himself as "Nieman" but was actually Czolgosz came to see Goldman. The police claimed that Czolgosz's act was inspired by Goldman. Using this flimsy connection, the Chicago police raided the Isaak home and arrested the parents, two of their children, and others working with the publishing group. They were imprisoned but soon released. Not long afterward the Isaaks moved to New York, where they published the newspaper until 1904.

In 1908 the Isaaks bought land near Lincoln, California, and began the Aurora Colony, an anarchist community that lasted only a few years. Like many communal societies of the time, only a few farmers, such as Abe Isaak, were able to make the land productive. Although the colony broke up, the Isaaks stayed on and remained anarchists until their deaths. Their grandson, Elmer B. Isaak, recalled during an interview with anarchist historian Paul Avrich that for Abe Isaak "anarchism was not just 'no government,' but society would be organized into committees to produce goods and services. Anarchism did not mean disorganization; it meant simply no formal government. But he never convinced me that it would work" (Avrich).

See also

Anarchist Press; Goldman, Emma; Parsons, Lucy

References
Ashbaugh, Carolyn, *Lucy Parsons: American Revolutionary* (Chicago: Charles H. Kerr, 1976).
Avrich, Paul, *Anarchist Voices: An Oral History of Anarchism in America* (Princeton: Princeton University Press, 1995).
Goldman, Emma, *Living My Life,* 2 vols. (New York: Knopf, 1933, reprint New York: Dover, 1970).

Italian Anarchism

From the mid-1800s through the early decades of the 1900s anarchist ideas have influenced many Italian radicals, including Luigi Galleani, Errico Malatesta, Carlo Tresca, Nicola Sacco, and Bartolomeo Vanzetti. "Ideologically, the Italian anarchists fell into four categories, anarchist-communist, anarcho-syndicalist, anarchist-individualist, and just plain anarchist, without the hyphen," wrote historian Paul Avrich, adding, however, that

> there were no hard-and-fast divisions between them. As followers of Galleani, Sacco and Vanzetti considered themselves anarchist-communists, rejecting not only the state but also the private ownership of property. The anarcho-syndicalists, among whom Carlo Tresca was a powerful influence, placed their faith in the trade-union movement, shunned by and large by the anarchist-communists, who feared the emergence of a boss, a padrone, endowed with special privileges and authority. (Avrich, 52)

In 1920 about 600,000 Italian workers were involved in takeovers of factories, mills, mines, breweries, and shipping companies. They continued production on their own. In addition, railway workers defied the government and managed freight lines in order to provide the means for transporting goods. "However, a growing aspiration for workers control, and for social transformation in an anticapitalist direction, ran head on into the growing bureaucratization of official Italian trade-unionism" (Wetzel). At the same time, dictator Benito Mussolini was gaining recruits among businesspeople, professionals, government workers, and property owners, all of whom feared the rise of the labor movement. Entire communities were terrorized by Mussolini's fascist squads.

The anarchist press and the anarchist movement itself were suppressed in Italy after the fascists seized power in 1922. Two years later, in the United States, immigration laws also severely restricted anarchist activities. However, "*L'Adunata* managed nonetheless to summon sufficient force to aid political prisoners, to rally Italian anti-Fascist refugees throughout the world, and to fight Fascism on the streets of Little Italies throughout America" (Wehling).

Over the decades, a number of Italian-language publications appeared in the United States and other countries. Among them was *La Questione Sociale,* initiated in part by Malatesta in 1895, and *L'Adunata dei Refrattari* (meaning "the call of the refractory ones"), which began in New York City in 1922 and continued until 1971. The name came from

> a defiant reference to words—*refrattario* (It.)/*refrattaire* (Fr.)—that had been used as a code by European governments before the turn of the century, during the heyday of "the propaganda of deed," to identify Anarchists in laws meant specifically to suppress their movement. The Anarchism propagated by *L'Adunata* reflected the exceptional influence of Galleani. *L'Adunata's* mixture of . . . belief in direct action and revolution, and absolute anti-organizationalism continually involved it in many a passionate debates within the Left and within the Anarchist movement itself. It played a major role in Anarchist activities not only in America but throughout the world, especially where concentrations of Italians were to be found. At its peak, during the anti-Fascist struggles in the 1930s, *L'Adunata* counted between 12,000 and 15,000 militants as its supporters. It always represented the dominant trend within the Italian Anarchist movement in America. (Wehling)

Today, two national anarchist federations are active in Italy: the Italian Anarchist Federation (FAI), founded in 1945, and the Federation of the Anarchist-Communists (FdCA), organized in 1986. FAI publishes the weekly newspaper

Umanita Nova. Numerous other anarchist newspapers and periodicals are published as well, but they do not necessarily have wide readership. By personal preference, most Italian anarchists are involved in activities at the local level.

See also

Anarchist Press; Anarchist-Communists; Anarcho-Syndicalism; Galleani, Luigi; Individualist Anarchists; Malatesta, Errico; Sacco, Nicola, and Bartolomeo Vanzetti; Tresca, Carlo

References

Avrich, Paul, *Sacco and Vanzetti: The Anarchist Background* (Princeton: Princeton University Press, 1991).

Wehling, Jason, "A Brief History of the American Anarchist Press" (March 1993), on the internet <http://www.teleport.com/~jwehling/APressHistory.html>.

Wetzel, Tom, "Italy 1920: When 600,000 Workers Seized Control of Their Workplaces" (1988), on the internet <http://users.uncanny.net/%7EWSA/ital1920.html>.

J

Jacobins

During the revolution in France between 1870 and 1871, Jacobins, who were "skilled, professional revolutionaries," helped make the Paris Commune of 1871 possible. The Jacobins of this period were "spiritual descendants of [Maximilien Robespierre]" (Williams, 134). During the late 1700s Robespierre had led the Jacobins, who took their name from the monastery of the Jacobins (Dominicans) in Paris, where they met. They became political revolutionaries who contended that the revolutionary process required a dictatorship of the minority under a powerful leader. They scorned the will of the majority. The Jacobins overthrew the French monarchy, established a new government, and conducted a "reign of terror," killing thousands of people, including aristocrats, clergy, and others who opposed them. Eventually the Jacobins themselves were suppressed.

The revolutionary Jacobin group that emerged in altered form during the 1800s detested followers of Louis Blanqui and Pierre-Joseph Proudhon, denouncing them as socialists (as opposed to revolutionaries). Nevertheless, these neo-Jacobins collaborated on the program of the Paris Commune, which was formed in Versailles after France suffered a humiliating defeat in the Franco-Prussian War of 1870–1871, ending Napoleon's rule. Jacobins were also involved in the Paris Commune's various committees, and Jacobin leader Charles Delescluze was given credit for writing the Paris Commune's manifesto, although followers of Proudhon played a role. Delescluze died at the barricades during the Bloody Week when the French army attacked and destroyed the Paris Commune, which had then existed for 71 days.

See also

Blanqui, Louis Auguste; Paris Commune of 1871; Proudhon, Pierre-Joseph

References

Nomad, Max, *Apostles of Revolution* (New York: Collier Books, 1961).

Williams, Roger L., *The French Revolution of 1870–1871* (New York: W.W. Norton, 1969).

Jones, Mary "Mother" (1830–1930)

Born Mary Harris in County Cork, Ireland, "Mother" Jones spent the last half of her long life organizing and speaking out for the rights of working people and the poor in the United States. She became totally dedicated to the cause of working people during the 1880s. Although she never considered herself an anarchist, she often attended anarchist meetings in Chicago during the push for the eight-hour workday.

Mary grew up in an atmosphere of protest. Her father was forced to leave Ireland, as he was a member of a group that protested living conditions of the county's poor by burning manors, barns, and crops and destroying the pastures of landowners who evicted peasants who could not pay the high rents. When Mary Harris was two, her grandfather was hanged because of protest activities; three years later her father left for North America to avoid the same end. When Mary was 11 her father sent for the family, and they relocated to Toronto, Canada, where she excelled in school. After graduating from high school, she studied at Toronto Normal School, then moved to the

United States to teach in Michigan. But she had to be more a disciplinarian than a mentor, so she left Michigan and moved to Chicago to become a dressmaker.

By 1860 Mary Harris had left Chicago to resume her teaching career in Memphis, Tennessee. There she met George Jones, an iron molder who was active in organizing workers and establishing a local chapter of the Iron Molders Union to demand improvements in the dangerous conditions of the foundry. The couple married and had four children. Union organizing was put on hold through the Civil War years as Memphis was occupied by Union forces, but soon thereafter George became a paid leader in the movement.

Just as their life was beginning to take shape a yellow fever epidemic swept through the city in 1867, taking the lives of hundreds of Memphians, including the Jones children as well as George himself. With some money raised by the Iron Molders Local, Mary Jones returned to Chicago and opened a seamstress shop that catered to the needs of the wealthy in the city. When visiting her clients' homes, she saw the opulence in sharp contrast to the conditions endured by her neighbors and most other Chicagoans. When the three-day Great Chicago Fire destroyed one-sixth of the city in 1871, conditions for the poor worsened considerably. Jones lost her home, her shop, and all of her possessions.

Wandering among the ruins one night, she happened upon a secret meeting of the Knights of Labor, its mission to unite all workers in an effort to change society through education and legislation. Employers fired any workers who were known to attend meetings or join the Knights of Labor. Nevertheless, the movement appealed to Jones, and she asked to join. In short order she was an organizer, speaker, and recruiter, being the only woman holding such leadership position in that group. She became a familiar face to the workers and poor of Chicago as she went throughout the neighborhoods spreading the word about the Knights and working together.

During the depression of the 1870s, Mary Jones's ideas as to how to bring about a better life for the underclass changed. Where the Knights preached persuasion over direct confrontation with the bosses, anarchists were advocating an opposite path. In Chicago they agitated for an eight-hour workday, which was also endorsed by the Knights of Labor. But when anarchists espoused the cause, the general public and employers became concerned. As Jones explained in her autobiography:

> The employers used the cry of anarchism to kill the movement. A person who believed in the eight-hour working day was, they said, an enemy to his country, a traitor, an anarchist. The foundations of government were being gnawed away by the anarchist rats. Feeling was bitter. The city was divided into two angry camps. The working people on one side—hungry, cold, jobless, fighting gunmen and police clubs with bare hands. On the other side the employers, knowing neither hunger nor cold, supported by newspapers, by the police, by all the power of the great state itself.
>
> The anarchists took advantage of the wide-spread discontent to preach their doctrines. . . . although I never endorsed the philosophy of anarchism, I often attended the meetings on the lake shore, listening to what these teachers of a new order had to say to the workers. (Parton, 18–19)

After Chicago's Haymarket affair in 1886 and the execution of the anarchist martyrs convicted of instigating the violence, Jones broke with the Knights of Labor. She could not abide the fact that the leaders, simply to protect the organization, distanced themselves from the men who were hanged. Jones left Chicago and went to the South, where she worked with coal miners and families who lived in extreme poverty.

In West Virginia during the 1890s, Jones became a full-time union organizer, a dangerous job considering mine owners often threatened organizers and fired miners who joined a union. Company guards and agents, hired by companies to break strikes, often brutally beat strikers and organizers. But Jones continued her work. She also gave away whatever money, food, and clothing she could spare to poor mining families, who soon began calling her "Mother."

Mother Jones helped organize the United Mine Workers (UMW) in West Virginia and was on the frontlines when the workers called a strike, which the company broke after 12 weeks. But from the late 1890s to the 1920s Mother Jones organized workers in other states. In 1903 she also led a "Crusade of the Mill Children," a march against child labor that called attention to the deformities and injuries young children suffered while performing hard factory labor for $2–$3 per week.

Eventually Mother Jones took over many responsibilities within the UMW, always as a leader and organizer of strikes and work actions. Threats from company guards and government agents had little effect on the tenacious woman. By her actions and bravery, she encouraged others to stand up for freedom, equality, and the rights of workers. Everything else in her life was subordinate to her work leading parades, marches, strikes, meetings, protests, and rallies from Virginia to California and countless stops in between. Although she worked for UMW, she also supported the Western Federation of Miners (WFM) in Colorado, where she spoke to miners involved in strikes that led to the Ludlow Massacre. She was arrested at age 83 and placed in a rat-infested cell in the basement of a jail for 26 days. She was arrested many other times, including once when she was almost 90 while supporting Pennsylvania steel workers. She was still speaking out on behalf of workers on her 100th birthday, just months before she died.

In the foreword to her autobiography, Clarence Darrow described Mother Jones as a woman of "deep convictions and fearless soul" who was jailed time and again but "never ran away. She stayed in prison until her enemies opened the doors. Her personal nonresistance was far more powerful than any appeal to force."

See also

Darrow, Clarence; Haymarket Affair; Ludlow Massacre

References

Atkinson, Linda, *Mother Jones: The Most Dangerous Woman in America* (New York: Crown Publishers, 1978).

Fetherling, Dale, *Mother Jones: The Miners' Angel* (Carbondale: Southern Illinois University Press, 1974).

Foner, Philip S., ed., *Mother Jones Speaks: Collected Writings and Speeches* (New York: Monad Press, 1983).

Long, Priscilla, *Mother Jones: Woman Organizer* (Boston: South End Press, 1976).

Parton, Mary Field, ed., *The Autobiography of Mother Jones* (Chicago: Charles H. Kerr, 1925, reprint 1972).

K

Kelly, Harry (1871–1953)

A dedicated anarchist for more than six decades, Missourian Harry Kelly became the "Moses" who led "a group of immigrants [anarchists and libertarians from New York] out into the wilderness of central New Jersey," as historian Laurence Veysey described him. Kelly was one of the founders of the modern school and colony in Stelton, New Jersey, and he established another modern school in Mohegan, New York.

Harry Kelly was born in St. Charles, Missouri, and spent his childhood in poverty. His father died before Harry was five, and he had to leave school after the fifth grade to help support the family. By his teens Kelly had learned the printing trade, which during the next 35 years provided a way to earn a living. However, he never stayed long in one place and liked to hop trains and live with hobos. Several times he traveled to Europe, visiting his father's relatives as well as social revolutionaries.

During the 1890s Kelly became a radical union organizer and in 1894 "permanently embraced the anarchist cause" after listening to a lecture by Charles W. Mowbray, a British anarchist. Mowbray was in Boston while on a speaking tour in the United States (Veysey, 93).

Kelly worked diligently for anarchism, but he was not an original thinker. Rather, he was more the type of person that Russian anarchist Peter Kropotkin envisioned would help form an ideal society. He became a regular contributor to Emma Goldman's anarchist magazine *Mother Earth,* which began publication in 1906. Goldman introduced Kelly to members of the Ferrer Association, formed in New York in 1910 in memory of martyred Spanish anarchist and modern school advocate Francisco Ferrer. Kelly, who had a talent for bringing people together, became a group leader of sorts, although he was never authoritarian and usually exhibited a sense of humor in human relations. He was also a practical person and was able to organize day-to-day activities.

During the early 1900s a series of violent incidents was linked to anarchists, and the New York police began to infiltrate anarchist meetings. Seeking safety, some members of the association made plans to move outside the city. Harry Kelly played a major role in selecting a farm up for sale in New Jersey. He heard about the site while visiting Mary Krimont, the woman he loved and who would eventually become his longtime partner. Krimont lived in a nearby socialist commune called Friendship Farm but soon became part of the Stelton Colony.

The New Jersey site, purchased by the Stelton group in 1916, included a farmhouse and barn about a mile and a half from the railroad line. Kelly and other leaders hoped the planned school and colony would be "the center of a new nationwide movement for libertarian education" (Veysey, 114).

For more than seven years Kelly, who made colonists feel a valuable part of the community, was involved in building the settlement, which by 1922 had grown to about 90 homes and a school with an enrollment of 120 children. In 1923, however, Kelly returned to New York City and learned about a parcel of land near Lake Mohegan, New York, that was for sale. At first Kelly thought the site could be a summer camp to bring additional income to the Stelton Colony, but he soon decided to develop another colony and modern school at Mohegan. By 1925 he also started another New York colony known as Mount Airy. Although Kelly maintained contact with Stelton, he broke away from the group entirely in 1927.

The Great Depression of the 1930s, a split among anarchists at that time (some opting for communism), and the beginning of World War II led to the demise of all three colonies. Although Kelly organized reunions for former colonists, his health gradually failed and he became blind. He died in 1953.

See also

Goldman, Emma; Modern School Movement; Stelton School and Colony

References

Avrich, Paul, *The Modern School Movement: Anarchism and Education in the United States* (Princeton: Princeton University Press, 1980).

Perrone, Fernanda, "History of the Modern School of Stelton," Special Collections and University Archives, Rutgers University Libraries, on the internet <http://www.libraries.rutgers.edu/rulib/spcol/modern.htm>.

Veysey, Laurence, *The Communal Experience: Anarchist and Mystical Communities in Twentieth-Century America* (Chicago: University of Chicago Press, 1978).

Kotoku Shusui (1871–1911)

The anarchist tradition never gained a strong foothold in Japan, but during the Russo-Japanese War of 1904 Kotoku Shusui emerged as that country's first real socialist leader. He rose to prominence from very humble beginnings as the house boy of Hayashi Yuzo, one of Tokyo's most progressive politicians at the end of the 19th century. Kotoku's exposure to the realities of politics inspired him to help found the Social Democratic Party in 1901.

During the early 20th century the Japanese ruling class began an imperialist drive into Asian countries and ruthlessly cracked down on opponents at home. The Social Democratic Party and Japanese anarchists were at the forefront of anti-imperialist agitation. Although the party was banned by the Japanese government before its ideas had an opportunity to spread, Kotoku, in association with a friend, Sakai Toshihiko, began publishing *Commoner's Newspaper.* They used it to rally opposition to Japan's involvement in the war with Russia and the occupation of Korea. Japanese rulers, already worried about the 1905 revolution in Russia, immediately shut down the paper and imprisoned its publishers.

While serving five months in jail Kotoku discovered the writings of Peter Kropotkin, and his conversion to anarchist principles began. After his release he had an opportunity to travel throughout the United States, where he met representatives of the Industrial Workers of the World (IWW). "Wobblies," as they were known, advocated direct action, and Kotoku learned their lessons well. Returning to Japan, he gathered disciples and influenced a number of Chinese who would become well known anarchist leaders in their own right. Kotoku took a lead role in criticizing the government and joined an underground conspiracy intent on assassinating the emperor. But he had actually withdrawn from the group when the plot was exposed; hundreds of radicals and anarchists were arrested and executed. Well-known anarchist Emma Goldman organized a protest movement in the United States to save Kotoku, his companion Kanno Sugako, and 24 other Japanese anarchists. Kotoku, however, was among a core of 11 men who were executed in 1911 for their part in the coup attempt. His death ended anarchist activity in Japan for many years, although Osugi Sakae attempted to carry on during the 1920s, developing his own anarchist ideas in his writings and anarcho-syndicalist activities until he, too, was killed by authorities.

See also

Anarcho-Syndicalism; Direct Action; Industrial Workers of the World; Kropotkin, Peter Alexeyevich; Osugi Sakae

References

Apter, David Ernest, and James Joll, eds., *Anarchism Today* (Garden City, NY: Doubleday, 1971).

"Kotoku Shusui," *Britannica Online* <http://www.eb.com:180/cgi-bin/g?DocF=micro/328/18.html>.

MacSimoin, Alan, "Korean Anarchism History," a speech to the Workers Solidarity Movement, Dublin (September 1991), on the internet <http://www.pitzer.edu/~dward/Anarchist_Archives/worldwidemovements/koreahis.html>.

Plotkin, I. L., *Anarchism In Japan: A Study of The Great Treason Affair, 1910–1911* (Lewiston, NY: E. Mellen Press, 1990).

Scalapino, Robert A., and G. T. Yu, "The Chinese Anarchist Movement," Berkeley Center for Chinese Studies, on the internet <http://www.pitzer.edu/~dward/Anarchist_Archives/worldwidemovements/scalapino.html>.

Kronstadt Uprising

As a result of the 1917 revolution in Russia, Nicholas II abdicated and the tsarist government toppled. Bolsheviks, a party of communist extremists led by Vladimir Ilich Lenin, gained power. A provisional government based on a constitution was set up, but the Bolsheviks were able to take control of workers' soviets (councils) and form their own so-called proletarian dictatorship—a rule by workers.

Although anarchists and Bolsheviks seemed to be working toward the same goals, many anarchists objected to the entire concept of power and to Lenin's view that "liberty is a luxury not to be permitted at the present stage of development." Anarchists became increasingly disillusioned when Bolsheviks suppressed most of their activities (Joll, 184).

Between late 1917 and mid-1921, there were many challenges to Bolshevik rule, and armed conflict—civil wars—erupted throughout the land. In early 1921 workers in Petrograd staged a massive strike, protesting their abject poverty and the many privileges that the ruling class enjoyed. Bolshevik leaders ordered the workers to return to their jobs, but the strikers refused. Many were arrested and imprisoned.

Nonetheless, the strike spread to other cities, and sailors meeting in Kronstadt joined the protest, demanding free speech and a free press. Fearing loss of control, Lenin ordered the army to put down the protest, and tens of thousands were massacred. The horrendous event convinced many anarchists, including Emma Goldman and Alexander Berkman, that they could no longer believe in the promise of the revolutionary cause in Russia. In fact, Goldman and Berkman each wrote a book describing their agonizing disappointment in crushed dreams. Berkman lamented: "Grey are the passing days. . . . The slogans of the revolution are forsworn, its ideals stifled in the blood of the people. The breath of yesterday is dooming millions to death; the shadow of today hangs like a black pall over the country. Dictatorship is trampling the masses underfoot. The revolution is dead; its spirit cries in the wilderness" (quoted in Joll, 191).

See also

Berkman, Alexander; Goldman, Emma; Russian Anarchism

References

Avrich, Paul, *The Russian Anarchists* (New York: W. W. Norton, 1978).

Avrich, Paul, ed., *The Anarchists in the Russian Revolution* (Ithaca: Cornell University Press, 1973).

Goldman, Emma, *Living My Life,* 2 vols. (New York: Knopf, 1933, reprint New York: Dover, 1970).

Joll, James, *The Anarchists* (Boston: Little, Brown, 1964).

Wexler, Alice, *Emma Goldman in Exile: From the Russian Revolution to the Spanish Civil War* (Boston: Beacon Press, 1989).

Kropotkin, Peter Alexeyevich (1842–1921)

Peter Kropotkin is one of the most important of the early anarchist theorists. He established the theory's scientific basis as the natural, positive consequence of humans' interactions when allowed to freely associate and make decisions based on self-interests. Given his family situation and his early education, however, one would have expected a far different role for this influential researcher and writer.

Kropotkin was born a prince in Moscow to a famous aristocratic military family. Young Peter, it was expected, would naturally take his place in the army as an officer and gentleman. He was an exceptional student in the Corps of Pages and was even chosen to be the personal page of Tsar Alexander. The beginnings of an illustrious career were certain. But at age 20 he threw this future away to pursue scientific studies.

Surprising everyone, Kropotkin chose assignment among the Cossaks in Siberia, where he would be free to study the effects of the autocratic government he was sworn to protect. In Siberia, Kropotkin spent his time studying geography and geology. His observations and reports helped correct maps of the region and earned him a reputation in scientific circles for his important contributions. But when he was 30, he made another life decision that seemed to fly in the face of good sense. He could have readily continued his work as a scientist, but the desire to make contributions on a political level superseded any consideration of this path. His extensive travels of more than 50,000 miles across the region brought him into contact with prisoners and exiles sent there for alleged subversive activities against the government.

During a meeting with the exiled poet Mikkailov, Kropotkin was introduced to the writings and ideas of Pierre-Joseph Proudhon. He soon realized that he agreed with Proudhon's views and was prepared to become an anarchist.

Kropotkin quit the army to continue his studies at university in St. Petersburg, but he left, at the same time being offered the head position of the Russian Geographical Society. But he simply could not ignore the plight of those without the same advantages life had afforded him. His first stop was Switzerland, where he joined the First International during the days of upheaval between the factions of Mikhail Bakunin and Karl Marx. Kropotkin sided with the federative elements but soon left to join other Russian anarchist exiles in the Jura Mountains. By the time he left that community of activists and scholars, he was an anarchist.

In 1874 Kropotkin was arrested and incarcerated at the Peter and Paul Fortress because of his agitating activities among workers in St. Petersburg. He advocated that peasants form armed bands. After he spent two years in prison his health deteriorated, and he was placed in a military hospital. With the help of friends, to whom he smuggled letters, Kropotkin organized "one of the most famous and dramatic escapes of the nineteenth century. A violin playing in the window of a house down the street gave the signal; a carriage was waiting; Kropotkin ran past the guard at the gate and was soon on his way abroad" (Joll, 127).

By 1882 Kropotkin was in a French jail for associating with those who were bombing and rioting in the streets to improve workers' conditions. The spectacular trial was used by the defense to preach the message of anarchy, and it was reported throughout the world. Although Kropotkin and his wife were convicted, they were eventually released because of Kropotkin's poor health and the mounting international protest. He moved to England, where he would make his home for the next three decades.

Kropotkin wrote and spoke out about his ideal society until his final days. Perhaps his most important work, *Mutual Aid,* was published in 1902 and presented a great deal of scientific data to support his idea that all species, humans included, did not tend to annihilate each other within the group to improve individual position, power, and prestige. He posited that the opposite was actually the case: Groups of animals naturally tended toward cooperation for the continuation of the species. The eternal internal motivation of the individual was the betterment of the whole of which he was a part. For Kropotkin, anarchism was simply the means of fulfilling the human promise of a better world.

In 1917 Kropotkin returned to Russia after the Bolshevik uprising, but he could not support the imposition of the new "peoples'" authority in place of the tsar's. He openly disagreed with Vladimir Lenin, and his last few years were not happy. However, upon his death, on February 8, 1921, it was reported that a procession more than five miles long followed his hearse to the grave.

See also

Bakunin, Mikhail A.; Marx, Karl; Proudhon, Pierre-Joseph

References

Harper, Clifford, *Anarchy: A Graphic Guide* (London: Camden Press, 1987).

Horowitz, Irving L., *The Anarchists* (New York: Dell, 1964).

Joll, James, *The Anarchists,* Boston: Little Brown (1964).

Kropotkin, Peter, *Memoirs of a Revolutionist* (Boston: Houghton Mifflin, 1899).

L

Labadie, Joseph A. "Jo" (1850–1913)

My empire is different than any other.
In so far as is possible mine is a self-
  determining entity,
And no one shall invade it but at his peril.
I am enemy of all invaders, and invader of
  none,
Being at peace with everyone who minds
  his own business and leaves mine to
  myself.

This excerpt is taken from one of more than 500 poems written by Joseph A. Labadie, who began composing poetry after he was 50. These few words encapsulate Labadie's fundamental ideals of individualist anarchism, a philosophical approach to life that he embraced as a follower of anarchist Benjamin Tucker.

Born in frontier Paw Paw, Michigan, at the midpoint of the 19th century, Labadie spent a great deal of time among the Pottowatomis working with his father, who was a translator for French missionaries. Before he was 18, and without any formal schooling to speak of, Labadie wandered the area working as a printer when he could find employment. At 22 he found regular employment as a printer for two Detroit newspapers, the *Tribune* and the *Post.* He settled in the city and married his cousin, Sophie Elizabeth Archambeau, in 1877.

That same year, Labadie became a member of the new Socialist Labor Party. Along with a partner (the only other member of the Socialist Labor Party who was not a German émigré), Judson Grenell, he began publishing *Detroit Socialist.* Their collaboration evolved into the Socialistic Tract Association, with the goal of printing and freely distributing pamphlets explaining the basic concepts of socialism. This led to the publication of the nationally read *Advance and Labor Leaf* and columns for other important socialist and labor periodicals. The next year, his advocacy of workers' issues brought him to the attention of Charles Litchman, an official of a secret society known as the Knights of Labor. Calling it the Washington Literary Society to hide its true purpose as a labor group, Labadie was able to organize Detroit's first Knights of Labor assembly in 1901. Concurrent with this activity, Jo Labadie also took an interest in the Greenback movement that was sweeping many parts of the nation and especially the Midwest. This movement, which lasted from 1868 to 1888, advocated the retention in circulation of paper money, "the greenback," as $450 million had been printed during the Civil War to finance the Union victory. But the greenbacks were not backed by gold, and prices thus rose due to the inflation resulting from so much currency in the economy.

Agricultural states like Michigan tended to support keeping the paper money in circulation because of the higher than normal prices it brought for farm products. Labadie actually ran for mayor of Detroit on the Greenback-Labor ticket, and he went to the Chicago political convention of that party as a delegate.

By 1883 Labadie was reassessing his commitment to socialism. In its stead he discovered anarchism. He was especially attracted to Benjamin Tucker's philosophy of individualist anarchism, and while he continued to advocate for workers' rights he forged an important alliance with Tucker. He often contributed pieces to Tucker's magazine, *Liberty.* He also arranged speaking engagements for Russian-born anarchist Emma Goldman during her visits to the city.

Labadie's anarchist views eventually began to conflict with positions taken by the Knights of Labor. When the Haymarket affair of 1886 created a backlash against anarchists of any stripe, Knights of Labor president Terrence Powderly vetoed an attempt by the organization to pass a clemency resolution in support of the condemned anarchists. Labadie, who had detoured to Chicago to see the men in prison on his way to the Knights of Labor convention in 1887, was furious and attacked the Knights leadership for its stand on the issue. He soon left the Knights to help form the Michigan Federation of Labor, an organization that eventually associated with Samuel Gompers.

Labadie continued to express his anarchist ideals through discussion clubs, lectures, and poetry. Despite his radical views, Jo Labadie was always a popular figure in Detroit. In 1894 during the span of a month he got in trouble with postal inspectors for placing anarchist quotations on his envelopes, and he was fired from his job in the city water department for expressing libertarian thoughts. When the people of Detroit heard about this, however, their uniform support brought about his reinstatement and exonerated him from any wrongdoing.

Labadie amassed a great deal of literature on the newly emerging field of labor relations as well as on anarchist and other radical materials. In 1911 he donated his library to the University of Michigan (a legacy now known as the Labadie Collection). It has been expanded considerably since Joseph Labadie's death in 1913 and includes

> a great variety of social protest literature together with political views from both the extreme left and the extreme right. Materials are now collected from all parts of the world. In addition, to anarchism, the Collection's strengths include: civil liberties (with an emphases on racial minorities), socialism, communism, colonialism and imperialism, American labor history through the 1930s, the IWW, the Spanish Civil War, sexual freedom, women's liberation, gay liberation, the underground press, and student protest. (U-M Special Collections Library)

See also

Goldman, Emma; Haymarket Affair; Individualist Anarchists; Socialism; Tucker, Benjamin R.

References

Anderson, Carlotta R., *All-American Anarchist: Joseph A. Labadie and the Labor Movement* (Detroit: Wayne State University Press, 1998).

"Labadie Website," on the internet <http://members.aol.com/labadiejo/>.

University of Michigan Special Collections Library, "Labadie Collection," on the internet <http://www.lib.umich.edu/libhome/SpecColl.lib/labadie>.

Labadie, Laurance (1898–1975)

Laurance Labadie, the son of famed labor organizer and individualist anarchist Joseph Labadie, carried on the ideas of his father as well as those of Benjamin Tucker. "From the early 1930s Laurance Labadie was the most polished exponent of this ideological tradition" (Martin). A self-taught individual with little formal schooling, Laurance Labadie became a proficient essayist and poet, self-publishing most of his writings. He was also a skilled craftsman in various trades, including toolmaking, building, typesetting, and mechanics.

For much of his adult life, Labadie worked for several companies and shops connected with Detroit's automobile industry. But after World War II he quit shop work and lived on savings from his various jobs and kept up lengthy correspondence and discussions with anarchists and other radicals at the University of Michigan, including the longtime curator of the Labadie Collection, Agnes Inglis, and anarchist historian James J. Martin, author of *Men Against the State* (1953).

When Laurance Labadie died in 1975, Martin declared that Labadie was "the last direct link to Benjamin R. Tucker," which "amounted to the virtual closure and the last episode in the socioeconomic impulse which became known in the early decades of the 20th century as 'Mutualism'" (Martin).

See also

Labadie, Joseph A. "Jo"; Mutualism; Tucker, Benjamin R.

References

Martin, James J., Introduction, "Laurance Labadie: Selected Essays," on the internet <http:// alumni.umbc.edu/~akoont1/tmh/laurance.html>.

Lawrence Textile Mill Strike

In 1912 Lawrence, Massachusetts, was the scene of a massive strike known as the "Bread and Roses" strike at the four textile mills owned by the American Woolen Company. The strike was organized by the Industrial Workers of the World (IWW), a radical organization that hoped to form one big union. Its aim was to overthrow capitalism and the wage system through anarchist tactics of direct action—strikes, boycotts, and industrial sabotage. However, IWW was not an anarchist group.

At the time of the Lawrence strike, adult workers were toiling 56 hours per week and earning an average of $7–$8 per week (Flynn). This was hardly enough for a family to survive even with the help of children, who often went to work before the legal age of 14. Children—about 15,000 of them in the mills—earned only 12 cents per hour.

The mill workforce was made up of recently arrived immigrants from Portugal, French Canada, England, Ireland, Russia, Italy, Syria, Lithuania, Germany, Poland, and Belgium. They lived in wretched, flammable wooden tenements that were overrun with vermin, sweltering in the summer and bitter cold in the winter. Because of the inhumane living and working conditions, more than one-third of adult workers at the mill died before they were 25 years old, and many child workers died after the first two or three years on the job.

On January 1, 1912, a Massachusetts law went into effect reducing the workweek by two hours for women and children. Although the law was designed to aid workers, it brought about the opposite effect. Mill managers simply increased the speed of machines so that the same amount of work could be done in less time. When a group of Polish women found their pay had been cut, they immediately stopped working and marched out into the street. The following day 5,000 workers at another mill quit, and within 24 hours all the mills in Lawrence were shut down.

IWW leaders were called in to help carry on the strike and to organize mass meetings and parades and also to help feed at least 50,000 striking workers, who made up the majority of the Lawrence population of 86,000 people. At the same time, the mayor called out the militia and the governor sent in the state police.

A few days after the strike began the militia attacked demonstrators by turning fire hoses on them in the frigid winter temperatures. Although many of the demonstrators were arrested and jailed, the strike continued with defiant marchers carrying signs reading, "We Want Bread and Roses Too," indicating they wanted not only better working conditions and a living wage but also respect.

A few weeks after the strike began, police attacked a picket line and shot to death a young woman who was marching. Although two labor organizers, Joseph Ettor and Arturo Giovannitti, were miles away, they were charged with being accessories to murder because they urged strikers to picket. Ettor and Giovannitti were eventually brought to trail but were found not guilty by the jury. Meantime, such labor leaders as Big Bill Haywood and Elizabeth Gurley Flynn arrived to speak to strikers and encourage them to carry on.

In February the strikers became concerned about the children who suffered from hunger and other deprivations because the food parcels and fuel handed out were insufficient for the thousands of families in need. The strikers would have to end their walkout if their children continued to suffer. After much careful and painful deliberation, strikers decided to send their children out of Lawrence to working-class families and sympathizers in other cities, where they would be safe and cared for. About 200 children went to New York City and were met by workers singing "Internationale," a popular rallying song of oppressed workers and anarchists worldwide.

Lawrence officials tried to pressure strikers to return to work by using a child-neglect statute to proclaim that no more children could leave the city. Nevertheless, on February 24, 40 children gathered at the train station to leave for Philadelphia. Police were waiting and began to beat the children and their parents with clubs, dragged mothers away, and arrested them. "The result was a Congressional investigation which was brought into being by Victor Berger, the Socialist congressman from Wisconsin, and the condition of those [Lawrence] workers were so exposed to the whole country that the employers were only too happy to call it a day and bring the strike to a close" (Flynn). The American Woolen Company finally offered to raise the pay of workers, and strikers voted to end the strike on March 12, 1912.

See also

Anarchist Songs; Direct Action; Flynn, Elizabeth Gurley; Haywood, William Dudley "Big Bill"; Industrial Workers of the World

References

Cameron, Ardis, *Radicals of the Worst Sort: Laboring Women in Lawrence, Massachusetts, 1860–1912* (Urbana and Chicago: University of Illinois Press, 1994).

Flynn, Elizabeth Gurley, "Memories of the IWW," Web edition of transcript by Eugene W. Plawiuk, on the internet <http://www.geocities.com/CapitolHill/5202/rebelgirl.html> (1997).

Meltzer, Milton, *Bread—and Roses: The Struggle of American Labor, 1865–1915* (New York: Knopf, 1967).

Libertarian Party

The third largest political party in the United States, the Libertarian Party (LP) was established in 1971, and its views are often confused with the libertarian philosophies espoused by anarchists. (The terms *libertarian* and *anarchist* have often been used synonymously.) Although the LP is based on a platform that supports individual rights and opposes government regulatory functions and services, the party does not advocate overthrowing the state or capitalism. In fact, it especially calls for a free-market economy and the return of government to local or state control.

The Libertarian Party has nominated candidates for the U.S. presidency for decades, and each candidate has called for huge cuts in government, repeal of numerous federal government regulations, and elimination of Social Security and federal income taxes.

In its statement of principles, the LP maintains that its members

> hold that all individuals have the right to exercise sole dominion over their own lives, and have the right to live in whatever manner they choose, so long as they do not forcibly interfere with the equal right of others to live in whatever manner they choose.
>
> Governments throughout history have regularly operated on the opposite principle, that the State has the right to dispose of the lives of individuals and the fruits of their labor. Even within the United States, all political parties other than our own grant to government the right to regulate the lives of individuals and seize the fruits of their labor without their consent.
>
> We, on the contrary, deny the right of any government to do these things, and hold that where governments exist, they must not violate the rights of any individual: namely, (1) the right to life—accordingly we support the prohibition of the initiation of physical force against others; (2) the right to liberty of speech and action—accordingly we oppose all attempts by government to abridge the freedom of speech and press, as well as government censorship in any form; and (3) the right to property—accordingly we oppose all government interference with private property, such as confiscation, nationalization, and eminent domain, and support the prohibition of robbery, trespass, fraud, and misrepresentation.
>
> Since governments, when instituted, must not violate individual rights, we oppose all interference by government in the areas of voluntary and contractual relations among individuals. People should not be forced to sacrifice their lives and property for the benefit of others. They should be left free by government to deal with one another as free traders; and the resultant

economic system, the only one compatible with the protection of individual rights, is the free market.

In August 1998 a former presidential candidate on the Libertarian Party ticket in 1995, Harry Browne, launched a nationally syndicated radio show on the Talk America Radio Network. Although the show focuses on politics and current events, its purpose is to air the views of Libertarians and to inform listeners about libertarian proposals that Browne claims can improve their lives and personally make them better off in a free society (LP news release).

References

Browne, Harry, *Why Government Doesn't Work* (New York: St. Martin's Press, 1995).
"Harry Browne Launches Syndicated Radio Show," LP News Release (September 1998).
"Libertarian Party—Statement of Principles," on the internet <http://www.lp.org/lp-sop.html>.

Libertarian Socialism

Traditionally, and still throughout Europe, the term *libertarian* is associated with those who advocate a leftist political/social/economic philosophy more correctly known as "libertarian socialism." According to the Anarchist FAQ on the internet, libertarian socialism is "a social system which believes in freedom of action and thought and free will, in which the producers possess both political power and the means of producing and distributing goods." For many whose personal beliefs found a resonance within the philosophies of Mikhail Bakunin, Pierre-Joseph Proudhon, Peter Kropotkin, and others, the term *anarchist* simply proved too negative. *Libertarian*—for these people and for others throughout the century—meant *anarchist* or, at the very least, *socialist*. During the 1930s, *libertarian communism* was a term used by Isaac Puente, who supported the anarchist-dominated Confederación Nacional del Trabajo (CNT) at the time of the Spanish Civil War and demonstrated his commitment to anarcho-syndicalism and direct action in a pamphlet he wrote in 1932.

A great deal of confusion exists today within the United States when the term *libertarian socialism* is used because it was co-opted by the American Libertarian political party, "anarcho-capitalists," and other so-called right-wing (i.e., conservative) libertarians. Following the philosophical lead of such influential free-market and extreme laissez faire capitalists as author Ayn Rand, the new libertarians advocate individual liberty within the market economy and abhor government when it contravenes attempts by the owners of capital to operate for maximum profit.

Anarchism (i.e., libertarian socialism) is not compatible with capitalism, which is a hierarchical system created and maintained for the ultimate benefit of the managers and owners. In the true historical sense of the term, and as far as anarchists believe today, these "right" libertarians are the opposite of libertarians, and anarchists do not want to be known in that sense of libertarianism. Indeed, anarcho-capitalism is an oxymoron.

See also

Anarcho-Capitalism; Anarcho-Syndicalism; Bakunin, Mikhail A.; Direct Action; Kropotkin, Peter Alexeyevich; Proudhon, Pierre-Joseph; Spanish Civil War

References

An Anarchist FAQ Version 7.2—22/05/98, on the internet <http://www.etext.org/Politics/Spunk/library/intro/faq/sp001547/index.html>.
"Libertarian Socialism" (1995), on the internet <http://www.tigerden.com/~berios/libsoc.html>.
Puente, Isaac, *Libertarian Communism* (Sydney, Australia: Monty Miller Press, 1985).

Lingg, Louis (1864–1887)

One of the eight Haymarket martyrs sentenced to die for the murder of police during the 1886 riot that followed a workers' demonstration in Chicago, Louis Lingg made clear in his statements to the jury that he was being tried for the fact that he was an anarchist, not for murder as charged. At his trial he declared his hatred for the court: "I despise you. I despise your order, your laws, your . . . authority. Hang me for it!" (David, 339).

Lingg was born in Mannheim, Germany, to parents who were able to provide fairly well for him and his younger sister. But his father, who worked in a lumberyard, was injured in an accident and because of poor health was forced to take a job that paid very little. He died in 1877 when Lingg was 13 and his sister seven. At this time, Lingg developed a bitter hatred for the way the rich exploited the poor. As he noted:

> It did not escape my observation that the former employer of my father grew continually richer, despite the extravagant life he and his family were leading, whilst, on the other hand, my father, who had performed his respective part in creating the wealth his employer possessed, and who had sacrificed his all, which was his health, in the effort to serve his master, was cast aside like a worn-out tool which had fulfilled its mission and could now be spared. (quoted in Foner, 170)

Lingg served as a carpenter's apprentice from 1869 until 1882, then traveled to cities in Germany and Switzerland to find work. When he refused to serve in the Swiss military, he wandered from town to town in an effort to stay out of the reach of police. With financial help from his stepfather—his mother had remarried in 1885—Lingg was able to sail to the United States, where he found work in Chicago. He joined the International Carpenters' and Joiners' Union and became a labor organizer, often espousing the view that force and revolution were necessary to bring about changes for the working class. His position may have been one reason for his arrest after the Haymarket affair. He was sentenced along with seven others to hang; he committed suicide less than two hours before his scheduled execution.

See also

Haymarket Affair

References

David, Henry, *The History of the Haymarket Affair* (New York: Russell and Russell, 1936).

Foner, Philip S., ed., *The Autobiographies of the Haymarket Martyrs* (Atlantic Highlands, NJ: Humanities Press, 1969).

Ludlow Massacre

In 1914, Ludlow, Colorado, was the scene of one of the most brutal reactions to a labor strike in the history of the United States, an event that led to anarchist demonstrations and protests across the country. Trouble surfaced in 1913 among coal miners employed by the Colorado Fuel and Iron Corporation; in 1914 the terrible tragedy that would become known as the Ludlow Massacre occurred. It was memorialized by Woodie Guthrie in a haunting folksong by the same name.

For years in the western states coal miners, most of them European immigrants, had tried to join the United Mine Workers (UMW) to demand a shorter workday, safe working conditions in the mines, and the right to form unions. But the coal mine operators, led by John D. Rockefeller Jr., opposed union organizing. Rockefeller hired guards and detectives to prevent unions from forming, and when a young labor organizer was shot to death by detectives, workers throughout mining towns in southern Colorado were outraged. They gathered at a mass meeting in Trinidad to listen to famed UMW organizer Mother Jones, who urged them to strike.

When the miners called a strike, the mining companies evicted the workers and their families from the miserable, company-owned shacks that miners were required to rent. With the help of the UMW Union, miners set up tent communities and carried on. According to one historian,

> The gunmen hired by the Rockefeller interests—the Baldwin-Felts Detective Agency—using Gatling guns and rifles, raided the tent colonies. The death list of miners grew, but they hung on, drove back an armored train in a gun battle, fought to keep out strikebreakers. With the miners resisting, refusing to give in, the mines not able to operate, the Colorado governor . . . called out the National Guard, with the Rockefellers supplying the Guard's wages. (Zinn, 346)

At first the miners cheered the arrival of the National Guard, but soon they learned the guardsmen were there to break the strike. The hired guns attacked the miners, their wives, and other women who were marching in protest along the streets of Trinidad.

Somehow the miners held out through the winter. In April 1914 the National Guard, armed with machine guns, circled and attacked the tent colony at Ludlow on the day miners were celebrating the Greek Easter. Miners fired back, and women and children tried to escape bullets by hiding in pits dug inside the tents. Then two companies of Colorado National Guardsmen along with thugs hired by the coal company poured gasoline on the tents and set them afire, burning to death eleven children and two women. After the massacre, strikers attacked the mines, and President Woodrow Wilson ordered federal troops to stop the violence.

When news of the Ludlow Massacre spread across the United States, protesters, including such anarchists as Carlo Tresca and Alexander Berkman, gathered on the streets and in meeting halls to denounce Rockefeller. Anarchists called for vengeance, and Berkman especially was ever more determined to use violence against capitalists.

See also

Berkman, Alexander; Jones, Mary "Mother"; Tresca, Carlo

References

Yellen, Samuel, *American Labor Struggles* (New York: Harcourt, Brace, 1936).

Zinn, Howard, *A People's History of the United States* (New York: New Press, 1997).

Luxemburg, Rosa (1870–1919)

Rosa Luxemburg was an influential leader of both the German and the Polish socialist parties. She advocated nonviolent, spontaneous revolution and was active in the Socialist International (also known as the Second International), which hoped to transform capitalist societies into socialist commonwealths and unify them in a world federation. The Socialist International had a great influence on the European labor movement during the late 1800s and early 1900s. Within the group, Luxemburg consistently argued against the trend toward nationalism among socialists. Unlike Vladimir Lenin, who advocated national self-determination, Luxemburg believed such a theory played into the hands of the bourgeoisie. In Luxemburg's view, workers should take part in direct mass action to help bring about an international socialist society. As she wrote:

> The working class must above all else strive to get the entire political power of the state into its own hands. Political power, however, is for us socialists only a means. The end for which we must use this power is the fundamental transformation of the entire economic relations.
>
> Currently all wealth—the largest and best estates as well as the mines, works and the factories—belongs to a few . . . private capitalists. The great mass of the workers only get . . . a meagre wage to live on for hard work. The enrichment of a small number of idlers is the aim of today's economy.
>
> This state of affairs should be remedied. All social wealth, the land with all its natural resources hidden in its bowels and on the surface, and all factories and works must be taken out of the hands of the exploiters and taken into common property of the people. The first duty of a real workers' government is to declare by means of a series of decrees the most important means of production to be national property and place them under the control of society. (Luxemburg, "1918")

Born in Zamosc, Poland, which was then part of Russia, Luxemburg was the youngest of five children in a Jewish family. From the time she was 16, Luxemburg was active in politics, joining an illegal student group. After graduating from the Warsaw Gymnasium, she joined the Proletariat, a revolutionary socialist party. In 1889 she, along with other revolutionaries, was forced to flee Poland because of her activities; she settled in Switzerland, where she enrolled in the University of Zurich. She began her studies in botany and political science and earned a Ph.D. in economics. While at the university she met Leo Jogiches, who instructed her on Marxism. Jogiches was Luxemburg's occasional lover throughout her lifetime, but he refused to allow her to disclose their relationship. The two founded the antinationalist Social Democratic Party (SDP) of Poland and Lithuania and urged workers to help overthrow the Russian tsar.

Luxemburg became a German citizen by marrying a German worker and joined the radical left wing of the German Social Democratic Party (SDP). By the early 1900s, she was known as a forceful orator, speaking on behalf of Germany's working class.

During the 1905 revolution in Russia, Luxemburg went to Warsaw to take part in the uprisings but was promptly jailed. After her release she taught at the SDP school in Berlin between 1907 and 1914. During that time, she published a pamphlet, *The Mass Strike,* which was widely read, and her most famous book, *The Accumulation of Capital,* which links the oppression of workers to imperial expansion of large industrial nations.

A staunch pacifist, Luxemburg publicly opposed World War I. In 1918 she and German socialist Karl Liebknecht founded the Spartacus League, a radical faction of the SDP, to counteract SDP's support for the war and to advocate revolution to end it. Because of her activities, Luxemburg was imprisoned, and after her release she and Liebknecht helped convert the Spartacus League into the German Communist Party. Yet she never agreed with Lenin and the Bolsheviks' centralist ideas and denounced their dictatorial powers. She insisted on democratic action among the proletariat, believing that workers would spontaneously organize themselves.

In 1919 Luxemburg and Liebknecht took part in a Spartacist uprising against the German government. They were arrested and shot by anticommunist German troops, who were later acquitted of the murders.

See also

Direct Action; Socialism

References

Abraham, Richard, *Rosa Luxemburg: A Life for the International* (Oxford and New York: Berg, 1989).

Ettinger, Elzbieta, *Rosa Luxemburg: A Life* (Boston: Beacon Press, 1986).

Luxemburg, Rosa, "1911: Rosa Luxemburg and Mass Action," on the internet <http://www.marx.org/Luxemburg/Archive/110829.htm>.

Luxemburg, Rosa, "1918: The Socialisation of Society," translated by Dave Hollis (1996), on the internet <http://www.marx.org/Luxemburg/Archive/181220.htm>.

"Luxemburg, Rosa" *Britannica Online* <http://www.eb.com:180/cgi-bin/g?DocF=micro/361/60.html>.

Shepherd, Naomi, *A Price Below Rubies: Jewish Women As Rebels and Radicals* (Cambridge: Harvard University Press, 1993).

M

Mackay, John Henry (1864–1933)

Despite the Scottish name, John Henry Mackay was a German, a poet, lyricist, novelist, and essayist whose written work had a major influence on European and American individualistic anarchists of his time. He is credited with bringing to prominence such individualists as Max Stirner, presenting Stirner's views in a biography, *Max Stirner, Sein Leben, und Sein Werk* (*Max Stirner, His Life, and His Work*). Mackay also helped disseminate the views of American Benjamin Tucker, an individualist and propagandist who rejected the idea of holding property in common and believed that a person had the right to own any property that his labor had produced or that he had received as a gift.

John Henry Mackay was born in Saarbrucken, Germany, to a Scottish father and German mother. His father died when Mackay was two, and he was brought up by his mother and German foster parent. His affluent family traveled widely, and Mackay was often in touch with intellectuals in Europe and the United States. According to one writer,

> Although he universally gave the impression of good breeding, taste, softness, and amiability, he . . . cherished a violent hate for the traditional Christianity and morality of Germany, a fear of the innate cruelty of churchgoers and people who considered themselves "good." His earliest poetry in the eighties [shows] a longing for death as an escape from the evil of life. His adoption of anarchism was clearly an attempt to find a weapon with which to combat his greatest fear, life itself." (Riley)

When Mackay was 23, he moved to London and lived for a year among communist anarchists, primarily political exiles from various European countries who espoused the views of Johann Most. Most believed that the masses had to rise in revolution to bring about a stateless society with property held in common.

In 1888 Mackay began to study the work of Max Stirner, who Mackey called the spiritual forefather of individualistic anarchism. Stirner rejected all political and moral ties of the individual and declared that egotism determines everything. After ten years of research, Mackay published his biography of Stirner, and today most accounts of Stirner's life are based on Mackay's work.

In 1889 Mackay met Benjamin Tucker in Paris. The two formed a friendship that lasted for 40 years, and Mackay translated into German a number of Tucker's propaganda pamphlets. Two of Mackay's novels show the influence of both Tucker and Stirner, especially his best known, *Die Anarchisten* (The Anarchist). In that book

> there are two contrasting characters, one of which represents a philosophy of life that is clearly communist-anarchism; the other, a more intellectual person, is an individualistic anarchist and an egoist. Through the eyes of these two men we see the horrors of life among the London poor in 1887 and the useless attempts of London radicals to wipe out the evils of the world by means of an effective social movement. Only by individualism *à la* Tucker and egoism *à la* Max Stirner can the world progress out of the misery, poverty, and

> wars produced by governments. The book is obviously aimed not only at the layman but also at the communist-anarchists, in an attempt to persuade them to drop their evil ways and come over to the camp of the Americans. It was translated into English by George Schumm immediately after its appearance and published by Tucker in Boston. (Riley)

Mackay's novel was highly touted in Tucker's periodical *Liberty* as "a poet's prose contribution to the literature of philosophic and egoistic Anarchism." Tucker explained that in the book Mackay traced his own mental development in London amid the exciting events of 1887, such as the rioting of the British unemployed and the executions of the Haymarket martyrs in Chicago. The antagonism between communism and anarchism was also emphasized in the book, Tucker noted (McElroy).

The Anarchist was translated into six other languages in addition to English, and more than 15,000 copies sold by the time of his death in 1933. But Mackay gained very little financially from his work, whether novels, poetry, or other publications. Indeed, he and his wife and child were poverty-stricken during the early 1900s, despite Herculean efforts by Tucker and other friends to sell Mackay's books in the United States.

Although Mackay refused to accept charity from anyone, in 1926 he received financial backing from Michael Davidovsky, a Russian millionaire who lived in France and was interested in Mackay's writings and anarchists such as Stirner. In 1926 Davidovsky financed the Stirner Publishing House in Berlin and set up a monthly pension for Mackay. But the venture lasted only two years, and the millionaire was no longer a benefactor. Mackay tried a few other publishing efforts, also failures. He died in poverty in 1933 not long after the Nazis assumed power in Germany.

See also

Anarchist Press; Haymarket Affair; Individualist Anarchists; Most, Johann; Stirner, Max; Tucker, Benjamin R.

References

McElroy, Wendy, "Liberty's Library," on the internet <http://alumni.umbc.edu/~akoont1/tmh/library.html>.

Riley, Thomas, "New England Anarchism in Germany," *New England Quarterly* (March 1945).

Magón, Ricardo Flores (1874–1922)

An outspoken advocate of anarchism, Ricardo Flores Magón is one of the martyrs of the Mexican Revolution and was the leader of a movement to which he dedicated his life: driving Mexican dictator Porfirio Diaz into exile in 1911. Despite the fact that Magón spent much of his adult life imprisoned in the United States, he was able to influence numerous Mexican revolutionaries who followed guerrilla leader Pancho Villa and peasant rebel leader Emiliano Zapata, calling for land and social reforms.

Magón was born in San Antonio Eloxochitlan in the state of Oaxaca. Although Ricardo was sent to Mexico City for advanced education, he was not intent on his studies, and along with his two brothers, Jesus and Enrique, became involved in political activities, including student demonstrations to protest the reelection of Diaz in 1892. This brought the first of many jail terms for Ricardo, who was 17 at the time.

In 1900, Ricardo, Jesus, and a friend founded *Regeneración,* a periodical that "played an important part in rousing the Mexican laborers, rural as well as urban, against the Diaz dictatorship" (Avrich, 208). About six months after founding the journal, Ricardo Magón became the sole editor, and until his death he used *Regeneración* to spread his brand of radicalism, which was based on the theories of Peter Kropotkin. Magón's followers, in fact, distributed thousands of copies of Kropotkin's work, *Conquest of Bread,* to win workers over to their cause.

Because *Regeneración* consistently criticized the Diaz government, authorities confiscated Magón's printing press. He was imprisoned again, and when he was released at the end of 1903 he was constantly harassed by police. So in early 1904, he and brother Enrique left Mexico for the United States. But the harassment did not end. After crossing the Rio

Grande into Texas, Magón spent the next few years, from 1904 to 1907, fleeing U.S. police, immigration officials, even private detectives. One time, a paid killer was sent from Mexico to stab him, but Enrique saved his life by throwing the thug out of the house. Enrique was then arrested and fined for disturbing the peace. Through all this, Magón managed to resume publication of *Regeneración,* which was then smuggled into Mexico.

Mexican dictator Diaz convinced U.S. authorities to continue their pursuit of Magón, and between 1907 and 1910 Magón served jail sentences in California and Arizona for violating U.S. neutrality laws. However, after his release he continued his agitation through his journal. In early 1911 his followers staged a revolt from Baja, California, but the uprising was soon put down. Magón was imprisoned once more, sentenced to nearly two years in federal prison on McNeil Island, Washington. It was close enough to the anarchist colony of Home that some colony residents were able to visit him.

Throughout this period (and after he was incarcerated—again—during the U.S. suppression of antiwar activists in 1918), Magón also received support from such anarchists as Emma Goldman, Alexander Berkman, and Voltairine de Cleyre and organizations like the Anarchist Red Cross (later the Anarchist Black Cross) and the Industrial Workers of the World. Magón received a 21-year sentence for violating the recently passed Espionage Act; his comrade, Librado Rivera, was sentenced to 15 years' imprisonment. When Magón's health steadily deteriorated, he was transferred from McNeil Island to Leavenworth. From there he sent dozens of letters to friends and his faithful lawyer, Harry Weinberger, who had defended Emma Goldman. In one letter he responded to Weinberger's request for "data regarding the sentence which ended on January 19, 1914." But he elaborated on his past so that Weinberger could determine whether he had "been the victim of a conspiracy bent on keeping in bondage the Mexican peon." In a 1921 letter, he described the persecution he had suffered ever since fleeing to the United States. In part, he wrote:

On February 18, 1917, I was arrested with my brother Enrique, for having published in *Regeneración* articles against the treachery committed by Carranza, then President of Mexico, against the workers, and for having written that the Mexicans who at the time were being assassinated by Texas rangers deserved justice rather than bullets. I got a sentence of one year and one day, for I was expected to live only a few more months, having been taken from a hospital bed to be tried. Enrique got three years. We appealed and finally succeeded in getting bond, under which we were released pending the appeal.

On the 21st of March, 1918, I was arrested with Rivera for having published in *Regeneración* the Manifesto for which I was given 20 years' imprisonment and Rivera 15. The wording and meaning of the Manifesto were construed as seditious by the prosecution, that is, as aiming at the insubordination and revolt of the military and naval forces of the United States. Any sensible person who happened to read the Manifesto would not draw such a conclusion, for in reality the Manifesto is only an exposition of facts and a fair warning to all mankind of the evils those facts might produce. In one of its paragraphs it is clearly stated that no one can make a revolution on account of it being a social phenomenon. The Manifesto was aimed at the prevention of the evils a revolution carries itself—the revolution being regarded from a scientific standpoint as a world-wide inevitable result of the unsettled conditions of the world. The Manifesto does not refer in the least to the policies of the American Government in the last war, nor gives aid and comfort to its enemies. It is neither pro-German nor pro-Ally, and does not single out the United States in its brief review of the world conditions. It was enough, however, to secure for me a life term behind prison bars. The persecution, this time, was exceedingly severe. My poor wife, Maria, was incarcerated during five months, and is now free on bond awaiting trial for having notified my friends of my

> arrest, that they should assist me in my legal defense. (Magón, *Collected Works*)

No matter what assistance his lawyer, friends, family, and comrades tried to provide, it was to no avail. Ricardo Flores Magón died in prison in November 1922. Two months later, a public funeral was held for him in Mexico City. His remains are interred there in the Rotunda of Illustrious Men.

See also

Anarchist Black Cross; Berkman, Alexander; de Cleyre, Voltairine; Goldman, Emma; Industrial Workers of the World; Kropotkin, Peter Alexeyevich; Zapata, Emiliano

References

Albro, Ward S., *Always a Rebel: Ricardo Flores Magùn and the Mexican Revolution* (Fort Worth: Texas Christian University Press, 1992).

Avrich, Paul, *Anarchist Portraits* (Princeton: Princeton University Press, 1988).

Cockcroft, James D., *Intellectual Precursors of the Mexican Revolution, 1900–1913* (Austin: University of Texas Press, 1968).

Hart, John M., *Anarchism and the Mexican Working Class, 1860–1931* (Austin: University of Texas Press, 1987).

MacLachlan, Colin M., *Anarchism and the Mexican Revolution: The Political Trials of Ricardo Flores Magùn in the United States* (Berkeley: University of California, 1991).

Magón, Ricardo Flores, *Collected Works—Letters—To Harry Weinberger* (March 9, 1921), on the internet <http://www.pitzer.edu/~dward/Anarchist_Archives/bright/magon/works/letters/harry050921.html>.

Wehling, Jason, "Anarchist Influences on the Mexican Revolution," on the internet <http://www.teleport.com/~jwehling/Anarchy.Mex.Rev.html>.

Makhno, Nestor Ivanovich (1889–1935)

Nestor Ivanovich Makhno was a legendary anarchist and heroic figure to the Ukrainian peasants and workers who revolted against the Bolsheviks in 1917. The Bolsheviks, led by Vladimir Ilich Lenin, had gained power in Russia after Nicholas II abdicated and the tsarist government toppled. Although a constitution-based, provisional government was set up, the Bolsheviks were able to take control of workers' soviets (councils) and form their own so-called proletarian dictatorship—a rule by workers.

Anarchists and Bolsheviks seemed to be working toward the same goals, but the two factions soon were at odds. Some anarchist groups objected to the entire concept of power and to Lenin's view that "liberty is a luxury not to be permitted at the present stage of development." Lenin acted on that premise, and Bolsheviks suppressed most Russian anarchist activities (Joll, 184).

Between late 1917 and mid-1921 there were numerous challenges to Bolshevik rule; armed conflict—civil wars—erupted throughout the land. Makhno led one insurgent force, an anarchist movement in his native village in the Ukraine, then a part of the Union of Soviet Socialist Republics (USSR).

Born into an extremely poor peasant family, Nestor Makhno was one of seven children. His father died when Nestor was less than a year old, and his mother reared all the children in the Ukrainian village of Gulyai Polye (or Guliai-Pole). Because of his family's extreme poverty, Makhno went to work as a shepherd at the age of seven. He attended school for about four years, then at 12 left to work as a farmhand for wealthy landowners; he later worked in a foundry.

During his early teens Makhno began to despise the "exploiters and dreamed of the way he would someday get rid of them," as a biographer stated. By the time he was 17 Makhno was "full of revolutionary enthusiasm and ready to do anything in the struggle for liberation of the workers" (Arshinov). He joined an anarcho-communist group in his village and took part in terrorist attacks against Marxists, who anarchists contended were perpetrating fraud against workers and peasants. In 1908 he was arrested for anarchist activities that resulted in the murder of a police officer, then sentenced to life in a Moscow prison. There he met a leading anarchist, Peter Arshinov, who had once been a member of the Bolshevik Party but defected due to its lack of response to workers' needs and aspirations. Arshinov was imprisoned for smuggling anarchist literature into Russia.

Makhno and Arshinov became good friends, and Arshinov, who was older and better educated than Makhno, taught the younger rebel basic anarchist doctrine as put forth by Russian political philosophers Peter Kropotkin and Mikhail Bakunin.

The provisional government granted the two prisoners amnesty in 1917, and Makhno returned to his village to build an anarchist movement. He organized a commune of farm workers, a farm workers' union, and a local peasant council and led the peasants in a seizure of property from the landed gentry of the region. He is best known, however, for his guerrilla army—the Revolutionary Insurgent Army of the Ukraine, often referred to as the Makhnovists. Its recruits were peasants and workers who elected officers and set up codes of discipline, although Makhno appointed top leaders. For a time the Bolsheviks supported Makhno's activities, even calling him a courageous and great revolutionary. But they later tried to use him for their own purposes and attacked him and his army.

After the Bolsheviks negotiated a 1918 peace treaty with Germany—the Treaty of Brest-Litovsk, which ended Russia's bloody involvement in World War I—Makhno denounced the Bolsheviks as traitors. The Germans demanded territory in exchange for peace, and German and Austrian armies occupied the Ukraine. The Makhnovists made daring attacks against the German and Austrian occupation forces, but they also at times fought the Bolsheviks. Occasionally they joined the Bolsheviks against common enemies such as the anti-Bolshevik White Guards, made up of elitists loyal to the former tsarist government, and the World War I Allies who intervened to support the Whites.

Makhno claimed that he and his insurgents were the only revolutionaries true to the cause of workers and peasants, and his purpose was always clear: to wage war against those who tried to put down the revolution. His army carried the black flag with the slogan "The Land to the Peasants, the Factories to the Workers" and became a terror to the local bourgeoisie as well as occupation authorities. As biographer Arshinov explained, landowners who were able to take back their estates and enslave the peasants

> found themselves suddenly under the merciless hand of Makhno and his partisans. Swift as the wind, intrepid, pitiless toward their enemies, they fell thunderously on some estates, massacred all the sworn enemies of the peasants, and disappeared as rapidly as they had come. The next day Makhno would be more than a hundred miles away, would appear in some town, massacre the *Varta* (security police), officers and noblemen, and vanish before the German troops had time to realize what had happened. (Arshinov, 56)

Makhno continued to wage war as land areas rapidly changed hands, controlled first by one army, then another. There was little opportunity to establish a social revolution. However, in the villages, towns, and cities liberated by the Makhnovists, restrictions of all types were lifted, except for political organizations that tried to dictate to the people. Freedom of speech, press, and assembly prevailed, prisoners were released from jails, and peasants and workers were able to organize their lives and their work as they saw fit.

During the 1920s the Bolsheviks enlisted the support of Makhno and his army to fight the Whites in exchange for the release of imprisoned anarchists. However, as the Bolshevik Red Army gained ever more victories in the civil war, they turned on the Makhnovists, attacking and killing many of Makhno's officers and arresting members of anarchist organizations. In November 1920 the Red Army attacked Makhno's headquarters in Gulyai Polye, capturing or shooting many insurgents. Makhno, his leg wounded, escaped with some of his army, which had been reduced from tens of thousands to 3,000; after almost a year of wandering, he eventually fled to Paris, France, in 1921. He died there in 1935, broken and embittered.

See also

Makhnovists and the Makhnovshchina; Russian Anarchism

References

Arshinov, Peter, Lorraine Perlman, and Fredy Perlman, trans., *History of the Makhnovist Movement, 1918–1921* (Detroit: Black and Red, 1974, orig. publ. Germany: The Group of Russian Anarchists, 1923).

Avrich, Paul, *The Russian Anarchists* (New York: W. W. Norton, 1978).
Joll, James, *The Anarchists* (Boston: Little, Brown, 1964).

Makhnovists and the Makhnovshchina

During the Russian Revolution, the Makhnovists took their name from Nestor Makhno, who had a leading role in the Ukrainian anarchist movement from 1917 to 1921. The Makhnovists were armed peasants and workers fighting the Bolsheviks or Communists (Reds) and forces of the tsar (Whites) and their supporters. They called themselves Makhnovists because they saw Makhno as a "faithful friend and leader . . . whose voice of protest against all oppression of the toilers rang out through the whole Ukraine, calling for a struggle against all the tyrants, marauders and political charlatans who were bent on deceiving us" (Avrich, 135).

During the insurrection (known as the Makhnovshchina) guerilla bands of Makhnovists not only fought the Reds and Whites but also freed prisoners in jails, established freedom of speech, and encouraged people to take charge of their own lives. They issued proclamation after proclamation, sometimes written on wrapping paper and pages from a ledger. Some were addressed "TO ALL WORKERS OF THE PLOW AND THE HAMMER!"; others attempted to encourage young people to take up the cause. One proclamation exhorted:

> Fellow workers! the Revolutionary Insurgent Army of the Ukraine (Makhnovist) was called into existence as a protest against the oppression of the workers and peasants by the bourgeois-landlord authority on the one hand and the Bolshevik-Communist dictatorship on the other.
>
> Setting for itself one goal—the battle for total liberation of the working people of the Ukraine from the oppression of various authorities and the creation of a TRUE SOVIET SOCIALIST ORDER, the insurgent Makhnovist army fought stubbornly on several fronts for the achievement of these goals. (Arshinov, 265)

Still other exhortations sought to convince soldiers in the Red Army that they were being told lies about the Makhnovists murdering captured Red Army men. "Captured Red Army men are immediately set free," a proclamation stated, ending with "Long live the Brotherly union of the Revolutionary Insurgent Makhnovists with the Peasant and Worker Red Army Men!" (Arshinov, 283). Despite calls for peasants, workers, and Red Army soldiers to fight with the insurgents, the Red Army defeated the Makhnovists, killing commanders and soldiers. By 1921 the leader of the Red Army, Leon Trotsky, had suppressed most anarchist activities in Russia.

See also
Makhno, Nestor Ivanovich; Russian Anarchism

References
Arshinov, Peter, Lorraine Perlman, and Fredy Perlman, trans., *History of the Makhnovist Movement, 1918–1921* (Detroit: Black and Red, 1974, orig. publ. Germany: The Group of Russian Anarchists, 1923).
Avrich, Paul, ed., *The Anarchists in the Russian Revolution* (Ithaca: Cornell University Press, 1973).
Harper, Clifford, *Anarchy: A Graphic Guide* (London: Camden Press, 1987).

Malatesta, Errico (1853–1932)

One of the primary leaders of the Italian anarchist movement, Errico Malatesta spent 60 years agitating to put anarchist ideas into practice. During the 1870s Malatesta, along with other anarchists, hoped that people in Italy would rise up as they had in France with the Paris Commune of 1871 and apply anarchistic principles. He wrote numerous articles and pamphlets and gave many speeches, spelling out his view that the state was unnecessary and by its very nature oppressive. He argued that individuals abdicate their own liberty when they give governors—kings, presidents, ministers, the clergy, teachers, and so on—the power to be masters. As he wrote in a pamphlet titled *Anarchy:*

> In all the course of history . . . government is either brutal, violent, arbitrary domination of the few over the many, or it is an instrument devised to secure domination

> and privilege to those who, by force, or cunning, or inheritance, have taken to themselves all the means of life, first and foremost the soil, whereby they hold the people in servitude, making them work for their advantage.

He argued further that whatever the name given to government, "its essential function is always that of oppressing and exploiting the masses" through its "indispensable instruments . . . the policeman and the tax collector, the soldier and the prison. And to these are necessarily added the time serving priest or teacher . . . supported and protected by the government, to render the spirit of the people servile and make them docile under the yoke."

Born in Santa Maria Capua Vetere in the province of Caserta, Italy, Malatesta was the son of an affluent landowner. He attended the University of Naples, where he was a medical student and for a time supported republicanism (as opposed to a monarchy). But he soon became a socialist. During the 1860s he was greatly influenced by Russian anarchist and activist Mikhail Bakunin, who lived in Italy at the time.

During his youth Malatesta was a strong advocate of "propaganda by deed," seizing land and organizing workers' revolts in the hope that widespread rebellions would result. Later in life, however, he emphasized syndicalism rather than armed insurrection as a means to attain anarchist goals. Anarchist historian and well-known author Murray Bookchin explained, "Although [Malatesta] eventually accepted anarcho-syndicalism with apparent reluctance, he continued to call for a far more expansive form of anarchist organization and practice than many syndicalists were prepared to accept. In practice, anarchist groups often came into outright conflict with anarcho-syndicalist organizations—not to speak of syndicalist organizations, many of which eschewed anarchism" (Bookchin).

In 1878, when an attempt was made to assassinate King Umberto I, Italian officials began to keep a close watch on anarchist leaders, often arresting and deporting them, which forced Malatesta to leave his homeland. In exile, Malatesta traveled throughout Europe for five years, continuing his revolutionary activities, but after he returned to Italy he was once more forced into exile. He spent 12 years in Argentina, organizing workers and publishing radical pamphlets and other materials. In 1895 he was part of an uprising in Spain and a general strike in Belgium. Because of his activities, Malatesta was often arrested and jailed; he served time in prison in England, France, and Switzerland and was expelled from all of these countries. In 1899 he went to the United States for a lecturing tour and began the anarchist journal *La Questione Sociale,* which became one of the most influential anarchist newspapers in the world. It originated as the channel for Italian anarcho-communists in Paterson, New Jersey, "to foster a class-conscious worker's union movement." Malatesta had previously initiated two other newspapers with the same name in Italy and Argentina (Wehling).

For 13 years Malatesta lived and worked in London. When World War I began he urged anarchists to stay out of the fight, seeing the conflict as a struggle between capitalists. In 1919, after the war, Malatesta returned to Italy. At that time, the anarchist movement was strong, and the daily anarchist newspaper *Umanita Nova*—which Malatesta had founded—boasted a circulation of 50,000. But when Mussolini became dictator, *Umanita Nova* and other radical publications were forced to close. The Italian anarchists went underground; Malatesta was under house arrest for the last five years of his life.

See also

Anarchist Press; Anarcho-Syndicalism; Bakunin, Mikhail A.; Italian Anarchism; Paris Commune of 1871

References

Bookchin, Murray, "Deep Ecology, Anarcho-syndicalism and the Future of Anarchist Thought" (1992), on the internet <http://www.lglobal.com/TAO/Freedom/book2.html>.

Horowitz, Irving L., *The Anarchists* (New York: Dell, 1964).

Malatesta, Errico, *Anarchy,* on the internet <ftp://etext.archive.umich.edu/pub/Politics/Spunk/anarchy_texts/writers/Malatest/Spunk415.txt>.

Wehling, Jason, "A Brief History of the American Anarchist Press" (March 1993), on the internet <http://www.teleport.com/~jwehling/APressHistory.html>.

Martí, José (1853–1895)

Known as the apostle of the Cuban revolutionary movement, José Martí was a poet and journalist who used his talents during the late 1800s to further the cause of *Cuba libre*—independence from Spanish rule. Although he never considered himself an anarchist, he was respected by many anarchists in Cuba, Europe, and the United States. Numerous Cuban and Spanish anarchists spread Martí's views on Cuban freedom.

José was born in Havana to Mariano and Leonor (Pérez) Martí of Spanish descent. His father worked as a tailor, providing a meager living for a family that included five sisters. Although the Martí family was not political, José was greatly influenced by Rafael Maria de Mendive, director of the Havana school. Mendive published pamphlets and propaganda against Spanish imperialism.

At 16 José was arrested and imprisoned for writing a letter to a friend criticizing him for joining the Spanish army. A Spanish judge convicted Martí of conspiracy. He was sentenced to six years in prison, but the sentence was changed to exile, and he was deported to Spain in 1871. During four years there he continued his education in law and the arts, became a rebel leader, and honed his rhetorical skills. From about 1874 to 1879 Martí spent his exile in Europe and in Mexico, where he met and married Carmen Zayas. The couple eventually had a daughter.

In 1879 Martí went to the United States and settled in New York, continuing to write and publish poetry and revolutionary articles and working for Cuban independence through the Cuban Revolutionary Party, which he initiated. From the time of the Ten Years War (1868–1878)—when Cubans fought for freedom but were overcome by the Spanish government—Cuban rebels had fled to the United States, settling in New York but particularly Florida. Martí helped organize Cuban exiles in Tampa, West Tampa, and Ybor City, Florida, uniting racial and labor factions to plan a war for Cuban independence. As he noted: "To all Cubans, whether they come from the continent where the sun scorches the skin, or from countries where the light is gentler, this will be the revolution in which all Cubans, regardless of color, have participated" (quoted in Greenbaum, 4).

Anarchists also joined Martí in the armed struggle for freedom that broke out in Cuba in 1895. In February of that year, Martí issued the *orden de levantamiento,* a manifesto calling for revolutionary action, which was delivered to rebels in Florida as well as to insurgent leaders in Cuba. A few months later, Martí was killed in the Cuban Revolutionary War, which did not end until 1898, when the United States intervened and defeated Spain in what is now called the Spanish-American War.

See also

Cuban Anarchism

References

Dolgoff, Sam, *The Cuban Revolution: A Critical Perspective* (Montreal: Black Rose Books, 1976).

Greenbaum, Susan, *Afro-Cubans in Ybor City: A Centennial History* (Tampa: University of South Florida, 1986).

Steffy, Joan Marie, *The Cuban Immigrants of Tampa, Florida, 1886–1898* (unpubl. thesis, University of South Florida, 1974).

Marx, Karl (1818–1883)

Karl Marx, along with lifelong collaborator Friedrich Engels, is generally credited with being the major theorist of modern socialism. He established the communist ideal or Marxism—scientific socialism as opposed to utopian theories.

Marx was born in Treves in the Rhine province of Prussia, where he was raised in a well-to-do, intellectual family of Jews who converted to the Protestant faith. His father was a lawyer, and Marx studied law, history, and philosophy in Bonn and Berlin, Germany. While earning his doctoral degree, Marx was strongly influenced by Ludwig Feuerbach and Bruno Bauer, and he joined the leftist Hegelian movement, at the time a group who tried to use Georg Wilhelm Hegel's ideas against organized religion and the Prussian autocracy. The Hegelians in their attempt to justify revolutionary action, gained converts throughout Germany's academic centers. Marx would eventually reject Hegel's idealism, but he had the ability to synthesize this tradition with the economic politics of Great Britain and the French socialist philosophy then gaining favor in the working class in Europe.

After receiving his doctorate in 1841, Marx edited *Rheinische Zeitung,* a newspaper established by a radical bourgeois group who opposed the feudal lords and wanted to protect their own economic interests. Under Marx's editorial direction, the newspaper became ever more radical in tone. He pointed out the terrible conditions of the working class and scornfully criticized the wealthy landowners who exploited peasants. In 1843 Marx was pressured to resign from the paper, and it soon ended publication. "Marx left the paper a completely transformed man." He had started as a "radical democrat, interested in the social and economic conditions of the peasantry. But he gradually became more and more absorbed in the study of the basic economic problems relating to the peasant question" (Riazanov). Marx left Germany and went to France with his wife, Jenny von Westphalen. In Paris, he and a fellow German published a radical magazine through which Marx began to formulate his basic communist philosophy.

In 1844 Marx met Friedrich Engels in Paris, and the two became good friends. Four years later they wrote the *Communist Manifesto,* a blueprint for the revolution, which they declared would eventually bring about the dictatorship of the proletariat. This work did not justify social change by citing natural law; instead it sought to use the evidence of historical imperative to argue that those who owned the means of production—the workers—would inherit the power.

When the revolutions of 1848 swept across Europe, Marx had high hopes that the working class would triumph. But the uprisings failed, and Marx was convinced that the solidarity of the working class could only come about through revolutionary parties.

In 1864 socialist organizations from across Europe met in London to establish the International Working Men's Association (IWMA). Karl Marx's personality dominated the First International, as it was known, from its inception, but not without a fight. In opposition to what he called Marx's authoritarian tendencies and policies, Mikhail Bakunin led a faction of anarchist-socialists in a fight for the heart and soul of the IWMA. Bakunin's critique of Marx's "dictatorship of the proletariat" as just another hierarchical structure that would lead to a corrupt form of government caused an irreparable rift among the participants. In reality, the mutualism and federalism philosophies of Proudhon—and Bakunin's ideal of the "collective" that grew from these—were the dominant themes of the eclectic organizations meeting in London at that time. In order for Marx to consolidate his personal power, and to redirect the mission of the First International to attain the status of a political party, he backed a campaign to malign Bakunin as a traitor to the cause of workingmen. Marx did rid the organization of the influence of the anarchists for that time, and he was able to establish a general council.

However, at the second congress the charges against Bakunin were completely repudiated, and Marx's plan to define a political structure out of the First International were rejected by the general membership. In defeat, Marx moved the general council to New York City, but without the support of the main European socialist groups and anarchists it ceased to be a power.

Yet Marx did not give up hope that revolution was at hand. Despite his dire poverty and having to seek refuge in the British Museum to write, he continued—with the support and some financial aid provided by his friend Engels—to work on his magnum opus, the voluminous *Das Kapital.* The work occupied much of his time over two decades, and the first volume of *Das Kapital* brought him some recognition. (Three other volumes were published after his death.) As one historian stated,

> It is the first volume of *Das Kapital,* and not the subsequent tomes, which plays such a unique role in socialist literature. . . . [It] has often been listed as one of the immortal classics of world literature at large. It has passages, pages, and chapters which no doubt will be "required reading" centuries hence as the best presentation of the inhuman methods by

> which the system of private capitalism came into existence and has maintained itself. (Nomad, 122)

Although *Das Kapital* and other works by Marx continue to be read and studied, Marx and Marxian theories generated great controversy before his death in 1883 and ever since. Communists see Marx as a hero. Some anarchists advocate various Marxist theories, whereas others, such as individualist anarchists, oppose Marxism altogether. Some scholars consider Marx a great economic theoretician, whereas others view him as someone who advocated the complete destruction of society.

See also

Anarchist-Communists; Bakunin, Mikhail A.; *Communist Manifesto*

References

Harper, Clifford, *Anarchy: A Graphic Guide* (London: Camden Press, 1987).

"N. Lenin, Karl Marx," *Granat Encyclopaedia,* 7th ed., vol. 28 (over the signature of V. Ilyin), on the internet <http://www.marx.org/Bio/Marx-Karl/Granat/1.htm>.

Nomad, Max, *Apostles of Revolution* (New York: Collier Books, 1961).

Riazanov, David, and Joshua Kunitz, trans., *Karl Marx and Frederick Engels: An Introduction to Their Lives and Work,* first published 1927, Monthly Review Press (1973), on the internet <http://www.marx.org/Riazanov/Archive/1927-Marx>.

"Socialism: MARX AND THE RISE OF SOCIAL DEMOCRACY: The Communist Manifesto," *Britannica Online* <http://www.eb.com:180/cgi-bin/g?DocF=macro/5007/6/4.html>.

Maximoff, Gregori Petrovich (1893–1950)

Gregori Petrovich Maximoff (or Maksimov) is listed among the famous anarcho-syndicalists who kept up a barrage of criticism against the Bolsheviks and Soviet government established after the revolutions in Russia during February and October 1917. He became a militant in the Russian trade unions, urging the formation of factory committees in place of unions, which, he declared, were too closely aligned with political parties, especially the Social Democrats. "Indeed, the influence of the parties on the unions is so strong that the unions merely imitate the parties, without attempting to create something new of their own," he wrote in 1917. He noted that "the factory committees, by contrast, are the product of the creativity of the working masses" (quoted in Avrich 1973, 73).

Maximoff was born and raised in the small peasant village of Mitushino, in the Russian province of Smolensk. Although there was an expectation that he would enter the priesthood upon completing his studies, he never realized that calling. Instead, he abandoned his theological degree to enter the Agricultural Academy in St. Petersburg. More important than establishing the basis for a career during this tenure, however, was his involvement in the student revolutionary movement at that time. Maximoff studied the works of Mikhail Bakunin and Peter Kropotkin and became an ardent propagandist.

After graduating as an agronomist in 1915, Maximoff was drafted into the army. But the Bolsheviks used the army for police work and to repress workers, and Maximoff could not abide this betrayal of the people he had learned to respect. Eventually, he simply refused to obey orders, prompting a court-martial and sentence of death. Steelworkers united and intervened, bringing about his release.

Maximoff joined the staff of *Golos Truda* (Voice of Labor), a journal of the Union of Russian Workers of the United States and Canada. The weekly originated in New York but was reestablished in the Russian capital when its editors, Vladimir Shatov and Vsevolod Mikhailovich Eikhenbaum (better known as Voline), returned to their homeland. The journal and, later, *Novy Golos Trouda* (New Voice of Labor), became the main organ for the Petrograd Union of Anarcho-Syndicalist Propaganda, which in 1917 adopted a manifesto calling for social and economic reconstruction, stating in part:

> The Anarcho-Syndicalists do not form a separate political party because they believe that the liberation of the working masses must be the task only of workers' and peasants' non-party organizations. They enter all such organizations and

> spread propaganda about their philosophy and their ideal of a stateless commune, which in essence merely represents the deepening and systematization of the beliefs and methods of struggle put forward by the working masses themselves. (quoted in Avrich 1973, 72)

Maximoff wrote numerous articles advocating anarcho-syndicalist principles and, along with Shatov and Voline, edited anarchist books published by *Golos Truda*. "The principal goal of the *Golas Truda* group was a revolution." They hoped to totally destroy the centralized state and replace it with worker committees, unions, and councils that were brought together in a free federation (Avrich, 140).

During the Kronstadt uprising in 1921, Maximoff and other anarchists were arrested and sent to a Moscow prison. They participated in an 11-day hunger strike, which led to an intervention by European syndicalists then attending a congress of the Red Trade Union International (the Profintern). The syndicalists negotiated with Bolshevik leader Vladimir Lenin to gain freedom for Maximoff and several of his colleagues, all of whom were later exiled from Russia.

While in exile Maximoff's first stop was Berlin, where he helped found a new workers' international known as the International Working Men's Association (IWMA), which took its name from the IWMA of 1864 (later known as the First International). A year later Maximoff went to Paris, and eventually he settled with his wife, Olga, in Chicago in 1926. He continued to edit syndicalist publications, including *Golos Truzhenika* (Worker's Voice) and later *Dielo Trouda-Probuzhdenie* (Labor's Cause-Awakening), which were widely read by Russian exiles. In 1933 he wrote his credo, clearly stating his belief that

> it behooves every honest man to urge the toiling masses not to let the flames of revolution be extinguished. On the contrary, their orbit should be widened, through a stimulated alertness and independence and the creation of free labour institutions. These should be of a type suitable to take into the workers' own hands, on the overthrow of capitalism, the organization of a free life upon the just principles of dignified work.
>
> I fully agree with the slogan of the First International: "The liberation of the workers must be the task of the workers themselves," and I believe in the class struggle as a powerful means to freedom. I believe that the proletariat is capable of attaining its full liberty only through revolutionary violence; that is, by direct action against capitalism and the state, and therefore I am a revolutionary.
>
> I believe that only a stateless form of society is compatible with human progress, and that only under such a form of commonwealth will humanity be able to attain full liberty, and therefore I am an anarchist.

Maximoff further stated his belief "that anarchy as a political form . . . is only feasible through the principle of federalisation," and that to obtain independence within a federation communes must be set up that strictly observe the "principle of the free individual. . . . Society has been established in order to satisfy the many and diverse needs of the human being, and these individual needs are by no means to be sacrificed to the community. Personality and its interests, and first of all its freedom, are the fundamentals of the new world of a free and creative society of workers." In Maximoff's view

> it is not enough to enjoy political liberty alone. In order to be free, in the real sense of the word, one must also be endowed with economic freedom. This kind of freedom, I am convinced, is unattainable without the abolition of private property and the organization of communal production on the basis of "from each according to his ability" and of communal consumption on the principle of "to each according to his needs."
>
> I believe that anarchism and communism are feasible on an international scale only, and I do not believe in them in one country alone. Therefore to my mind it is

> urgently necessary that the proletariat should be organised in the form of international producers' unions (or associations). I consider that only by direct action, based upon international proletarian solidarity, can the rule of the bourgeoisie and the state be overcome, and that only by the international of productive workers' unions can the moribund capitalist world be superseded. (Maximoff, "My Social Credo")

Maximoff's written works included several books, among them *The Guillotine at Work* and a compilation of Mikhail Bakunin's writings entitled *The Political Philosophy of Bakunin: Scientific Anarchism*. Although his time and influence in the cause of anarchism were short-lived—Maximoff died of heart disease in 1950—his personal impact upon those who had come to know him was great. As anarchist Rudolf Rocker noted, Maximoff "was not only a lucid thinker, but a man of stainless character and broad human understanding. And he was a whole person, in whom clarity of thought and warmth of feeling were united in the happiest way. He lived as an Anarchist, not because he felt some sort of duty to do so, imposed from outside, but because he could not do otherwise, for his innermost being always caused him to act as he felt and thought" (Rocker).

See also

Anarcho-Syndicalism; Bakunin, Mikhail A.; Direct Action; Eikhenbaum, V. M. (Voline); First International; Kropotkin, Peter Alexeyevich; Rocker, Rudolf

References

Avrich, Paul, *The Russian Anarchists* (New York: W. W. Norton, 1978).

Avrich, Paul, ed., *The Anarchists in the Russian Revolution* (Ithaca: Cornell University Press, 1973).

Maximoff, Gregori, "My Social Credo," on the internet <http://www.xchange.anarki.net/~huelga/credo.htm>.

Rocker, Rudolf, "Prominent Anarchists and Left-Libertarians," on the internet <http://www.tigerden.com/~berios/libertarians.html>.

May 1968

The 1960s were a time of rebellious actions in many countries as students followed the lead of American protesters agitating against U.S. involvement in Vietnam and of such Latin American revolutionaries as Fidel Castro and Che Guevara. Workers and students in France, some of whom called themselves anarchists, took part in an event known today as "May 1968."

Although in 1968 France was enjoying peace and prosperity after years of colonial wars in French Indochina and then Algeria, universities were overcrowded with a student population ten times greater than that before World War II. Students at the Sorbonne University began to protest overcrowded facilities, lack of access to teachers, and the inflexible rules and regulations established by university officials. Fearing violent confrontations, the rector of the Sorbonne suspended classes and called in police. When police arrested protesters, other students attacked the officers, who responded with tear gas and flailing batons, injuring hundreds. This escalated the confrontation.

Students built barricades and occupied the Sorbonne, creating a commune reminiscent of the Paris Commune of 1871. The unrest spread to other universities, and street fighting erupted. Then factory workers joined the fray with strike after strike. Eventually 10 million workers were on strike, paralyzing France for two weeks. The insurrection threatened the very existence of the nation, and the government soon initiated labor and political reforms. By fall students went back to school, and the revolutionary movement lost its momentum. Today, historians argue over whether the May 1968 uprising was truly a revolution, but the date is commemorated by many anarchists as an example of successful direct action and the relevance of anarcho-syndicalist ideas.

See also

Anarcho-Syndicalism; Guevara, Ernesto Che; Paris Commune of 1871

References

Associated Press, "France Fights Legacy of May '68," *New York Times* electronic version (April 29, 1998).

"Paris, May 1968," on the internet <http://128.100.124.81/library/exhibitions/posters>.

May Day

In many countries the first day of May is associated with worker and socialist causes. In these places, the secular May Day festival is Labor Day. The ultimate example of this modern holiday occurred in the Soviet Union. May Day was the time when all things "soviet" were on display and celebrated for the benefit of national pride and for its considerable international propaganda value. Although it is true that ancient Greek and Roman societies incorporated a May Day ritual as part of the spring season, this is not the precedent for the modern labor holiday. The Hellenistic tradition was a sacred honoring of the "great mother" and the rebirth of nature after the cold winter. This springtime celebration is still carried on in various parts of the globe where the Maypole, the May king and queen, and the carrying of garlands are often used to harken the pre-Christian fertility festivals.

The origin of the international labor day is much more recent, however. Peter J. McGuire, a founding member of the Knights of Labor, proposed a holiday honoring the American worker in New York. The first festival occurred in New York City when 10,000 laborers marched on September, 5, 1882. Two years later the American Federation of Trades and Labor Unions called for a general strike to attain an eight-hour workday. Action would begin on May Day 1886 in Chicago. At that time, the anarchist International Working People's Association (IWPA) urged workers to take to the streets in a demonstration against the increasing power of the owners of American industries such as steel, iron, and railroads. Since the mid-1870s so-called robber barons and capitalists had seen unparalleled profits from their enterprises, and labor was convinced that profits came on the backs of workers. The union's plan for the 1886 May Day rallies was to call for an end to the 12-hour shift. Their chant of the day was "eight hours for work, eight hours for sleep, and eight hours for what we will!"

On May 1, 1886, 80,000 people marched down Michigan Avenue in Chicago; the next day 30,000 gathered in Grant Park for a rally. When anarchist and labor leader August Spies spoke to a meeting of lumber workers the next day, he happened to be very close to the McCormick manufacturing plant where a strike was under way. The audience moved to that site after Spies's talk and a riot ensued. On May 4 a mass rally was called for Haymarket Square to discuss the previous day's events; this led to a major police assault and eventually the conviction and execution of Spies and others who became known as the Haymarket martyrs.

May Day 1889 was designated a worldwide labor day by the International Socialist Congress to remember the events at Haymarket and, more importantly, to honor the Haymarket martyrs. In the United States and Canada, Labor Day has been moved to September and disassociated with the socialist strife of the late 19th century. In other parts of the globe, however, May Day still retains some of its original intent. In Mexico, May 1 is actually celebrated as the Day of the Martyrs.

See also

Haymarket Affair; Haymarket Anarchists; International Working People's Association; Lingg, Louis; Parsons, Albert; Spies, August

References

Adelman, Bill, "Talk of the Nation" (National Public Radio) (April 30, 1998).

"United States of America: History: The Transformation of American Society, 1865–1900: Industrialization of the U.S. Economy," *Britannica Online* <http://www.eb.com:180/cgi-bin/g?DocF=macro/5006/47/94.html>.

Meltzer, Albert (1920–1996)

Anarcho-syndicalist Albert Meltzer declared that the least anyone could say about him was that he never gave up. For 60 years he was a class-struggle anarchist, and in his view anyone who did not want to destroy the class structure and form a stateless society could not rightly be called an anarchist.

Meltzer was born into a working-class family in London, and like many boys in the neighborhood he soon became streetwise. He began taking boxing lessons at 15 and claimed that his political views developed because of boxing, a sport that friend and fellow journalist-publisher Stuart Christie noted "made him a shrewd judge of opponents' strengths and weaknesses" (Christie). At his first anarchist meeting in 1935 Meltzer defended boxing against an opponent of the sport, well-known anarchist speaker Emma Goldman, who called Meltzer a "young hooligan" and a "rascal" with no understanding of anarchism. However, he soon became an outspoken participant at anarchist meetings. As a young adult Meltzer earned a living as a fairground promoter, theater manager, and warehouseman. Later he was a bookseller, typesetter, and eventually copy taker for the *Daily Telegraph*.

Whatever his occupation, his commitment to anarchism continued throughout his life. During the Spanish Civil War, which began in 1936, he helped smuggle arms to anarcho-syndicalists who hoped to bring about a social revolution, and he was the contact for the Spanish anarchist intelligence service.

During the late 1940s Meltzer championed "anarchism as a revolutionary working class movement," which led to conflict with numerous groups. "Many otherwise politically incompatible people were drawn to anarchism because of its militant tolerance. Albert was vehemently opposed to the repackaging of anarchism as a broad church for academia-oriented quietists and single issue pressure groups" (Christie).

Meltzer often argued vituperatively against those he declared were not true anarchists. In *Anarchism: Arguments For and Against,* he wrote:

> bourgeois academics borrow the name "Anarchism" to give expression to their own liberal philosophies or, alternatively, picking up their cue from journalists, assorted objects of their dislike. For some professors and teachers, "Anarchism" is anything from Tolstoyism to the IRA, from drug-taking to militant-trade unionism, from nationalism to bolshevism, from the hippy cult to Islamic fundamentalism, from the punk scene to violent resistance to almost anything! This is by no means an exaggeration but a sign of academic illiteracy, to be distinguished from journalists who in the 1960s obeyed a directive to call anything Marxist-Leninist that involved action as "Anarchist" and anything Anarchist as "nationalist." (Meltzer)

During the 1960s, Meltzer edited *Cuddon's Cosmopolitan Review,* a satirical magazine addressing cultural as well as political issues. In 1967 Meltzer and Stuart Christie, who had been imprisoned for running arms to anarchists in Spain, founded the Anarchist Black Cross (ABC), an organization that has supported jailed anarchists and political prisoners worldwide. The following year, the two began publishing the ABC's monthly *Bulletin,* which later became *Black Flag,* providing information on the international anarchist movement. Since ABC was founded, various local branches have been set up throughout Great Britain and in other countries.

Meltzer also was a major contributor to the Kate Sharpley Library, named for a World War I anarchist and antimilitary activist. The library, which consists of donations from the private collections of anarchists, is in Northamptonshire, England, and includes several thousand publications—books, pamphlets, newspapers, journals, flyers, essays, and unpublished manuscripts—in more than 20 languages.

Among Meltzer's published works are *The Floodgates of Anarchy,* written with Stuart Christie, *The Anarchists in London,* and his 1995 autobiography *I Couldn't Paint Golden Angels.* In the latter work, Meltzer declared that he wanted "to die in dignity" but expected to have a jovial funeral. He advised people to throw "snowballs if in season (tomatoes if not)"; and "should anyone of a religious mind offer pieces of abstract consolation they should be prepared to dodge pieces of concrete confrontation" (quoted in Coull).

Meltzer died of a stroke in 1996, but his life has been commemorated with an anarchist imprint, the Albert Meltzer Press. Fifty percent of the profits from the publishing house go to the Kate Sharpley Library.

See also

Anarchist Black Cross; Anarcho-Syndicalism; Spanish Civil War

References

Christie, Stuart, "Albert Meltzer—Anarchy's Torchbearer," *The Guardian* (May 8, 1996).

Coull, Dave, "Albert Meltzer's Funeral," on the internet (May 1996) <http://calvin.pitzer.edu/~dward/anarchy/rebelworker/funeral.html>.

Meltzer, Albert, *Anarchism: Arguments For and Against,* on the internet <http://spunk.etext.org/library/writers/meltzer/sp001500.html>.

Michel, Louise (1830–1905)

Anarchist Louise Michel believed that the entire social structure had to be torn down and rebuilt. She maintained that a new society without government, in which justice and love prevailed, could be set up with small groups contributing to the general good, the needs of all being supplied from a public store. She was a participant in the Paris Commune of 1871 and became known for her revolutionary zeal and her passionate struggle for women's rights. She contended that career women should reject marriage, as she herself did, which earned her the sobriquet "the Red Virgin."

Louise was born out of wedlock at the Chateau de Vroncourt; Michel's father was said to be a member of the aristocracy, her mother was one of his servants. Shortly after Michel's birth, her father left the chateau, and she was raised by her mother and grandparents. The latter provided her with a comfortable lifestyle and a liberal education at a boarding school in Chaumont. There she "began to write poetry, focusing upon nature and freedom as literary themes—as she would continue to do during her later anarchist experience in the 1880s and 1890s" (Varias, 68).

Trained as a teacher, Michel rejected her first offer as a schoolmistress because the position required that she pledge allegiance to Napoleon III. But in 1853 she opened a libertarian or free school with an emphasis on students learning to think for themselves, first in the village of Audeloncourt, then two years later in Millieures. She was forced to close the schools because of police harassment, and eventually she went to Paris. There she began her revolutionary career, becoming part of the Paris Commune of 1871, fighting with the National Guard to defend the commune against the Versailles government troops. The commune was put down within a short time, and about 50,000 were arrested, Michel among them. At her trial she demanded to be shot, saying, "Since it seems as if every heart that beats for liberty has only the right to a little lead, I too demand my share" (O'Carroll). Instead, she was deported with about 4,500 others to the remote islands of New Caledonia, a French colony in the southwestern Pacific.

While in New Caledonia Michel met and became friends with Charles Malato; both became anarchists, influenced in part by the rebellion of colonists against French imperialism. The two believed that "they had witnessed important episodes in the historic universal struggle for freedom" which would help bring about a revolution that would be global in scope (Varias, 69–70).

When Michel and Malato were released in 1880, they returned to Paris; Michel lectured throughout France. She was arrested and imprisoned again in 1883 for inciting a riot, but her reputation was greatly enhanced as a revolutionary. Between 1886 and 1896 she lived in London and opened a free school. However, police closed the school, charging that they had discovered bomb-making equipment in the basement, although Louise Michel was not implicated (Shotton, 33–35). She returned to France and conducted lecture tours until her death.

See also
Paris Commune of 1871

References
O'Carroll, Aileen, "The Paris Commune" (a talk presented October 1993), on the internet <http://flag.blackened.net/revolt/talks/paris.html>.
Shotton, John, *No Master High or Low: Libertarian Education and Schooling, 1890–1990* (Bristol: Libertarian Education, 1993).
Varias, Alexander, *Paris and the Anarchists: Aesthetes and Subversives During the Fin de Siècle* (New York: St. Martin's Press, 1996).

Modern School Movement

Since the beginning of the 20th century, modern or alternative schools have been a component of the anarchist movement. Students, teachers, and parents self-manage such schools, rejecting the authoritarian educational systems established by the state or church. Even before the 1900s, however, libertarian forms of education were promoted by earlier anarchists such as

William Godwin, Pierre-Joseph Proudhon, and Mikhail Bakunin.

The modern school movement in the United States stems from the ideas of anarchist martyr Francisco Ferrer y Guardia of Spain. Beginning in 1901 with his first school, Escuela Moderna, Ferrer established a number of private, progressive schools in Spain. He believed that education should be free of church and state authority, and his network of schools was an alternative to the church-controlled education, a system operated by clerics who emphasized rote instruction and discipline. Ferrer's schools were coeducational and democratic; class attendance was voluntary.

After Ferrer was accused of insurrection and executed in 1909, a group of about two dozen anarchists in the United States under the leadership of Emma Goldman and Alexander Berkman founded the Francisco Ferrer Association. Goldman had no use for an authoritarian educational system that had little, if any, regard for personal freedom and original thought. In her view, the school system was "for the child what the prison is for the convict and the barracks for the soldier—a place where everything is being used to break the will of the child, and then to pound, knead, and shape it into a being utterly foreign to itself" (quoted in Schulman, 116).

The Francisco Ferrer Association supported a cultural center and day school in New York with "a threefold purpose: to publish and disseminate Ferrer's works, to organize memorial meetings on the first anniversary of his death, and to establish Modern Schools in cities throughout the country to be administered by local branches of the Ferrer Association," according to Fernanda Perrone, who arranged and described a special collection of modern school manuscripts for Rutgers University Libraries.

The Ferrer Center and Modern School in New York opened in 1911 and became an important center for libertarians, anarchists, and other radicals. Among those associated with the school were author and popular philosopher Will Durant, artist Max Weber, authors Jack London and Upton Sinclair, feminist Margaret Sanger, and labor organizer Elizabeth Gurley Flynn. Because of political upheavals and an unintentional bombing nearby that was actually planned for anarchist enemy John D. Rockefeller Jr., the center eventually moved to Stelton, New Jersey. But it served as a model for other schools established in cities across the United States, including Chicago, Salt Lake City, Seattle, and Los Angeles. Most of the schools closed within a few years, but the schools at Stelton and at Mohegan, New York, operated for decades. The latter two were part of anarchist colonies committed to racial and sexual equality and educational freedom.

Most modern schools had no formal curriculum, and students pursued hands-on learning such as painting, metalwork, printing, and handcrafts and often went on outdoor expeditions. Attendance was voluntary. Such free schools began to fade from the scene during World War II, but a few continued until the late 1950s. During the 1960s libertarian schools appeared once more across the United States, some established under the guidance of alumni of modern schools. Such alumni still meet on a yearly basis to recall old times.

See also

Bakunin, Mikhail A.; Berkman, Alexander; Ferm, Alexis and Elizabeth; Flynn, Elizabeth Gurley; Proudhon, Pierre-Joseph; Stelton School and Colony

References

Avrich, Paul, *Anarchist Voices: An Oral History of Anarchism in America* (Princeton: Princeton University Press, 1988).

Avrich, Paul, *The Modern School Movement: Anarchism and Education in the United States* (Princeton: Princeton University Press, 1980).

Bookchin, Murray, "Francisco Ferrer's Modern School," excerpt from *The Spanish Anarchists,* on the internet <http://flag.blackened.net/revolt/spain/ferrer.html.

Perrone, Fernanda, "History of the Modern School of Stelton," Special Collections and University Archives, Rutgers University Libraries, on the internet <http://www.libraries.rutgers.edu/rulib/spcol/modern.htm>.

Shulman, Alix Kates, ed., *Red Emma Speaks: Selected Writings and Speeches by Emma Goldman* (New York: Random House, 1972).

Sonn, Richard D., *Anarchism* (New York: Twayne/Macmillan, 1992).

Veysey, Laurence, *The Communal Experience: Anarchist and Mystical Counter-Cultures in America* (New York: Harper and Row, 1973).

Montseny, Federica

See Confederación Nacional del Trabajo

Most, Johann (1846–1906)

A German immigrant and anarcho-communist, Johann Most came to the United States at a time when Germans made up a large portion of organized labor. In fact, his arrival in the United States in 1882 was a triumph for New York City's German workers, many of whom had been part of socialist movements in their homeland.

Johann Most was born in Augsburg, Bavaria. His mother had once been a governess, and his father was a copyist in a legal office, earning barely enough to provide a living. At the age of seven, Hans, as he was called, suffered an infection of the jawbone, and after botched treatments part of his jaw had to be removed to save his life. The surgery left him permanently disfigured.

Johann's mother died when he was nine; his father later remarried. His stepmother treated Johann cruelly, adding to the misery already endured due to his misshapen face. Throughout most of his childhood, Johann was taunted and jeered because of his disfigurement, but as an adult he was able to cover his jaw with a beard.

A rebel at an early age, Most organized a strike against a brutal teacher and was expelled from school, which prevented him from becoming a member of the educated middle class. As a result he had to learn a trade, and at 15 he became an apprentice to a bookbinder. When he was 17 he set out to find work, walking from city to city as was the custom. He traveled across Germany, Austria, Switzerland, and northern Italy, but he was often rebuffed and told that his face would repel customers. "Such humiliations . . . filled him with bitterness which was to pervade his whole life," one historian wrote. That bitterness "found its expression in a fanatical hatred of the privileged classes. In his later years, when all hope was gone, it took the shape of an all-embracing contempt for the human race" (Nomad, 258).

In 1867 Most joined the Swiss branch of the International Working Men's Association and became a zealous organizer and protester against injustices in the economic system. Most left Switzerland in 1868 and went to Vienna, Austria, where he became a popular speaker at workers' meetings. His invective against the privileged and ruling classes brought on the wrath of authorities, and Most landed in jail for a month. His continued agitation in Austria brought another prison term in 1870.

Most was expelled from Austria in 1871, but he went to Berlin and became active with the German socialist movement. In 1874, on the third anniversary of the Paris Commune of 1871, Most delivered a speech praising the group, which hoped to establish a society organized from the bottom up by workers. His speech prompted another arrest and a two-year jail term. After his release in 1876, the ruling authorities in Germany began a campaign to suppress all socialist activities, and Most heeded the advice of friends to emigrate to London to escape further arrests.

In 1879, with the support of radical workers, Most founded a socialist newspaper, *Die Freiheit* (Freedom). The paper, published in London, was smuggled into Germany for circulation among workers, and it became ever more strident in its revolutionary tone. In 1881 Most published a passionate editorial calling for the assassination of the Russian tsar, Alexander II. The editorial created adverse public opinion in England and made arrest a certainty. Most once again served a prison term—this time for 16 months. Upon his release he received an invitation to come to the United States for a lecture tour. In his most famous speech, "The Beast of Property," delivered in 1884, Most declared,

> The richer a man, the greater his greed for more. We may call such a monster the "beast of property." It now rules the world, making mankind miserable, and gains in cruelty and voracity with the progress of our so called "civilization." This monster we will in the following characterize and recommend to extermination.
>
> Look about ye! In every so-called "civilized" country there are among every 100 men about 95 more or less destitute and about 5 money-bags.

> It is unnecessary to trace all the sneaking ways by which they have gained their possessions. The fact that they own ALL, while the others exist, or rather vegetate merely, admits of no doubt, that these few have grown rich at the expense of the many. Either by direct brute force, by cunning, or by fraud, this horde has from time to time seized the soil with all its wealth. The laws of inheritance and entail, and the changing of hands, have lent a venerable color to this robbery, and consequently mystified and erased the character of such actions. For this reason the "beast of property" is not fully recognized, but is, on the contrary, worshipped with a holy awe.

For more than a decade, Most spread his revolutionary ideas—"propaganda by deed"—wherever he could in the United States. One of his followers was a young Russian immigrant, Emma Goldman, who became a well-known anarchist in the United States. When Most discovered Goldman's talent for oratory, he arranged for her to become a spokesperson for the anarchist cause. Most also shared a flat in New York City with Goldman and three other comrades.

Most reestablished *Freiheit* in New York and hoped to ignite a terrorist movement that would intimidate if not destroy the ruling class. Most urged workers to use force to free themselves from oppression. This was part of his message at the Pittsburgh Congress of anarchists, which he helped organize in the fall of 1883. That year he founded the International Working People's Association, which he hoped would bring together various anarchist factions, but after only five years the organization was crushed by authorities.

At first authorities looked on Most as a harmless zealot, but that view changed when anarchists began to agitate for an eight-hour workday and Most urged workers to arm themselves with guns, bombs, and other weapons. Most was arrested in 1886 and convicted of holding an unlawful assembly. He served a one-year prison term on Blackwell's Island, a penitentiary where other anarchists were also imprisoned.

Most was also jailed in 1891 because of an impassioned speech he gave denouncing the execution of the Chicago martyrs who were convicted of murdering police officers during the notorious Haymarket affair. About the time Most was released in 1892, Alexander Berkman followed a bomb-making pamphlet written by Most to assemble a device intended to kill Henry Clay Frick, head of the Carnegie Steel Company. Anarchists hated Frick because he had ordered a malicious attack on strikers in Homestead, Pennsylvania.

Although Berkman's experiment failed, Most's pamphlet as well as his articles telling readers how to manufacture nitroglycerine could be and were considered efforts to incite violence. But Most apparently did not expect people to take him literally. When Berkman went to Frick's office and tried unsuccessfully to shoot him, Most denounced Berkman and his attempt to kill the industrialist. This infuriated numerous anarchists, including Emma Goldman, who had once looked to Most as her mentor. Most attempted to justify his views by saying he no longer found terrorism an effective way to advance the revolutionary movement.

Most continued publishing *Freiheit,* but circulation steadily declined, and he had to earn a living as an editor of a German daily newspaper in Buffalo, New York. He left after a short time and returned to New York City; he was in New York when President William McKinley was assassinated by self-described anarchist Leon Czolgosz. On the day Czolgosz shot McKinley, Most's *Freiheit* reprinted an article often used as a filler by German-American radical newspapers. The article, by a then-deceased revolutionary, urged readers to "save humanity through blood and iron, poison and dynamite!" (Nomad, 296). That article led to one more arrest and a year of imprisonment.

Most spent his last years trying to keep his newspaper going, but he had to mount a speaking tour to keep it afloat. He was on such a tour in 1906 when he became ill and died at age 60 in Cincinnati.

See also

Berkman, Alexander; Czolgosz, Leon; Goldman, Emma; Haymarket Affair; Paris Commune of 1871; Pittsburgh Manifesto

References

Goldman, Emma, *Living My Life,* 2 vols. (New York: Knopf, 1933, reprint New York: Dover, 1970).

Jacker, Corinne, *The Black Flag of Anarchy: Antistatism in the United States* (New York: Charles Scribner's Sons, 1968).

Most, Johann, "The Beast of Property," on the internet <http://www.fyi.net/~basemans/beast.html>.

Nomad, Max, *Apostles of Revolution* (New York: Collier Books, 1961).

Mother Earth

See Goldman, Emma

Mujeres Libres

During the Spanish Civil War (1936–1939), militant women who were active in the Spanish anarcho-syndicalist movement formed Mujeres Libres (Free Women), mobilizing more than 20,000 women to liberate and empower themselves as well as build a sense of community. Even before the revolution in Spain, groups of women had attempted to change the inferior status of women not only within the general society but also within such organizations as the Federación Ibérica de Juventudes Libertarias (FIJL), an anarchist youth group, and the Confederación Nacional del Trabajo (CNT) or National Confederation of Labor. Although anarchists believe that men and women should interact as equals, women were seldom treated with respect and were in many cases expected to maintain their "proper" roles as wives and mothers.

Professor Martha Ackelsberg, an expert on women's political activism, interviewed numerous men and women in the Spanish anarchist movement and found that views on male-female relationships ranged from "acceptance of women's secondary status" to "insistence that women were the equals of men and ought to be treated as such in all social institutions." However, most of the women interviewed complained that male anarchists, no matter how committed they were to the cause, "expected to be 'masters' in their homes" (Ackelsberg, 89).

Mujeres Libres actually began as two factions, one in Barcelona and the other in Madrid. In Barcelona, a group of women anarchists began in 1934 to work toward a more active role for women within the CNT and the anarcho-syndicalist movement. They organized networks of women anarchists and attempted to deal with sexist behavior through direct action, such as educational and propaganda tours to explain that men did not have the right to rule over women and that women should be independent.

In Madrid three anarchist women were instrumental in establishing Mujeres Libres—Lucía Sánchez Saornil, a poet; Mercedes Comaposada, a lawyer; and Amparo Poch y Gasecón, a physician. Together they edited the journal *Mujeres Libres,* first published in May 1936 and designed to raise women's consciousness about the subordination and economic exploitation of women and to encourage social action. The journal was popular across the country and read by many working-class women, spurring some to activism.

Mujeres Libres became an official federation—the National Federation of Mujeres Libres—in 1937, and through its newspaper strongly advocated the freedom of women from ignorance, subservient roles, and gender-based discrimination in the workplace. The organization, however, rejected feminism, a theory they believed was bent on setting up a female hierarchy in place of male domination. One of the primary campaigns of the organization was literacy, which would help women gain self-confidence and take part in the movement to change society. Mujeres Libres also conducted numerous projects to help women become skilled workers and to obtain well-paying occupations previously reserved for men. In addition, the organization ran clinics and hospitals to meet the specific medical needs of women.

During the Spanish Civil War, which began in July 1936, Mujeres Libres worked with anarcho-syndicalists and other groups to bring about the dream of an egalitarian society while fighting to preserve the Spanish republic against nationalists—military leaders, the aristocracy, and fascists. Anarchists and other activists took over factories and government buildings, organized democratic militias (without a ranking structure), established rural collectives, set up communal kitchens and arranged other means to feed people, and transformed educational facilities into free institutions. Activities of anarchists, including Mujeres Libres, were quashed when nationalists, with the help of German and Italian fascists, won out in 1939, ushering in the dictatorship of General Francisco Franco. With Franco in power until his death in 1975, a rigid, centralized government supported by the Catholic Church was set up; many anarchists were imprisoned or executed. Some found safety in France and Mexico. Mujeres Libres, however, left a legacy that many anarchists would like to emulate, demonstrating the effects of direct action and the importance of the individual in communities.

See also

Anarcho-Syndicalism; Spanish Anarchism; Spanish Civil War

References

Ackelsberg, Martha A., *Free Women of Spain: Anarchism and the Struggle for the Emancipation of Women* (Bloomington: Indiana University Press, 1991).

Sonn, Richard D., *Anarchism* (New York: Twayne/Macmillan, 1992).

Mutualism

Mutualism is the term coined by Pierre-Joseph Proudhon to describe his philosophy of revolutionary economic reordering. Mutualism equaled anarchism for Proudhon. The name derives from a secret society of weavers in the city of Lyon, France, who called themselves the Mutualists. Proudhon was swept up in the citywide movement to establish workers' associations to run local factories when he arrived to take a position at a water transport company. This new style of revolutionary thought, with its emphasis on economic goals rather than violent overthrow of government structures, was in line with Proudhon's own philosophy of change. He would never support the replacement of one form of dictatorship for another.

See also

Proudhon, Pierre-Joseph

N

Neebe, Oscar

See Haymarket Anarchists

New England Labor Reform League

In 1869 two antistatists, William Bradford Greene—who had long been influenced by Pierre-Joseph Proudhon's mutual banking and labor reform ideas—and Ezra Heywood—a strong individualist anarchist who was affected by worker unrest after the American Civil War—helped establish the New England Labor Reform League (NELRL). Greene and Heywood drafted the League's Declaration of Sentiments, which essentially championed free speech, free credit, free markets, and free land as well as equality for women.

NELRL was supported by other anarchist-individualists of the time, such as Lysander Spooner, Stephen Pearl Andrews, Benjamin Tucker, and Josiah Warren. In 1873 Greene became vice president. From the NELRL grew the American Labor Reform League, founded in 1871 and led by anarchists for more than two decades.

See also

Greene, William Bradford; Heywood, Ezra Hervey Hoar; Individualist Anarchists; Mutualism; Proudhon, Pierre-Joseph; Spooner, Lysander; Tucker, Benjamin R.; Warren, Josiah

References

Avrich, Paul, *Anarchist Portraits* (Princeton: Princeton University Press, 1988).

Jacker, Corinne, *The Black Flag of Anarchy: Antistatism in the United States* (New York: Charles Scribner's Sons, 1968).

New England Non-Resistant Society

The New England Non-Resistant Society (NRS) was formed in 1838 by abolitionist and antistatist William Lloyd Garrison and several friends who shared his views. Their philosophy "was anarchistic in the sense that it visualized the destruction of all human law and government as well as all human authority and the construction of a new order in which the individual enjoyed absolute freedom" (Schuster, 70–71).

Members of the society, never more than 200, were primarily religious anarchists—Christian anarchists—who maintained that people should be guided by the love of God and that God's laws as laid out in the Golden Rule and the Sermon on the Mount replaced civil laws. Human government was wrong, they argued, because it was based on violence and the dominion of certain humans—such as lawmakers, police, and similar officials—over other humans.

Although NRS members differed on many issues, they held basic principles in common. They would not vote or hold public office, and they were adamantly opposed to slavery, capital punishment, and war. They believed that a new society based on brotherhood would be formed if people followed their principles. Their views were disseminated through *Non-Resistance*—published twice a month for about three and a half years—other publications, and lectures.

NRS met stiff criticism throughout its 11-year existence (being branded as "anti-God" and "incendiary"). Opponents were convinced that the existing order was "not only divine but necessary. They were afraid to trust human nature . . . to live by the Golden Rule. Others feared nonresistance, because the absence of government to them meant chaos, disorder, bloodshed, and the destruction of the family" (Schuster, 74). Such constant criticism and then the onset of the Civil War contributed to the disintegration of the society. Most members were unable to publicly justify their stance against war, as they were abolitionists, and the impending armed conflict would settle the issue of slavery in America. By 1849 the society dissolved. Yet nonresistance as a philosophy has surfaced since then in movements led by Leo Tolstoy in Russia, Mohandas Gandhi in India, and Martin Luther King Jr. in the United States.

See also

Gandhi, Mohandas "Mahatma" Karamchand; Religious Anarchism; Tolstoy, Count Lev (Leo) Nikolayevich

References

Jacker, Corinne, *The Black Flag of Anarchy: Antistatism in the United States* (New York: Charles Scribner's Sons, 1968).

Schuster, Eunice M., *Native American Anarchism: A Study of Left-Wing American Individualism* (Northampton, MA: Smith College, 1932, reprint New York: AMS Press, 1970).

New Left

During the 1960s and 1970s anarchist ideas—which had faded into the background after the 1917 Russian Revolution and were suppressed in Spain after the Civil War of 1936–1939—reemerged worldwide. Student activists and other radical groups, inspired by older philosophers such as Peter Kropotkin and anarchist critiques of Karl Marx's theories, rose in dissent, opposing the established political, social, and economic orders. Most opposition came from middle-class youths in a movement of radical activists advocating revolutionary changes. Dubbed the "New Left," the movement was felt in Asia, Europe, and the Americas.

Antiauthoritarian and anarchist books, magazines, and newspapers appeared, such as the British *New Left Review* (its first issue was published in 1960), and *Anarchy,* established in 1961. British-based Freedom Press, founded in England in 1886, continued to publish magazines, pamphlets, and books on anarchist theory and anarchist propaganda as counterculture interest in anarchist ideas increased during the 1960s.

Because of the New Left movement and focus on anarchist views during the 1960s and 1970s, commercial publishers in Britain and other European countries as well as in North America issued many books about anarchists and radicals, including such figures as Mikhail Bakunin, Dorothy Day, Mohandas Gandhi, Emma Goldman, Peter Kropotkin, Errico Malatesta, Pierre-Joseph Proudhon, Rudolf Rocker, Lysander Spooner, and many others.

During the early 1960s sit-downs were also common. In Great Britain, the Committee of 100, for example, staged protests against nuclear arms. The "Committee of 100 was an illustration of the kind of politics pointed to by the New Left—and which of course had always been advocated by anarchists: an ad hoc spontaneous organization, unhampered by an authoritarian structure, applying direct action for change" (in Apter and Joll, 87).

Student activism in the United States during the 1960s focused on support for civil rights for blacks and on opposition to the Vietnam War. Much of the direct action taken by students was initiated by the Student Nonviolent Coordinating Committee (SNCC), formed in 1960 in Raleigh, North Carolina, to stage sit-in demonstrations for civil rights. Not long afterward, a small group of northern students joined SNCC efforts by founding Students for a Democratic Society (SDS). In 1962 SDS, which had about 800 members, met in Port Huron, Michigan, to write its founding principles, a manifesto that became known as the Port Huron Statement. It called for a New Left "with real intellectual skills, committed to deliberativeness, honesty, reflection as working tools." Furthermore, the manifesto, written primarily by Tom Hayden, outlined the way the New Left would work through the university:

> A new left must be distributed in significant social roles throughout the country. The universities are distributed in such a manner.
>
> A new left must consist of younger people who matured in the postwar world,

> and partially be directed to the recruitment of younger people. The university is an obvious beginning point.
>
> A new left must include liberals and socialists, the former for their relevance, the latter for their sense of thoroughgoing reforms in the system. The university is a more sensible place than a political party for these two traditions to begin to discuss their differences and look for political synthesis.
>
> A new left must start controversy across the land, if national policies and national apathy are to be reversed. The ideal university is a community of controversy, within itself and in its effects on communities beyond.
>
> A new left must transform modern complexity into issues that can be understood and felt close up by every human being. It must give form to the feelings of helplessness and indifference, so that people may see the political, social, and economic sources of their private troubles, and organize to change society. In a time of supposed prosperity, moral complacency, and political manipulation, a new left cannot rely on only aching stomachs to be the engine force of social reform. The case for change, for alternatives that will involve uncomfortable personal efforts, must be argued as never before. The university is a relevant place for all of these activities. (Hayden)

As U.S. war efforts continued, SDS tactics became increasingly confrontational and radical; a more violent SDS faction, the Weather Underground, emerged, its members often involved in terrorist acts. As a result, authorities cracked down on students, and in 1970 the National Guard confronted protesters at Kent State University in Ohio; the guardsmen shot into a crowd of students, injuring dozens and killing four. Not long afterward many colleges and universities across the nation were shut down because of student and faculty protests.

Authorities also confronted other radical groups such as the Black Panthers and the Youth International Party (the Yippies), the latter led by Abbie Hoffman, whose "radicalism was of deed, not word." As Eric Foner wrote in the foreword to a Hoffman biography, "Unlike the authors of SDS's Port Huron Statement, Abbie Hoffman had little interest in offering a blueprint for a new society." Instead, "Hoffman challenged the way the Left had traditionally communicated with a mass constituency, introducing humor, theatricality, and studied irreverence into the repertoire of protest" (quoted in Raskin, xiv).

All of those characteristics were present at the so-called Chicago conspiracy trial in 1969. Several defendants—known as the Chicago Eight—were on trial for actions during the riots during the 1968 Democratic National Convention: Hoffman and Hayden of SDS; Rennie Davis, coordinator for the National Mobilization to End the War in Vietnam; longtime leftist and antiwar activist David Dellinger; Yippies cofounder Jerry Rubin; John Froines and Lee Weiner, antiwar academicians; and Bobbie Seale of the Black Panthers. The Chicago Eight were charged with planning and leading violent demonstrations and clashing with police. In indicting these eight, the federal government "planned to portray all those fighting to end racism, injustice, and the war in Vietnam as part of a deeper, darker conspiracy. The government hoped for a Soviet-style show trail, one that would paint the entire Left as anti-American and show Americans that these leading activists were mere criminals" (Hoffman and Simon, 120). Although the defendants were acquitted of the conspiracy charges, Hoffman, Rubin, Dellinger, Davis, and Hayden were convicted of crossing state lines to incite a riot; all the convictions were later thrown out by an appeals court. Years later, files released through the Freedom of Information Act showed that in numerous instances the judge in the case, Julius Hoffman (no relation to Abbie Hoffman), "had acted as an FBI operative" at the trial (Hoffman and Simon, 146; see also Jezer, 200).

Throughout the 1970s, agents of the Federal Bureau of Investigation and other law enforcement officers infiltrated New Left groups, gathering information and even trying to provoke illegal actions so that activists could be arrested. High costs of legal defense helped bring about the demise of the New Left movement, as did the end of the Vietnam War, a central rallying issue.

See also

Bakunin, Mikhail A.; Day, Dorothy; Gandhi, Mohandas "Mahatma" Karamchand; Goldman, Emma; Kropotkin, Peter Alexeyevich; Malatesta, Errico; Marx, Karl; Proudhon, Pierre-Joseph; Rocker, Rudolf; Spanish Civil War; Spooner, Lysander

References

Apter, David Ernest, and James Joll, eds., *Anarchism Today* (Garden City, NY: Doubleday and Company, 1971).

Hayden, Tom, "Port Huron Statement," on the internet <http://207.229.128.100/tribe/insiders/huron.html>.

Jezer, Marty, *Abbie Hoffman: American Rebel* (New Brunswick, NJ: Rutgers University Press, 1992).

Miller, James, *"Democracy Is in the Streets": From Port Huron to the Siege of Chicago* (New York: Simon and Schuster, 1987).

Raskin, Jonah, *For the Hell of It: The Life and Times of Abbie Hoffman* (Berkeley: University of California Press, 1996).

Noyes, John Humphrey (1811–1886)

One of the well-known individualist and religious anarchists in the United States during the 19th century was John Humphrey Noyes, who founded a doctrine called "perfectionism"—attaining perfect love with God. Many radicals became followers, among them Christian anarchist and abolitionist William Lloyd Garrison.

John Noyes was born in Brattleboro, Vermont, where his father was a successful merchant and part of the elite. For two years, the elder Noyes was a U.S. representative, but he retired at an early age and settled his family in Putney, Vermont. John was educated in private schools and at 15 enrolled in Dartmouth College. He graduated with high honors and joined his brother-in-law's law firm. However, after a prolonged revival meeting in Putney, he claimed to be converted and decided to become a minister. He attended Andover Theological Seminary for a year; he found the school too conservative and transferred to Yale. He began to preach and write about his belief that an individual could attain perfection on Earth and after salvation could not fall from grace. In his view, a person should be guided by inner convictions, not the authority of the church.

Noyes converted several family members to his cause, and for several years he traveled throughout the Northeast delivering his message and seeking other converts. In 1838 he married one of them, Harriet A. Holton, who helped him gather an informal association of followers. As his followers increased, Noyes established an anarcho-communistic society in which participation was entirely voluntary. About three dozen people, including nine children, joined the group; they supported themselves by operating a store and two farms, which were part of an inheritance Noyes received from his father. Three households were set up, and according to researcher Maren Lockwood Carden, members of the community "voted unanimously for the 'theocratic' government of John Noyes, who allowed no opposition to his doctrines or to his organization of the three households. Even his sisters submitted to his choice of husbands for them" (Carden, 19).

The group remained intact for about four more years, during which Noyes developed his ideas about complex marriage based on his interpretation of a biblical statement: "In the resurrection they are neither married nor given in marriage" (Matthew 22:30). Although most biblical scholars understand the verse to mean that resurrected people are sexless, Noyes claimed just the opposite. In his view, the biblical verse referred to an ideal system of marriage in which everyone is equally loved and all men are married to all women. In the afterlife, monogamous marriage did not exist. According to his doctrine, any man and woman might freely cohabitate, provided there was mutual consent.

Along with his system of complex marriage, Noyes advocated "male continence"—a practice of self-control during which the male interrupts sexual intercourse in order to prevent pregnancy. This practice developed because Noyes was opposed to "random procreation" but favored what he called "scientific propagation," whereby sexual relationships were governed to produce "spiritually superior" people.

The community at Putney began to experiment with Noyes's ideas, which brought a great deal of condemnation and hostility from neighbors and others in the "outside" world. In 1847 Noyes was arrested for the illegal marriage system practiced at Putney. Before his trial, his legal counsel warned that there might be mob action against the community and advised Noyes to leave the state. Noyes immediately left, convinced that the practices he advocated could exist only in a kind of Utopia separated from the rest of the world. Accordingly, in 1848 he bought land on the former Oneida Indian Reserve in Madison County, New York, where he established the Oneida Community, with all property held in common and members paying for necessities from a common fund.

Based on agriculture and including small industries such as blacksmith shops and lumber mills, the community suffered severe hardships, but it was saved from financial ruin by Sewell Newhouse, an inventor of steel animal traps. After Newhouse joined the Oneida Community, he helped establish trap manufacturing. This and later industries improved the community's economy. As the commune prospered, branches were organized in several New England states, but these later closed. The Oneida Community and a settlement at Wallingford, Connecticut, became the center of the Perfectionist experiment, with the two communities operating as one. About 250 members lived in Oneida, another 50 in Wallingford.

During the 1860s a large brick mansion was built to house most of the Oneida members. Children lived in one wing, beginning as infants until their early teens. Parents visited their children often, but nurses and other caretakers were responsible for their upbringing.

During its three decades of communism, the Oneida Community was disciplined and managed by a system of mutual criticism. If a member had a moral problem or felt a sense of guilt about some "sinful" act, he or she could request criticism by a committee of members or by the entire community. The person being criticized remained silent during the session, afterward making a public confession and resolving to follow community recommendations for improvement. As researcher Carden pointed out: "Members' self-esteem depended almost exclusively upon their fellow Perfectionists' approval. They only left the 'home domain' occasionally, and they were frowned on for talking too freely with local outsiders working in the Community businesses. . . . A member had only his private or Community standards by which to judge his actions" (Carden, 71).

By the 1870s some members of the Oneida Community became dissatisfied with the religious zeal of the founders and the communistic way of life. In addition, the community had been under constant attack from leaders of religious denominations and some academics, who labeled the Perfectionists immoral because of their complex marriage system. Eventually, Noyes was forced to leave Oneida once again, seeking refuge in Canada. He also proposed that the complex marriage system be renounced in deference to the growing public criticism of his community.

In 1879 the community gave up its sexual practices, and many couples married. Although the community attempted to sustain communism, that system too was abandoned. In 1881 the community reorganized as the Oneida Community Limited, and shares of stock were divided among 226 members.

Some members remained at Oneida, whereas others left to join orthodox Christian groups. A few attempted to set up a new communistic society, but it did not materialize. As a legal company, the Oneida Community continued to manufacture a variety of products, and by 1920 Oneida silverware and stainless steel tableware were known for quality worldwide.

See also

Anarchist-Communists; Religious Anarchism

References

Carden, Maren Lockwood, *Oneida: Utopian Community to Modern Corporation* (New York: Harper and Row, 1971, orig. publ. Baltimore: Johns Hopkins University Press, 1969).

Jacker, Corinne, *The Black Flag of Anarchy: Antistatism in the United States* (New York: Charles Scribner's Sons, 1968).
Nordhoff, Charles, *The Communistic Societies of the United States: From Personal Observations* (New York: Harper and Brothers, 1875, reprint New York: Dover, 1966).
Schuster, Eunice M., *Native American Anarchism: A Study of Left-Wing American Individualism* (Northampton, MA: Smith College, 1932, reprint New York: AMS Press, 1970).
Woodcock, George, *Anarchism: A History of Libertarian Ideas and Movements* (Cleveland: World Publishing Company, 1962, reprint New York: New American Library, 1974).

O

Orwell, George (1903–1950)

George Orwell is the pseudonym of Eric Arthur Blair, who became a world-renowned author during the 1940s for his brilliant anti-totalitarian satire *Nineteen Eighty-Four* and an earlier work, *Animal Farm.* He claimed for a time to be an anarchist but was more in tune with socialism—or the type of communism that was not corrupted by totalitarian practices such as advocated by Joseph Stalin. A veteran of the Spanish Civil War, Orwell fought at the Aragón front in 1937 and observed the worker revolution in Catalonia, which he described in detail in *Homage to Catalonia.*

Born in Motihari, India, to parents who were members of the Indian Civil Service, Eric Blair moved often during his childhood between India and England. He grew up in an atmosphere of "impoverished snobbery" and with the aid of scholarships was educated in exclusive British schools, including Eton College, where Aldous Huxley was a temporary assistant master in English and French. Although the expected next step would be to enroll at Oxford or Cambridge, in 1922 Blair chose to go along with his father's wishes and serve the British Empire. He joined the Indian Imperial Police in Burma, where he served for five years; bitterly disillusioned, he resigned. Near the end of this period he began writing his novel *Burmese Days,* which he saw primarily as a documentary attacking British imperialism and rule over the Burmese.

After resigning from the imperial police, Blair began calling himself an anarchist. According to his biographers, to assuage his guilt he lived among the poor in Paris and London, which eventually led to the 1933 publication *Down and Out in Paris and London.* His novel-documentary *Burmese Days* was published the following year. These publications, bearing the pen name of George Orwell, successfully launched his prolific writing career. Between 1934 and 1935 Orwell operated a bookshop and continued to write and publish. In 1936 he married Eileen Maud O'Shaughnessy, a socialist in her convictions but not a member of any political party.

When General Francisco Franco led a coup against the Spanish government in 1936, sparking the Spanish Civil War, Orwell went to Barcelona, in Catalonia, to observe and write about the fighting. He decided to stay and fight against Franco and fascism, because "at the time and in that atmosphere it seemed the only conceivable thing to do," he later wrote in *Homage to Catalonia.* In Barcelona, Orwell saw for himself

> a town where the working class was in the saddle. Practically every building of any size had been seized by the workers and was draped with red flags or with the red and black flag of the anarchists; every wall was scrawled with the hammer and sickle and with the initials of the revolutionary parties; almost every church had been gutted and its images burnt. . . . Every shop and café had an inscription saying it had been collectivized; even the bootblacks has been collectivized and their boxes painted red and black. Waiters and shop-walkers looked you in the face and treated you as an equal. Servile and even ceremonial forms of speech had temporarily disappeared. (Orwell, 5)

Orwell was given the choice between joining a militia group of the anti-Stalinist Partido Obrero de Unificación Marxista (POUM) or the anarchist-dominated Confederación Nacional del Trabajo (CNT), a federation of Spanish workers' and peasants' unions. He chose POUM, but he had no idea that communists, who had gained control in government and were receiving money and arms from Russia, would undermine the militia's efforts by continually circulating rumors that POUM members were fascists and traitors. Orwell "was under the impression that one militia was more or less the same as the next and that they were united by the common goal of defeating the fascists" (Shelden, 252).

Orwell went to the Aragón front with a POUM unit in early 1937; after nearly four months in the trenches he was granted leave. His wife met him in Barcelona, where he recuperated and made plans to leave POUM and join the International Brigade fighting on the Madrid front. But before he could carry out his plan, he became embroiled in a government attack on May 3, 1937, on Barcelona's central telephone exchange, operated by CNT. Workers took up arms, and fighting spread throughout the town, with government and communist troops on one side and anarchists on the other, both shooting at POUM, which had been falsely labeled "Franco's Fifth Column."

When the fighting ended after four days, Orwell decided he would not join the International Brigade because it was controlled by Communist Party leaders. As his biographer notes:

> Suddenly, the complexities of left-wing Spanish politics mattered very much to him. He was willing to die in a fight against fascism but not in some pointless squabble over left-wing loyalties. It did not take him long to realize that a communist bullet might get him before a fascist one. The communists were looking for ways to strengthen their power in the Republic, and the street fighting gave them a pretext for intensifying their hate campaign against the POUM. (Shelden, 267)

When Orwell returned with POUM to the front, he was gravely wounded by a rifle shot in the neck. He was sent back to Barcelona at the end of May for recovery, but he and his wife soon were forced to leave, fearing for their lives. The government had outlawed the POUM and arrested, tortured, and murdered leaders. Within a month the two had escaped to England, where Orwell's impassioned *Homage to Catalonia* was published in 1938.

During the next decade, Orwell continued writing, and his fiction and nonfiction works reflected his hatred of totalitarianism and distrust of communism. Among those works were *Animal Farm,* which attacks Stalinism, and *Nineteen Eighty-Four,* which shows the dangers of bureaucracy and Big Brother's rule.

During World War II Orwell worked for the British Broadcasting Corporation; he died in 1950 at the age of 46. Some of his articles and essays written during the war years are included in *Collected Essays, Journalism, and Letters of George Orwell* (1968), published long after tuberculosis cut his life short.

See also

Confederación Nacional del Trabajo; Huxley, Aldous Leonard; Spanish Civil War

References

Crick, Bernard, *George Orwell: The First Complete Biography* (Boston: Atlantic/Little Brown, 1980).

Gross, Miriam, ed., *The World of George Orwell* (New York: Simon and Schuster, 1971).

Orwell, George, *Homage to Catalonia* (New York: Harcourt, Brace, 1952, orig. publ. England, 1938).

"Orwell, George," *Britannica Online* <http://www.eb.com:180/cgi-bin/g?DocF=micro/442/50.html>.

Shelden, Michael, *Orwell: The Authorized Biography* (New York: HarperCollins, 1991).

Stansky, Peter, and William Abrahams, *The Unknown Orwell* (New York: Knopf, 1972).

Osugi Sakae (1885–1923)

A rebel, an anarchist, a martyr is how the translator of Osugi Sakae's autobiography described a prominent twentieth-century Japanese anarchist. Osugi succeeded Japanese anarchist Kotoku Shusui (1871–1911)—who was executed—as an antiwar activist and radical leader.

Sakae was born into a military family. He was the eldest son of Osugi Azuma, an army officer described as "loyal, patriotic, devoted to the military spirit." After attending elementary and middle school, Osugi Sakae was sent to military cadet school at age 14; two years later he was expelled for fighting.

In 1902 Osugi left his family home and went to Tokyo to study. He also began reading left-wing materials, which included articles by Kotoku Shusui. Kotoku's pen, as Osugi described it, was exactly like a "naked blade" that cut its "way wherever his beliefs led him. I was absolutely awed by his merciless attacks on militarism and the military. I, born to a military family, raised among military men, given a military education, and then coming to curse the blind obedience and binding fetters of that military life, was enchanted by these qualities of Shusui's antimilitarism" (Osugi, 98).

Osugi became one of Kotoku's followers in the Commoners' Society, a circle of socialists, Marxists, and labor organizers who sought social reforms and an end to Japanese imperialism. From the time of the Japanese war with Russia (1904–1905), Osugi began to develop his ideas on anarcho-syndicalism. He took part in protests against the oppression of workers, actions that resulted in several arrests and jail terms between 1906 and 1909. In one incident he and others were arrested for singing revolutionary songs and waving flags displaying "Anarchism" and "Communism." For that demonstration, he received a two-and-a-half-year jail term. He was imprisoned at the same time that Kotoku and at least two dozen other anarchists were behind bars, convicted of treason.

While Osugi was in prison he read the works of such anarchists as Mikhail Bakunin, Peter Kropotkin, and Errico Malatesta. After his release in 1910, the government suppressed his activities. Yet during World War I Osugi became an editor and contributor for anarchist publications and translated Russian anarchist Peter Kropotkin's work, gaining a reputation as a leading anarchist.

In 1922 Osugi went to Europe to meet anarchists; the following year he took part in a May Day celebration in a Paris suburb. He was arrested and deported to Japan. Two months later, he was kidnapped and murdered by members of the military police. He was 39 years old.

See also

Anarcho-Syndicalism; Bakunin, Mikhail A.; Kotoku Shusui; Kropotkin, Peter Alexeyevich; Malatesta, Errico

References

Apter, David Ernest, and James Joll, eds., *Anarchism Today* (Garden City, NY: Doubleday and Company, 1971).

Osugi Sakae, *The Autobiography of Osugi Sakae,* trans. Byron K. Marshall (Berkeley: University of California Press, 1992).

Owen, Robert (1771–1858)

A Welsh industrialist, Robert Owen was among the social reformers of the 1800s who are considered to be the forerunners of socialism. Owen envisioned utopian socialist communities where universal happiness could be achieved through education and communal living. Although not an anarchist, he was a strong advocate of labor reforms, arguing that man should not be subservient to or in competition with machines. Such a situation—prevalent during the Industrial Revolution then under way—was the cause of social distress and poverty, Owen theorized. Josiah Warren, the first American anarchist, belonged to Owen's socialist community in the United States. Owen purchased the land for his community from a religious group called the Rappites, which had failed in its attempt to establish a utopian commune. Owen used the community as a laboratory for his own economic experiments.

Born in Newtown, Montgomeryshire, Wales, Owen was educated in local schools until he was ten years old, "when he became an apprentice to a clothier. His employer had a good library, and young Owen spent much of his time reading. He did so well in business that by the time he was 19 he had become superintendent of a large cotton mill in Manchester, which he soon molded into one of the foremost establishments of its kind in Great Britain.

In 1799 Owen and two partners bought the textile mills in New Lanark, Scotland, a town of about 2,000 people. There Owen was able to apply his social and economic ideas. In his view, people did not behave in an evil manner because of original sin or deep-rooted personality disorder. Instead, he theorized, defective institutions were the cause of social evils. Thus, he devised a plan for model communities based on cooperation and humane education, which in turn would help increase industrial production. Applying these ideas to the mill town, he theorized that the crime and deep discontent in New Lanark were brought on by the general problems of society. So he set out to improve his employees' living and working conditions through educational programs (including a nursery school that he opened in 1816), shorter working hours, and funds for ill workers. Stores were set up so that workers could buy quality goods at reasonable prices.

Owen publicly advocated his ideas in articles and speeches, proposing that communities of 500 to 2,000 people could be set up in a scientific manner worldwide. These communities, he theorized, would replace the family as a form of social organization. He shared some of his concepts during a period of several years in letters and publications he sent to George Rapp, founder of a religious commune called Harmonie in the United States. The correspondence prompted Rapp to send a representative to England to see Owen and propose that he buy Harmonie. Owen eventually moved with his family to the United States, and in 1824 he purchased the Rappite community for $150,000.

Renaming the village New Harmony (Indiana), Owen formed the Preliminary Society of New Harmony with the stated purpose of promoting "the happiness of the world." He hoped to set up an "empire of peace and goodwill," which he thought would lead "in due season, to that state of virtue, intelligence, enjoyment, and happiness which it has been foretold by the sages of the past would at some time become the lot of the human race" (Holloway, 105). He also expected that his ideas for community life would spread worldwide.

Owen appointed a committee to manage the society's affairs and outlined numerous provisions for membership. For example, members were expected to willingly provide their services for the good of society. However, the constitution for the Preliminary Society was vague, and no one could be sure exactly what kind of community Owen planned to establish.

One month after the Preliminary Society was formed in 1825, Owen left for England, not returning until January 1826, six months later. Not long afterward, a group of scientists and teachers arrived on what became known as the "boatload of knowledge." The community was reorganized under a second constitution that awarded equal privileges to all members rather than according to the worth of an individual's services (as provided in the first constitution); a skilled laborer received the same amount as an unskilled worker.

Due to lack of leadership and no binding force such as religion to hold the members together, the society failed to become a true community. In less than two years, New Harmony failed. Nevertheless, in 1839 Owen established Queenwood in Hampshire, England, but that community experiment only lasted until 1845, failing primarily because of conflicts among members of the commune.

Despite the community failures, Owen's influence was felt among British workers, who organized numerous labor unions during the 1830s. This prompted the government, courts, and employers to repress union activities and stop expansion of the labor movement. But decades later, in 1864, French mutualists met with British followers of Owen at a mass meeting in London. They formed the International Working Men's Association, later known as the First International.

See also

First International; Mutualism; Socialism; Warren, Josiah

References

Bestor, Arthur, *Backwoods Utopias: The Sectarian Origins and the Owenite Phase of Communitarian Socialism in America, 1663–1829,* 2d enlarged ed. (Philadelphia: University of Pennsylvania Press, 1970).

Gay, Kathlyn, *Communes and Cults* (New York: Twenty-First Century Books/Holt, 1997).

Holloway, Mark, *Heavens on Earth: Utopian Communities in America, 1680–1880,* 2d ed. (New York: Dover, 1966).

"Owen, Robert," *Britannica Online* <http://www.eb.com:180/cgi-bin/g?DocF>.

P

Paine, Thomas (1737–1809)

Thomas Paine shared a philosophy similar to that of Thomas Jefferson, with whom he corresponded regularly. Paine adamantly espoused his belief that people should control their own lives. He became well known during the American Revolution for his 1776 pamphlet "Common Sense," in which he asserts that government at its best is a "necessary evil" and at its worst is "intolerable." His pamphlet pointed out that it was a matter of common sense for British colonists in America to separate themselves from a repressive government, which imposed taxes on colonists but did not give them the right to be represented in the British Parliament.

Although Paine never claimed to be an antistatist or anarchist, his widely distributed pamphlet and others in a series (called "The Crisis") were effective propaganda tools in the American rebellion and fight for independence from British rule. His words encouraged rebels to remain loyal to the American Revolution.

Paine claimed allegiance to no nation, but he was born at Thetford in Norfolk, England. The son of a Quaker, Paine received a basic education, spent some time at sea, then began work as an excise officer in London. However, he was fired from his job, perhaps because he was outspoken on many issues then considered radical. Paine married Mary Lambert, but she died in childbirth, as did their child. His second marriage was unhappy, and the couple soon separated. Paine was forced to turn over all his possessions to creditors. He was in this miserable state when he met American printer, statesmen, and philosopher Benjamin Franklin, who was in England working for better relationships between Great Britain and its American colonies.

Following Franklin's advice, Paine emigrated to America in 1774, settling in Philadelphia, Pennsylvania, and becoming a journalist. In 1775 he became coeditor of *Pennsylvania Magazine;* that same year he wrote and published *African Slavery in America,* criticizing slavery as inhumane and unjust. After "Common Sense" was published in 1776, he continued to write pamphlets encouraging American patriots to fight the British.

After the Revolutionary War, Paine returned to England, where between 1791 and 1792 he published several editions of *The Rights of Man,* which he wrote in response to Edmund Burke's attack on the French Revolution. In his treatise, Paine defended the revolution and also analyzed the discontent then prevailing in Europe. He blamed public dissatisfaction on government, unemployment, poverty, and war.

Paine was accused of treason and no doubt would have been arrested, but he was already on his way to France. He had become a French citizen and had been elected to the National Convention. When Maximilien Robespierre, who headed the Committee of Public Safety, led a brutal campaign known as the Reign of Terror (1793–1794) against people considered rebels or enemies of France, Paine was imprisoned because he insisted that the revolution should be democratic and merciful. He had voted against the execution of Louis XVI, the dethroned king. Tens of thousands of French people were ruthlessly killed during the Reign of Terror, and the National

Convention finally ordered the arrest of Robespierre, who was tried and executed.

While in prison Paine wrote the first part of his book *Age of Reason.* In that work, Paine spelled out his belief that organized religion was corrupt—which many clergy interpreted as an atheistic view—in equal rights for laborers, redistribution of land, a free press, and public education. Paine was released from prison in 1794 and stayed in France for the next eight years, returning to the United States in 1802. He was unwelcome due to *Age of Reason.* In addition, business interests disliked him because of his prolabor views, and Federalists attacked him in efforts to discredit his cohort, Jefferson, who as a Democratic-Republican had long opposed Federalist views. Although Paine had been a major force in the American Revolution, he was ridiculed and in his later years, forgotten by the independent republic he had helped bring about. Paine died in poverty in 1809.

References

Katz, Jon, "The Age of Paine," *Wired,* on the internet <http://www.wired.com/wired/3.05/features/paine.html> (May 1995).

Paine, Thomas, "Common Sense," on the internet <http://odur.let.rug.nl/~usa/D/1776–1800/paine/CM/sense02.htm>.

Thomas Paine National Historical Association, on the internet <http://www.mediapro.net/cdadesign/paine>.

Palmer Raids (1919–1920)

The Palmer Raids were named for Alexander Mitchell Palmer, who became U.S. attorney general just after World War I. During his two years in that office, Palmer initiated raids in 33 cities, rounding up and arresting thousands of citizens and aliens he claimed were subversives. The raids occurred at the height of the Red Scare, when authorities detained radicals, often for many weeks, without charging them, against basic civil rights.

The fear of radicalism stemmed from the Russian Revolution of 1917. Americans, spurred by heated rhetoric from many sources—liberal and conservative—became increasingly concerned that revolutionaries would attempt to overthrow the U.S. government as the Bolsheviks had in Russia. During World War I, pacifists, among them many anarchists, communists, and religious dissenters, had been against military involvement and had staged protests against the draft. The U.S. Congress passed the Espionage Act of 1917 and the Sedition Act of 1918, which virtually outlawed any criticism of or protests against U.S. government war policies. Under these laws, numerous citizens were arrested and imprisoned and aliens were deported. Socialist leader and presidential candidate Eugene V. Debs was one victim, as were members of the Industrial Workers of the World (IWW), a radical labor union that Debs helped establish. Debs received a ten-year prison sentence, and while in jail he ran for president, receiving nearly 1 million votes. Debs was pardoned by President William Harding in 1921.

After the war, the United States suffered an economic crisis as industries, with little direction from the government, attempted to retool for peacetime. Millions of military personnel returning from the war were now in the workforce. Although the economy seemed to boom for a time, inflation rose sharply. Strikes became common. There was also racial unrest that led to riots, with the worst one occurring over a six-day period in Chicago during summer 1919. Attorney General Palmer, who often accused people he disliked of being Bolshevik agitators, blamed the riots on communists.

A series of bombings and attempted bombings of government officials (including Palmer himself) and multimillionaire heads of industries added to the tense situation. Although anarchists were connected to some bombings, the terrorist acts were not part of a widespread plot to overthrow the U.S. government. But Palmer immediately jumped to the conclusion that socialists, anarchists, members of the IWW, and communists were a threat to the nation, declaring that the whole country was infested by anarchists and Bolsheviks. He ordered arrests of members of the Russian Workers Union, most of whom were innocent of any crime and had to be released. Russian-born Emma Goldman and Alexander Berkman were among 249 anarchists who were arrested and deported from the United States and sent to the Soviet Union. In early 1920 Palmer ordered raids on meetings of communists across the United States, and thousands of people were arrested and jailed.

The Palmer Raids encouraged hysteria, suspicion, and the persecution of innocent citizens. By mid-1920, however, Palmer was under heavy criticism from prominent jurists and writers and an organization called the National Popular Government League, which charged the U.S. Department of Justice with numerous offenses and violations of constitutional rights. Although Palmer was eventually discredited and the fervor subsided, the "radical" label in the United States still engenders suspicion for many.

See also

Debs, Eugene Victor; May Day; Sedition Act of 1918

References

Drexel, John, ed., *The Facts on File Encyclopedia of the 20th Century* (New York: Facts on File, 1991).

Hoyt, Edwin P., *The Palmer Raids, 1919–1920: An Attempt to Suppress Dissent* (New York: Seabury Press, 1969).

Jacker, Corinne, *The Black Flag of Anarchy: Antistatism in the United States* (New York: Charles Scribner's Sons, 1968).

Tindall, George Brown, *America: A Narrative History, vol. 2,* 2d ed. (New York: W. W. Norton, 1968).

Paris Commune of 1871

The Paris Commune was formed in 1871 after France suffered a humiliating defeat in the Franco-Prussian War of 1870–1871, which ended Napoleonic rule. Although the commune lasted only 71 days, it was the first practical effort to show that a revolutionary government organized from the ground up could work.

When France was defeated, the National Assembly headed by Adolphe Thiers was set up in Versailles. Thiers had negotiated the peace details with Prussia, turning over Alsace and part of Lorraine to Germany. France also had to pay Germany a huge sum—5 billion francs—in reparations. The French government then had to gain control of Paris. Parisians would not accept a Prussian victory and highly resented Thiers and his government, which, in the view of Parisians, had brought about France's defeat.

Controlling Paris meant disarming the Parisian National Guard, which was on alert, ready to attack any invading Prussians who still occupied northern France. The National Guard was armed with German cannons, left behind following a Prussian siege of the city then placed in strategic spots in various precincts. The government troops' attempt to capture the cannons sparked a major uprising, and masses of people gathered in the streets to jeer at the French soldiers. The guardsmen refused to obey orders from government commanders and instead turned their guns on the officers. This was the beginning of the commune.

Parisians elected a council, or central committee, which claimed that Paris was sovereign and called for other communes, or communities, to be set up throughout France. However, members of the elected committee could not agree on how to organize. Some members were followers of Louis Auguste Blanqui, who had been at the center of the 1848 uprisings in France. Their main goal was to get Blanqui released from jail so that the revolution could go forward. Other members were more concerned about implementing basic education for all and creating cooperatives to produce needed goods. At the same time, all in the commune were subject to an attack by the French forces from Versailles.

Even though the commune was heavily armed and had a strong military force, Parisians were not prepared for a civil war. When Theirs and his soldiers attacked on May 1, Parisians were massacred in street fighting. Some Parisians built barricades of stone and bricks, mattresses, overturned buses, and whatever they could find, but they had to retreat before the French army. Numerous buildings were set afire as communards retreated, and those who were captured by the national forces were shot. By May 28 the commune was destroyed, leaving an estimated 30,000 dead. Tens of thousands of communards were arrested and sentenced to death. About 4,500, among them a well-known anarchist, Louise Michel, were deported to New Caledonia, a French colony off the coast of Australia.

The demise of the commune brought on years of repression for the French labor movement. Many working-class activists were jailed, killed, or forced into exile.

See also

Blanqui, Louis Auguste; Michel, Louise

References

Nomad, Max, *Apostles of Revolution* (New York: Collier Books, 1961).
"Paris Commune," on the internet <http://www.geocities.com/CapitolHill/2419/pariscom.html>.
Williams, Roger L., *The French Revolution of 1870–1871* (New York: W. W. Norton, 1969).

Parsons, Albert (1848–1887)

Albert Parsons was one of the Haymarket martyrs, several anarchists wrongly accused and convicted of events stemming from a riot in Chicago in 1886. He spent many years of his life with labor, socialistic, and anarchistic groups. He eventually was arrested, convicted of being an accessory in the killing of a police officer, and executed.

Born in Montgomery, Alabama, Albert Parsons was the son of an owner of a shoe and leather factory. His ancestors were some of the earliest American settlers, whose descendants took an "active and useful part in all the social, religious, political and revolutionary movements in America." His mother, Parsons reported, was "of great spirituality of character, and known far and near as an intelligent and truly good woman." Besides Albert, there were nine other children in the family (see Foner, 27). Both of Albert's parents died when he was a youth, so he went to live with his married brother, William, in Texas. In 1859 he lived with a sister and her husband in Waco, where he attended school for about a year; he then served for seven years as an apprentice printer at the *Daily News.*

During the Civil War, when he was 15, Albert joined a Texas cavalry brigade under the command of his brother, Maj. Gen. William Parsons. After the war he returned to Waco and attended the university there, gaining a technical education in the printing trade. In 1868 he founded and edited a weekly called *The Spectator,* in which he supported the constitutional amendments that provided civil rights for blacks. His stance brought on the wrath of neighbors and friends, and his newspaper did not survive long. In 1869 he became a traveling correspondent for Houston's *Daily Telegraph*. During a news-gathering trip through northwestern Texas he reportedly met Lucy, "the charming young Spanish Indian maiden who, three years later, became my wife" (quoted in Foner, 30). However, their 1872 interracial marriage was probably not legal, since at that time miscegenation laws forbade marriage between whites and members of other races.

Albert Parsons became involved in political activities, registering black voters, which brought lynching threats. In 1873 he decided that he and Lucy should move to Chicago, where he immediately became a member of Typographical Union No. 16 and worked for the *Times.* He also began to investigate a scandal surrounding the Relief and Aid Society of Chicago, which had collected millions of dollars to aid people impoverished by the Great Chicago Fire of 1871. Working people claimed the society was corrupt and that people in need had not been receiving aid. Although the Chicago press defended the Relief and Aid Society and claimed that detractors were communists and robbers, Parsons found that the complaints "against the society were just and proper." From that time on he was active in the labor movement, which led to contacts with socialists who were caught up in the problems of the working class, which was hard hit by the economic depression that began in 1873 and dragged on for years. Thousands were unemployed and homeless. By 1877 workers had become increasingly radicalized by socialist and anarchist ideas, prompting one of the greatest mass strikes in U.S. history. At first, textile workers and coal miners struck, followed by railroad workers. Owners of railroad companies had forced workers to labor long hours at low pay, and across the United States railroad workers walked off the job.

When strikes took place in Chicago, Albert Parsons, one of the leaders in the Workingmen's Party (later called the Socialist Labor Party), urged workers to join his political party and vote against the ruling class. As a result of his activities, Albert lost his job as a newspaper printer with the *Chicago Sun* and was blacklisted in the trade. Lucy had to open a dress shop to earn a living for the family, which eventually included two children.

Parsons was active in the Socialist Labor Party for a number of years and was a "strenuous advocate" for the eight-hour workday. But he became disillusioned with the idea that the political system could be reformed through the ballot box. He became convinced, as did many workers, that moneyed interests controlled government and that laws were passed so that the propertied class could coerce and exploit workers. He withdrew from the Socialist Labor Party in 1880 but continued to campaign for shorter work days and publicly denounced government. About this time, the mainstream press began to label Parsons and others with similar views as anarchists and enemies of law and order. To such charges, Parsons answered that

> anarchists do not advocate or advise the use of force. Anarchists disclaim and protest against its use, and use of force is justifiable only when employed to repel force. Who, then, are the aiders, abettors and users of force? . . . Are they not those who hold and exercise power of their fellows? They who use clubs and bayonets, prisons and scaffolds? The great class conflict now gathering throughout the world is created by our social system of industrial slavery. Capitalists could not if they would, and would not if they could, change it. This alone is to be the work of the proletariat, the disinherited, the wage-slave, the sufferer. (quoted in Foner, 45)

In 1884 the International Working People's Association (IWPA), which a year before had issued the Pittsburgh Manifesto, calling for proletarians to unite, founded a weekly newspaper in Chicago called *The Alarm*. Parsons was chosen to be the editor, a position he held until police confiscated the paper in 1886 after the May 6 Haymarket affair, which began as a rally to protest police brutality the day before during a strike at the McCormick manufacturing plant. In protest, workers gathered near Haymarket Square; when police tried to disperse them, a bomb thrown into the crowd exploded, causing a riot (some historians characterize it as a police riot). One policeman was killed and dozens more were injured. Police immediately began to fire on the crowd, killing and wounding an unknown number of civilians.

Parsons had spoken at the rally, as had anarchists August Spies and Samuel Fielden. When police began rounding up and arresting many people—most were not connected with the Haymarket meeting—friends of Parson urged him to leave the city and offered to help him get out of the country. For nearly two months he found refuge with friends in Wisconsin, then voluntarily returned to face trial with Spies, Fielden, and five other comrades. Parsons characterized the trial as "a travesty on justice," adding:

> Every law, natural and statute, was violated in response to the clamor of the capitalist class. Every capitalist newspaper in the city, with one exception, called for our blood before the trial began, demanded our lives during the trial and since. A Class jury, class law, class hate, and a court blinded by prejudice against our opinions, has done its work, we are its victims. Every juryman swore he was prejudiced against our opinions; we were tried for our opinions and convicted because of them. (in Foner, 56)

Albert Parsons and seven of his comrades were convicted of being accessories to murder even though the actual bomber was never identified. Four of the men, Albert included, were sentenced to death by hanging; one committed suicide just prior to his scheduled execution; three were imprisoned but later pardoned by Governor John Peter Altgeld.

See also

Haymarket Affair; International Working People's Association; Parsons, Lucy; Pittsburgh Manifesto; Spies, August

References

Ashbaugh, Carolyn, *Lucy Parsons: American Revolutionary* (Chicago: Charles H. Kerr, 1976).

Avrich, Paul, *The Haymarket Tragedy* (Princeton: Princeton University Press, 1984).

Foner, Philip S., ed., *The Autobiographies of the Haymarket Martyrs* (Atlantic Highlands, NJ: Humanities Press, 1969).

Parsons, Lucy (1853–1942)

History has often ignored Lucy Parsons, primarily because she was thought to have devoted her life to her husband, Albert, one of the eight Haymarket martyrs, men convicted of murder charges stemming from the 1886 Haymarket Square riot in Chicago. But Lucy was a strong revolutionary activist and spent nearly 70 years fighting for the oppressed and the rights of women, workers, people of color, and political prisoners.

According to most accounts, Lucy was born in Texas around 1853, but little is known about her early life except that her heritage included African American, Native American, and Mexican ancestry. Lucy claimed to have been orphaned at age three, and it is likely that her parents were slaves. She often denied her African American heritage and claimed to be of Mexican ancestry, calling herself Lucy Gonzales, although she used numerous surnames. About 1870, Lucy lived with Oliver Gathings, a former slave. She met Albert Parsons that year, and they soon married. Their interracial marriage was probably not legal, as miscegenation laws forbade marriage between whites and members of other races.

Albert Parsons became involved in political activities, registering black voters, which brought lynching threats, so the couple left Texas and moved to Chicago, where the Parsons settled in a socialist neighborhood and became involved with the Social Democratic Party. Along with thousands of other Chicagoans, they were caught up in the problems of the working class, which was hard hit by the economic depression that began in 1873 and dragged on for years. Thousands were unemployed and homeless. By 1877 workers had become increasingly radicalized by socialist and anarchist ideas, prompting one of the greatest mass strikes in U.S. history. At first, textile workers and coal miners struck, followed by railroad workers. Owners of railroad companies had forced workers to labor longer hours at lower pay, and across the United States railroad workers walked off the job.

When strikes took place in Chicago, Albert Parsons, one of the leaders in the Workingmen's Party, urged workers to join the party and vote against the ruling class. As a result of his activities, Albert lost his job as a newspaper printer with the *Chicago Sun* and was blacklisted in the trade. Lucy had to open a dress shop to earn a living for the family, which eventually included two children.

Both Albert and Lucy Parsons were involved in trade union organizing, and Lucy became known for her speeches on behalf of the Working Women's Union as well as her writings in *Socialist* and other publications. She played a major role in the International Working People's Association (IWPA), which promoted direct action to achieve a stateless society. Lucy Parsons often wrote for IWPA's weekly newspaper, *The Alarm,* urging violent action against the wealthy, some of whom influenced police to repress workers.

To Lucy Parsons, the revolution was based on class, and she differed sharply with the Knights of Labor, even though she and her husband were members of that organization. "In general," one biographer wrote, "the Knights advocated working within the system to establish alternative institutions. In dealing with capitalists, they favored arbitration over strikes, legislative lobbying over direct action on the job" (Ashbaugh, 50).

She strongly agreed with Johann Most, a German anarchist who arrived in the United States in 1882 and had a major impact on the U.S. anarchist movement. Most advocated "propaganda by deed," and in 1883, along with Albert Parsons, he helped form the IWPA in Pittsburgh. Lucy lived by the principles of the IWPA as expressed in its Pittsburgh Manifesto, which declared that the ruling class would not give up power unless forced to do so; force was the only recourse for the proletariat.

When Albert Parsons was implicated in the 1886 Haymarket affair in Chicago, friends and family urged him to go into hiding. Dozens of Chicago radicals had been arrested and were due to stand trial. Albert Parsons was sheltered by anarchist friends in Wisconsin but wrote a letter to newspapers saying he would surrender for the trial when needed. Meanwhile, Lucy Parsons and her children were subjected to police harassment, invasion of their home, and physical attacks. Albert Parsons returned for a notoriously biased trial and was convicted. Lucy, along with many others who were convinced that the trial was fraudulent, worked to stir public opinion and bring about a pardon, but Albert and three of his comrades were hanged.

Lucy Parsons turned her grief into revolutionary revenge and became a tireless speaker and writer for the cause, which she considered much more important than her own interests. She continually fought for the right of free speech, which she championed with more success in the East than in the Midwest. She also mounted a speaking tour in Great Britain for the Socialist League of England. Returning to Chicago in late 1888, Lucy Parsons was scheduled to speak on the labor movement in England, but police barred her and several dozen other radicals from the hall where they intended to meet.

By 1889, exposés of the Chicago police revealed the corrupt practices of an inspector and a captain on the force and resulted in their dismissal. In addition, a Chicago court ruled that anarchists had the right to freedom of speech. Nevertheless, Lucy Parsons was continually in conflict with people in authority who wanted to prevent her from exercising her right.

When the United States declared war on Spain in 1898, sending troops to fight in Cuba, Lucy Parsons publicly opposed the imperialist invasion, urging young men to resist the call to enlist. When her 18-year-old son enlisted despite his mother's adamant denunciations of the war, "Lucy Parsons committed her son to the Illinois Northern Hospital for the Insane," testifying against him in court. Although hospital doctors found nothing wrong with Albert Jr., he "deteriorated mentally and physically" while confined and died of tuberculosis in 1919. Apparently, Lucy Parsons never saw her son alive again after committing him. As Parson's biographer wrote: "She had put her political commitments first and had attempted to make Albert Jr. a part of her larger political vision. When he failed to measure up to her expectations, and began to actively fight her, she put him away" (Ashbaugh, 208).

As years passed, Lucy Parsons found herself at odds with anarchists and other radicals such as Emma Goldman and Johann Most. She denounced propaganda by deed as well as free love, which many anarchists of the time advocated. Instead, Lucy concentrated on unionism and the labor struggle. She and her friend, Lizzy Holmes, edited *Freedom: A Revolutionary Anarchist-Communist Monthly.* In the early 1900s she was one of the founding members of the Industrial Workers of the World (IWW), believing that revolution would come about only through well-organized workers who took over production. She edited the IWW paper, *The Liberator,* supporting not only labor but also a woman's right to birth control and divorce.

During the last years of her life, she worked with the Communist Party and touted the party line that the end justified the means, never questioning executions of Russian anarchists or the lack of freedom for workers. She lectured continuously, distributed pamphlets, marched in May Day parades in support of workers, and wrote many articles in the cause of free speech. In 1942, at the age of 89, she died in an accidental fire in her home. None of her papers and books survived, but they had not been destroyed by the fire. Rather, the Chicago police claimed that officials of the Federal Bureau of Investigation had confiscated Parson's papers, still trying to silence this woman even after death.

See also

Goldman, Emma; Haymarket Affair; Industrial Workers of the World; International Working People's Association; Most, Johann; Parsons, Albert; Pittsburgh Manifesto

References

Ashbaugh, Carolyn, *Lucy Parsons: American Revolutionary* (Chicago: Charles H. Kerr, 1976).

Lowndes, Joe, "Lucy Parsons (1853–1942): The Life of an Anarchist Labor Organizer," *Free Society,* vol. 2, no. 4 (1995).

Rice, Jon F., "Lucy Parsons: Chicago Revolutionary," *People's Tribune,* electronic edition, February 13, 1995.

Pelloutier, Fernand (1867–1901)

A French social organizer and one of the most influential philosophers of the labor movement, Fernand Pelloutier affected workers' organizations in his country and beyond. He was called the father of revolutionary syndicalism (or anarcho-syndicalism) and was a strong advocate of workers taking direct action through general strikes. For most of his life, he worked to create an organizational foundation for an autonomous working-class movement. His books and articles contended that money was the source of nearly all evils and that capitalism operated in the interests of those who had the wealth, not in the interests of consumers and producers, who, in his view, were usually exploited.

Pelloutier started life in a family of some privilege, and early on he chose a career in journalism, working in the same town where he attended college, Saint-Nazaire, France. His interests soon turned to social issues and the Marxist approach to solving the problems of workers' welfare. He joined the country's largest Marxist party of the day, Parti Ouvrier Francais (French Workers' Party) but soon became disillusioned with its reliance on the state to supply the main organizing mechanism for social change. He especially lamented the fact that the Marxist leadership would not support the notion of a general strike.

Pelloutier quit Parti Ouvrier Francais in 1892 to join the Federation of Bourses du Travail, and there he began to incorporate libertarian ideas into his philosophical structure. In his "Letter to the Anarchists," he wrote "we are . . . full-time rebels, truly godless men, without master or homeland, incorrigible enemies of all despotism, moral or collective, that is to say, of laws and dictatorships, including that of the proletariat" (Pelloutier).

The Bourses (a loose federation that functioned as a workers' social club and labor union exchange), according to Pelloutier, was to become the basis of what Mikhail Bakunin called the "free association of producers," the syndicalism on which the new social contract would be based. Pelloutier helped define the syndicalist movement that was first outlined in the Charter of Amiens (1906).

See also
Anarcho-Syndicalism; Bakunin, Mikhail A.

References

"Fernand Pelloutier and Revolutionary Syndicalism: Part One," on the internet <http://flag.blackened.net/huelga/pell1.htm>.

Pelloutier, Fernand, "Anarchism and the Workers Unions," on the internet <http://flag.blackened.net/huelga/workers.htm>.

"Pelloutier, Fernand" *Britannica Online* <http://www.eb.com:180/cgi-bin/g?DocF=micro/457/59.html>.

Pissarro, Camille

See French Anarchism

Pittsburgh Manifesto

According to one labor historian, "The Pittsburgh Manifesto occupies a prominent place in the history of American radicalism even though . . . it is poorly written and suffers from obscurity and infelicity of expression" (David, 100). Whatever its faults, the manifesto was created in 1883 during a conference in Pittsburgh, Pennsylvania, that attempted to unite workers and the various factions of so-called revolutionary socialists (otherwise known as anarchists) in the United States. Among the 26 delegates to the Pittsburgh Congress, as it was known, were leaders Johann Most, Albert Parsons, and August Spies.

Participants at the conference represented groups with disparate ideas, but they were unanimous in their view that the nation's social problems could not be solved through the political process or cooperation with capitalists. Representatives also agreed that any national organization had to be a loose federation, allowing autonomy for each group within it.

The Pittsburgh Congress voted to name the new federation the International Working People's Association (IWPA). Representatives also agreed to publish a manifesto—the Pittsburgh Manifesto—in three languages: English, German, and French. It was drawn up by a committee that included Most, Parsons, and Spies and addressed "Workingmen of America."

The manifesto begins with a paragraph

from the Declaration of Independence stating that it is the people's right and duty to throw off despotism. "This thought of Thomas Jefferson was the justification for armed resistance by our forefathers, which gave birth to the Republic," the manifesto states, then asks "Do not the necessities of the present time compel us to re-assert their declaration?"

Denouncing the capitalist society and its repression of the working class, the manifesto espouses "agitation" and "rebellion" to bring about social change because

> the political institutions of our time are the agencies of the propertied class; their mission is the upholding of the privileges of their masters; any reform in your [labor's] behalf would curtail these privileges . . . there remains but one recourse—FORCE! . . .
>
> By force our ancestors liberated themselves from political oppression, by force their children will have to liberate themselves from economic bondage. "It is, therefore, your right, it is your duty," says Jefferson—"to arm!"

Finally the manifesto spelled out what the IWPA would achieve "plainly and simply":

> *First:*—Destruction of the existing class rule, by all means, i.e., by energetic, relentless, revolutionary and international action.
>
> *Second:*—Establishment of a free society based upon cooperative organization of production.
>
> *Third:*—Free exchange of equivalent products by and between the productive organizations without commerce and profit-mongery.
>
> *Fourth:*—Organization of education on a secular, scientific and equal basis for both sexes.
>
> *Fifth:*—Equal rights for all without distinction to sex or race.
>
> *Sixth:*—Regulation of all public affairs by free contracts between the autonomous (independent) communes and associations, resting on a federalistic basis. (David, 99–100)

Despite the Pittsburgh Congress and its manifesto, many IWPA members were against insurrection, although they often armed to protect themselves against attacks by authorities. Among those who actively recruited for IWPA were Spies, Parsons, and Samuel Fielden—who in 1886, along with five others, were convicted and executed for inciting a riot during the infamous Haymarket affair in Chicago. The men successfully organized affiliated groups in industrial cities of the Midwest, but by 1888 the militant organization was repressed in the wake of the Haymarket affair.

See also

Haymarket Affair; Haymarket Anarchists; International Working People's Association; Lingg, Louis; Most, Johann; Parsons, Albert; Spies, August

References

Avrich, Paul, *The Haymarket Tragedy* (Princeton: Princeton University Press, 1984).

David, Henry, *The History of the Haymarket Affair* (New York: Russell and Russell, 1936).

Foner, Philip Sheldon, ed., *The Autobiographies of the Haymarket Martyrs* (Atlantic Highlands, NJ: Humanities Press, 1969).

Propaganda by Deed (or Propaganda of the Deed)

The terms *propaganda by deed* or *propaganda of the deed* refer to anarchist actions during the 25-year period following the Paris Commune of 1871 and the deaths of some 30,000 dissident anarchists who took part in that revolt. After many leaders had been imprisoned or executed, members of anarchist and socialist causes in France and Europe operated underground for fear of police reprisals. Capitalists, flush with a new sense of confidence, continued to consolidate centuries-old crafts into new factories and the industrial-production paradigm. In the name of progress and efficiency, workers toiled at low-paying piecework and repetitive assembly stations to produce cheaper products. Former skilled entrepreneurs were forced from their traditional livelihoods to work 10- and 12-hour days in unsafe conditions for poverty wages.

Frustrated by the government's role in denying workers the right to form unions or to take their grievances to factory managers, anarchists developed a new method to make their statements of protest. "Placid and carefree sleeps the bourgeoisie, but the day of shuddering and fear, of ferocious tempests, of bloody revenge is approaching. The savage, blinding light of explosions begins to light up its dreams" (Harper, 65). And so began the era of propaganda by deed.

In his attempt to inflame workers to take action, German anarchist Johann Most articulated his views on propaganda by deed whenever and wherever he could in the United States during the late 1800s, although he apparently did not intend that his words be taken literally, as he denounced some terrorist acts. Near the turn of the 19th century, dozens upon dozens of violent incidents against capitalists, politicians, clergy, royalty, and property were recorded around the world. The most famous of these actions were Alexander Berkman's attempt to assassinate Henry Clay Frick, chairman of the board of Carnegie Steel, in 1892; the shooting of King Umberto in Italy in 1900; and the murder of U.S. President William McKinley in 1901.

However, the tactics of anarcho-syndicalists under the leadership of Frenchman Fernand Pelloutier and Italian Errico Malatesta, who organized workers into syndicates of direct action, were perhaps more effective. They organized boycotts, attacks against managers and bosses, and sabotage of machinery. These tactics, they contended, would speed the day when a massive general strike would bring down the capitalist system and the governments it supported.

By the early 1900s propaganda by deed had become more a detriment than a help to anarchist causes. The fear of bombers and terrorists of all kinds was pervasive throughout the United States and Europe, and many anarchist philosophers (though not all) began to publicly condemn terrorism. In addition, "the legal and constitutional machinery for obtaining social reform and economic improvement was more efficient [in industrialized countries] than it had been at any time since the industrial revolution. . . . Therefore, it seemed more sensible to join a political party or a trade union and to agitate legally for piecemeal reforms rather than to make the apocalyptic gestures of the anarchists" (Joll, 145).

See also

Berkman, Alexander; Direct Action; Malatesta, Errico; Most, Johann; Paris Commune of 1871; Pelloutier, Fernand

References

Harper, Clifford, *Anarchy: A Graphic Guide* (London: Camden Press, 1987).

Jacker, Corinne, *The Black Flag of Anarchy: Antistatism in the United States* (New York: Charles Scribner's Sons, 1968).

Joll, James, *The Anarchists* (Boston: Little, Brown, 1964).

Proudhon, Pierre-Joseph (1809–1865)

French mutualist Pierre-Joseph Proudhon was one of the first philosophers during the 19th century to call himself an anarchist. Although others such as William Godwin had formulated an anarchist political philosophy during the late 1700s, Proudhon became famous for his view that the foundation of society should be a voluntary contract between persons. He advocated doing away with the state, which he described as a "fictitious being, without intelligence . . . without morality" (Carr, 47).

Proudhon became well known for his statement that "property is theft," a concept he developed in a pamphlet entitled "What is Property," published in Paris in 1840. Proudhon held that it was right and proper for individuals to have "possessions," those items that are kept for personal use. In fact, possessions are a prerequisite of individual liberty. But he denounced nonproducers who controlled the means of production (property) such as factories, mines, and raw land and exploited the labor of others.

One of Proudhon's major ideas was the mutual bank organization, based on the concept of voluntary participation. Through a mutual bank, producers of goods "would be able to exchange products at a cost value by means of labor checks that would represent the hours of labor needed to produce the merchandise in question" (Jacker, 65). A similar idea (the Time Store) had been developed by Josiah Warren in the United States. Proudhon's thinking struck a chord with communists during this period, but he was not a communist-anarchist, and he soon broke with communists over the issue of individual independence.

Born to a poor family in Besançon, France, Proudhon's father, Claude-Francois, was a brewer and innkeeper but never made more than a subsistence living. Despite the family's poverty, Proudhon's mother, Catherine, helped him enter the local high school, where he won a scholarship to study in Paris at age 19. However, he was forced to return home because of his family's poverty and near starvation. He became an apprentice in the printing trade, working as a proofreader and compositor. While preparing manuscripts for publication, he taught himself Latin, Hebrew, and Greek; he also associated with authors and intellectuals, helping him acquire a broad education. One of the books he worked on was Charles Fourier's *The New Industrial World,* which introduced Fourier's elaborate schemes for a utopian society. Fourier hated the social problems associated with industrialization and believed that all classes of people should work together cooperatively through a series of occupational groups organized into what he called phalanxes. Individuals chose their occupations and varied them by working with other groups in order to become completely self-fulfilled. Although Proudhon was influenced by Fourier's ideas, he later denounced all Utopias.

Eventually, Proudhon was able to pursue his academic studies full time and began writing and publishing. During the 1840s Proudhon's published books and pamphlets became well known throughout radical circles in France and other countries, and he gained fame as a revolutionary pamphleteer. At the time, radicals throughout the world hoped that France, which had suffered a bloody revolution, would lead in devising economic reforms to benefit workers. None of Proudhon's writing brought him much income, however, and in 1843 he went to work in Lyon for a shipping company, where he was "in charge of all correspondence, of negotiations with customers and with the authorities, and notably of all business disputes and lawsuits" (Hyams, 68).

During the three-year period he worked in Lyon, Proudhon had enough free time to continue his studies and writing and to travel to Paris, where he met many intellectuals of the period, among them Karl Marx and Mikhail Bakunin. Proudhon himself became the leading intellectual in France and then in Europe.

In February 1848 a workers' revolution overthrew the monarchy in France, and Proudhon supported the revolt with his pamphlets and the newspaper *Le People.* He was also elected to the National Assembly but voted against the constitution not only because he disapproved of its content but also because it was a constitution. He hoped to convince the assembly to reform the system of taxation and to confiscate private funds of the wealthy to establish free credit and subsidies for peasants and workers. He also attempted to found a people's bank, similar to what Josiah Warren had tried to establish in the United States about the same time.

While a member of the National Assembly, Proudhon wrote a cynical piece, often reprinted, on the meaning of government:

> To be ruled is to be kept an eye on, inspected, spied on, regulated, indoctrinated, sermonised, listed and checked-off, estimated, appraised, censured, ordered about, by creatures without knowledge and without virtues. To be ruled is, at every operation, transaction, movement, to be noted, registered, counted, priced, stamped, surveyed, assessed, licensed, permitted, authorised, apostolised, admonished, prevented, reformed, redressed, corrected. It is, on the pretext of public utility and in the name of the common good, to be put under contribution, exercised, held to ransom, exploited, monopolised, concussed, pressured, mystified, robbed; then, at the least resistance and at the first hint of complaint, repressed, fined, vilified, vexed, hunted, exasperated, knocked-down, disarmed, garroted, imprisoned, shot, grape-shot, judged, condemned, deported, sacrificed, sold, tricked; and, to finish off with, hoaxed, calumniated, dishonoured. Such is government! (in Hymas, 149–150)

By June the revolt in France was crushed, and Louis Napoleon Bonaparte was elected president. Liberties were suppressed, and the press was censored. Although Proudhon considered the president to be a friend, he published a fierce attack on Napoleon, which led to charges of sedition. For a time, he escaped arrest in Belgium, but he returned to Paris and was tried and convicted. He spent three years in prison, where he continued to study and write.

Before his imprisonment, Proudhon had planned a marriage that would be without passion but would allow him to have a family and a "complete life." He married a poor seamstress, Euphrasie Piégard, who was an excellent manager and steadfast throughout many difficulties. During his imprisonment, Proudhon was allowed three-day paroles each month to visit his wife, who lived nearby, and the couple had their first child, a daughter, in fall 1850. (Two other daughters were born; one died during a cholera epidemic.)

Proudhon's work influenced French workers in the First International and succeeding Internationals (meetings to discuss the problems of working-class people). They defended his solutions, which aimed at free credit and equality of exchange without a dictatorship of the proletariat. Marx first admired this enemy of property, then attacked him, undermining Proudhon's prestige and virtually eclipsing him; syndicalist Fernand Pelloutier would revive interest in his theories. Proudhon's many published works included *System of Economic Contradictions or the Philosophy of Poverty, Confessions of a Revolutionary,* and *The Principle of Federation and the Need to Rebuild the Revolutionary Party.*

Proudhon's greatest book, according to biographer Edward Hyams, was *Justice in the Revolution and the Church,* published in 1858. Justice, Proudhon proclaimed, was not defined in legal terms but rather meant "the rightness of things. It is the master-principle of the universe . . . equilibrium . . . ecological balance . . . logic . . . equality or equation . . . the rule governing our rights and obligations" (Hyman, 212). In Proudhon's view, there was no need for God or theology because, simply put, justice is an innate quality in humankind.

Justice was soon condemned by government officials, the church, and the press, and Proudhon was warned to leave France or face imprisonment. From late 1858 until he died, in January 1865, Proudhon took refuge in Belgium with his wife and two daughters. While in exile, Proudhon's health deteriorated, although he continued to write during the final months of his life, completing all but the last chapter of a book arguing against workers taking part in any parliamentary government. A friend finished the work for him just before Proudhon's death.

See also

Bakunin, Mikhail A.; First International; Fourierism; Godwin, William; Marx, Karl; Mutualism; Pelloutier, Fernand; Warren, Josiah

References

Carr, Edward Hallet, *Studies in Revolution* (New York: Barnes and Noble, 1962).

Hyams, Edward, *Pierre-Joseph Proudhon: His Revolutionary Life, Mind, and Works* (New York: Taplinger Publishing, 1979).

Jacker, Corinne, *The Black Flag of Anarchy: Antistatism in the United States* (New York: Charles Scribner's Sons, 1968).

Joll, James, *The Anarchists* (Boston: Little, Brown, 1964).

R

Rand, Ayn

See Anarcho-Capitalism

Rebels at Ruesta

An international meeting of anarchists and libertarians was organized by Alternative Libertaire of France and held in Ruesta, Spain, in 1995. Ruesta is a village owned by an anarcho-syndicalist union.

The conference brought together anarchists and libertarians who saw themselves coming from a tradition that includes ideas formulated by followers of Spanish anarchist Buenaventura Durruti and the controversial Manifesto of Libertarian Communism as spelled out in 1926 by Dielo Trouda, an anarchist group of Russian exiles in France. Although the majority of delegates were from France and Switzerland, others represented Poland, Italy, Lebanon, and Sweden. Delegates discussed such activities as union organizing and the possibility of an international federation of libertarian communist organizations. At the end of the conference, participants issued a declaration, stating that the international meeting

> allowed anarchists, militants, sympathisers, libertarian socialists, libertarian communists, anarcho-syndicalists and revolutionary syndicalists to discuss our analyses of and methods of intervention in the social movements (i.e., the struggles against unemployment, sexism, imperialism, racism etc. and in the unions).
>
> Discussions from different viewpoints also took place around ex-Yugoslavia and the rebellion in Chiapas. The debates showed there was a common wish to transform a world now dominated by many forms of oppression (Capitalism, imperialism & sexism). They also revealed differences in how we analyse and fight these oppressions.
>
> Exploring these differences opens up a way for improving each group's understanding. It gave each organisation a chance to reflect on its practice and current position. The meeting was a small step forward in the construction of a new international political culture, one based on libertarian and revolutionary values. One also determined to bring together the oppressed to strengthen future revolts and struggles to create a new society. ("International Anarchist Declaration")

See also

Anarcho-Syndicalism; *Dielo Trouda* (Workers' Cause); Durruti, Buenaventura; Libertarian Socialism

References

"International Anarchist Declaration," on the internet <http://flag.blackened.net/revolt/rbr/decrbr2.html>.

"Rebels at Ruesta: International Libertarian Meeting," on the internet <http://flag.blackened.net/revolt/rbr/reusrbr2.html>.

Reclus, Elisée

See French Anarchism

Religious Anarchism

One of the oldest forms of anarchy was created by religious and spiritual dissidents. Virtually every organized religion, at some point in history, has experienced movements that "reject all authority, whether temporal or spiritual, and claim complete liberty to act in accordance with an inner light" (Joll, 17). Over the centuries numerous sects have challenged established religious doctrine and the state. To religious anarchists, civil authority is evil, the only moral law being that of God. Because of the antiauthoritarian stance, religious dissidents have often been called the precursors of the 18th-, 19th-, and early-20th-century radicals (including American revolutionaries) who initiated armed rebellions against governments.

Certainly throughout history some religious sects have engaged in violent insurrections, but most religious anarchists disputing orthodox Christian doctrines have been pacifists. They attempted to live by the precepts of Christian love and nonviolence; the state, in their view, is a violent institution because it provokes and engages in war, represses the masses, and holds people in bondage by controlling natural resources and the products of labor for the benefit of the few. In the words of Englishman Gerrard Winstanley, who announced in his manifesto for the English Diggers during the 1600s:

> Every single man, Male and Female, is a perfect Creature of himself; and the same Spirit that made the Globe, dwells in man to govern the Globe; so that the flesh of man being subject to Reason, his Maker, hath him to be his Teacher and Ruler within himself, therefore needs not run abroad after any Teacher and Ruler without him, for he needs not that any man should teach him, for the same Anoynting that ruled in the Son of man, teacheth him all things. (Winstanley)

In the 1800s the great Russian writer Leo Tolstoy articulated Christian anarchism (although he never used that label) in some of his published works. Many religious and spiritual anarchists have more recently practiced nonviolent direct action or passive nonresistance as formulated by Mohandas Gandhi in India (e.g., sit-ins to protest a civil law or government policy), often leading authorities to forcibly remove protesters.

Countless religious anarchists have also been antiwar activists. In the United States, they protested involvement in military conflicts ranging from the Spanish-American War of 1898 to the Korean, Vietnam, and Persian Gulf Wars of the 20th century. Religious anarchists have been conscientious objectors, refusing to obey military draft laws or to pay taxes to support war efforts. Some have sabotaged military installations and damaged weapons plants. Arrests and jail sentences were sometimes the result, yet religious anarchists have traditionally been willing to pay that price to demonstrate the anarchist precept that government represents violence.

Since the 1600s American religious anarchists have included such figures as Anne Hutchinson, who was expelled as a heretic from the Massachusetts Bay Colony; numerous abolitionists of the Civil War era who denounced the government for supporting slavery; and founders of religious communal societies of the 1800s, such as John Humphrey Noyes. During the 19th century many religious anarchists in the United States tried to live the philosophy of nonresistance, which

> was anarchistic in the sense that it visualized the destruction of all human law and government as well as all human authority and the construction of a new order in which the individual enjoyed absolute freedom, was "inspired" by the Love of God and was guided only by the Golden Rule. While the "individualist anarchists," Josiah Warren, William Bradford Greene, Lysander Spooner, and Benjamin Tucker would supplant existing law by the laws of nature, the non-resistants would substitute the laws of God as simply set forth by the Golden Rule and by Christ in the Sermon on the Mount—a difference only in name. (Schuster, 70–71)

Christian anarchists have long differed in

the ways to bring about a new society and take control of their own lives. Yet they all shared a belief in the sanctity of the individual and generally are guided by the Golden Rule and Christ's Sermon on the Mount. As historian Eunice Schuster wrote:

> They declared that since they were guided by inner consciousness, they were not subject to the laws, to government, or to any coercive authority in the world. Some of them even constructed and prepared for a new world where [people] would live peacefully without an external authority over their intellectual, social, or moral life. Their speculations and aspirations for the most part lay in the ethical and social field. Within this area they definitely built up a philosophy of Christian Anarchism. (Schuster, 86)

See also

Gandhi, Mohandas "Mahatma" Karamchand; Greene, William Bradford; Hutchinson, Anne Marbury; Noyes, John Humphrey; Spooner, Lysander; Tolstoy, Count Lev (Leo) Nikolayevich; Tucker, Benjamin R.; Warren, Josiah; Winstanley, Gerrard

References

Joll, James, *The Anarchists* (Boston: Little, Brown, 1964).

Schuster, Eunice M., *Native American Anarchism: A Study of Left-Wing American Individualism* (Northampton, MA: Smith College, 1932, reprint New York: AMS Press, 1970).

Winstanley, Gerrard, "The True Levellers Standard Advanced: The State of Community Opened, and Presented to the Sons of Men" (1649), on the internet <http://www.vancouver.net/home/campbell/Leveller.htm>.

Revolutions of 1848

Anarchists who believed in direct action, such as Mikhail Bakunin, took part in revolutionary activities that erupted across Europe during 1848–1849. Anarchists were not the only participants; many others, increasingly intolerant of crop failures and a decline in national economies, joined them. There was general dissatisfaction among the emerging middle class, creating an unstable situation for European monarchies. Liberal and nationalistic groups took advantage of the unrest, leading revolutionary uprisings in almost every European capital. The only unaffected countries were Finland, Sweden, Russia, and Spain; the latter two nations would experience violent changes 70 years later.

A minor local revolution in January 1848 on the island of Sicily signaled the beginning, but the most significant movement took place in Paris a month later. Workers and the middle class joined forces to drive King Louis Phillippe from the throne, and for a time "national workshops" were established to redistribute the workforce and to lower unemployment. However, disagreements between the *republique democratique* (democratic republic) and the supporters of *republique democratique et sociale* (social democratic republic) led to workers' full-scale revolt in June.

In Great Britain, Ireland, the Netherlands, and Denmark the revolutionary movement manifested in peaceful demonstrations and lawful pressure for democratic reforms. As in Paris, monarchs in Germany and Austria were powerless to quell mobs that took control of capital cities and government institutions. However, the advances of these liberalizing forces, though dramatic, were short-lived.

The Austrian empire saw a rapid breakdown of control as ethnic German ministers, inspired by events in Paris, took power in Vienna. By March, Hungary broke free from the empire, Croatia was planning to do the same, and Italy saw its chance to loosen the Austrian hold on its land. Eventually, a working-class revolt took the Austrian capital, but it soon lost out to a new prime minister. In December Francis Joseph succeeded to the throne, and by April 1849 a new authoritarian government was firmly in charge of the old empire. In Berlin, liberals had intended to establish an empire that incorporated ethnic German areas then under Austrian control. When it became apparent that the Austrian empire would hold, the dream soon died.

Monarchies were reestablished in Germany, Austria, and Italy with the help of armies loyal to the sovereigns. And with the support of the middle classes and the clergy—more frightened of the new socialist ideas than the old ways—they increased police forces and squelched the popular press. In France, a violent counterattack swept liberals from power and reestablished the hereditary empire under Napoleon III in 1852.

It can be said that the restoration was not complete, as universal suffrage was not abolished in France, the elective assembly stayed in Prussia, and some other minor gains were maintained. For the most part, however, leaders of the revolutions of 1848 were hounded into hiding, and authoritarian governments remained very much in control throughout Europe.

See also

Bakunin, Mikhail A.; Direct Action; French Anarchism

References

"1848, Revolutions of," *Britannica Online* <http://www.eb.com:180/cgi-bin/g?DocF=micro/187/51.html>.

Joll, James, *The Anarchists* (Boston: Little, Brown, 1964).

Robertson, Priscilla, *The Revolutions of 1848: A Social History* (Princeton: Princeton University Press, 1952).

Rocker, Rudolf (1873–1958)

Considered one of the major anarcho-syndicalist theorists, Rudolf Rocker was also the most influential figure in the Jewish anarchist movement during the late 1800s and early 1900s. However, Rocker was not Jewish. He was born into a liberal Catholic family in Mainz, Germany, and when his parents died young, the five-year-old Rocker was sent to a Catholic orphanage. Although he was not abused in the orphanage, Rocker in later years compared his experience "to being exiled to the desert, away from everything that was dear to him or that he cared for." Rocker ran away from the orphanage twice but was forced to return, which, in the opinion of a biographer, "contributed to a considerable extent to Rocker's subsequent philosophy of rejecting authoritarianism and institutionalism" and advocating anarchism (Graur, 17–18).

After completing school and an apprenticeship, Rocker became a journeyman in the bookbinding trade, traveling for several years. His political life began at 17 when he joined the German Social Democratic Party (SDP), but he became disenchanted when the party, in its official publication, attacked the anarchists in the 1886 Chicago Haymarket affair as enemies of workers. Rocker became involved in an SDP opposition group called Die Jungen (The Young), whose views caused a rift within the party. "Both sides proved extremely keen in pointing out the moral faults in the leaders of the rival faction. . . . While the 'Jungen' charged the party's leadership with corruption, opportunism, and petty-bourgeois mentality, the heads of the SDP retaliated, claiming the 'Jungen' were nothing more than a collection of literati divorced of any real connections with the proletariat on whose behalf they professed to speak" (Graur, 27).

Rocker was an outspoken critic of SDP leaders and was soon expelled from the party, but that did not prevent the bookbinders' union from electing him its representative at the 1891 socialist congress, known as the Second International. The congress was held in Brussels, and there Rocker met a German anarchist who introduced him to anarchist writings, including the works of Mikhail Bakunin and Peter Kropotkin. Rocker was especially influenced by their ideas, and after returning to Germany he founded an anarchist group.

In 1892, just before he turned 20, Rocker was forced to flee Germany to escape police harassment. He lived in exile for the next 25 years, first in Paris and then London. In Paris he was joined by a German woman named Charlotte, with whom he had a son, Rudolf. But the couple separated, and Charlotte returned to Germany, taking Rudolf with her. When young Rudolf was 6, his mother sent him to London to live with Rocker and his companion, Milly Witkop, and their son, Fermin.

Witkop was from an orthodox Jewish family but became active in the radical Jewish movement centered in London's East End. Rocker, although a Gentile, was also involved in the Jewish anarchist movement and lived in the Jewish community. He met Milly when she was 18, and they quickly found they were soulmates, establishing a relationship that lasted for 58 years. Following anarchist principles, they refused for 30 years to formalize their relationship, but they were finally forced to marry legally in order to obtain passports.

Within the Jewish anarchist movement, Rocker was a prominent speaker and writer, editing several Yiddish newspapers. In 1907 he represented the anarchist Jewish movement at the International Anarchist Congress in Amsterdam. There he and fellow anarchists, including Errico Malatesta of Spain and John Turner of England, set up the International Anarchist Bureau. Its purpose was to coordinate anarchist activities and distribute information on the anarchist movement worldwide. But it failed the mission because of difficulties in establishing contacts with anarchist groups.

When World War I broke out in 1914, Rocker expressed his opposition to both sides, a stand that conflicted with that of friend and mentor Peter Kropotkin, who urged anarchists to support France's fight against German invaders. This contradicted Kropotkin's consistent argument against all wars, which he had previously labeled a means to exploit the masses and enrich capitalists. Kropotkin's pronouncements created a split in the anarchist movement, with some supporting his view and others, such as Rocker, Alexander Berkman, Emma Goldman, and Errico Malatesta, contending that all wars should be condemned and that anarchists should concentrate on liberating the masses. Within a few months Rocker was imprisoned as an enemy alien. In 1916 Milly was also imprisoned because of her antiwar stance.

In March 1918 the British released prisoners who were in poor health, Rocker among them, and deported them to the Netherlands. His wife was not released until August, and she and their son Fermin were then able to join Rocker in Amsterdam.

Like many other anarchists of the time, Rocker at first supported the Bolshevik Revolution in 1917, declaring it better than no revolution at all. In Rocker's view, "anarchists should take an active part in the effort to create a new society, but at the same time try to divert it from the centrist tendencies adopted by the Bolsheviks." But that was impossible to accomplish because the Bolsheviks deported, jailed, and executed anarchists, destroying their influence. As a result of that repression, Rocker quickly changed his views when he realized the "true meaning of the Soviet state, and for the rest of his life he remained a relentless and unequivocal critic of the Soviet system" (Graur, 133). His criticism of the Soviets preceded that of Emma Goldman, who wrote about her disillusionment with Russia in 1922.

In 1933 Rudolf and Milly Rocker and their son Fermin and his wife escaped from Nazi persecution in Germany and eventually settled in the United States. Rocker lectured throughout North America and wrote many articles, pamphlets, and books attacking the evils of fascism and communism. His English-language book-length works include *Nationalism and Culture* (1937), *The Six* (1938), *Anarcho-Syndicalism* (1938), *Pioneers of American Freedom* (1949), and a section of his autobiography called *The London Years* (1956).

When World War II broke out, Rocker, like Kropotkin before him, took a promilitary stance and sided with the Allies, justifying the war as the means to preserve libertarian values. His arguments created a breach in the anarchist movement just as Kropotkin's stand had during World War I. Yet "he was the best-known anarchist in the country until his death" in 1958 at the age of 85 (Walter).

See also

Anarcho-Syndicalism; Berkman, Alexander; Goldman, Emma; Malatesta, Errico; Turner, John

References

Graur, Mina, *An Anarchist "Rabbi": The Life and Teachings of Rudolf Rocker* (New York: St. Martin's Press, 1997).

Walter, Nicolas, "The Life of Rudolf Rocker," Introduction to the 1988 Freedom Press edition of *Anarchism and Anarcho-Syndicalism* by Rudolf Rocker.

Russian Anarchism

The Russian anarchist movement flourished for about 25 years during the late 1800s and early 1900s. However, long before the beginning of the 20th century and the 1905 and 1917 revolutions in Russia, radicals and peasants took direct action in attempts to overthrow hierarchical and repressive governments. As professor Paul Avrich explained: "Over the centuries, the Russian borderlands had been the scene of wild popular uprisings with strong anarchic overtones. Although the rebellious peasants had reserved their venom for the landlords and officials, and had continued to venerate the Tsar or some false pretender, this heritage of mass revolts . . . was a rich source of inspiration to [Mikhail] Bakunin, [Peter] Kropotkin, and their anarchist disciples."

Such anarchists were also inspired by religious dissidents as well as by Leo Tolstoy and his followers, who formed anarchistic groups during the 1800s. Most religious anarchists were pacifists who rejected any type of violent action. Nevertheless, they "spurned the official hierarchy of the Russian Orthodox Church, and they often avoided paying taxes and refused to take oaths or bear arms" (Avrich 1978, 35).

During the early 1900s Russia suffered a terrible famine and economic depression, and war with Japan compounded economic and social problems. In addition, as people migrated from rural to urban areas in attempts to find work in factories, discontent grew. Small anarchist groups formed in various parts of Russia and distributed articles by Kropotkin and Bakunin as well as materials written by anarchists in other countries.

By early 1905 great masses of people were primed for direct action. When a few workers in a St. Petersburg factory were fired, thousands of other workers and their families in the city and surrounding suburbs jammed the streets. They marched in protest to the Winter Palace, hoping to present a petition for an eight-hour workday and an end to war. But they were greeted by Russian soldiers who opened fire and gunned down nearly a thousand people in what became known as "Bloody Sunday." The massacre prompted strikes, uprisings, and mutinies. During the revolution, various types of anarchist groups sprang up across Russia—anarcho-communists, anarcho-syndicalists, and individualist anarchists.

By October 1905 workers had elected many revolutionary committees called soviets, and these councils planned militant action, forcing Emperor Nichols II to promise a duma, or representative government. Although the 1905 revolution was put down within two months, the stage had been set for anarchist action in the future.

So when the second revolution broke out in 1917, workers took over factories. A provisional government was formed, forcing Nicholas II to relinquish the throne. But the Bolsheviks, or communists, led by Vladimir Illich Lenin, gained power and took control of the government, creating a proletarian dictatorship that suppressed most anarchist activities. Between late 1917 and mid-1921, anarchists challenged Bolshevik rule, and civil wars broke out across Russia. Nestor Makhno led one anarchist force in the Ukraine, which was then a republic of the Union of Soviet Socialist Republics (USSR). Makhno's army was eventually overcome, and he was forced into exile in 1921, as were many other Russian anarchists, including the celebrated V. M. Eikhenbaum (Voline). Voline played an important role in Makhno's movement, but he was a propagandist—a prolific writer—not a fighter (Avrich 1978, 125).

The Russian anarchist movement soon died out as the communists held firm control. Although small anarchist groups sprang up during the years after World War II, they were soon put down by the Committee for State Security, the KGB. With perestroika (economic restructuring) and glasnost (openness) initiated by Mikhail Gorbachev during the 1980s, a few small anarchist groups formed again. Some exist today in such cities as Moscow and St. Petersburg and in the Ukraine, focusing primarily on publishing anarchist magazines and papers.

See also

Anarchist-Communists; Anarcho-Syndicalism; Bakunin, Mikhail A.; Eikhenbaum, V. M. (Voline); Individualist Anarchists; Kropotkin, Peter Alexeyevich; Makhno, Nestor Ivanovich; Tolstoy, Count Lev (Leo) Nikolayevich

References

"After the Fall: A New Beginning for Russian Anarchism?" *Red and Black Revolution* (1996).

Avrich, Paul, *The Russian Anarchists* (New York: W. W. Norton, 1978).

Avrich, Paul, ed., *The Anarchists in the Russian Revolution* (Ithaca: Cornell University Press, 1973).

S

Sacco, Nicola (1891–1927), and Bartolomeo Vanzetti (1888–1927)

The names Sacco and Vanzetti are forever linked as the two men who were tried in a controversial murder case in 1920. Like the Haymarket affair decades before, their case took place in a hostile, bigoted atmosphere, in a court with a publicly prejudiced judge and biased jury ready to convict anarchists and other social revolutionaries.

Both were born in Italy and emigrated to the United States in 1908. They came from rural families and did not know each other. Sacco was born and raised in southern Italy, Vanzetti in northern Italy.

In the United States, Sacco and Vanzetti settled in Massachusetts and worked at various jobs. Sacco eventually became a shoemaker, married, and fathered children. Vanzetti remained a bachelor, held construction jobs, and worked for a time in a rope factory. He eventually became a fish peddler. Always eager to learn, he was an avid reader and self-educated.

Sacco and Vanzetti, who well knew the indignities and poverty suffered by the working class, joined anarchist groups not long after their arrival in the United States. But they did not meet personally until 1917 while attending a meeting of anarchists in Boston about six weeks after the United States entered World War I. The meeting was led by Luigi Galleani, a foremost Italian anarchist-communist in the United States during the 1910s and 1920s. Galleani urged his followers to repudiate the war and avoid the draft if eligible for conscription. Since Sacco and Vanzetti were antimilitary and believed the war was being fought by the poor for the rich, they joined other Italian anarchists going to Mexico. The group lived communally for a few months, but their funds ran short, and they returned to the United States to find work.

By the time America entered the war, it was engulfed by patriotic fever and fears of foreigners and radicals. After the war, Attorney General A. Mitchell Palmer initiated a series of raids on those he accused of planning a "red," or communist, uprising and the Red Scare swept the country. Those who agitated against capitalism and for the rights of working people were labeled subversives by superpatriots and authorities. Many foreign-born radicals were arrested and deported. This climate prevailed in 1920 when a paymaster and guard in a Braintree, Massachusetts, shoe company were murdered while being robbed of a payroll. A similar theft had taken place a few months earlier, and a witness identified the robbers as Italians, leading police to conclude that an Italian gang was responsible.

Although Sacco and Vanzetti had alibis, and numerous witnesses testified to their whereabouts at the time of the crime, they were convicted of the murders on thin evidence. Both were carrying guns at the time of their arrests, but there was no proof that their weapons were used in the robbery. In addition, no stolen money was ever found, and another convicted criminal confessed to the murders.

After the trial of Sacco and Vanzetti and during their seven-year imprisonment and appeals, many people worldwide concluded that the men were innocent and had been unjustly treated. Italian anarchists in the United States as well as many other groups campaigned to save the two men, calling for a new trial (which was denied) and clemency. Sacco and Vanzetti were electrocuted in 1927 because—as supporters contended then and still assert today—of their political beliefs and foreign birth. "Just like now, the country was in an anti-immigrant, anti-union mood," noted 92-year old Jack Spiegel, who was interviewed by a *Chicago Tribune* columnist in 1997. Spiegel was active with a 1927 committee that tried to save Sacco and Vanzetti from the electric chair (Grossman 1997).

During the years since the executions, prominent men and women have tried to clear Sacco and Vanzetti. Finally, in 1977, Massachusetts Governor Michael Dukakis issued a proclamation declaring that the trial of the two men "was permeated by prejudice against foreigners and hostility toward unorthodox political views; and . . . the conduct of many of the officials involved in the case shed serious doubt on their willingness and ability to conduct the prosecution and trial . . . fairly and impartially." Governor Dukakis proclaimed "that any stigma and disgrace should be forever removed from the names of Nicola Sacco and Bartolomeo Vanzetti, from the names of their families and descendants" (Young and Kaiser, 3–4).

See also

Galleani, Luigi; Haymarket Affair; Italian Anarchism; Palmer Raids

References

Avrich, Paul, *Sacco and Vanzetti: The Anarchist Background* (Princeton: Princeton University Press, 1991).

Ehrmann, Herbert B., *The Case That Will Not Die: Commonwealth vs. Sacco and Vanzetti* (Boston: Little, Brown, 1969).

Frankfurter, Felix, *The Case of Sacco and Vanzetti: A Critical Analysis for Lawyers and Laymen* (Boston: Little, Brown, 1927).

Grossman, Ron, "Sacco and Vanzetti," *Chicago Tribune*, Tempo Section, August 27, 1997.

Young, William, and David E. Kaiser, *Postmortem: New Evidence in the Case of Sacco and Vanzetti* (Amherst: University of Massachusetts Press, 1985).

Sanctuary Movement (United States)

Some call the sanctuary movement anarchy and others contend that it is a humanitarian effort. In short, the sanctuary movement in the United States provides refuge for people fleeing violent repression in their homelands whether in Asia, Africa, Latin America, or Europe.

The concept of providing sanctuary is centuries old, dating to biblical times. In the United States, the sanctuary movement has included activists of diverse persuasions and has manifested in a variety of ways, such as the Underground Railroad of Civil War days when citizens defied laws to protect runaway slaves escaping to freedom.

Since the 1980s the U.S. sanctuary movement has practiced civil disobedience similar to that of religious anarchists and helped refugees from Central America—primarily Guatemala and El Salvador—who have fled persecution and violence. But sanctuary activists have come up against the U.S. Immigration and Naturalization Service (INS), the agency that enforces immigration laws such as the Refugee Act of 1980. That law provides asylum for those who leave their country of origin and are unable to return because of persecution due to racial, religious, political, or national reasons. However, the law does not protect illegal aliens who come to the United States for economic purposes, and during the 1980s INS declared that most Central American refugees were economic aliens. Numerous church groups involved in the sanctuary movement vehemently disagreed, insisting that civilians in El Salvador and Guatemala were being massacred by armies trained and supplied by the U.S. government. Sanctuary activists began helping refugees from these countries come into the United States across the Mexican border and provided sanctuary for them in hundreds of U.S. and Canadian churches.

National attention focused on the movement in 1985 when the Rev. John Fife, pastor of Southside Presbyterian Church in Tucson, Arizona, and Jim Corbett and 14 others were indicted in federal court in Arizona on charges of conspiracy and transporting and harboring illegal aliens, a felony. Eleven of the sixteen went to trial in 1986, and in his opening statements Special Assistant U.S. Attorney Donald Reno Jr. charged that four of the defendants—Corbett, Fife, a church employee, and a Catholic nun—were "generals" or "chief executive officers" in an "underground railroad" that smuggled aliens from Mexico into Arizona and on to other states (quoted in Becklund). The defendants countered that they were acting out of humanitarian and religious concerns and that the federal government was breaking federal laws and international agreements by refusing to grant refugee status to people who were fleeing political repression and, in some cases, torture or certain death in El Salvador and other Central American countries.

Several years before the trial, Reverend Fife had declared his church a sanctuary. "It was a classic David/Goliath situation: a mission chapel measuring 30 by 75 feet against the might of the United States," reported one participant. "The stakes were high. Anyone convicted would face five years imprisonment and a $2,000 fine for each alien aided. Yet in a short time we had more than 200 declared sanctuaries around the country and a support community of more than 2,000 churches and synagogues. . . . Hundreds of thousands of refugees were spared deportation" (MacEoin).

Fife and seven other activists were convicted on various charges of conspiracy, transporting and harboring aliens, and aiding illegal entry of aliens. All received probation, with the proviso that they no longer harbor refugees. But the defendants continued to work for the sanctuary movement, as have activists in other areas of the United States and Canada.

The sanctuary movement has played a major role in urging the U.S. Congress to modify strict U.S. immigration policies that went into effect with passage of the Illegal Immigration Reform and Immigrant Responsibility Act of 1996. The law eliminates a provision that suspends deportation of aliens who have lived continuously in the United States for at least seven years and would be persecuted if deported. In December 1997 the U.S. Congress passed and the president signed the Nicaraguan Adjustment and Central American Relief Act of 1997, which allows Cubans and Nicaraguans meeting certain criteria to apply for permanent residence and also permits certain Salvadorans, Guatemalans, and Eastern Europeans to apply for cancellation of the deportation ruling put in place with the 1996 law.

References

Becklund, Laurie, "Sanctuary Movement Leaders Assailed," *Los Angeles Times,* November 16, 1985.

Collins, Sheila D., "The New Underground Railroad," *Monthly Review* (May 1986).

Crittenden, Ann, *Sanctuary: A Story of American Conscience and the Law in Collision* (New York: Weidenfeld and Nicholson, 1988).

Davidson, Miriam, *Convictions of the Heart: Jim Corbett and the Sanctuary Movement* (Tucson: University of Arizona Press, 1988).

MacEoin, Gary, "Sanctuary Movement Lives on in New Interest, Commitment," *National Catholic Reporter,* April 3, 1998.

Schwab, Michael

See Haymarket Anarchists

Sedition Act of 1918

The U.S. Sedition Act of 1918 amended the Espionage Act passed a year earlier. These laws were designed to identify and arrest alleged spies and others suspected of disloyalty or threatening the U.S. government's military efforts before and during World War I. Section 3 of the Sedition Act:

> Whoever, when the United States is at war, shall willfully make or convey false reports or false statements with intent to interfere with the operation or success of the military or naval forces of the United States, or to promote the success of its enemies, or shall willfully make or convey false reports, or false statements . . . or incite insubordination, disloyalty, mutiny, or refusal of duty, in the military or naval forces of the United States, or shall willfully obstruct . . . the recruiting or enlistment service of the United States, or . . . shall willfully utter, print, write, or publish any disloyal, profane, scurrilous, or abusive language about the form of government of the United States, or the Constitution of the United States, or the military or naval forces of the United States . . . or shall willfully display the flag of any foreign enemy, or shall willfully . . . urge, incite, or advocate any curtailment of production . . . or advocate, teach, defend, or

> suggest the doing of any of the acts or things in this section enumerated and whoever shall by word or act support or favor the cause of any country with which the United States is at war or by word or act oppose the cause of the United States therein, shall be punished by a fine of not more than $10,000 or imprisonment for not more than twenty years, or both.

Although many government officials and American citizens were convinced of the necessity for espionage and sedition laws, free speech and the civil rights of citizens were put at risk. As one historian noted:

> The impact of the acts fell with most severity upon Socialists and other radicals. Victor Berger, Socialist congressman from Milwaukee, got a twenty-year sentence for editorials in the *Milwaukee Leader* which called the war a capitalist conspiracy. Eugene V. Debs, who had polled over 900,000 votes for president in 1912, got twenty years for statements that had a "tendency" to bring about resistance to the draft. [He was pardoned in 1921.] . . .
>
> Just after the war the Supreme Court upheld the Espionage and Sedition Acts. *Schenck v. United States* (1919) upheld the conviction of a man for circulating anti-draft leaflets among members of the armed forces. In this case Justice Holmes said: "Free speech would not protect a man in falsely shouting fire in a theater, and causing a panic." The act applied where there was "a clear and present danger" that speech in wartime might create evils congress had a right to prevent. (Tindall, 1006)

See also

Debs, Eugene Victor; Socialism

References

Jacker, Corinne, *The Black Flag of Anarchy: Antistatism in the United States* (New York: Charles Scribner's Sons, 1968).

Tindall, George Brown, *America: A Narrative History, vol. 2,* 2d ed. (New York: W. W. Norton, 1988).

Seldes, George (1890–1995)

He has been called "the inventor of modern investigative reporting," and his name stands with the more famous I. F. Stone and Lincoln Steffens as the three most influential independent journalists of the 20th century. Although he was not an anarchist, he corresponded with such noted anarchists as Emma Goldman, and he was able to point out, as many anarchists have done, how government and business issues affect daily lives and infringe liberties. His uncompromising reporting showed that government is free to operate in a manner that optimizes its own perpetuation rather than working on behalf of freedom for the masses.

Seldes's weekly newsletter *In Fact* began publication in 1940, a decade after he ended a 20-year career as a globetrotting, influential reporter for mainstream papers like the *Pittsburgh Leader,* the *Atlanta Constitution,* and the *Chicago Tribune.* He quit this promising career to follow the words of Abraham Lincoln, who said: "I am a firm believer in the people. If given the truth, they can be depended upon to meet any national crisis. The great point is to bring them the real facts."

Seldes contended that the mainstream press manipulated and controlled news and that the truth was getting through by only accident. In 1910 he gathered evidence for a story about a Pittsburgh department store heir suspected of raping one of the store's saleswomen. The story never appeared, however, and he noted that larger, more expensive advertisements ran regularly in the newspaper immediately following his investigation.

This incident as a cub reporter was the first but hardly the only one that gave him pause about the moral character of his chosen profession and its relationship to business and government. The most important event came just after Germany surrendered in World War I. Seldes was then a reporter for the *Chicago Tribune* covering the war in Europe. He got an exclusive interview with German Field Marshal Paul von Hindenburg, who admitted Germans lost the war because of the presence of American reinforcements and overwhelming military forces.

The story was suppressed by General John

Pershing's censors in retaliation for Seldes gaining access to Hindenburg behind the lines. He and a few other reporters were court-martialed for breaking the Armistice, and they were forbidden to even report about the interview. In the absence of the truth, an alternative explanation for German losses eventually took hold in postwar Germany, and communists, socialists, and Jews inside the country were blamed for undercutting the war effort. As Seldes wrote in his autobiography, *Witness to a Century,*

> If the Hindenburg interview had been passed by Pershing's censors at the time, it would have been headlined in every country civilized enough to have newspapers and undoubtedly would have made an impression on millions of people and become an important page in history. . . . I believe it would have destroyed the main planks on which Hitler rose to power, it would have prevented World War II, the greatest and worst war in all history, and it would have changed the future of all mankind.

He continued to cover international stories for the *Tribune* until 1929, when he could no longer abide the paper's editorial decision-making. He quit to work as an independent journalist and to publish two influential books about how the press covered stories: *You Can't Print That!* (1929) and *Can These Things Be!* (1931). In 1932 he married Helen Larkin, who would help with all his subsequent writing, including *In Fact,* until her death in 1979.

In Fact was not shy in the way it criticized mainstream media masking the full truth. His paper's mission was "An Antidote for Falsehood in the Daily Press," and when fellow reporters had trouble getting stories published in their own papers, they would feed their information to Seldes, for they knew the facts would at least see the light of day. For the entire life of the paper, which ceased publication in 1950 because of intensive Red-baiting by the Federal Bureau of Investigation, Seldes promulgated information he knew was critical for a free society to thrive. His was the first publication to expose the link between cancer and tobacco, for example, but this knowledge, like so much of what he reported on, had little effect on the general public. People relied instead on the mass media.

Seldes died with little fanfare at the age of 104. But his life stands as an example of the power of truth and the need for the public to have the facts.

See also

Goldman, Emma

References

Berlet, Chip, "George Seldes: Muckraker, Journalism Critic, Antifascist," on the internet <http:www.publiceye.org/pra/glossary/seldes.html>.

Goldsmith, Rick, "Tell the Truth and Run: George Seldes and the American Press," New Day Films (1996) on the internet <http://www.e-media.com/seldes/>.

Holhut, Randolph T., "Tell the Truth and Shame the Devil: The Story of *In Fact*" (Adapted from George Seldes's 1968 book *Never Tire of Protesting*), on the internet <http:www.e-media.com/seldes/infact1.html>.

Walljasper, Jay, "George Seldes," Passages, *Utne Online* (September 1996), on the internet <http:utne.com/lens/mt/16mtseldes.html>.

Shays's Rebellion

Between 1784 and 1789 in the United States, a major economic depression set the stage for an uprising that became known as Shays's Rebellion, what some historians have erroneously called an attempt to establish a Bolshevik or Marxist society. However, the rebel uprising, like insurrections of some anarchist groups throughout history, was a reaction to the tyranny of elite lawyers and merchants who controlled the financial system and courts.

Prices of goods, which had been inflated during the American Revolutionary War, steadily fell during the depression. Farmers, who had enjoyed prosperous times during the war and at the urging of money lenders mortgaged their farms to make improvements or to buy more land, were particularly hard hit. When the prices of their crops declined, many could no longer pay debts and faced foreclosures and high taxes; laws and court decisions—debtors were subject to jail terms—were considered by some to be unjust. Thousands of farmers, including many Revolutionary War veterans, were sued for debts.

Along with other debtors, they protested unjust legal practices and the lack of a stable monetary system.

Daniel Shays, a captain during the Revolutionary War, led a Massachusetts group in uprisings beginning in August 1786. To prevent the trials and imprisonment of debtors, Shays and his followers closed down the court in Northampton on August 31. About a month later, rebels stormed the state supreme court in Springfield, but they were driven off by state militia. Then, in January 1787 Shays and more than a thousand men planned to attack the federal arsenal at Springfield; again militia repulsed the protesters. Some of them, including Shays, escaped to Vermont.

During this turbulent time, Thomas Jefferson, then a member of the Continental Congress, became increasingly alarmed about authorities' overreaction to what he believed was a short-lived tax revolt. He "was afraid that a counterrevolution in America would concentrate power in the hands of a despotic minority, as in Europe. Most of all, he feared repression of any kind, and he was not afraid of popular resistance to government measures" (Randall, 480–481). He believed people should voice their grievances, and in late January 1787 he wrote a letter to fellow congressman James Madison, declaring that "a little rebellion now and then is a good thing. . . . a medicine necessary for the sound health of government."

References

Jefferson, Thomas, to James Madison, "A Little Rebellion Now and Then Is a Good Thing," *The Early America Review* (Summer 1996), electronic version.

Randall, Willard Sterne, *Thomas Jefferson: A Life* (New York: HarperCollins, 1993).

Shelley, Percy Bysshe (1792–1822)

Percy Bysshe Shelley is considered to be one of the great English romantic poets, but his connection to anarchist thought and principles is not often discussed. Most analysis of his poetry looks at the influence of Neoplatonism and Shelley's quest for the ideal life for humans on Earth. In that sense, he was always a radical thinker. In fact, he wrote:

> The man
> Of virtuous soul commands not, nor obeys:
> Power, like a desolating pestilence,
> Pollutes whate'er it touches, and obedience,
> Bane of all genius, virtue, freedom, truth,
> Makes slaves of men, and, of the human frame,
> A mechanized automaton.

These lines point up the view of anarchists, who place a high priority on liberty—for themselves and others—and on individuality.

The eldest child of Timothy and Elizabeth (Pilfold) Shelley, Percy was born in Sussex, England, and grew up with four younger sisters and a brother. He began his education at age six, learning Latin and Greek; at ten he left home to be educated at an academy near Brentford. He had little respect for the strict discipline of the academy and protested the indignity of floggings. In 1804 Shelley enrolled in Eton, where he seldom fit in with boisterous schoolmates who often harassed him.

Shelley was expected to take his place as a wealthy country squire but rebelled against this role. He attended Oxford in 1810; he was expelled from the university in 1811 when he and a friend published a pamphlet entitled "The Necessity of Atheism," which began with the words, "There is no God." At 19, Shelley married 16-year-old Harriet Westbrook, a classmate of his sister's, and the two went to Ireland to live, where Shelley became a strong critic of the British government's treatment of the Irish. The couple had two children but drifted apart; in 1814 they separated.

Meanwhile, Shelley continued his work on "Queen Mab," his first long poem, an attack on religious orthodoxy and political oppression. At the time, he corresponded with William Godwin, who had developed a political philosophy that would become known as anarchism. Shelley eventually went to meet the man who had penned *Political Justice.* At the author's humble home, he met Godwin's daughter, Mary, whose mother was Mary Wollstonecraft, an avid feminist. The couple fell in love, eloping two years later. They were married in 1816 after Shelley's first wife committed suicide.

The relationship between Godwin and Shelley was critical to the development of the poet's maturing philosophy regarding the perfectibility of humanity when left to its own will. This influence can best be seen in the poems "Queen Mab," "Ode to Liberty," "The Revolt of Islam," "The Masque of Anarchy," and "Prometheus Unbound." This body of work marks Shelley as the first "anarchist" poet.

After he wedded Mary Wollstonecraft, Shelley tried to gain custody of his children, who were with Harriet Westbrook's family. But the courts intervened and placed them in the care of guardians, claiming that Shelley was immoral and an atheist. He was allowed to see the children only 12 times a year. In 1818 Shelley and Wollstonecraft moved to Italy, where their three children were born (two of whom died). Shelley perished at sea in a boating accident in 1822.

See also

Godwin, William; Wollstonecraft, Mary

References

Marshall, Peter, ed., *The Anarchist Writings of William Godwin* (London: Freedom Press, 1986).

"Percy Bysshe Shelley," *Groliers Encyclopedia* electronic version (1994).

Scrivener, Michael Henry, *Radical Shelley: The Philosophical Anarchism and Utopian Thought of Percy Bysshe Shelley* (Princeton: Princeton University Press, 1982).

Scudder, Horace E., ed., *The Complete Poetical Works of Percy Bysshe Shelley* (Boston and New York: Houghton Mifflin, 1901), on the internet <http://www.cc.columbia.edu/acis/bartleby/shelley/index.html>.

Social Ecology

Social ecology theories are associated primarily with the writings of ecoanarchist Murray Bookchin, who cofounded the Institute for Social Ecology in Vermont. The institute states that

> social ecology integrates the study of human and natural ecosystems through understanding the interrelationships of culture and nature. It advances a critical, holistic world view and suggests that creative human enterprise can construct an alternative future, reharmonizing people's relationship to the natural world by reharmonizing their relationship with each other. This interdisciplinary approach draws on studies in the natural sciences, feminism, anthropology and philosophy to provide a coherent radical critique of current anti-ecological trends, and to offer a reconstructive, communitarian and ethical approach to social life. In response to the challenge of creating an ecological society, social ecology provides a critical analysis and suggests a process for building sustainable community structures through the integration of theory and practice. Using Central Vermont as a laboratory, the Institute explores bioregional solutions to global problems.

In Bookchin's many articles and books written since the 1960s, he has emphasized that ecological destruction is the result of authoritarian, hierarchical social structures. He stresses the need to replace the competitiveness of a capitalist system with a free, cooperative society, following the anarchistic principle that government should be eliminated because individuals can manage their own affairs without being dominated by authorities. In Bookchin's words:

> What literally defines social ecology as "social" is its recognition of the often overlooked fact that nearly all our present ecological problems arise from deep-seated social problems. Conversely, present ecological problems cannot be clearly understood, much less resolved, without resolutely dealing with problems within society. To make this point more concrete: economic, ethnic, cultural, and gender conflicts, among many others, lie at the core of the most serious ecological dislocations we face today—apart, to be sure, from those that are produced by natural catastrophes.
>
> If this approach seems a bit too "sociological" for those environmentalists who identify ecological problems with the

> preservation of wildlife, wilderness, or more broadly, with "Gaia" and planetary "Oneness," it might be sobering to consider certain recent facts. The massive oil spill by an Exxon tanker at Prince William Sound, the extensive deforestation of redwood trees by the Maxxam Corporation, and the proposed James Bay hydroelectric project that would flood vast areas of northern Quebec's forests, to cite only a few problems, should remind us that the real battleground on which the ecological future of the planet will be decided is clearly a social one.
>
> Indeed, to separate ecological problems from social problems . . . would be to grossly misconstrue the sources of the growing environmental crisis. The way human beings deal with each other as social beings is crucial to addressing the ecological crisis. Unless we clearly recognize this, we will surely fail to see that the hierarchical mentality and class relationships that so thoroughly permeate society give rise to the very idea of dominating the natural world. (Bookchin, "What is Social Ecology?")

Bookchin was warning Americans about an environmental crisis and ecological pollution brought on by capitalist demands as early as the 1950s, positing that the use of carcinogenic chemicals as well as the abuse of natural resources stemmed from a profit-oriented society, not the needs of the public. Since the 1960s he has elaborated on the social causes of ecological devastation and has consistently called for a union of anarchism and ecology to create a society that is humane, libertarian, cooperative, and decentralized. As one writer puts it:

> In its range and depth, Bookchin's dialectical synthesis of anarchism and ecology, which he called social ecology, had no equal in the postwar international Left. The first major effort to fuse ecological awareness with the need for fundamental social change, and to link a philosophy of nature with a philosophy of social revolution, it remains the most important such effort to this day. (Biehl)

See also

Bookchin, Murray; Ecoanarchists

References

Biehl, Janet, ed., *The Murray Bookchin Reader* (London: Cassell, Wellington House, 1997).

Bookchin, Murray, *The Philosophy of Social Ecology* (Montreal: Black Rose Books, 1990).

Bookchin, Murray, "What Is Social Ecology?" on the internet <http://www.tao.ca/~ise/library/b_soceco.html>.

Bookchin, Murray, "Will Ecology Become 'The Dismal Science'?" *The Progressive* (December 1991).

Evanoff, Richard, "Social Ecology: Basic Principles, Future Prospects—An Interview with Murray Bookchin," *Japan Environment Monitor* (1996), on the internet <http://www.yin.or.jp/user/rdavis/bookchin.html>.

Socialism

Dictionary definitions of *socialism* usually refer to a social system in which people work cooperatively for the benefit of all; producers have the political power and the means to produce and distribute goods. As an economic theory, socialism challenges capitalism and the sanctity of private property.

Many forms of socialism have fallen under this broad concept. They range from idealistic utopian communities, such as those established by individualist anarchist Josiah Warren in the United States and the schemes touted by Frenchman Charles Fourier, to the brand of socialism advocated by Karl Marx and Friedrich Engels, who believed that class conflict would inevitably bring about revolution. Anarchists of various persuasions—from individualists to social anarchists—have also claimed to fit under the socialist umbrella, because they are opposed to capitalism and because the term *socialism* originally included anyone who believed that an individual had the right to whatever he or she produced. In the now well-known words of Frenchman Louis Blanqui, who set forth a primary socialist principle in the 1840s: "From each according to his abilities, to each according to his needs."

Socialism as it is known today was a response to the Industrial Revolution that began in Great Britain during the 18th century and spread to Europe and the United States. Many factory owners gained great wealth while factory workers earned low wages and often lived in squalid urban conditions. Social critics of industrialization sought to eliminate injustices that workers suffered and establish more equitable societies in Europe and the United States. Socialist groups in the United States included the Socialist Labor Party, formed in 1874, and the Socialist Party of America, established in 1901. However, socialists—whatever their organization or country of origin—did not agree on how society should be restructured.

Idealistic social planners wanted to reorganize society so that the abundance of industry would be equally distributed for the benefit of all. Such utopian schemes sometimes included communal living; the terms *communism* and *socialism* were often used synonymously. This was particularly true in communal religious societies established in the United States during the 1800s (Gay).

During the late 1840s Marx and Engels attacked utopian ideas and called for militant socialism—class warfare. Whereas anarchists and other radicals pressed for the revolutionary approach, others in the socialist movement called for a gradual reform of the political process. The revolutionists—Bolsheviks—became the dominant force, however, and during the Russian Revolution of 1917 brought about a split that led to the formation of the Communist Party, led by Vladimir Ilich Lenin and Leon Trotsky. Lenin and his cohorts seized control of the Russian government and formed the Union of Soviet Socialist Republics (USSR), soon beginning a ruthless extermination of people considered enemies of the communist government, a pattern that continued during the more than thirty years while Joseph Stalin was dictator.

After World War I socialists in Europe and other parts of the world cooperated with national governments, and socialism was adopted as an alternative to the private enterprise system in some European, Asian, and Latin American countries. Following World War II, as working-class people increasingly gained benefits and political power, socialism lost its revolutionary zeal and became an established system in many nations.

See also

Fourierism; Marx, Karl; Socialist Party of America/Socialist Party USA; Warren, Josiah

References

Gay, Kathlyn, *Communes and Cults* (New York: Twenty-First Century Books/Holt, 1997).

Holloway, Mark, *Heavens on Earth: Utopian Communities in America, 1680–1880,* 2d ed. (New York: Dover, 1966).

Jacker, Corinne, *The Black Flag of Anarchy: Antistatism in the United States* (New York: Charles Scribner's Sons, 1968).

"Socialism," *Britannica Online* <http://www.eb.com:180/cgi-bin/g?DocF=macro/5007/6.html>.

Socialist Party of America/ Socialist Party USA

Socialists in the United States of various backgrounds and views came together in 1901 at a "Unity Convention" held in Indianapolis, Indiana, to form the Socialist Party of America (SPA), the forerunner of today's Socialist Party USA (SPUSA). Among the delegates were individualist anarchists who believed that individuals had the right to possess or own what they produce, sharing the socialist concept that a society should be established in which producers own and control the means of production. Some delegates were religious anarchists or communal Christians (so-called Christian socialists) and those who accepted socialism as an alternative to establishing utopian cooperative communities.

Other delegates were former members of the Socialist Labor Party (SLP), created in 1877 from various German labor groups in the United States. SLP was later controlled by Daniel De Leon, who used the group to meld his idea of Marxism and syndicalist doctrine. De Leon's SLP was primarily intellectual, and his followers hoped to wrest power from capitalists through voting and strikes. Some SLP members became disenchanted with De Leon's authoritarianism and left the party to help form the SPA.

When the SPA formed there was widespread public disgust with corrupt corporations and so-called robber barons who controlled most of the country's wealth. As a result, the SPA membership grew rapidly, from 10,000 at the outset to 150,000 in 1912 (*Britannica*).

At the Unity Convention, the party set forth its demands:

> (1) public ownership of transportation, communications, utilities, monopolies and trusts, (2) reduced hours and increased wages for labor, (3) workman's compensation and insurance in case of accident, unemployment, sickness or want in old age, (4) a system of public industries, (5) education of all children up to age 18 with aid for books, clothing and food, (6) equal civil and political rights for all men and women, (7) more widespread use of proportional representation, initiative, referendum, and recall. (Zeidler)

Except for public ownership of industries, most of the party's concepts have become part of American life, and since 1904 numerous socialists have been elected to government offices. Eugene Victor Debs, founder of the American Railway Union and well-known orator and labor organizer, became a member of SPA and was a five-time presidential candidate. Debs and other well-known figures, such as poets Carl Sandburg and Vachel Lindsay, were influential as socialist organizers.

However, throughout history, SPA and socialism itself have not been readily accepted in the United States, particularly when the general public and the press associated the party with communists. Early communists called themselves socialists, and Karl Marx and Friedrich Engels labeled their ideas for a collective society "scientific socialism" in order to differentiate their doctrine from socialists who advocated utopian communal societies. In 1919 communists split from the SPA and formed the American Communist Party.

According to Frank Zeidler, former national chair of the Socialist Party and former mayor of Milwaukee, the SPA also "found itself in some difficult relations" with the Industrial Workers of the World (IWW), which was formed in 1905 by labor leaders like Debs, Big Bill Haywood, and others.

> The organization was based on the concept that there was an irrepressible conflict between the working class and the capitalist class and that the working class must defend itself if necessary through force. Government action also was eschewed as a means of changing society and no political party should be supported. The platform denounced craft unionism and favored industrial unionism. Debs resigned in 1906 because of the belief that the group was advocating violence, but other members continued to be active. (Zeidler)

Haywood, in fact, continued his support for the type of direct action that anarchists and other radicals espoused. As an IWW leader, Haywood insisted that socialists could not be law-abiding citizens. In his view, IWW was a "fighting organization," its purpose to overthrow capitalism, "becoming conspirators then against the United States government" (Preston, 48–49).

Conflicts within the party also surfaced before and during World War I. SPA at first took a neutral stance toward the war, but in 1917, when the United States declared war, the party, "after intense debate adopted a resolution . . . declaring unalterable opposition to the war," which "put the party immediately in a stance of confrontation" with the administration of President Woodrow Wilson, who brooked no opposition to the war effort. The administration as well as the press and educators attacked antiwar activists, and socialist publications were harassed, nearly causing them to fail (Zeidler).

Internal divisions caused SPA to split again in the 1970s; one group became the Socialist Democrats USA, changing the name to the Democratic Socialist Organizing Committee in 1973 and then the Democratic Socialists of America in 1982. This faction moved to the right politically, supporting republicans Richard Nixon and Ronald Reagan. In 1973 the Socialist Party of America reorganized as the Socialist Party USA (SPUSA), still in existence. (Because of its name, SPUSA has been erroneously linked to the German National Socialist Workers Party in the United States. However, there is no connection with the Nazi organization.) SPUSA has long worked for a cooperative society and a way to settle international disputes without warfare. The party's strongest support is in the Midwest and California.

See also

Anarchism; De Leon, Daniel; Haywood, William Dudley "Big Bill"; Marx, Karl; Religious Anarchism; Socialism

References

Preston, William Jr., *Aliens and Dissenters: Federal Suppression of Radicals, 1903–1933,* 2d ed. (Urbana and Chicago: University of Illinois Press, 1994).

"Socialism: Other Socialist Tendencies Before World War I: Socialism in the United States," *Britannica Online* <href=http://www.eb.com:180/cgi-bin/g?DocF=macro/5007/6/12.html>.

Zeidler, Frank P., "History of the Socialist Party" (July 18, 1991), on the internet <http://www.pitnet.net/spwis/sphistory.html>.

Socialist Party USA

See Socialist Party of America/Socialist Party USA

Spanish Anarchism

For most of its history, Spain experienced periodic peasant revolts, and from the late 1860s until World War II anarchism enjoyed popular support in Spain. As Murray Bookchin explained:

> It is essential to emphasize that Spanish anarchism was not merely a program embedded in a dense theoretical matrix. It was a way of life: partly the life of the Spanish people as it was lived in the closely knit villages of the countryside and the intense neighborhood life of the working class barrios; partly, too, the theoretical articulation of that life as projected by Bakunin's concepts of decentralization, mutual aid, and popular organs of self-management. (Bookchin)

One of Mikhail Bakunin's disciples, Italian Giuseppe Fanelli, played a primary role in laying a foundation for anarchism in Spain. Bakunin's followers found common ground in the concepts of French anarchist Pierre-Joseph Proudhon. Spaniard Pi y Margall had translated many of Proudhon's books into Spanish, spreading Proudhon's concept of a society of self-governing communes joined in a loose federation.

Fanelli went to Spain after the revolution of 1868 brought about the abdication of Queen Isabella II. A weak constitutional monarchy was established, and many Spaniards called for a decentralized federal republic. In 1869 Fanelli contacted "a group of young intellectuals who were already familiar with the doctrines of [Charles] Fourier and Proudhon, and were anxious to use the overthrow of the monarchy and the creation of a new republic as an opportunity for social revolution" (Joll, 112).

Fanelli was able to form a Spanish section of the International Working Men's Association, or the First International, founded in London in 1864 and led by Karl Marx. However, the Spanish group was based on the Bakunin Alliance, which emphasized fomenting a revolution by proletariats with nothing to lose, who would set up their own committees and a universal union of free associations. In contrast, the First International espoused Marx's view, that is, an elite council of Bolsheviks should control workers until they were able to control their own destinies and the worker movement then sweeping Europe. The conflict between Bakunin and Marx eventually forced Spanish anarchists to choose sides, and the majority opted to follow Bakunin.

When the Spanish monarchy was reestablished, anarchists were forced to operate clandestinely, but the movement grew. Anarchist activities were prevalent among workers in Catalonia, particularly Barcelona, where the Confederación Nacional del Trabajo (CNT) was founded. CNT was a federation of Spanish workers' and peasants' unions dedicated to the establishment of an anarchist-communist society. Anarchism also gained converts in Andalusia, where "a grass-roots movement of peasants and workers . . . grew and flourished between 1868 and 1903" within the northern

Cádiz province (Kaplan, 3). Andalusian anarchists were often involved in violent insurrections, yet many dedicated anarchists led austere, even prudish lives and became martyrs to the cause.

From the 1870s through the 1890s anarchism was repressed in Spain, although revolutionary ideas were never wiped out. By the 1890s "propaganda by deed" spurred anarchist activity, which "consisted both of support for any sort of strike or rising springing spontaneously from below and of individual acts of terrorism and symbolic vengeance" (Joll, 233). As a result, government authorities cracked down on anarchists, often imposing harsh, sometimes unjust sentences.

One victim of the repression was Francisco Ferrer, a self-labeled "philosophical anarchist" who founded a number of progressive schools free of church and state authority. The Catholic clergy became increasingly agitated by Ferrer's activities, but the church was unable to restrict Ferrer's work until a Spanish workers' protest in Barcelona erupted into a rebellion known as the Tragic Week of July 1909. Numerous churches and convents were desecrated or burned, and Spanish authorities accused Ferrer of inciting an insurrection. During his trial no evidence connected him to the rebellion, yet Ferrer was convicted and executed, creating protests around the world.

Despite such coercion, anarchists continued to spread ideas and to organize workers in factories and farms through CNT and the militant anarchist group the Federación Anarquista Ibérica (FAI) or the Anarchist Federation of Iberia. When King Alfonso XIII abdicated in 1931, a somewhat reformist government was established, but those reforms were reversed between 1934 and 1936. Then politicians of the Popular Front, a coalition of liberals, syndicalists, and communists, won elections and once again pressed for reforms, such as separation of church and state and redistribution of large landholdings among peasants. But forces on the right—the church, the military, the upper class, and fascists—were adamantly opposed to such reforms, and by July 1936 they consolidated their efforts and supported a military uprising led by General Francisco Franco—the beginning of the Spanish Civil War and revolution.

CNT and FAI urged workers to prepare for a general strike and arm themselves in order to resist fascists and communists who supported Franco and his military uprising. However, because of their antiauthoritarian doctrines, CNT and FAI opposed any form of government or political activities. During the first year of the revolution, workers and peasants encouraged by CNT and FAI were able to appropriate land, set up communes, and operate factories in hundreds of villages in Andalusia, Catalonia, and Levante. But as the war progressed and Franco's troops stacked up victories, many Spaniards living in republican-dominated areas "did not understand why all the political parties and social movements did not constitute a united antifascist front regardless of their ideological differences. The people wanted the CNT and the much less important FAI to join the united front government which was, for them, absolutely necessary to guarantee the defeat of fascism" (Dolgoff).

Indeed, some CNT and FAI leaders began to cooperate with government officials "in order to win the war and save the people of the world." Such collaboration has been condemned by some anarchist writers while others have seen "sound practical reasons" for joining the government in an attempt to "contribute to unity on the republican side and to have a say in the actual running of the war" (Joll, 263).

Nevertheless, anarchist influence quickly diminished as the government became more centralized and fascists and communists gained ever more control. The Franco offensive succeeded in taking Barcelona in 1939, ending the revolution but not necessarily the anarchist tradition in Spain.

See also

Bakunin, Mikhail A.; Bookchin, Murray; Confederación Nacional del Trabajo; Ferrer, Francisco y Guardia; First International; Fourierism; Marx, Karl; Propaganda by Deed; Proudhon, Pierre-Joseph; Spanish Civil War

References

Bolloten, Burnett, *The Spanish Civil War: Revolution and Counterrevolution* (Chapel Hill: University of North Carolina Press, 1991).

Bookchin, Murray, "To Remember Spain: The Anarchist and Syndicalist Revolution of 1936" (1993), on the internet <http://www.spunk.org/library/writers/bookchin/sp001642/overview.html>.

Dolgoff, Sam, "Controversy: Anarchists in the Spanish Revolution," from *Fragments: A Memoir* (Cambridge: Refract Publications, 1986), on the internet <http://flag.blackened.net/liberty/dolgoff-controv.html>.

Fraser, Ronald, *Blood of Spain: An Oral History of the Spanish Civil War* (New York: Pantheon Books, 1986).

Joll, James, *The Anarchists* (Boston: Little, Brown, 1964).

Kaplan, Temma, *Anarchists of Andalusia, 1868–1903* (Princeton: Princeton University Press, 1977).

Spanish Civil War

Following years of rule by a monarchy and then a six-year dictatorship, Spain became a republic in 1931. A republican-socialist government tried to create an egalitarian society, attempting to wrest power from the church, wealthy landholders, and the military. But the coalition government did not take strong action against established institutions "for fear of alienating them entirely and provoking a military coup." Although the government established some moderate land reforms, limited the military, supported secular education and separation of church and state, "workers and agricultural laborers who were living in a state of near destitution became increasingly frustrated by the lack of change" (Ackelsberg, 66–67). At the same time, those in power wanted to retain their privileges, and they helped elect a new center-right government that curbed revolutionary activities and was in control from 1933 to 1935. But the following year the Popular Front government tried once more to institute reforms.

The government did not enjoy widespread support. Worker organizations—especially the anarcho-syndicalist trade union Confederación Nacional del Trabajo (CNT) and the socialist federation Unión General Trabajadores (UGT)—demanded more radical changes. In rural areas agricultural workers expropriated land and organized cooperatives; in cities workers staged strikes and in some cases seized factories. Spain became increasingly polarized, and assassinations of leaders of both the left and right were common.

Such a climate set the stage for civil war, which began with a military revolt in July 1936 led by General Francisco Franco. The rebels, known as nationalists, also included political conservatives and extreme rightists. Opposing the military uprising were CNT and UGT as well as various communist, socialist, and republican groups, a coalition known as republicans or loyalists.

During the early days of the war, the army gained control of the western and southern provinces, but not the major cities of Madrid, Barcelona, and Valencia. Loyalists held these cities as they did most of eastern Spain, where many collectives were formed in industries and agriculture.

In late July 1936 anarchists claimed a victory in Barcelona, defeating the army after two days of fighting. "From July 1936 until May 1937 the anarcho-syndicalists worked to prosecute the war and simultaneously to realize their long-held dreams of social revolution." Anarchists, socialists, and Marxists defended their territory with volunteer militias who lacked military knowledge of logistics and were short on supplies. "The anarchist militias had to overcome an inherent antimilitary bias and hoped to make up in enthusiasm what they lacked in professionalism, training, and discipline" (Sonn, 88).

Less than a year after the Spanish Civil war began, it became an international conflict. Nationalists received aid from Nazi Germany, which sent bombers and weapons, and fascist Italy, which sent ground forces. On the other side, International Brigades made up of volunteers from Europe and the United States went to Spain to fight fascism, and the Soviet Union sent advisers and weapons to support the republic. The Spanish Civil War became an ideological struggle between freedom (democracy) and tyranny (fascism).

Although loyalists held out against Franco's forces throughout 1936, they were plagued by strife between socialist and communist factions. Both factions opposed the anarchists and radical Marxists, but they increasingly quarreled over military involvement, food distribution, and workers' control of industry. In May 1937 armed conflict between the factions broke out in Barcelona, and after a month of fighting—with hundreds killed and wounded—the radical element was defeated. Communists, who gained control over the loyalists, increasingly repressed revolutionary workers' organizations.

Communists continued to seek aid from the USSR, but Soviet supplies dwindled in 1938, and nationalists gained the military advantage. By early 1939 Franco's forces, with the support of German dictator Adolf Hitler and Italian fascist Benito Mussolini, quickly won territory. The United States, Britain, and France refused to provide aid to the republic, and Britain and France signed a nonintervention pact, hoping to prevent armed conflict in other parts of Europe. The nonintervention policy allowed Franco's forces to wear down republicans. Franco captured Madrid on March 28, 1939, ending the war. The pattern of Allied appeasement and German and Italian testing of military tactics (which were used during World War II) have led numerous historians to label the Spanish Civil War a "dress rehearsal" for the later world conflict. Yet anarchist historian Murray Bookchin has taken issue with such a depiction, writing in a 1986 issue of *New Politics:*

> Spain was seized by more than a civil war: it was in the throes of a profound social revolution. Nor was this revolution, like so many self-styled ones of recent years, simply the product of Spain's struggle for modernization. If anything, Spain was one of those very rare countries where problems of modernization helped inspire a *real* social revolution rather than a reaction or adaptation to Western and Eastern Europe's economic and social development. This seemingly "Third World" feature of the Spanish Civil War and, above all, the extraordinary alternatives it posed to capitalism and authoritarian forms of socialism make the revolution hauntingly relevant to liberation movements today. In modernizing the country, the Spanish working class and peasantry literally took over much of its economy and managed it directly in the form of collectives, cooperatives, and union-networked syndicalist structures. Democratically-run militias, free of all ranking distinctions and organized around a joint decision-making process that involved the soldiers as well as their elected "commanders," moved rapidly to the military fronts.
>
> To have stopped Franco's [Army] composed of foreign legionnaires and Moorish mercenaries . . . and its well-trained Civil Guards and police auxiliaries, would have been nothing less than miraculous once it established a strong base on the Spanish mainland. That hastily formed, untrained, and virtually unequipped militiamen and women slowed up Franco's army's advance on Madrid for four months and essentially stopped it on the outskirts of the capital is a feat for which they have rarely earned the proper tribute from writers on the civil war of the past half century.

See also

Anarcho-Syndicalism; Bookchin, Murray; Confederación Nacional del Trabajo; Mujeres Libres; Spanish Anarchism

References

Ackelsberg, Martha A., *Free Women of Spain: Anarchism and the Struggle for the Emancipation of Women* (Bloomington: Indiana University Press, 1991).

Bolleten, Burnett, *The Spanish Civil War: Revolution and Counterrevolution* (Chapel Hill: University of North Carolina Press, 1991).

Bookchin, Murray, "To Remember Spain: The Anarchist and Syndicalist Revolution of 1936" (1993), on the internet <http://www.spunk.org/library/writers/bookchin/sp001642/overview.html>.

Creveld, Martin van, ed., *The Encyclopedia of Revolutions and Revolutionaries: From Anarchism to Zhou Enlai* (New York: Facts on File, 1996).

Dolgoff, Sam, ed., *The Anarchist Collectives: Workers' Self-Management in the Spanish Revolution, 1936–1939* (New York: Free Life eds., 1974, reprint Montreal: Black Rose Books, 1990).

Sonn, Richard D., *Anarchism* (New York: Twayne/Macmillan, 1992).

Wexler, Alice, *Emma Goldman in Exile: From the Russian Revolution to the Spanish Civil War* (Boston: Beacon Press, 1989).

Spies, August (1855–1887)

August Spies was one of the most outspoken of the eight martyrs convicted of the 1886

Chicago Haymarket murders. After he was sentenced to hang, Spies declared to the court: "If you think that by hanging us you can stamp out the labor movement . . . if this is your opinion, then hang us! Here you will tread upon a spark, but there and there, and behind you and in front of you, and everywhere, flames will blaze up" (quoted in Falk, 17).

Spies was born in central Germany and was educated for a career in government service. But when he was 17 his father died suddenly, and he left school in order to spare his family the expense. In 1872 he emigrated to the United States and stayed with wealthy relatives in New York for a time. He learned the upholstery business and moved on to Chicago, opening his own shop there in 1876. His mother, three brothers, and a sister emigrated to the city, and Spies took over their care. About this time, Spies began studying everything he could find on socialism, whether pro or con, and soon became a member of the Socialist Labor Party. In 1880 he began managing the German workingmen's paper *Arbeiter-Zeitung,* later becoming its editor.

Throughout the 1880s tens of thousands of industrial workers across the United States organized and struck for an eight-hour workday. At first many anarchists did not support the eight-hour movement, primarily because they wanted to entirely abolish the wage system. However, by 1886 anarchists were agitating for the shorter workday; Chicago became the major center of this movement.

When workers at the McCormick Harvester Machine Company outside Chicago staged a strike in 1886, McCormick hired nonunion laborers to replace strikers. On May 3 August Spies addressed a group of strikers near the McCormick plant, and police came to break up the crowd by clubbing and shooting people. One worker was killed and others were severely injured. The brutality outraged Spies, and the following day he published a pamphlet urging workingmen to arm themselves as protection against their "thieving masters." He and other anarchists called for a protest meeting on the evening of May 4 at Haymarket Square in Chicago. After Spies and others had spoken, police came once again to break up the workers, and within seconds a bomb was thrown by an unknown person. A force of 176 policemen began firing wildly on a crowd of about 200. One policeman was killed and dozens more were injured.

Over the next few days, police without warrants raided homes and offices of labor activists and anarchists. Spies and seven others were arrested and convicted of murder, despite no evidence linking them to the bombing or police fatalities. One of the men, Oscar Neebe, was sentenced to 15 years in prison; the other seven were sentenced to hang. The defendants appealed but lost their case. However, Illinois Governor John Peter Altgeld commuted the sentences of two men, Samuel Fielden and Michael Schwab, to life imprisonment. Louis Lingg committed suicide just prior to his scheduled execution. Spies and three others were executed, but before he was hanged Spies predicted, "The day will come when our silence will be more powerful than the voices you are throttling today." Those words are inscribed on a monument to the Haymarket martyrs in the German Waldheim Cemetery in Chicago.

See also

Haymarket Affair; Lingg, Louis

References

Falk, Candace Serena, *Love, Anarchy, and Emma Goldman* (New Brunswick, NJ: Rutgers University Press, 1990).

Foner, Philip Sheldon, ed., *The Autobiographies of the Haymarket Martyrs* (Atlantic Highlands, NJ: Humanities Press, 1969).

Spooner, Lysander (1808–1887)

An individualist, Lysander Spooner was a strong critic of formal laws and believed in a system of natural law, which he said was the "science of justice," and "the science of all human rights; of all a man's rights of person and property; of all his rights to life, liberty, and the pursuit of happiness . . .. It is the science which alone can tell any man what he can, and cannot, do; what he can, and cannot, have; what he can, and cannot, say, without infringing the rights of any other person" (Spooner).

Born in a rural area near Athol, Massachusetts, Spooner showed a distaste for authority early in life. He studied law in Worcester, but after completing his reading course "he found that admission to the bar was permitted only to those who had studied for three years, except in the case of college graduates. He considered the ruling obnoxious and worked [successfully] to have it removed from the Statute books" (Schuster, 144).

In 1844 Spooner challenged the monopolistic practices of the U.S. Postal Service. He objected to the postal rate of 12.5 cents to send a letter from New York to Boston and 25 cents to send a letter from Boston to Washington, D.C. In Spooner's view, the government charged high rates because it held a monopoly on letter carrying. He proved that the service could be operated less expensively, opening his own American Letter Mail Company, which carried mail for five cents. His business was so successful that the government feared other postal services would soon be started. After overwhelming government harassment, Spooner was forced to close his postal system. However, his actions prompted the U.S. Congress to pass a law reducing postal rates.

A fervent abolitionist, Spooner argued in his pre–Civil War book *The Unconstitutionality of Slavery* that according to natural justice each person was the sole owner of self. Therefore, slavery was unconstitutional. His book had an influence on numerous reformers and politicians, but some abolitionists such as William Lloyd Garrison strongly disagreed with Spooner. Garrison and his followers denounced all government and its laws as evil and inconsistent with Christian doctrine. Yet the differences between Spooner and Garrison may have been due to temperament, as Garrison did not like to compromise and Spooner was a methodical, analytical lawyer (Schuster, 145).

Spooner attacked government in a treatise that was intended as a six-part series. For unknown reasons, only three were actually printed under the same title, *No Treason: The Constitution of No Authority.* The first part was published in 1870 in Boston. In the 1966 reprint of the pamphlet, James J. Martin's introduction explains that

> Spooner strips away the support from any and all who conjure up one or another persuasive explanation of the Constitution as a contract, or as an agent facilitating a contract theory of government. A practicing jurist all his adult life, Spooner puts the Constitution to the test of contracts "on general principles of law and reason," such as prevailed in public affairs and in the market place where he worked with people from day to day, and concludes that it does not meet any of the basic criteria for contracts at all, and was not valid or binding on anyone. The sort of mystical osmosis, akin to telepathy, perhaps, by which Americans were supposed to have contracted with one or another to function under the document at the launching of the post–Revolutionary War American State, evaporates in Spooner's path as he assembles his argument, line by line, in nineteen carefully reasoned sections. Spooner does not find that the Constitution "says" anything, because it cannot talk. But he does see it as a device through which judges talk, explaining what it "said" to those who live under it. (Martin, 1966)

Spooner believed that individuals should determine their own destinies rather than allow government to continually expand its authority, making people virtual slaves. As he wrote in *Trial by Jury,* "If the people have invested the government with power to make laws that absolutely bind the people, and to punish the people for transgressing those laws, the people have surrendered their liberties unreservedly into the hands of the government" (Spooner, 1852).

In Spooner's view, the U.S. Congress should disperse, burn the law books, and allow people to rule themselves. In 1882 Spooner wrote and published an open letter to Senator Thomas Bayard of Delaware, challenging Congress's legislative power over the people. Four years later, Spooner published a letter to President Grover Cleveland, attacking all aspects of the federal government.

Like many individualist anarchists in the United States, Spooner "envisioned a society of preindustrial times in which small property owners gathered together voluntarily and were assured by their mutual honesty of full payment of their labor." Individuals would live together "in pursuit of their natural rights—life, liberty, property, and happiness." These rights were inalienable and could not be transferred, but with enactment of the U.S. Constitution basic rights were surrendered to a central authority. Spooner maintained that when men forced "obedience to the laws based upon [the Constitution], they were usurping the power of the individual" (Jacker, 82–83).

See also
Individualist Anarchists

References

Jacker, Corinne, *The Black Flag of Anarchy: Antistatism in the United States* (New York: Charles Scribner's Sons, 1968).

Martin, James J., "Introduction," *No Treason: The Constitution of No Authority* (1966), on the internet <http://alumni.umbc.edu/~akoont1/tmh/jjmintr.html>.

Schuster, Eunice M., *Native American Anarchism: A Study of Left-Wing American Individualism* (Northampton, MA: Smith College, 1932, reprint New York: AMS Press, 1970).

Spooner, Lysander, *Natural Law or the Science of Justice*, pt. 1, chap. 1 (Boston: by the author, 1870), on the internet <http://www.mind-trek.com/treatise/ls-nl.htm>.

Spooner, Lysander, *Trial By Jury*, chap. 1 (1852), on the internet <http://ipf.simplenet.com/eeta/htm–01/lsjury.shtml>.

Statism

Often referenced in anarchist literature, statism is a concept that is an opposite philosophy and social organizational paradigm from the ideals of anarchism. It was the rise of capitalism and the complicity of the state in exploiting individuals to give up "the means of production" that initially gave rise to the protestations (or antistatism) of William Godwin, Max Stirner, Pierre-Joseph Proudhon, and others. A strong central government that demands allegiance and sacrifice on the part of its citizenry (whether it calls itself theocratic, democratic, fascist, or communist) for the purpose of perpetuating the hierarchical structure of governance and the maintenance of economic power in the hands of a few is statism.

See also
Godwin, William; Proudhon, Pierre-Joseph; Stirner, Max

Steimer, Mollie (1897–1980), and Simon Fleshin (1894–1981)

Mollie Steimer and Simon Fleshin were well known among anarchists in the United States and Russia during the first half of the 20th century. They were rebels and idealists during their youths and dedicated their lives to liberty and justice, fighting for more than 60 years against authority and privilege.

Mollie Steimer was born in 1897 in Dunaevtsy, a village in the Ukraine. When she was 15, she emigrated with her parents and five siblings to the United States. To help support her family, she immediately went to work in one of New York's many garment factories (often referred to as "sweatshops"). Sweatshops were poorly ventilated, unsanitary, and hazardous, and workers earned meager wages.

Although Steimer soon learned firsthand about the harsh conditions of workers, she also began reading anarchist literature condemning worker oppression. By 1917 she was an avowed anarchist and met regularly with a Harlem anarchist group of Eastern European Jews. The collective shared a six-room apartment and in secret published an antiwar and prorevolution newspaper. As the newspaper masthead stated: "The only just war is the social revolution" (Bluestein, 5).

Steimer and comrades Jacob Abrams, Hyman Lachowsky, Samuel Lipman, and Jacob Schwartz were eventually arrested, indicted on conspiracy charges, and tried and convicted under the Espionage Act of 1917. Passed after the United States entered World War I, the espionage law made it illegal to obstruct the war effort in any way. Some historians condemn the Abrams case, named after defendant Jacob Abrams, as a flagrant violation of civil rights. Defense arguments were often brushed aside; Abrams and Schwartz were brutally beaten in jail, and Schwartz died while the trial was pending.

Before Steimer's trial ended, she was able to deliver a speech explaining her beliefs about anarchism, which she called "a new social order, where no group of people shall be governed by another group of people." She explained that

> individual freedom shall prevail in the full sense of the word. Private ownership shall be abolished. Every person shall have an equal opportunity to develop himself well, both mentally and physically. . . . No one shall live on the product of others. Every person shall produce as much as he can, and enjoy as much as he needs—receive according to his need. . . . we, the workers of the world, shall stretch out our hands towards each other with brotherly love; to the fulfillment of this idea I shall devote all my energy, and, if necessary, render my life for it. (Bluestein, 8)

Steimer and the others were released on bail pending appeal to the U.S. Supreme Court. Because she continued her anarchist activities, Steimer was constantly under police surveillance; she was arrested and released and rearrested at least eight times during an 11-month period. Twice during her imprisonments she staged hunger strikes, and while locked up on Blackwell's Island—barred from all contact with other prisoners and the outside world—she protested by singing anarchist songs.

The U.S. Supreme Court upheld the convictions, although Justices Louis Brandeis and Oliver Wendell Holmes strongly dissented. As Holmes wrote: "Sentences of twenty years' imprisonment have been imposed for the publishing of two leaflets that I believe the defendants have had as much right to publish as the Government has to publish the Constitution of the United States" (Bluestein, 11). Months after the decision, the defense lawyer obtained the defendants' release on the condition they be deported to the Soviet Union—the Union of Soviet Socialist Republics (USSR), as Russia became known after the communists took power in 1917.

Not long after arriving in the USSR in 1921, Steimer met Simon (Senya) Fleshin, and the two quickly fell in love; they became lifelong companions. Fleshin, who had also emigrated to the United States from Russia as a teen, had returned to his homeland in 1917 to join fellow anarchists involved in the revolution. But the communists in power continually harassed, arrested, and imprisoned groups of anarchists, Fleshin among them.

When Steimer and her comrades arrived in the USSR they were deeply disappointed to find many workers and peasants under the control of a Soviet dictatorship. Steimer and Fleshin organized the Society to Help Anarchist Prisoners, but they too were arrested and jailed, although they were soon released after threatening a hunger strike.

For almost a year (from late 1922 to September 1923) Steimer and Fleshin continued their work in Petrograd and elsewhere on behalf of fellow anarchists; they were rearrested and jailed. Again the two, along with 13 other anarchists, staged a hunger strike; eventually all were released. Most anarchists were exiled to areas outside Petrograd province, but Steimer and Fleshin were deported to Germany. Steimer later wrote that even though she had been happy to be deported from America to Russia, she was distressed that she was forced to leave her homeland despite the fact that "the hypocrisy, intolerance, and treachery of the Bolsheviks aroused in me a feeling of indignation and revolt" (Bluestein, 15).

In Germany, Mollie and Senya were befriended by Emma Goldman and Alexander Berkman, well known anarchists who had left Russia earlier, disenchanted with the Soviet system and the suppression of dissidents. During the 1930s, when Nazi dictator Adolf Hitler gained power in Germany, Steimer and Fleshin fled to France, where Fleshin became a professional photographer. But World War II erupted in 1939, and Germany occupied most of France. Because of their Jewish origins and anarchist activities, Steimer and Fleshin were soon under police surveillance. Steimer was arrested and sent to an internment camp in May 1940 but after six months somehow managed a release and escaped to unoccupied France. There she was reunited with Fleshin, who with the help of French comrades had been able to elude police.

In fall 1941 Steimer and Fleshin sailed for Mexico, a haven for many exiles. The couple maintained a photography business in Mexico for more than 20 years, and their home was a center for social activists—freedom lovers from around the world. They continued to advocate anarchism for the rest of their lives, even after they retired due to poor health. Mollie Steimer died in July 1980 at her home in Cuernavaca, Mexico; Simon Fleshin died less than a year later, in June 1981.

See also

Abrams v. United States; Berkman, Alexander; Espionage Act of 1917; Goldman, Emma

References

Avrich, Paul, *Anarchist Portraits* (Princeton: Princeton University Press, 1988).

Bluestein, Abe, ed., *Fighters for Anarchism: Mollie Steimer and Senya Fleshin, a Memorial Volume* (Minneapolis, MN: Libertarian Publications Group, 1983).

Marsh, Margaret S., *Anarchist Women, 1870–1920* (Philadelphia: Temple University Press, 1981).

Stelton School and Colony

An outgrowth of the Ferrer modern school movement of the early 20th century, the modern school in Stelton, New Jersey, was founded in 1914 by anarchists and libertarians, some of whom eventually established a small anarchist colony, about 30 miles from New York. The Ferrer school began in New York City in 1910 and was named for Spanish anarchist Francisco Ferrer, who believed that schools should be free of church and civil authority. In defiance of the church, which controlled Spain's educational system, he established "modern" or progressive schools in his homeland.

When Ferrer was executed (some say unjustly) for inciting an insurrection in Spain, a cry of outrage erupted worldwide. In Ferrer's memory, prominent anarchists such as Emma Goldman and Alexander Berkman helped found the Francisco Ferrer Association and a day school in New York City. But a series of violent incidents linked to industrial unrest occurred during the next few years, including the massacre of striking miners and their families in Ludlow, Colorado. In New York, three anarchists were killed when a bomb they were making accidentally exploded, and rumors spread that anarchists planned a bomb for industrialist John D. Rockefeller Jr., who was blamed for the killings at Ludlow. Police began to infiltrate anarchist meetings, and several New York anarchists decided to move the Ferrer day school to a rural area in New Jersey.

Harry Kelly, an anarchist printer and contributor to Emma Goldman's magazine *Mother Earth,* played a major role not only in the Ferrer Association but also at the Stelton school. He helped select the site, a farm for sale about a mile and a half from the railroad line. Kelly and other leaders hoped the planned school and colony would be "the center of a new nationwide movement for libertarian education" (Veysey, 114).

The land for the school and colony was purchased by the Stelton group, then sold to individual colonists at fair market value, enabling the group to set aside acreage for the school. "The individual ownership of plots of land was entirely in keeping with the anarchist belief in volunteerism. No one was to be compelled to remain in the colony any longer than he wished; he could always sell out his holdings and leave. Anarchists, unlike orthodox Marxists, had no single attitude toward the holding of private property; some approved of it, while others wanted ultimately to abolish it" (Veysey, 117). For the first few years, the modern school in Stelton struggled. But in 1916 William Thurston Brown, a socialist who had already established several modern schools, was appointed principal, and the school at Stelton began to flourish.

> Like the school in New York, attendance was voluntary, there was no discipline, punishment, or formal curriculum. As well as learning from books, the students participated in outdoor activities and made handicrafts. . . . In addition to the students who lived with their parents in the colony, thirty to forty children boarded at the Modern School. The farmhouse was converted into a boarding house, next to which was built an open-air dormitory,

> which was icy cold in winter. Margaret Sanger's daughter Peggy contracted pneumonia while at the boarding house, and had to be removed to a hospital in New York where she died. Conditions improved, however, after the arrival of Jim and Nellie Dick in the spring of 1917. (Perrone)

Nellie and James Dick dedicated their lives to anarchist ideas on freedom and spontaneity in education and concepts developed by Spanish anarchist Ferrer, setting up modern schools in their native England as well as the United States. At Stelton, the Dicks ran the boardinghouse, called the Living House, for children, instilling discipline and a sense of responsibility in their wards.

In 1920 Elizabeth and Alexis Ferm took over as coprincipals of the school. Previously, they had operated their own schools in New York.

> At Stelton, the Ferms promoted manual and creative work, such as printing, weaving, carpentry, basket-making, pottery, metal work, gardening, singing, dancing and other sports; they built a series of workshops in the schoolhouse, although the children still had the choice of studying academic subjects with Jim Dick in the library. This program led to a remarkable creative flowering among the children, who produced, among other things, the *Voice of the Children,* which they wrote, illustrated and printed entirely themselves. Eventually, however, the Ferms came into conflict with some of the parents who wanted a more radical, politicized education for their children, and objected to the lack of attention paid to academics. Refusing to modify their methods, the Ferms left in 1925.
>
> After the Ferms' departure, the Modern School went through a difficult period of transition, until Jim and Nellie Dick returned in 1928 as co-principals. The Dicks renovated the Living House, which had fallen into disrepair, revived *Voice of the Children,* and reintroduced a full range of activities for adults. Jim and Nellie had always wanted to start their own school, however, and in 1933, they left Stelton to found a Modern School in Lakewood, New Jersey, which lasted until 1958. They were replaced by the Ferms, who were persuaded to return as co-principals. (Perrone)

During the Great Depression of the 1930s, the school began to decline as many parents lost jobs and could not afford to keep their children in the school. There was further decline after the U.S. government bought land next to the colony to build a military base, causing problems for the Stelton group. After Elizabeth Ferm died in 1944 and Alexis Ferm retired four years later, only 15 students remained. In 1953 the school closed permanently.

See also

Ferm, Alexis and Elizabeth; Goldman, Emma; Kelly, Harry; Ludlow Massacre; Modern School Movement

References

Avrich, Paul, *Anarchist Voices: An Oral History of Anarchism in America* (Princeton: Princeton University Press, 1995).

Avrich, Paul, *The Modern School Movement: Anarchism and Education in the United States* (Princeton: Princeton University Press, 1980).

Perrone, Fernanda, "History of the Modern School of Stelton," Special Collections and University Archives, Rutgers University Libraries, on the internet <http://www.libraries.rutgers.edu/rulib/spcol/modern.htm>.

Veysey, Laurence, *The Communal Experience: Anarchist and Mystical Communities in Twentieth-Century America* (Chicago: University of Chicago Press, 1978).

Whitehead, Andrew, "A Real Anarchist," *New Statesman and Society* (May 14, 1993).

Stirner, Max (1806–1856)

Johann Kaspar Schmidt, who went by his student nickname Max Stirner, has been called the father of individualist anarchism. He is known principally for his work *The Ego and His Own,* in which he presented his philosophy that "nothing is more to me than myself." Published in 1845, it was hailed as most revolutionary for its time, and Stirner became an overnight sensation in radical and philosophical circles. The book (republished in some editions as *The Ego and Its Own*) influenced anarchist thinking for years, especially among artists and more creative individuals, who saw in Stirner's words justification for their "Bohemian" lifestyle. To many scholars, his work served as a foundation for twentieth-century existentialism.

In Stirner's view, the individual (the ego) was the only finite, objective quantification of human society. As he stated: "Away with every concern that is not altogether my concern. You think at least the 'Good Cause' must be my concern? What's good? What's bad? Neither has meaning for me. The divine is God's concern; the human is down to humans. My concern is neither the divine nor the human, not the true, good, just, free, etc., but is unique, as I am. Nothing is more to me than myself!" (quoted in Harper, 34).

Stirner was born to a poor family in Bayreuth, Bavaria. His father died the year after Stirner was born; his mother remarried in 1809. The family moved to Prussia, and ten years later Stirner went back to Bayreuth to live with an aunt and attend a prestigious gymnasium. Later he studied the classics, philosophy, and modern languages at several universities, completing his studies in 1834. The following year his mother was committed to a mental institution.

Stirner married Agnes Klara Kunigunde Butz in 1837, who died a year later in childbirth; the child was stillborn. He intended to teach and at first had difficulty obtaining a position, but eventually he was hired by the Gropius Institute for the Instruction and Cultivation of Superior Girls after spending two years as an volunteer instructor. The security of his teaching position and relatively tranquil life at the institute belied the foment and exciting ideas then circulating throughout Europe.

Stirner's working-class roots gave him an empathy for the labor struggle and the political unrest all around him. As a result, he joined the Free Ones in 1841. This group of radical intellectuals included the likes of Karl Marx and Friedrich Engels and met in Hippel's Cafe in Berlin. One of the frequent visitors to this rowdy bunch, which often finished the night carousing in nearby brothels, was a wealthy 25-year-old, Marie Daenhardt. During this time, Marie and Max became close, and they finally wedded in 1843. With newfound financial independence thanks to his wife's money, Stirner concentrated on his writing. *The Ego and His Own* was published about two years later (in late 1844 but bearing a publication date of 1845).

Stirner wrote chiefly for the working-class reader, who he believed could be trained to achieve an adequate level of self-awareness that would create "true individuals." It was the free association or "union of egoists" that Stirner held up as the goal that would lead to the creation of a new society. States, classes, and even the "masses" were, for him, mere abstractions. And nothing but the reality of the ego was worthy of concentrated effort. Although this egoist philosophy is related to anarchism, in that egoists reject the state and all authority, it is unlike anarchism in that the will of the individual alone determines relationships and how issues are resolved. Anarchists usually emphasize social reform.

In his seminal work, "Stirner throws down his challenge to thousands of years of religious, philosophical and political depreciation of the individual," as S. E. Parker wrote in the introduction to a 1982 Rebel Press edition. From his

> uncompromisingly egocentric stand-point, Stirner proceeds to criticize mercilessly all those doctrines and beliefs that demand subordination of the interests of the individual to those of State, God, Humanity, Society, or some other fiction. He investigates what these terms mean; what, if anything, they are based on; and clears away the mental rubbish that surrounds them. He exposes the bondage of the individual to fixed ideas. He declares his hostility to every creed that would crush or deny individuality. His call to self-liberation is no mealy-mouthed carping about this or that restriction placed upon us by one or another authority. It is not designed to set up a new authority in place of the old. His message is to those who wish to affirm

> their self-sovereignty to the fullest extent of their power—here and now. To those who want to remain members of a herd, who feel an imperative need to merge themselves into some present or future collectivity, his philosophy will have no appeal. (Parker)

After his book was published, Stirner quit his teaching position and used his wife's money to open a dairy business, which quickly failed. Disgusted with the way her money had been squandered, Marie left Stirner, who was soon impoverished. He attempted to earn a living by translating, but it brought little income. Twice between 1853 and 1854 he was sentenced to debtors' prison for not paying his creditors. He died from a poisonous insect bite at 49, and his friends had to collect money for his burial.

See also
Individualist Anarchists; Marx, Karl

References
"The Ego and His Own: S. E. Parker's Introduction" (March 1982), on the internet <http://alumni.umbc.edu/~akoont1/tmh/separker.html>.

Harper, Clifford, *Anarchy: A Graphic Guide* (London: Camden Press, 1987).

"Max Stirner," on the internet <http://alumni.umbc.edu/~akoont1/tmh/huneker.html> and <http://www.math.uio.no/~solan/Stirner/stirner-netscape.html#index>.

"Stirner, Max" *Britannica Online* <http://www.eb.com:180/cgi-bin/g?DocF=micro/567/9.html>.

Stone, I. F. (1907–1989)

Never an anarchist but admired by many libertarians, antiauthoritarians, and truth-seekers, Isidor Feinstein Stone was most famous for his newsletter *I. F. Stone's Weekly* (later changed to *I. F. Stone's Bi-Weekly*). He believed in an uncompromising look at politics and government. Following the lead of groundbreaking independent journalist George Seldes, Stone's influence was much broader than the small readership his paper claimed. In a tribute written in 1989 upon Stone's passing, Ralph Nader noted he was like the activist and major force in the American Revolution, a modern-day Thomas Paine "as independent and incorruptible as they come. He knew what was important and what was fluff. And he tied these facts to a ferocious practice of the First Amendment" (Nader).

Stone would not compromise his principles of seeking out the truth and reporting what he discovered. With his wife Esther, he began publishing his own paper when it became apparent to him that working on newspapers like the *New York Star* and the *New York Daily Compass* or even as editor of the liberal magazine *The Nation* did not allow free dissemination of unvarnished truth. He took on Senator Joseph McCarthy and his accusations against suspected communists and exposed the U.S. military-industrial complex. He exposed liberals and conservatives alike when he found out they were trying to manipulate the truth for their own ends. From 1952 to 1967 *I. F. Stone Weekly* (1967–1971, *Biweekly*) was found in some of the most influential homes in America.

See also
Paine, Thomas; Seldes, George

References
Nader, Ralph, "A Tribute to I. F. Stone," *Multinational Monitor* (July 1989), on the internet <http://www.essential.org/monitor/hyper/issues/1989/07/mm0789_12.html>.

"Stone, I(sidor) F(einstein)" *Britannica Online* <http://www.eb.com:180/cgi-bin/g?DocF=micro/567/71.html>.

Students for a Democratic Society

See New Left

T

Taborites

The Taborites were a radical group of Hussites who revolted after leader Jan Huss was executed during the 1400s. These radicals set up religious communist centers in the hills—known as tabors in biblical terms—of Bohemia. Their main political and military center was called Tabor, and the insurgents who lived there began calling themselves Taborites. They were dedicated to striking out against the increasingly corrupt German-controlled church and the repressive institutions of the clergy and nobility. In an explanatory note to Friedrich Engel's *The Peasant War in Germany,* professor David Riazanov explained:

> All the classes of the Bohemian people arrayed themselves against the power of the pope—for a church reform, and against the Germans—for national independence. In this nationalist religious struggle the masses of the people revealed their social hatred for the propertied classes. At the beginning, however, all classes of Bohemia acted in unison. The slogan of the struggle was the demand for communion under two forms. The rites of the Catholic Church gave to the layman in communion bread alone, and to the priests bread and wine. The masses rising against the privileges of the Church demanded equality in communion. "A chalice for the layman!"

The Taborites were led by John Ziska, who belonged to the inferior nobility of southern Bohemia and had distinguished himself as an undaunted fighter and excellent leader. He led the rebel Taborite army as it seized several towns and controlled whole areas in what is the present-day Czech Republic. People burned their own dwellings and joined the movement as it constructed a radical new society where property was held in common. At their height, the Taborites reached as far as Nuremberg. By 1434, however, the movement was effectively crushed by government forces.

Taborite ideas were kept alive in this part of Europe for at least another century through pamphlets and occasional threats of peasant revolution. Several leaders attempted to incite mass uprisings among the poorest of their people, with calls for justice and the right of all people to live freely. Such leaders were burned at the stake for their efforts.

See also

Free Spirit Movement; Religious Anarchism

References

Catholic Encyclopedia electronic version (1996), New Advent Catholic Website <http://www.csn.net/advent/cathen/07585a.htm>.

Riazanov, David, "Introductory Notes" to 1926 edition of Frederick Engels, *The Peasant War in Germany,* on the internet <http://www.marx.org/Archive/1850-PWG/Notes/09.html>.

Walter, Nicolas, "Anarchism and Religion," in *The Raven,* on the internet <http://black.cat.org.au/spunk/library/pubs/freedom/raven/sp000614.txt>.

Thoreau, Henry David (1817–1862)

Known for his book about Walden Pond, his 1840s experiment in simple living in the woods near Concord, Massachusetts, Henry David Thoreau has long been quoted by libertarians and anarchists. Some of Thoreau's most famous words come from his essay "On the

Duty of Civil Disobedience," which begins with his hearty acceptance of the motto that "government is best that governs the least," enlarging upon this with his own belief "that government is best which governs not at all." He added:

> Government is at best but an expedient; but most governments are usually, and all governments are sometimes, inexpedient. The objections which have been brought against a standing army, and they are many and weighty, and deserve to prevail, may also at last be brought against a standing government. The standing army is only an arm of the standing government. The government itself, which is only the mode which the people have chosen to execute their will, is equally liable to be abused and perverted before the people can act through it. (Thoreau, 222)

Born in Concord, Massachusetts, Thoreau was the third child of John and Cynthis Dunbar Thoreau. His father was a businessman who owned a pencil factory. As a young boy, Henry tramped through the woods and fields near his home and learned to love nature. In 1828 Henry's parents sent him to Concord Academy, where he prepared for college. At 16 he entered Harvard University, and although he was a good student, he paid no attention to the school's ranking system. Instead he used the school library to become proficient in the English classics and in Greek and Latin. He graduated in 1837.

About a year later Thoreau, with the help of his brother, John, started a small progressive school in Concord. They were forced to close the school after three years, however, because of John's illness. John died of lockjaw in 1842. Thoreau then became a handyman for and disciple of the philosopher Ralph Waldo Emerson. With Emerson's encouragement, Thoreau began writing poetry, publishing some of his numerous poems in *The Dial,* a magazine that Emerson edited for other transcendentalists.

A lifelong bachelor, Thoreau had once proposed marriage to a young woman visiting Concord. The engagement was called off at the insistence of the woman's parents. Not long afterward, Thoreau began his successful experiment to live by the work of his own hands. At 27 he borrowed an ax to build a wooden hut on the edge of Walden Pond. For a little more than two years he carefully noted the survival skills and habitats of animals, contemplated the ways of humankind, and kept journals of his observations.

While at Walden Pond Thoreau was arrested and jailed because he refused to pay poll taxes. Thoreau did not want to support the Mexican-American war, which he declared was being waged by the United States for imperialist purposes. He also protested the U.S. government's support of slavery. Thoreau was released after one night when an unknown benefactor paid the tax owed. The incident prompted Thoreau to write his now famous "On the Duty of Civil Disobedience," a protest against government interference with human liberty. He also opposed the rule of the majority because the majority rules by virtue of its power—"they are physically the strongest." Thus, in Thoreau's view, "majority rule in all cases can not be based on justice." He concluded that "we should be men first, and subjects afterward. It is not desirable to cultivate a respect for the law, so much as for the right. The only obligation which I have a right to assume is to do at any time what I think right" (Thoreau, 223). His essay was so widely read that it came to the attention of Mohandas Gandhi, who used it as a basis for his nonresistance movement in India. Later, it influenced Martin Luther King Jr. and his nonviolent civil rights movement in the United States.

Thoreau believed that the law of equal justice was the only valid law, and he ardently protested slavery and defended minority rights. In 1859 he wrote a defense of the anarchist-type direct action taken by John Brown, an abolitionist, who with his followers captured the U.S. arsenal at Harpers Ferry, Virginia (now West Virginia), as part of a plan to free slaves. Thoreau contended that John Brown had acted without fear of government and that Brown's actions were inspired by motives far higher than those who condemned him. After Brown was executed, Thoreau declared that the future of the nation depended not on government but on individuals who do not seek guidance from "legislatures and churches" but rather from "inspirited or inspired" persons. As historian Eunice Schuster put it, Thoreau's defense "was a powerful one, and particularly courageous when it is remembered that the majority of the people of the time—even ardent abolitionists—condemned [Brown's action] as an insane act" (Schuster, 49).

Along with his essays, Thoreau wrote several journals that recounted trips he made from 1849 to 1853. These were published posthumously in book form with the titles *Excursions, The Maine Woods,* and *A Yankee in Canada.*

See also

Direct Action; Gandhi, Mohandas "Mahatma" Karamchand; Individualist Anarchists

References

Schuster, Eunice M., *Native American Anarchism: A Study of Left-Wing American Individualism* (Northampton, MA: Smith College, 1932, reprint New York: AMS Press, 1970).

Thoreau, Henry David, *Walden or, Life in the Woods and On the Duty of Civil Disobedience* (New York: New American Library, 1960).

"Thoreau, Henry David" *Britannica Online* <http://www.eb.com:180/cgi-bin/g?DocF=micro/592/9.html>.

Tolstoy, Count Lev "Leo" Nikolayevich (1828–1910)

Count Leo Tolstoy is best known for some of the world's greatest literary works, such as *War and Peace, Anna Karenina,* and "The Death of Ivan Illych." But in anarchist circles he is also known for his radical antigovernment ideas, which developed about the time he was 50 years old. His writings and views had (and still do have) a great influence on religious anarchists, although Tolstoy never called himself an anarchist. Among his disciples was the famous Mohandas Gandhi, who practiced nonviolent civil disobedience in India. Many prominent Americans, including Clarence Darrow and Jane Addams, were also influenced by Tolstoy's philosophy of love and his tactic of nonresistance as the proper response to aggression.

Lev Nikolayevich Tolstoy was born in Yasnaia Poliana, south of Moscow, into a family of Russian nobility. He was orphaned, however, at age nine—his mother died before he was two years old and his father died seven years later. His grandmother took custody until she died, then an aunt raised him along with his four siblings. As was typical of aristocrats of his rank, he was educated by tutors until he enrolled in the University of Kazan at 16. Two years later he left the university without earning a degree and returned to his family estate, living a dissipated life in Moscow and St. Petersburg. Between 1852 and 1855 he served in the army and wrote the first parts of an autobiographical trilogy, "Childhood" and "Boyhood," published in the journal *Contemporary.*

In 1862 Tolstoy married Sophia Anreyevna Bers, and the couple raised a large family at the Yasnaia Poliana estate, where Tolstoy was able to write his famous novels. Over the years he also underwent serious soul-searching and questioned the meaning of his life. He studied the biblical teachings of Jesus and converted to the doctrine of Christian love and opposition to violence of any kind. When he was about 50, he wrote *Confession,* which summed up his early adult years as a time of

> horror, loathing and heartache. I killed men in war and challenged men to duels in order to kill them. I lost at cards, consumed the labor of the peasants, sentenced them to punishments, lived loosely, and deceived people. Lying, robbery, adultery of all kinds, drunkenness, violence, murder—there was no crime I did not commit, and in spite of that people praised my conduct and my contemporaries considered and consider me to be a comparatively moral man.

Other books based on his newfound faith followed, and for his remaining years he dedicated himself to spreading his view of Christianity and faith. In his written works he espoused the simple life and, in the manner of other religious anarchists before and after, opposed the government and the church as institutions of force and violence. His major work on Christian anarchism is *The Kingdom of God Is Within You.* However, because anarchism was associated with violence, Tolstoy never referred to his beliefs and principles as anarchistic.

Tolstoy put his beliefs into practice and relinquished all his material goods, which led to a serious conflict with his wife and children. Only one of his daughters sided with him, and she accompanied her father when he left their home in 1910. But Tolstoy did not travel far. He had contracted pneumonia and died of heart failure at the railroad station.

See also

Gandhi, Mohandas "Mahatma" Karamchand; Religious Anarchism

References

Avrich, Paul, *The Russian Anarchists* (New York: W. W. Norton, 1978).

Bridgwater, William, and Seymour Kurtz, *The Columbia Encyclopedia,* 3d ed. (New York and London: Columbia University Press, 1963).

Morris, Brian, "Tolstoy and Anarchism," in *The Raven,* on the internet <http://www.etext.org/Politics/Spunk/library/pubs/freedom/raven/sp001746.html>.

Tolstoy, Leo, *A Confession,* electronic book, on the internet <http://www.dis.org/daver/anarchism/tolstoy/conf2.html>.

Tresca, Carlo (1879–1943)

Carlo Tresca was one of the leading Italian anarcho-syndicalists of the early 1900s, although his friend, poet Arturo Giovannitti, wrote that "from the point of view of pure doctrine he was all things to all men and in his endless intellectual vagabondage he never really sought any definite anchorage or moorings" (Gallagher, xii).

Born in the small town of Sulmona, Italy, Carlo was the sixth of eight children. His parents, Filippo and Filomena, were prominent citizens who lived on an inherited estate and were owners of two businesses. But in the 1880s, when Carlo was a teen, the nation's agricultural industry suffered an economic downturn that affected the entire country. The Trescas, along with many others, lost their lands and businesses.

Carlo had hoped to obtain a university education, but the family could not afford it, so his mother arranged for him to go to a seminary to study for the priesthood. However, Carlo despised the clergy and advocated free thought. He soon left the seminary to become active in politics, joining the Socialist Party and organizing peasants in the area surrounding his hometown. By 1900 he was secretary of the Railroad Workers Union and had started writing for the local socialist newspaper, *Il Germe.* He became editor of the paper and used it as a platform to attack the clergy, city officials, and others he considered corrupt. His harsh criticism eventually brought charges of libel and a two-month jail sentence. He continued his attacks, however, and in 1904 he was again convicted of libel. Although he could have appealed his case, he decided to emigrate to the United States, leaving behind a young wife, Helga, whom he had recently married. Helga joined Carlo a year later.

In the United States, Tresca lived for a short time in New York, where his brother, Ettore, who had emigrated from Italy earlier, had set up a medical practice. But Carlo hated New York and moved to Philadelphia. He lived there with Helga and their first child, daughter Beatrice, born in 1906.

Tresca became editor of the Italian Socialist Federation newspaper, *Il Proletario,* but he soon became disillusioned with the Socialist Party, which did little to advance the cause of workers. He was jailed once more for libel and resigned from the newspaper. Not long after serving his three-month sentence, Tresca was able to start his own newspaper, *La Plebe,* publishing articles condemning the capitalist system of production that resulted in terrible working and living conditions for miners and their families in western Pennsylvania.

Tresca's publishing ventures included another newspaper, *L'Avvenire,* which attacked the clergy and championed workers. As biographer Dorothy Gallagher explained: "Six years after his emigration he was a well-known agitator among Italian workers in Pennsylvania as well as Ohio, New England, and Illinois. In the fall of 1910 he was making speeches to steel workers at McKees Rocks, Pennsylvania. At the Westmoreland mines he documented his accusations that officials of the United Mine Workers were in league with the coal operators" (Gallagher, 33).

Tresca's agitation in deed and in print was a pattern he followed for the rest of his life. By 1912 Tresca was ready to take on the plight of textile workers in Lawrence, Massachusetts. Most of the workers were European immigrants attracted by recruiters promising wealth and happiness. Instead the workers were forced to live in disease-ridden tenements and work long hours in foul factories, earning less than a living wage. The Industrial Workers of the World (known as the Wobblies), which was based on the principle of direct action, led a strike at the Lawrence mill. Among the strike leaders were Elizabeth Gurley Flynn and Big Bill Haywood, who often worked with anarchists but did not necessarily espouse their cause. Tresca was called in to help organize, staying in Lawrence for months.

During the summer and fall of 1912, Flynn and Tresca worked closely together in Lawrence and soon fell in love. Although Tresca returned home to Helga and Beatrice for a time, he was called to New York in 1913 for a hotel workers' strike and never went back to his family. Helga and Carlo divorced years later.

Tresca and Flynn continued their relationship, which Flynn described in her memoir as "tempestuous, undoubtedly because we were both strong personalities with separate and often divided interests." They took part in another now-famous strike of silk workers at Paterson, New Jersey, and along with such anarchists as Emma Goldman and Alexander Berkman agitated for workers—and the masses of unemployed—throughout the nine years they were partners.

When World War I broke out, Tresca used his newspaper to condemn U.S. involvement, which prompted the U.S. Department of Justice to prosecute Tresca for violations of the Espionage Act. His newspaper was banned, but he began another under the masthead *Il Martello.*

During the 1920s and 1930s Tresca became increasingly involved in the Italian anarchist movement and antifascist activities in the United States. In *Il Martello* he published many articles against Italian fascist leader Benito Mussolini, who by the early 1920s had gained power, leading a radical right movement supported by many landowners, industrialists, and army officers. In 1922 Mussolini and the fascists formed a coalition government with King Victor Emmanuel III, and several years later he took over the government, imposing a dictatorship. Throughout the 1920s the U.S. government and the press, along with many Italians in the United States, supported Mussolini, viewing him as a heroic savior of the people.

Tresca, meanwhile, published his paper, smuggling some copies into Italy. Mussolini sent officials to the United States to protest Tresca's continued attacks on the Italian government and to ask the U.S. Federal Bureau of Investigation (FBI) to find evidence that would allow the United States to deport Tresca back to Italy. The FBI's case was flimsy, but it used a federal obscenity law in 1923 to arrest Tresca. He was charged with distributing pamphlets on birth control, which was illegal at the time, and convicted and sentenced to a year and a day in the penitentiary in Atlanta. Although Tresca and Flynn had parted company by this time, she along with the American Civil Liberties Union, of which she was a founding member, and several Italian trade union locals in New York helped get Tresca's sentence reduced to three months.

The remainder of Tresca's life, spanning the Spanish Civil War and World War II, was a constant battle against tyranny of all types. As a result, he had numerous enemies, including not only fascists and government officials but also groups of anarchists who opposed his views. He was shot to death on a New York street in January 1943.

See also

Anarcho-Syndicalism; Flynn, Elizabeth Gurley; Haywood, William Dudley "Big Bill"; Industrial Workers of the World; Italian Anarchism; Lawrence Textile Mill Strike; Sacco, Nicola, and Bartolomeo Vanzetti

References

Avrich, Paul, *Sacco and Vanzetti: The Anarchist Background* (Princeton: Princeton University Press, 1991).

Flynn, Elizabeth Gurley, *The Rebel Girl: An Autobiography; My First Life, 1906–1926* (reprint New York: International Publishers, 1973).

Gallagher, Dorothy, *All the Right Enemies: The Life and Murder of Carlo Tresca* (New Brunswick, NJ: Rutgers University Press, 1988).

Tucker, Benjamin R. (1854–1939)

Like Josiah Warren and other individualist anarchists before him in the United States, Benjamin Tucker believed that individual liberty was the highest good. He is credited with producing a published work that most clearly describes individualist anarchism: *Instead of a Book: By a Man Too Busy to Write One.* Tucker was king among U.S. individualists during the late 1800s and early 1900s, disseminating his ideas through many publications, including his own periodical, *Liberty,* started in 1881. A prolific writer, Tucker, like most anarchists, was convinced that "government is invasion, and the State is the embodiment of invasion in an individual, or band of individuals, assuming to act as representatives or masters of the entire people within a given area. The Anarchists are opposed to all government, and especially to the State as the worst governor and chief invader" (C.L.S.).

Benjamin Tucker was born in South Dartmouth, Massachusetts, the son of Abner R. Tucker, who owned whaling ships and later was a grocer in New Bedford. His mother, Caroline A. Cummings, was his father's second wife; Benjamin was their only child. Benjamin was undoubtedly influenced by his mother, an admirer of Thomas Paine and considered to be a progressive, even radical woman. According to the editor of a compilation of Tucker's writings, "At two years Tucker was reading English fluently and at four gleefully discovered that the Episcopal Prayer Book had misquoted the Bible. At sixteen he had finished the course at the Friends' Academy, and, while at first refusing to go to any college, he finally spent two years at the Massachusetts Institute of Technology" (MIT) (C.L.S.).

In 1872, during his second year at MIT, Tucker became involved with the New England Labor Reform League (NELRL), which was promoting the free speech movement. At the time, Tucker heard Josiah Warren speak and met other individualist anarchists such as William Bradford Greene, Ezra Heywood, and Lysander Spooner. During an NELRL convention in Boston, Tucker heard Greene quote French anarchist Pierre-Joseph Proudhon, which prompted Tucker's further interest in anarchism.

While involved with the NELRL, Tucker met and fell in love with anarchist and ardent suffragist Victoria Woodhull, who was a lecturer on free speech and free love. Woodhull often faced opposition during her lecture tours, and Tucker helped arrange her appearances. In the fall of 1873 Tucker did not return to MIT, and instead went to New York and stayed with Woodhull and her family until summer 1874. The following year Tucker went to Europe with the Woodhulls, but when Victoria returned to the United States Tucker stayed on until early 1875.

After returning to the United States, Tucker worked for more than a year with anarchist Ezra Heywood on his magazine *The Word,* published in Princeton, Massachusetts. By 1877 Tucker was ready to establish his own periodical and founded *The Radical Review,* which lasted only a short time due to lack of funds. Tucker needed to earn a living and went to work as a reporter for the *Boston Daily Globe,* and by 1881 he had saved enough money to launch the longest-lived anarchist publication in the United States, known as *Liberty.*

With his masthead, *Liberty: Not the Daughter but the Mother of Order,* Tucker succinctly stated his philosophy and also defined anarchy in the journal with these words: "The Anarchists are simply unterrified Jeffersonian Democrats. They believe that 'the best government is that which governs least,' and that which governs least is no government at all" (Wehling). In 1882, Tucker moved to New York, where for more than 25 years he published his journal, including many of his own articles. He also edited *The Engineering Magazine.*

Unlike such anarchists as Johann Most, Tucker was opposed to "propaganda by deed." He believed that working people could reform capitalism in nonviolent ways through strikes and free credit. In his view an ideal society could be created with businesspeople, farmers, craftsmen, and cooperative associations based on mutual banking, as suggested by Warren and Proudhon. He believed workers' strikes should be encouraged by those who supported labor. This would indicate that people understood their rights and were willing to take risks to maintain them.

Tucker went to great lengths to explain what he saw as similarities and differences between two schools of socialistic thought: state socialism and anarchism. The first represented authority, the latter liberty. As he wrote, state socialism is

> the doctrine that all the affairs of men should be managed by the government, regardless of individual choice. [Karl] Marx, its founder, concluded that the only way to abolish the class monopoly was to centralize and consolidate all industrial and commercial interests, all productive and distributive agencies, in one vast monopoly in the hands of the State. The government must become banker, manufacturer, farmer, carrier, and merchant, and in these capacities must suffer no competition. . . . To the individual can belong only the products to be consumed, not the means of producing them. (C.L.S.)

In contrast, Tucker described anarchism as "the doctrine that the affairs of men should be managed by individuals or voluntary associations and that the State should be abolished." He pointed out that

> when Warren and Proudhon, in prosecuting their search for justice to labor, came face to face with the obstacle of class monopolies, they saw that these monopolies rested upon Authority, and concluded that the thing to be done was, not to strengthen this Authority and thus make monopoly universal, but to utterly uproot Authority and give full sway to the opposite principle, Liberty, by making competition, the antithesis of monopoly, universal. (C.L.S.)

Tucker's writings covered numerous topics, especially the concept of equal liberty for all and that "minding your own business" should be the only law in the anarchistic scheme. Tucker logically demonstrated that the application of these principles would benefit society, because each person's power would be limited by the exercise of the equal rights of all others. Tucker wrote as well on the relationship of the state to the individual and what allegiance a person owes to the state; the power of the state to tax; the concept that freedom means nothing if it is not total; a definition of property according to anarchist precepts; and how society could be organized without privilege or invasion.

Along with publishing *Liberty,* Tucker set up a printing operation and warehouse in New York City to publish low-cost editions of other anarchists' works, including his translation of Pierre-Joseph Proudhon's *What Is Property?,* Leo Tolstoy's *The Kreutzer Sonata,* and Mikhail Bakunin's *God and the State.* He also printed works by numerous other radicals, such as Max Stirner and philosopher and evolutionist Herbert Spencer, who were great influences on Tucker.

In 1907 Tucker opened Benj. R. Tucker's Unique Book Shop, several blocks away from his warehouse. The bookstore carried a variety of radical literature. A fire in 1908 completely destroyed Tucker's warehouse, printing equipment, and extra stock of books. As a result, Tucker, who carried no insurance, was out of business. He left the United States for France and gave up his anarchist activities.

When World War I began, he moved to Great Britain and broke with his pacifist stand, declaring he favored the Allies and their war effort because, as he wrote, the war had been caused by the German "nation of domineering brutes bent on turning the whole world into a police-ridden paradise of the Prussian pattern" (Jacker).

After the war, Tucker moved to Monaco, living there for 20 years and "becoming more and more pessimistic as he saw the rise of one authoritarian State after another," from the birth of the communist state in Russia to Nazism in Germany (Jacker). Tucker died at the age of 85 just before World War II began.

See also

Anarchist Press; Greene, William Bradford; Heywood, Ezra Hervey Hoar; Individualist Anarchists; Mackay, John Henry; Paine, Thomas; Proudhon, Pierre-Joseph; Spooner, Lysander; Woodhull, Victoria Claflin

References

Blatt, Martin Henry, *Free Love and Anarchism: The Biography of Ezra Heywood* (Urbana: University of Illinois Press, 1989).

C.L.S., ed., excerpts from *Individual Liberty: Selections from the Writings of Benjamin R. Tucker* (New York: Vanguard Press, 1926, reprint Millwood, NY: Kraus Reprint Co., 1973), on the internet <http://flag.blackened.net/daver/anarchism/tucker/tucker1.html>.

Jacker, Corinne, *The Black Flag of Anarchy: Antistatism in the United States* (New York: Charles Scribner's Sons, 1968).

Marshall, Peter, *Demanding the Impossible: A History of Anarchism* (London: HarperCollins, 1992).

Schuster, Eunice M., *Native American Anarchism: A Study of Left-Wing American Individualism* (Northampton, MA: Smith College, 1932, reprint New York: AMS Press, 1970).

Wehling, Jason, "A Brief History of the American Anarchist Press" (March 1993), on the internet <http://www.teleport.com/~jwehling/APressHistory.html>.

Turner, John

See Antianarchist Laws (United States); Rocker, Rudolf

W

Warren, Josiah (1798–1874)

Called the "American Proudhon" and the "first American anarchist," Josiah Warren developed a philosophy of individualism and theory of anarchism that included economic as well as spiritual and moral aspects. He published the first anarchist newspaper in the United States and founded several anarchist colonies.

Warren was born in Boston to a distinguished family—his father was a Revolutionary War general—but little else is known about his early life, except that he was a talented musician. Josiah and his brother, George, became professionals and played in local bands.

When Josiah was 20 he married, and not long afterward he left Boston to seek his fortune in Cincinnati, Ohio. There Warren became an orchestra leader and during his leisure time experimented with various mechanical devices and inventions. In 1823 he patented a new lamp and set up a lamp manufacturing company in Cincinnati. The following year, however, his life changed dramatically.

In 1824 Warren attended lectures by Robert Owen, a successful industrialist and social reformer in Great Britain who had purchased what was once a religious utopian community of Rappites in Indiana. Owen had established a secular community called New Harmony, where he declared there would be universal happiness achieved through education and communal living. He hoped to set up an "empire of peace and goodwill" that he thought would lead "in due season, to that state of virtue, intelligence, enjoyment, and happiness which it has been foretold by the sages of the past would at some time become the lot of the human race" (Holloway, 105).

Warren moved with his family to New Harmony, living there for two years and meeting renowned intellectuals from Europe and the United States. Although New Harmony failed to meet its goals and many communalists left, Warren was able to "study the problems of government, property, and industry, together with the relation of the individual to society" (Lockwood, 295). When New Harmony broke up in 1827, Warren hoped to put to use what he had learned, particularly the concept of human liberty that Owen conveyed. However, Warren criticized the lack of individuality, initiative, and personal responsibility in New Harmony. The community awarded equal privileges to all members rather than according to the worth of an individual's services; a skilled laborer, for example, received the same amount as an unskilled worker. Decisions were made by the majority, an authoritarian body. In contrast, Warren believed that social reform had to be based on complete individual freedom, which to him meant that "every one should be free to dispose of his person, his property, his time, and his reputation as he pleases—but *always at his own cost;* this qualification of the principle . . . is the core, as it were, of his philosophy" (Lockwood, 296).

To put his theories into practice, Warren returned to Cincinnati and began an experiment with labor notes, that is, to make labor the basis of currency. He opened what became known as a Time Store. "The storekeeper exchanged his time for an equal amount of the time of those who purchased goods from him. The actual cost of the goods bought was paid for in cash, the labor note of the customer was given to the merchant to pay for his service" (Lockwood, 296). Labor was evaluated not only by the time involved but also according to its "repugnance" or disagreeableness. "A street-cleaner's hour of labor was worth more than that of a college professor," for example. "As an economic experiment it was an attempt to break the monopoly power of the merchant-capitalist who, by virtually controlling the media of exchange, prevented the exchange of commodities according to labor cost" (Schuster, 103–104).

Warren expanded on his labor and individualist theories by establishing a village called Equity in Tuscarawas County, Ohio, where he hoped to teach young people the trades. To prepare for the experiment he taught himself various skills such as metalworking and printing. In 1833 Warren began publishing the first anarchist newspaper, a four-page weekly called *The Peaceful Revolutionist.* He invented his own cylinder press, the first to print from a roll of paper, and made type molds and plates that "were cast over the fire of the same stove at which [his] wife cooked the family meals" (Lockwood, 298). The publication primarily described the principles of equity and lasted only a few months. After two years, Equity itself had to be abandoned because of outbreaks of malaria in the region.

Undaunted, Warren in 1847 founded a second anarchist colony in Ohio called Utopia, where he published another newspaper, *The Peaceful Anarchist.* Each family in Utopia owned their own property but cooperated wherever possible in other ventures of the colony.

> Warren's efforts were for those whose only means was their labor force, and his purpose was to demonstrate that such people, with free access to natural resources, could, by exchanging their labor on equitable terms, by means of labor notes, build their own houses, supply their prime necessities, and attain to comfort and prosperity without dependence on capitalists, or any external authority, for the means of life. (Lockwood, 301)

Although the colony progressed during a four-year period, people moved on to other states where land was less expensive and readily available.

In 1850 Warren began a lecture tour in New York and Boston and gained a number of followers, among them Stephen Pearl Andrews, who wrote *Science of Society,* espousing Warren's ideas. Andrews also supported Warren's next colony, Modern Times, set up in 1851 about 40 miles from New York on Long Island. A year later, in 1852, he published *Practical Details in Equitable Commerce.*

Because of its proximity to New York City, the colony attracted reporters who wrote articles about Modern Times, prompting many people to visit the village. Some of the visitors stayed, although they knew little about Warren's theories or the views of the original settlers who lived by the principles of equity. Some of the newcomers exhibited eccentric behavior patterns and became an aggravation. But true to their belief in equal rights, the pioneers tolerated silliness and oddities as long as the strangers did not infringe on others' rights. The New York press, however, published sensational articles about the colony, creating unwanted notoriety. Yet the pioneers prospered despite "the persistent misrepresentations and the withering slanders" (Lockwood, 303). Still, they changed the name of their colony to Brentwood. While his anarchist colony developed, Warren published a record of his movement in *Periodical Letters* from mid-1854 to late 1858.

The economic depression of 1857 destroyed a manufacturing company that was the mainstay of Modern Times/Brentwood; when the nation was torn asunder by civil war, the anarchist colony could no longer thrive. Warren left Brentwood in 1860 and spent his remaining years writing. In 1863 he published *True Civilization,* containing his theories on absolute individual sovereignty and voluntary cooperation in society. Many of his ideas were forerunners for the more profound works of Pierre-Joseph Proudhon. Warren lived with friends near Boston until his death in 1874.

See also

Andrews, Stephen Pearl; Proudhon, Pierre-Joseph

References

Holloway, Mark, *Heavens on Earth: Utopian Communities in America, 1680–1880,* 2d ed. (New York: Dover, 1966).

Lockwood, George B., *The New Harmony Movement* (New York: D. Appleton and Company, 1905).

Schuster, Eunice M., *Native American Anarchism: A Study of Left-Wing American Individualism* (Northampton, MA: Smith College, 1932, reprint New York: AMS Press, 1970).

Wilson, Charlotte

See Freedom Press

Winstanley, Gerrard (1609–1676?)

Gerrard Winstanley, a religious dissenter, is known for leading a small group of rural men known as Diggers. Historians know very little about Winstanley's life prior to the Digger movement, except that he was born in Lancashire and became a tradesman, selling cloth. His business failed during the 1640s, probably because of the civil war in England, an armed conflict between Parliament and the monarchy. The war ended royal rule, and a moralistic leader of a bitterly divided Parliament, Oliver Cromwell, eventually appointed himself Lord Protector. Cromwell dissolved Parliament and became dictator, ruling until his death in 1658.

In 1649 Winstanley and William Everard established a Digger commune of 20–30 men and women at St. George's Hill, Walton-on-Thames, Surrey. Later, another commune was set up in nearby Cobham.

Winstanley announced the Diggers' intentions in a pamphlet entitled "A Declaration from the Poor oppressed People of England, directed to all that call themselves, or are called Lords of Manors." The pamphlet declared that Winstanley and his followers,

> in the name of all the poor oppressed people in *England,* declare unto you, that call your selves lords of Manors, and Lords of the Land, That in regard the King of Righteousness, our Maker, hath inlightened our hearts so far, as to see, That the earth was not made purposely for you, to be Lords of it, and we to be your Slaves, Servants, and Beggers; but it was made to be a common Livelihood to all, without respect of persons: And that your buying and selling of Land, and the Fruits of it, one to another, is *The cursed thing,* and was brought in by War; which hath, and still does establish murder, and theft, In the hands of some branches of Mankinde over others, which is the greatest outward burden, and unrighteous power, that the Creation groans under: For the power of inclosing Land, and owning Propriety, was brought into the Creation by your Ancestors by the Sword; which first did murther their fellow Creatures, Men, and after plunder or steal away their Land, and left this Land successively to you, their Children. And therefore, though you did not kill or theeve, yet you hold that cursed thing in your hand, by the power of the Sword; and so you justifie the wicked deeds of your Fathers; and that sin of your Fathers, shall be visited upon the Head of you, and your Children, to the third and fourth Generation, and longer too, till your bloody and theeving power be rooted out of the Land. (Winstanley)

Although the Digger commune never included more than 50 members, it was a major threat to local authorities. Winstanley and his followers were attacked and beaten, and he was jailed more than once. By 1650 the experiment was over; the Diggers abandoned their burned cottages and destroyed crops. Shortly thereafter Winstanley moved to London, but no one knows what happened to him there.

The major importance of Winstanley's life, however, was the communal experience of the Diggers, which he used as the basis for the first document outlining anarchist-communism principles. Published under the title *The Law of Freedom* in 1652, the work called for the abolition of private property and for the establishment of a cooperative system of employment. Winstanley also wrote *The New Law of Righteousness,* published in 1649, which spelled out his ideas on religion. In his words: "Reason was an active force guiding love, justice, and wisdom. Without Reason there would be madness and disorder" (Sutherland).

There is no record of when, where, or how Winstanley died, although some historians speculate he may have been the Quaker Gerrard Winstanley whose death was recorded in 1676. Nevertheless, his writings and the activities of the Diggers (and the related Levellers) are kept alive today by a number of anarcho-communist groups, who maintain websites and disperse Winstanley's ideas.

See also

Anarchist-Communists; Diggers; Religious Anarchism

References

"Digger," *Britannica Online* <http://www.eb.com:180/cgi-bin/g?DocF=micro/170/34.html>.

Roberts, John Morris, *History of the World* (New York and Oxford: Oxford University Press, 1993).

Sutherland, Donald R., "The Religion of Gerrard Winstanley and Digger Communism," on the internet <http://viva.lib.virginia.edu/journals/EH/EH33/suther33.htm>.

Winstanley, Gerrard, "A Declaration from the Poor oppressed People of England, directed to all that call themselves, or are called Lords of Manors," on the internet <http://www.tlio.demon.co.uk/poor.htm>.

Wobblies

See Industrial Workers of the World

Wollstonecraft, Mary (1759–1797)

Called the "mother of the England's feminist movement," author Mary Wollstonecraft was well known for her fierce independence, free-love views, and eventually her marriage to William Godwin, who developed a set of philosophical principles that would be called anarchism. Her daughter, also named Mary, became a renowned British literary figure and married poet Percy Bysshe Shelley.

Mary Wollstonecraft was born in London and was the second child of John Edward Wollstonecraft, a gentry farmer, and Elizabeth Dickson. She had an older brother, Edward, and four other siblings who were born after her: James, Charles, Eliza, and Everina. Throughout the decade following Mary's birth the family moved to several different farms, settling for a time in Yorkshire and Wales, eventually returning to London.

Educated in the traditional day school, Mary also developed intellectually by studying with a neighboring clergyman. Her family experiences were teaching tools as well. At an early age she began protecting her mother from her father's tyranny and abuse and made no secret of the resentment she felt for her brother's favored position. Mary clearly exhibited her independence when at age 19 she became a paid companion, defying the established custom for gentry women, who never worked outside the home. Soon afterward she vowed never to marry.

In 1780 Wollstonecraft returned home to be with her ill mother, who died in 1782. That same year, Wollstonecraft's sister, Eliza, married, and Mary went to live with Francis "Fanny" Blood, a close friend from her teen years. Wollstonecraft was called upon again to care for a family member in 1784, when Eliza suffered a mental breakdown after a difficult childbirth. Apparently, Eliza's husband was abusive, and Mary helped her sister escape the marriage even though Eliza had to leave her child behind. Hoping to become independent, Mary and Eliza and Fanny Blood opened a school in Islington. Later the other Wollstonecraft sister, Everina, joined them.

In 1785 Fanny Blood married in Lisbon. She became pregnant, and when she suffered complications she called for Wollstonecraft, who was at her friend's side when Fanny and her baby died during a premature birth. Wollstonecraft returned to England, closed the school—which had deteriorated because of her absence—and began writing. She also worked as a governess over the next few years but was bored with her job and wrote a largely biographical book, *Mary, a Fiction*. After its publication the book was hardly noticed and was not reprinted.

Wollstonecraft's book *Thoughts on the Education of Daughters* was published in 1786, the year she became a full-time writer and editor for *The Analytical Review*, a monthly magazine in London. When the French Revolution of 1789 began, Wollstonecraft became interested for the first time in politics and the humanitarian values espoused by radicals of the day. She hoped, as did many intellectuals, that the revolution in France would result in the emancipation of women. She was soon disappointed, however, and as a result she wrote *A Vindication of the Rights of Woman,* the first social study arguing that "if women are not permitted to enjoy legitimate rights, they will render both men and themselves vicious to obtain illicit privileges." Although the book was too revolutionary for mainstream readers, Wollstonecraft succeeded in focusing public attention on women as a social force.

After publication of her book, Wollstonecraft went to France, where she met American businessman Gilbert Imlay. They began an affair that lasted for several years. Although they never married, they registered as husband and wife with the American embassy to protect Wollstonecraft from imprisonment or even death. In 1794 the couple had a daughter, Fanny. Contrary to her views on sexual freedom, Wollstonecraft began to expect Imlay to establish a more serious commitment to the relationship. But he left her, and Wollstonecraft followed and attempted to rekindle the relationship; she was rejected and attempted suicide twice.

By early 1796 she was no longer infatuated with Imlay and became involved with novelist and philosopher William Godwin, who she had met five years earlier. Late that year, Mary Wollstonecraft was pregnant, and she and Godwin married in 1797 even though both had decried marriage. Godwin called the institution one of society's worst monopolies yet agreed to marry the pregnant Wollstonecraft to protect her from the type of scorn she had received when her first child was likewise born out of wedlock.

During the summer of 1797 Wollstonecraft began writing *The Wrongs of Women: Or Maria* while awaiting the birth of her child, Mary, who arrived at the end of August. Wollstonecraft, however, died of an infection known as "childbed fever" less than two weeks later. Godwin began the process of raising Mary and Fanny and to write *Memoirs of the Author of the Vindication of the Rights of Women,* which was published in 1798.

See also
Godwin, William; Shelley, Percy Bysshe

References
"The Famous Feminist—Mary Wollstonecraft," on the internet <http://www.netaxs.com/~kwbridge/feminist.html>.

"Mary Wollstonecraft: Mother of England's Feminist Movement," on the internet <http://www.suite101.com/articles/article.cfm/6533>.

Wollstonecraft, Mary, *A Vindication of the Rights of Woman with Strictures on Political and Moral Subjects* (Boston: Peter Edes for Thomas and Andrews, 1792), in the public domain, on the internet <http://wiretap.spies.com/ftp.items/Library/Classic/woman.txt>.

Wollstonecraft, Mary, *The Wrongs of Women: Or Maria,* in the public domain, on the internet <ftp://sailor.gutenberg.org/pub/gutenberg/etext94/maria10.txt>.

Woodcock, George (1912–1995)

Much of George Woodcock's work as a poet, writer, historian, and editor illuminated his anarchistic views. Although he was not an anarchist philosopher, he wrote many essays, pamphlets, and books about anarchists and the anarchist movement. Woodcock's more than 140 publications include biographical works on such celebrated figures as Peter Kropotkin, Pierre-Joseph Proudhon, Mahatma Gandhi, Aldous Huxley, and George Orwell. His most well-known books on anarchy are *Anarchism* and *The Anarchist Reader,* the latter in print since 1977 and translated into several languages.

Woodcock's 1961 work *Anarchism* has been criticized because it presents anarchism as a lost cause with no possibility of rebirth. Following the 1960s student rebellions in Europe and North America, Woodcock corrected himself in *Anarchism Revisited* (1977). Peter Marshall, who also wrote a major work on anarchism (*Demanding the Impossible: A History of Anarchism*), explained that Woodcock admitted he

> had been "rash in so officiously burying the historic anarchist movement" and explained that the work was, largely, a reckoning with his own youth. He had been disillusioned at the time with certain English anarchists who resorted to violence and was fearful with George Orwell that

"anarchist intolerance might create a moral dictatorship." But he still insisted that the renewal of anarchism did not add up to a movement. He approved of the new radicals' rejection of the state, their stress on direct action, decentralisation and popular participation, but saw it merely as a manifestation of the anarchist 'idea' in new forms. It was still his belief that the anarchists would never create their own world and therefore their aim should be "to preserve as much freedom as possible for men as they are rather than dream a hypothetical total freedom for men as they at present are not."

In a new postscript to *Anarchism* in 1975 Woodcock further acknowledged his rashness and in the introduction to *The Anarchist Reader* in 1977 he described anarchism as a phoenix in an awakening desert. But he continued to insist on the distinction between the "movement" and the "idea." His approach not only underestimated the continuity of the anarchist movement between the '50s and '60s but turned a useful distinction into a rigid and distorting framework. There is no dialectical recognition that a movement shapes ideas or that ideas shape a movement. (Marshall)

George Woodcock was born in Winnipeg, Canada, but his parents took him as an infant to England. He was unable to afford a university education, so he went to work as a railway clerk and at the same time attempted to establish himself as a freelance writer. During the 1930s he edited an antiwar newspaper, *War Commentary,* and also worked for the anarchist publisher Freedom Press, which has been in existence since the 1800s. He strongly supported the Spanish anarchist movement and the revolutionary efforts during the Spanish Civil War that began in 1936. Although he was embittered by the defeat of the Spanish anarchists, he never lost faith in the ability of working-class people to fundamentally change society in line with anarchistic ideas on individual liberty and voluntary cooperation.

During World War II Woodcock was a conscientious objector and worked as a farm laborer. After the war, in 1949, Woodcock and his wife, Ingeborg, moved to Canada, settling in British Columbia. He taught at the University of Washington in Seattle during the mid-1950s, then became an associate professor at the University of British Columbia in Vancouver. In 1963 he began writing full time.

In his writing and his personal life, Woodcock "preached the politics not of the left or the right but of the dignity of free individuals who, he insisted, could lead organically useful lives if not thwarted by authority. He believed in staying small and avoiding impersonal institutions; his life was an example of how great things can be accomplished by one person working away steadfastly" (Fetherling).

Woodcock remained steadfast to his own antigovernment principles and refused to accept honors and awards from the Canadian government. He continued to write until his death at age 82.

See also

Gandhi, Mohandas "Mahatma" Karamchand; Huxley, Aldous Leonard; Kropotkin, Peter Alexeyevich; Orwell, George; Proudhon, Pierre-Joseph

References

Fetherling, Douglas, "Eloquent Anarchist: George Woodcock's Mind—and Heart—Were Expansive," *Maclean's* (February 13, 1995).

Marshall, Peter, "Woodcock Obituary," on the internet <http://www.tao.ca/~freedom/marshall.html>.

"Woodcock, George" *Britannica Online* <href=http://www.eb.com:180/cgi-bin/g?DocF=micro/644/9.html>.

Woodhull, Victoria Claflin (1838–1927)

Biographers have described Victoria Woodhull variously as notorious spiritualist, faith healer, psychic, suffragist, reformer, stockbroker, one-time prostitute, presidential candidate, terrible siren. She apparently fit each description at one time or another, but she was also known as a supporter of individualist anarchist theories, especially those espoused by Stephen Pearl Andrews.

Victoria was born in Homer, Ohio, the sixth child of Buckman ("Buck") and Roxy Claflin, who were itinerant medicine-show performers and often in trouble with the police. Victoria and her sister, Tennessee, became part of the medicine show at an early age, performing "spiritual healings." Victoria also became a medium, going into trances to communicate with the spirit world. She and her sister were soon supporting their family with their "spiritual gifts." At 15, Victoria married a man almost twice her age, Dr. Canning Woodhull, who turned out to be a drunk. She had to care for not only him but their severely disabled child as well. The couple divorced in 1864.

Victoria and Tennessee continued to work with the traveling medicine show throughout the Midwest and then in New York City, where multimillionaire Cornelius Vanderbilt met them and in 1870 offered to help them set up a brokerage firm. With the help of "supernatural stock tips," the sisters gained great wealth and power, and Woodhull began speaking out on women's rights and for the suffragist movement.

In 1870 Woodhull joined a group led by individualist anarchist and intellectual Stephen Pearl Andrews. His group was based on a theory called pantarchy, which rejected conventional marriage and advocated free love, a single standard of morality for men and women, and communal living. Andrews and Woodhull's lover, Colonel James H. Blood (whom she in fact may have married), helped Woodhull and her sister begin a journal, *Woodhull and Claflin's Weekly,* publishing articles on women's rights and free love. Some historians speculate that Andrews was the ghostwriter for many of the articles.

In 1871 Woodhull and her sister became leaders in a U.S. faction of Karl Marx's International Working Men's Association (IWMA), founded in London in 1868 and known as the First International. The sisters' weekly was the first to publish an English translation in the United States of the *Communist Manifesto,* by Marx and Friedrich Engels.

By the end of 1871 Woodhull was involved in politics. She became the first woman to appear before a committee of the U.S. House of Representatives, arguing for women's suffrage. Then, in 1872, she and her supporters founded the Equal Rights Party after she parted ways with the National Woman Suffrage Association, whose members were not pleased with her scandalmongering. Woodhull ran as her party's candidate for the U.S. presidency, being history's first woman to do so. Frederick Douglass was her running mate, but he refused to campaign with Woodhull because of her radicalism.

About this time, Woodhull and her sister published stories in their weekly accusing a well known and powerful clergyman, Henry Ward Beecher, of having an affair with one of his parishioners, Elizabeth Tilton, who was married. Although Woodhull supported free love, she was disgusted with the cover-up of the affair and exposed the hypocrisy in her newspaper. That led to an indictment for libel and for "sending obscene material through the mail." Both sisters were jailed but later acquitted. However, there was little if any public support for the two, and in 1877 they moved to England, where Woodhull met and in 1833 married a wealthy businessman, John Martin. Her sister was married two years later to a prosperous merchant. The two continued to publish and lecture both in England and the United States, spending their final years in England.

See also

Andrews, Stephen Pearl; *Communist Manifesto;* First International; Individualist Anarchists; Marx, Karl

References

Gabriel, Mary, *Notorious Victoria: The Life of Victoria Woodhull, Uncensored* (Chapel Hill: Algonquin Books, 1998).

Goldsmith, Barbara, *Other Powers: The Age of Suffrage, Spiritualism, and the Scandalous Victoria Woodhull* (New York: Knopf, 1998).

Helmer, Diana Star, *Women Suffragists* (New York: Facts on File, 1998).

Sachs, Emanie, *"The Terrible Siren": Victoria Woodhull, 1838–1927* (New York: Harper, 1928).

Underhill, Lois Beach, *The Woman Who Ran for President: The Many Lives of Victoria Woodhull* (Bridgehampton, NY, and Lanham, MD: Bridge Works, 1995).

Workers Solidarity Movement

Founded in Dublin, Ireland, in 1984, the Workers Solidarity Movement (WSM) is an Irish anarchist group that came about because local anarchists were convinced there was a need to be organized nationally. "At that time with unemployment and inequality on the rise, there seemed every reason to argue for anarchism and for a revolutionary change in Irish society. This has not changed," the WSM declares on its website.

The WSM contends, as do most socialists and anarchists, that capitalism must end and that

> the wealth of society should be commonly owned and that its resources should be used to serve the needs of humanity as a whole and not those of a small greedy minority. But, just as importantly, we see this struggle against capitalism as also being a struggle for freedom. We believe that socialism and freedom must go together, that we cannot have one without the other. As Mikhail Bakunin, the Russian anarchist said, "Socialism without freedom is tyranny and brutality."

Although advocating, as all anarchists do, for individual freedom, WSM also works for democracy in the workplace and espouses worker control of all industry: "The only real alternative to capitalism with its ongoing reliance on hierarchy and oppression and its depletion of the world's resources." Since the group formed, members have taken part in direct action, ranging from fights for abortion rights to protests against racism. WSM also publishes *Workers Solidarity, Red and Black Revolution*—"an anarchist magazine of libertarian communism theory and history"—and numerous pamphlets. In addition, the group organizes speaking tours, including a 1997 tour for Black Panther Lorenzo Kom'boa Ervin, a U.S. anarchist and former political prisoner.

> WSM members see themselves as part of a long tradition that has fought against all forms of authoritarianism and exploitation, a tradition that strongly influenced one of the most successful and far reaching revolutions in this century—in Spain in 1936–37. The value of this tradition cannot be underestimated today. With the fall of the Soviet Union there is renewed interest in our ideas and in the tradition of libertarian socialism generally. We hope to encourage this interest with Red & Black Revolution. We believe that anarchists and libertarian socialists should debate and discuss their ideas, that they should popularise their history and struggle, and help point to a new way forward. (WSM website)

See also

Bakunin, Mikhail A.; Black Panthers; Spanish Civil War

References

"About the Workers Solidarity Movement," on the internet <http://flag.blackened.net/revolt/once/about_wsm.html>.

"Red and Black Revolution," on the internet <http://flag.blackened.net/revolt/rbr.html>.

Z

Zapata, Emiliano (1879–1919)

A hero of the Mexican Revolution (1911–1917), Emiliano Zapata was a leader of a peasant army that sought agrarian reform and overcame Porfirio Diaz's dictatorship, which was established in 1876. Zapata took up arms on behalf of the peasants. His charter called for "land and liberty" and helped shape the revolution; years after his murder, the revolutionary Zapatista National Liberation Army took his name and declared that Zapata still lives in them, particularly his anarchistic cry for freedom: "It's better to die on your feet than to live on your knees."

Emiliano Zapata was born in the Mexican state of Morelos. For centuries, communal Indian lands had been steadily taken over by owners of large plantations, and land and water supplies for the Morelos peasants were in short supply. Although by no means wealthy, the Zapata family was better off than most of the villagers. Emiliano's family farmed a small plot and raised cattle and horses.

Although he often worked on the farm, Emiliano was able to attend school on an irregular basis. He loved the land, and in 1897 he joined a village protest against wealthy plantation owners who had appropriated Indian territory. He was arrested and pardoned; a born leader, he continued to agitate. As a result, he was drafted and served six months in the army. After his discharge, he worked for a landowner, training horses.

In 1909 villagers elected Zapata president of a defense group attempting to gain back peasant lands. When all efforts failed, Zapata and his friends took over their communal lands by force.

About the same time, Francisco Madero, a reformer and champion of democracy whose family owned a vast estate in the north, ran for president, advocating social reforms and democracy. His opponent, Diaz, won a mock election in 1910 by imprisoning Madero, who was then released and took refuge in the United States, declaring himself president and calling for a revolt. With the help of peasant guerrillas, Madero returned to Mexico, and Zapata and his small defense force decided to back him.

While Zapata led his army in the north, revolutionary troops under Francisco "Pancho" Villa and Venustiano Carranza forced Diaz to resign. Madero became president and insisted that Zapata's guerrillas lay down their arms in exchange for money to buy communal land. Zapata refused the offer of money but did begin to disarm his troops—until Madero sent the army against them.

Zapata, who in 1910 had formulated his own plan for agrarian reform called the Plan de Ayala, declared that a revolutionary junta had organized to carry out the promises of the revolution. In 1911 Zapata and some of his followers declared Madero unfit to carry out the revolution because of his "lack of integrity" and the fact that "he left standing most of the governing powers and corrupted elements of oppression of the dictatorial government of Porfirio Diaz" (quoted in Womack, 400–404). As the rebel fighting continued, Zapata's troops distributed land taken from the plantation owners. In some cases he was often ruthless, killing landowners, extorting money from the wealthy, and stealing weapons from the army. But thousands of peasants followed him and fought for him.

After Madero was deposed and assassinated by another faction of rebel forces, several succeeding governments promised reforms, but there was little change. By the end of 1911 Zapata and his guerrillas had taken control of most of the state of Morelos and major portions of other areas as well as the capital, Mexico City.

The revolutionary war wore on, and Carranza, a moderate politician, was able to take over the federal government and declare himself president. He called for revolutionary forces to unite, but the rebel factions fought among themselves; Zapata and Villa, who demanded that the Plan de Ayala be put into effect, combined their forces against Carranza. Throughout the next few years bloody battles took place as rebel leaders attempted to gain power. Carranza remained in power by killing off his enemies, including Zapata, who was ambushed in 1919 and shot to death by Carranza's soldiers. Today, legends, ballads, and poems celebrate Zapata's life and deeds, and the Zapatista National Liberation Army carries on in his name.

See also

Zapatista National Liberation Army

References

Screenan, Dermont, "Zapata Lives!" on the internet <http://flag.blackened.net/revolt/ws/zapata41.html. >

Welker, Glenn, "Emiliano Zapata," on the internet <http://www.indians.org/welker/zapata.htm>.

Womack, John Jr., *Zapata and the Mexican Revolution,* "The Plan de Ayala" (New York: Vintage Books, 1968), excerpt, on the internet <http://www.msstate.edu/Archives/History/Latin_America/Mexico/ayala.html>.

Zapatista National Liberation Army

On January 1, 1994, the day the North American Free Trade Agreement (NAFTA) went into effect, a group of mostly indigenous Mexican peasants attacked four small towns in the state of Chiapas. In anarchist fashion, under the leadership of the masked Subcomandante Marcos, the self-proclaimed Zapatista National Liberation Army (EZLN) surprised government forces and captured the villages. Rebels demanded fair treatment for the country's Indian populations and called for the resignation of President Carlos Salinas de Gortari. The action shocked the nation and became headline news throughout the world.

The EZLN, severely outnumbered, was desperate to take a stand against a government it believed was working to enrich the wealthy at the expense of the poor. The attack on the day NAFTA went into effect was symbolic because the EZLN saw the trade agreement as one more wedge widening the economic chasm between the classes.

The conflict escalated days later when bombs exploded in Mexico City and Acapulco. By January 10 the government, under intense pressure to resolve the situation, negotiated a peace settlement with EZLN leadership. One year later, newly elected President Ernesto Zedillo broke the truce by ordering an attack against the Zapatistas in the area of Chiapas they had captured. The intent was to break the back of the leadership by exposing and capturing the charismatic Subcomandante Marcos. Marcos was identified as Rafael Sebastián Guillén Vicente, a philosopher and college professor.

Marcos led his followers into the Lacandona jungle as Mexican troops pushed into Chiapas. From his hideout, he used the internet to continue a dialog with the world and to publish a series of declarations that laid out the principles of a new governmental and social structure based on liberty, freedom, and equality.

Use of the internet has become a major communication channel for supporters of the Zapatistas, not only throughout Mexico but also in countries such as Australia, Italy, Canada, and the United States. Internet lists, conferences, newsgroups, and websites have proliferated since early 1994. Chiapas-L is the main list for discussion of struggles in Chiapas, but many pro-Zapatista activists post messages on sites such as the one maintained by the Accion Zapatista group in Austin, Texas (go to <http://www.utexas.edu/ftp/student/nave>, which contains links to many other sites).

See also

Frente Zapatista de Liberación Nacional

References

"Book of the Year (1996): Biography: Marcos, Subcomandante," *Britannica Online* <http://www.eb.com:180/cgi-bin/g?DocF=boy/96/J00355.html>.

"Zapatistas in Cyberspace: A Guide to Analysis and Information," an Accion Zapatista Report, on the internet <http://www.eco.utexas.edu/faculty/Cleaver/zapsincyber.html> (no date).

Zasulich, Vera Ivanovna (1849–1919)

A militant revolutionary, Vera Zasulich was a heroine in the eyes of many Russians. She was idolized by Emma Goldman, who became a well-known anarchist in Europe and North America.

Zasulich was the youngest of three daughters born into an impoverished noble family. Vera's father died when she was three years old, leaving a small estate, which did not provide enough income to raise a family. Vera's mother sent her daughter to the village of Biakolovo to live with wealthy relatives. She spent her childhood under the care of a governess, and at age 17 she completed school and went to work in St. Petersburg, a center of student radicalism. Many students were Nihilists, believing it was necessary to destroy the existing economic and social system through such direct action as assassination and arson. In 1866 a student Nihilist, who contended that the recently emancipated serfs had not been treated fairly, attempted to assassinate the tsar. Throughout the 1860s student activists demonstrated and agitated for social and economic reforms. Zasulich soon became radicalized, and in 1869 she was arrested for her connection with the student revolutionary movement. She spent four years in prison and was exiled. She continued to work underground.

During the 1870s there was widespread unrest throughout Russia, and police arrested and imprisoned numerous political activists. In 1873, 193 activists were imprisoned and held without trial until 1877–1878. The Trial of the 193, as it has been called, got under way, and the accused gained public sympathy because of their long imprisonment and the fact that "no less than twenty-one of them had either put an end to their lives by suicide or become insane," anarchist philosopher Peter Kropotkin reported in his memoirs. Some of the prisoners were given lenient sentences because they had already endured severe punishment. "It was confidently expected that the Emperor would still further mitigate the sentences. It happened, however, to the astonishment of all, that he revised the sentences only to increase them" (Kropotkin, 415).

About this time, Zasulich was again in St. Petersburg, where she became involved in a bizarre incident. The St. Petersburg governor and police chief, General Trepov (or Trépoff), became incensed when a political prisoner, student revolutionary Arkhip Bogolyubov, did not take off his hat in deference. The general flew at the prisoner, "gave him a blow, and, when the prisoner resisted, ordered him to be flogged. The other prisoners, learning the fact in their cells, loudly expressed their indignation, and were in consequence fearfully beaten by the warders and the police" (Kropotkin). The public was outraged by the general's action, and when Zasulich heard about the brutal treatment she went to Trepov's office with a revolver and shot him, wounding him. Zasulich never knew the prisoner who had been beaten, and she never denied her guilt. But as Kropotkin reported, because Trepov had so many enemies at St. Petersburg,

> the jury acquitted [Zasulich] unanimously; and when the police tried to rearrest her, as she was leaving the court house, the young men of St. Petersburg, who stood in crowds at the gates, saved her from their clutches. She went abroad and soon was among us in Switzerland.
>
> This affair produced quite a sensation throughout Europe. I was at Paris when the news of the acquittal came, and had to call that day on business at the offices of several newspapers. I found the editors fired with enthusiasm, and writing powerful articles to glorify the girl. (Kropotkin, 415–416).

While in Switzerland during the 1880s Zasulich corresponded with Karl Marx and Friedrich Engels and helped found the Emancipation (or Liberation) of Labor, the first

Russian Marxist group. The group spread Marxist ideas throughout Russia by translating and distributing such works as *Manifesto of the Communist Party* by Marx and Engels, *Wage-Labour and Capital* by Marx, and *Socialism: Utopian and Scientific* by Engels.

In 1900 Vladimir Lenin, founder of Bolshevism, conferred with Zasulich and other members of Emancipation of Labor in regard to possible contributors to his Social-Democratic working-class newspaper, *Iskra,* and the scientific and political magazine *Zarya*. Zasulich helped edit the newspaper and sat on its editorial board.

In 1903 Lenin was responsible for a split in the Russian Social-Democratic Workers' Party to which Zasulich belonged. Although Lenin espoused the idea that only a party of professional revolutionaries could bring socialism to Russia, Zasulich was part of the faction known as Mensheviks (the minority), which advocated a loosely organized mass party. The Mensheviks argued that a bourgeoisie regime had to be developed before the proletariat could take over and rule the country. When the Bolsheviks seized power in the revolution of 1917, Zasulich opposed them and continued to do so until her death two years later.

See also
Marx, Karl; Russian Anarchism

References

Engel, Barbara Alpern, and Clifford N. Rosenthal, eds. and trans., *Five Sisters: Women Against the Tsar* (New York: Knopf, 1975).

Kropotkin, Peter, *Memoirs of a Revolutionist* (Boston: Houghton Mifflin, 1899).

Zeno of Citium (342 B.C.–ca. 267 B.C.)

A Greek philosopher responsible for Stoicism, Zeno of Citium developed a concept that arose about 300 B.C. and had a major influence throughout the empires of Greece and Rome for centuries. Stoics are credited with developing the notion of natural law, or the idea that all human beings live in a world governed by universal precepts that define moral and immoral activity. The Stoic declared that the goal of life was to find happiness by living morally, in conjunction with natural law and through service to the community. Peter Kropotkin mentions Zeno in his article on anarchism that appeared in *Encyclopaedia Britannica* for decades. An excerpt follows:

> The best exponent of anarchist philosophy in ancient Greece was Zeno . . . from Crete, the founder of the Stoic philosophy, who distinctly opposed his conception of a free community without government to the state-utopia of Plato. He repudiated the omnipotence of the state, its intervention and regimentation, and proclaimed the sovereignty of the moral law of the individual—remarking already that, while the necessary instinct of self-preservation leads man to egotism, nature has supplied a corrective to it by providing man with another instinct—that of sociability. When men are reasonable enough to follow their natural instincts, they will unite across the frontiers and constitute the cosmos. They will have no need of law-courts or police, will have no temples and no public worship, and use no money—free gifts taking the place of the exchanges. Unfortunately, the writings of Zeno have not reached us and are only known through fragmentary quotations. However, the fact that his very wording is similar to the wording now in use, shows how deeply is laid the tendency of human nature of which he was the mouthpiece.

See also
Kropotkin, Peter Alexeyevich

References

Kropotkin, Peter, "Anarchism," *The Encyclopaedia Britannica* (1910), on the internet <http://www.etext.org/Politics/Spunk/library/intro/sp001636.html>.

"Stoicism," *Britannica Online* <http://www.eb.com:180/cgi-bin/g?DocF=micro/567/42.html>.

Appendix: Internet Anarchism

"Anarchy and the Internet," is a unique course at Pitzer College in Claremont, California, taught by Dana Ward. His course combines research and discovery about anarchists and anarchism concepts with a skill component that trains students how to publish and collaborate with peers using the internet as a medium of exchange. As he explains it in the course description, "Although unintended, the internet is the quintessential example of a large scale anarchist organization. There is no hierarchical authority controlling the internet, the subunits participate voluntarily, information flows freely, individuals join and exit associations at will. . . . Just as Pierre-Joseph Proudhon, the first theorist to call himself an anarchist, acquired much of his education as a by-product of working as a printer, you will learn what the classic anarchists had to say as you prepare their words for publication on the World Wide Web." Ward's classes have added to a growing "anarchy archive" that makes information on anarchism available to almost any interested person. The website for these efforts is found at http://www.pitzer.edu/~dward/classes/Anarchy/anarchyinternet.html.

There are numerous other websites, created by individuals and organizations who want to keep the philosophical questions raised by anarchism alive and evolving. The internet today is very much like the free pamphlet of the past, and the potential for reaching a huge audience is undeniable. The internet is the most affordable means to communicate ideas to supporters and doubters alike. And regardless of the rampant stereotype of the bomb-thrower that emerged during the era of "propaganda by deed," anarchists are interested in the intellectual assault on complacency that has led to one class dominating another. The web could be a conduit for exposing the modern state.

During the late 1990s, the anarcho-indigenous movement in Chiapas, Mexico, gained strength through internet exposure. One web site, the Zapatista Net of Autonomy and Liberation (http://www.actlab.utexas.edu/~zapatistas/index.html), includes several links to websites that relate the history of this struggle for autonomy. The "ZapNet" offers visitors the chance to contribute to the communities in Mexico and on the internet:

> You/we compose this space. We have learned to speak and to listen, to walk without exclusions, to respect the distinct levels and thinkings, to not impose our ideas and not to decree obedience to history, but above all to recognize and correct our errors. And it is from all of you from whom we have learned all of this.
>
> We seek dialogue, to establish connections and pathways. All of you have taught us that we are not alone, that our truth can not be imposed as an absolute truth. That to recognize our errors does not make us less, and that to talk of our failures does not dirty our words. No few times we have talked and acted as if the truth and the right did not have any other place than ours, as if we were the possessors of the better road, as if we were the only ones and the best ones.
>
> Contribute to the construction of this discursive community with your words and thoughts. Learning we continue to

> develop and make ourselves new. . . . The EZLN [Zapatista National Liberation Army] is no longer only the army with a majority of its members indigenous people who rose up in arms against the supreme government. The EZLN is, now and forever, a hope. And the hope, like the heart, is on the left side of the chest. We are now the product of all of you, of your word and of your nourishment.
>
> Share your ideas. Challenge us to challenge ourselves. Today it is no longer "all of you" and "we." We are the same. We are.

Interactive exchange also takes place in internet mail lists and via Usenet and other news and conference groups. The mail lists and newsgroups have a longer history than the world wide web. A very small listing of some of the more useful sites is included below; keep in mind that websites and addresses quickly change or vanish entirely.

An Anarchist FAQ Webpage (Version 7.2) <http://www.spunk.org/library/intro/faq/sp001547/index.html> is the website for an anarchist FAQ (frequently asked questions). "Its aim is to present what anarchism really stands for and indicate why you should become an anarchist. This website is the creation of many anarchists across the globe and is a classic example of the power of freedom, equality, and mutual aid. If you want to contact some of those responsible, then send email to anarcho@geocities.com."

Spunk Press: An Online Archive of Anarchist and Alternative Materials <http://au.spunk.org> is a well-developed archive that "collects and distributes literature in electronic format, with an emphasis on anarchism and related issues." It houses the Anarchist FAQ, described above, as well as a myriad of texts from well-known and lesser-known anarchist writers.

The Emma Goldman Papers <http://sunsite.berkeley.edu/Goldman/> is under the direction of Dr. Candace Falk, who initiated the Emma Goldman Papers Project. The project has collected, organized, and edited tens of thousands of documents by and about Goldman from around the world. Emma Goldman papers and sources are housed in libraries across the country and internationally. This website includes excerpts from the collection.

The Noam Chomsky Archive <http://www.worldmedia.com/archive/> includes links to text excerpts from Chomsky's writings, as well as audio excerpts from some of his more memorable interviews and speeches.

The Anarchy Organization <http://www.tao.ca> is a Canadian group known as tao communications, "a regional federation of local autonomous collectives and individuals involved in communications and media, radical activism and social work." This activist site also includes the archives of Freedom Press, "the longest lasting alternative publisher in the world," specializing in literature on anarchism since 1886.

The Portland Anarchist Web <http://www.teleport.com/~jwehling/LongAnarchistSites.html> has compiled an exceptional index of useful anarchist websites.

The Sixties Project <http://lists.village.virginia.edu/sixties/HTML_docs/Sixties_Proj_entry.html> is a collective of humanities scholars working together on the internet to use electronic resources to provide routes of collaboration and make available primary and secondary sources for researchers, students, teachers, writers, and librarians interested in the 1960s. It is sponsored by the Viet Nam Generation, Inc., and the Institute of Advanced Technology in the Humanities at the University of Virginia–Charlottesville.

A-INFOS NEWS is a list with reports and commentary from international news agencies that have an anarchist bent. To join, send email to majordomo@tao.ca with "SUBSCRIBE A-INFOS" in the body of the message. A separate discussion list for commenting on A-INFOS is also available. To join, include the phrase "SUBSCRIBE A-INFOS-D" to the same address. An archive is located at http://www.tao.ca/ainfos/ainfos_arch.html.

AIT-IWA-TALK is a discussion group on international syndicalism. To access this list, send email to AIT-IWA-talk-request@list.uncanny.net with the subject line "SUBSCRIBE."

ALTERNATIVE NETWORK FOR

EASTERN EUROPE is a list of the Polish Anarchist Federation. It can be accessed by sending email with the message "SUBSCRIBE ALTER-EE" to listserv@plearn.edu.pl.

ANARCHIST PROPAGANDA LIST can be joined by sending a blank message to geton.anarchoprop@cat.org.au. This list has been designed to post, discuss, and criticize current anarchist propaganda that is directed at nonanarchists. Archives of the important threads are located on the web at http://www.cat.org.au/aprop.

ANARCHY-IRELAND is, as the name suggests, a discussion of Irish events and history with a libertarian and anarchist point of view. Send email to anarchy-ireland-request@unamerican.com with only the word "SUBSCRIBE" as the subject.

ANARCHY-LIST, which can be joined with a message to anarchy-list-request@cwi.nl discusses many aspects of anarchism. Send a message asking to subscribe, accessing http://www.cwi.nl/cwi/people/Jack.Jansen/anarchy/anarchy.html.

ANARQ-LAT is a Spanish-language mail list that deals with anarchist subjects in Latin America. To join, send email to majordomo@majordomo.ucv.edu.ve without a subject line but with the words "SUBSCRIBE ANARQLAT" in the body of the message.

ANETDEV has been established to create a method for establishing international online connections between established anarchist websites, BBSs, and the like. Email should go to majordomo@tao.ca with "SUBSCRIBE ANETDEV" in the message.

ANOK4U2 is accessed through http://www.anok4u2.org/anok4u2-list/. This list caters to anarchist punks.

ANOKED is a list dedicated to the way anarchist thought and action can modify or be altered by the education processes. It discusses various facets of anarchist thought, specifically as to education. Send email with "SUBSCRIBE ANOKED-L" to majordomo@boink.clark.net.

A SPECTACLE is at http://www.nothingness.org/listedit.html. The focus is on the history of situationist theory and its recent influence.

ATLANTIC ANARCHIST CIRCLE has been created to meet the special regional needs of Atlantic Coast North American anarchists. Send email to majordomo@tao.ca to join; include "SUBSCRIBE AAC" in the body of the message.

AUSANET is an Australian anarchism list available for subscription via email to ausanet-request@lyst.apana.org.au. Ask to be added to the distribution list.

AUT-OP-SY has been chartered to discuss class and struggles associated with social structure within the international working environment. To subscribe, send email to majordomo@jefferson.village.virginia.edu with the message "SUBSCRIBE AUT-OP-SY."

BLACKFLAG-L is an English anarchist discussion list. To join, send the message "SUBSCRIBE BLACKFLAG-L" to listserv@qnet.org.uk.

CHIAPAS95 has been created to disseminate news and reports on the Zapatista movement in Mexico. Send email to majordomo@eco.utexas.edu to join; include "SUBSCRIBE" in the body of the message. CHIAPAS-L is a related list to discuss events and issues of the Zapatistas. Email should be directed to majordomo@profmexis.sar.net and include "SUBSCRIBE" in the message.

CONFEDERATION OF ANARCHIST YOUTH is a list based out of the University of California–San Diego for new and younger anarchists. In order to subscribe, send a message to listserv@burn.ucsd.edu with "SUBSCRIBE CAY yourfirstname yourlastname" in the body.

IWW-NEWS has been established by IWW to disseminate alternative news. To join, send email to majordomo@igc.apc.org and include "SUBSCRIBE IWW-NEWS" in the message.

MUJERESLIBRES has been established as a meeting place for anarchist feminists. It can be found via the web at http://www.geocities.com/Paris/2159/mujeres_mail.html.

ONEUNION is a mail list that centers on libertarian socialism and syndicalist issues. It can be joined by emailing OneUnion-request@list.uncanny.net with "SUBSCRIBE" in the subject line.

ORGANIZE is a private list that can be joined only by invitation. In order to become a member of this group of self-styled "class struggle anarchists," email platform@geocities.com and ask for the guidelines.

NOAM CHOMSKY was established to discuss the work, speeches, and writings of the contemporary world's preeminent linguists and best known anarchists. To join the discussion, email the message "SUBSCRIBE CHOMSKY" to LISTSERV@ MAELSTROM. STJOHNS.EDU.

RESEARCH ON ANARCHISM at listserv@bred.univ-montp3.fr is a moderated list that may make it more useful than the ANARCHY-LIST for many. To subscribe, email the message "SUBSCRIBE RA-L FIRSTNAME LASTNAME."

WSA-TALK is accessed by emailing "SUBSCRIBE" in the subject line to WSA-talk-request@list.uncanny.net. This is the online email discussion list of the IWA's American section.

Bibliography

Abraham, Richard. *Rosa Luxemburg: A Life for the International.* Oxford and New York: Berg, 1989.

Ackelsberg, Martha A. *Free Women of Spain: Anarchism and the Struggle for the Emancipation of Women.* Bloomington: Indiana University Press, 1991.

Adelman, William J. *Haymarket Revisited.* Chicago: Illinois Labor History Society, 1976.

Albro, Ward S. *Always a Rebel: Ricardo Flores Magùn and the Mexican Revolution.* Fort Worth: Texas Christian University Press, 1992.

Altgeld, John P. *Reasons for Pardoning the Haymarket Anarchists.* Chicago: Charles H. Kerr, 1986.

American Civil Liberties Union. *The Trial of Elizabeth Gurley Flynn.* Edited by Corliss Lamont. New York: Horizon Press, 1968.

Anarchism and Anarcho-Syndicalism: Selections Karl Marx, Frederick Engels and V. I. Lenin. New York: International Publishers, 1974.

Anderson, Carlotta R. *All-American Anarchist: Joseph A. Labadie and the Labor Movement.* Detroit: Wayne State University Press, 1998.

Anderson, Jon Lee. *Che Guevara: A Revolutionary Life.* New York: Grove Press, 1997.

Apter, David Ernest, and James Joll, eds. *Anarchism Today.* Garden City, NY: Doubleday, 1971.

Arshinov, Peter, Lorraine Perlman, and Fredy Perlman, trans., *History of the Makhnovist Movement, 1918–1921.* Detroit: Black and Red, 1974, originally published in 1923 by the Group of Russian Anarchists in Germany.

Ashbaugh, Carolyn. *Lucy Parsons: American Revolutionary.* Chicago: Charles H. Kerr, 1976.

Ashe, Geoffrey. *Gandhi.* New York: Stein and Day, 1968.

Atkinson, Linda. *Mother Jones: The Most Dangerous Woman in America.* New York: Crown Publishers, 1978.

Avrich, Paul. *An American Anarchist: The Life of Voltairine de Cleyre.* Princeton: Princeton University Press, 1978.

———. *The Russian Anarchists.* New York: W. W. Norton, 1978.

———. *The Modern School Movement: Anarchism and Education in the United States.* Princeton: Princeton University Press, 1980.

———. *The Haymarket Tragedy.* Princeton: Princeton University Press, 1984.

———. *Anarchist Portraits.* Princeton: Princeton University Press, 1988.

———. *Sacco and Vanzetti: The Anarchist Background.* Princeton: Princeton University Press, 1991.

———. *Anarchist Voices: An Oral History of Anarchism in America.* Princeton: Princeton University Press, 1995.

Avrich, Paul, ed. *The Anarchists in the Russian Revolution.* Ithaca: Cornell University Press, 1973.

Bakunin, Mikhail Aleksandrovich. *The Political Philosophy of Bakunin: Scientific Anarchism,* edited by G. P. Maximoff. Glencoe, IL: Free Press, 1953.

———. *The Confession of Mikhail Bakunin.* Trans. Robert C. Howes. Ithaca: Cornell University Press, 1977.

———. *The Basic Bakunin: Writings, 1869–1871,* Ed. and trans. Robert M. Cutler. Buffalo, NY: Prometheus, 1992. Originally published as *From Out of the Dustbin.* Ann Arbor, MI: Ardis, 1985.

Barber, Benjamin. *Superman and Common Men: Freedom, Anarchy and the Revolution.* New York: Praeger, 1971.

Barbour, Bloyd B., ed. *The Black Power Revolt.* Toronto: Collier-Macmillan, 1968.

Barsky, Robert F. *Noam Chomsky: A Life of Dissent.* Cambridge: MIT Press, 1998.

Becklund, Laurie. "Sanctuary Movement Leaders Assailed." *Los Angeles Times,* November 16, 1985.

Bedford, Sybille. *Aldous Huxley: A Biography.* New York: Knopf, 1974.

Beevor, Anthony. *The Spanish Civil War.* New York: Peter Bedrick Books, 1983.

Benjamin R. Tucker, C.L.S., ed. *Individual Liberty: Selections from the Writings of Benjamin R. Tucker.* New York: Vanguard Press, New York, 1926, Kraus Reprint Co., Millwood, NY, 1973.

Berkman, Alexander. *Prison Memoirs of an Anarchist.* New York: Mother Earth Publishing Association, 1912.

———. *Now and After: The ABC of Communist Anarchism.* New York: Vanguard Press, 1929.

———. *What Is Communist Anarchism?* New York: Dover, 1972.

———. *The Bolshevik Myth.* Boulder: Westview Press, 1989.

Berman, Paul, ed. *Quotations from the Anarchists.* New York: Praeger, 1972.

Bernstein, Samuel. *Auguste Blanqui and the Art of Insurrection.* Woodstock: Beekman Publishers, 1971.

Bestor, Arthur. *Backwoods Utopias: The Sectarian Origins and the Owenite Phase of Communitarian Socialism in America: 1663–1829.* American Historical Association, 1950. Reprint second edition Philadelphia: University of Pennsylvania Press, 1970.

Biehl, Janet, ed. *The Murray Bookchin Reader.* London: Cassell, Wellington House, 1997.

Blatt, Martin Henry. *Free Love and Anarchism: The Biography of Ezra Heywood.* Urbana: University of Illinois Press, 1989.

Blatt, Martin Henry, ed. *The Collected Works of Ezra Heywood.* Weston, MA: M and S Press, 1985.

Bluestein, Abe, ed., *Fighters for Anarchism: Mollie Steimer and Senya Fleshin, a Memorial Volume.* Minneapolis, MN: Libertarian Publications Group, 1983.

Bolloten, Burnett. *The Spanish Civil War: Revolution and Counterrevolution.* Chapel Hill, NC: University of North Carolina Press, 1991.

Bookchin, Murray. *Post-Scarcity Anarchism.* Berkeley, CA: Ramparts, 1971. Montreal: Black Rose Books, 1986.

———. *The Spanish Anarchists: The Heroic Years, 1868–1936.* New York: Free Life Editions, 1977.

———. *The Ecology of Freedom: The Emergence and Dissolution of Hierarchy.* Palo Alto, CA: Cheshire, 1982.

———. *The Philosophy of Social Ecology.* Montreal: Black Rose Books, 1990.

———. "Will Ecology Become 'The Dismal Science'?" *The Progressive,* December 1991.

———. *The Spanish Anarchists.* San Francisco, CA: AK Press, 1994.

Brenan, Gerald. *The Spanish Labyrinth.* Cambridge: Cambridge University Press, 1943.

Bridgwater, William, and Seymour Kurtz. *The Columbia Encyclopedia,* Third Edition. New York and London: Columbia University Press, 1963.

Brissenden, Paul F. *The IWW: A Study of American Syndicalism.* New York: Russell and Russell, 1957. Originally published in 1919. New York: Columbia University Press.

Brogan, Dennis William. *Proudhon.* London: H. Hamilton, 1934.

———. *The American Character.* New York: Alfred A. Knopf, 1944.

Brooks, John G. *American Syndicalism: The IWW.* New York: Arno Press, 1969.

Brown, Judith M. *Gandhi: Prisoner of Hope.* New Haven: Yale University Press, 1989.

Brown, Susan. *The Politics of Individualism: Liberalism, Liberal Feminism and Anarchism.* Montreal: Black Rose Books, 1993.

Browne, Harry. *Why Government Doesn't Work.* New York: St. Martin's Press, 1995.

Buckley, Stephen. "Berrigan Released While Appealing Contempt Term." *The Washington Post,* March 28, 1992.

Butler, M. *Burke, Paine, Godwin, and the Revolution Controversy.* Cambridge: Cambridge University Press, 1984.

Cahm, Caroline. *Kropotkin and the Rise of Revolutionary Anarchism, 1872–1886.* Cambridge: Cambridge University Press, 1989.

Cameron, Ardis. *Radicals of the Worst Sort: Laboring Women in Lawrence, Massachusetts, 1860–1912.* Urbana and Chicago: University of Illinois Press, 1994.

Camp, Helen C. *Iron in Her Soul: Elizabeth Gurley Flynn and the American Left.* Pullman: Washington State University Press, 1995.

Carden, Maren Lockwood. *Oneida: Utopian Community to Modern Corporation.* New York: Harper and Row, 1971, orig. publ. Baltimore: Johns Hopkins University Press, 1969.

Carr, Edward Hallet. *Studies in Revolution.* New York: Barnes and Noble, 1962.

Chalberg, John. *Emma Goldman: American Individualist.* New York: HarperCollins, 1991.

Chan, Ming K., and Arif Dirlik. *Schools Into Fields and Factories: Anarchists, the Guomindang, and the National Labor University in Shanghai, 1927–1932.* Durham and London: Duke University Press, 1991.

Chaplin, Ralph. *The General Strike.* 1933. Reprint, Chicago: Industrial Workers of the World, 1986.

Chomsky, Noam. *American Power and the New Mandarins.* New York: Pantheon Books, 1969.

———. *For Reasons of State.* New York: Vintage Books, 1973.

———. *Powers and Prospects: Reflections on Human Nature and the Social Order.* Boston: South End Press, 1996.

Clark, J. P. *The Philosophical Anarchism of William Godwin.* Princeton: Princeton University Press, 1977.

Clark, John. *The Anarchist Moment.* Montreal: Black Rose Books, 1984.

Coates, James. *Armed and Dangerous: The Rise of the Survivalist Right.* New York: Hill and Wang, 1987.

Cockcroft, James D. *Intellectual Precursors of the Mexican Revolution, 1900–1913.* Austin: University of Texas Press, 1968.

Cohen, Joseph J. *In Quest of Heaven: The Story of the Sunrise Co-operative Farm Community.* New York: Sunrise History Publishing Committee, 1957.

Cohen, Joseph J., and Alexis C. Ferm. *The Modern School of Stelton.* Stelton, NJ: The Modern School Association of North America, 1925.

Collins, Sheila D. "The New Underground Railroad." *Monthly Review,* May 1986.

Comfort, Alex. *Against Power and Death: the Anarchist Articles and Pamphlets of Alex Comfort.* Edited by David Goodway. London: Freedom Press, 1994.

Conlin, Joseph R. *Bread and Roses, Too.* Westport, CT: Greenwood Press, 1969.

Corcoran, James. *Bitter Harvest: The Birth of Paramilitary Terrorism in the Heartland.* New York: Viking Penguin, 1990, 1995.

Cowan, Geoffrey. *The People v. Clarence Darrow: The Bribery Trial of America's Greatest Lawyer.* New York: Times Books/Random House, 1993.

Coyote, Peter. *Sleeping Where I Fall.* Washington: Counterpoint Press, 1998.

Crick, Bernard. *George Orwell: The First Complete Biography.* Boston: Atlantic/Little Brown, 1980.

Crittenden, Ann. *Sanctuary: A Story of American Conscience and the Law in Collision.* New York: Weidenfeld and Nicholson, 1988.

Crowder, G. *Classical Anarchism: The Political Thought of Godwin, Proudhon, Bakunin, and Kropotkin.* Oxford: Clarendon Press, 1991.

Currie, Harold W. *Eugene V. Debs.* Boston: Twayne Publishers, 1976.

Darrow, Clarence. *The Story of My Life.* New York: Charles Scribner's Sons, 1932.

David, Henry. *The History of the Haymarket Affair.* New York: Russell and Russell, 1936.

Davidson, Miriam. *Convictions of the Heart: Jim Corbett and the Sanctuary Movement.* Tucson: University of Arizona Press, 1988.

Day, Dorothy. *The Long Loneliness.* Chicago: Saint Thomas More Press, 1993.

De Caux, Len. *The Living Spirit of the Wobblies.* New York: International Publishers, 1978.

de Cleyre, Voltairine. *The Selected Works of Voltairine de Cleyre.* Edited by Alexander Berkman. New York: Mother Earth, 1914.

———. *Anarchism and American Traditions.* Chicago: Free Society Group, 1922.

———. *The First Mayday: The Haymarket Speeches, 1895–1910.* Over-the-Water, Sanday, Orkney, UK: Cienfuegos Press; New York: Libertarian Book Club, 1980.

De Leon, Daniel. *As to Politics: A Discussion Upon the Relative Importance of Political Action and of Class-conscious Economic Action, and the Urgent Necessity of Both.* 1907. Reprint. New York: New York Labor News, 1956.

De Leon, David. *The American as Anarchist: Reflections on Indigenous Radicalism.* Baltimore: Johns Hopkins University Press, 1978.

Debs, Eugene. *Writings and Speeches of Eugene V. Debs.* New York: Hermitage Press, 1948.

Dees, Morris, with James Corcoran. *Gathering Storm: America's Militia Threat.* New York: HarperCollins, 1996.

Dellinger, David. *From Yale to Jail: The Life of a Moral Dissenter.* New York: Pantheon Books, 1993.

Detre, J. *A Most Extraordinary Pair: Mary Wollstonecraft and William Godwin.* Garden City, NY: Doubleday, 1975.

Dewitt, Rebecca. "Abe Bluestein: An Anarchist Life." *Perspectives on Anarchist Theory Newsletter,* Institute for Anarchist Studies, Spring 1998.

Dirlik, Arif. *Anarchism in the Chinese Revolution.* Berkeley: University of California Press, 1991.

Dolgoff, Sam. *The Cuban Revolution: A Critical Perspective.* Montreal: Black Rose Books, 1976.

———. *The Relevance of Anarchism to Modern Society.* Minneapolis, MN: Soil of Liberty, 1977.

———. *Bakunin on Anarchism.* Montreal: Black Rose Books, 1980.

Dolgoff, Sam, ed. *The Anarchist Collectives: Workers' Self-Management in the Spanish Revolution, 1936–1939.* New York: Free Life Editions, 1974. Reprint Montreal: Black Rose Books, 1990.

Dorsey, Gary. "Jonah House Under Seige: Convicts of Strong Conviction." *Christian Century,* April 15, 1998.

Drinnon, Richard. *Rebel in Paradise: A Biography of Emma Goldman.* Chicago: University of Chicago Press, 1961.

Duberman, Martin. *Mother Earth: An Epic Drama of Emma Goldman's Life.* New York: St. Martin's Press, 1991.

Dubofsky, Melvyn. *We Shall Be All: A History of the Industrial Workers of the World.* New York: Quadrangle Books, 1969.

Dulles, John W.F. *Anarchists and Communists in Brazil, 1900–1935.* Austin: University of Texas Press, 1973.

Edwards, Stewart. *Selected Writings of Pierre-Joseph Proudhon.* New York: Doubleday, 1969.

Ehrlich, Howard J., ed. *Reinventing Anarchy, Again.* San Francisco: AK Press, 1994.

Ehrlich, Howard J., ed. *Reinventing Anarchy: What Are Anarchists Thinking These Days?* London: Routledge and K. Paul, 1979.

Ehrmann, Herbert B. *The Case That Will Not Die: Commonwealth vs. Sacco and Vanzetti.* Boston: Little, Brown, 1969.

Eisenstein, Zillah R. *The Radical Future of Liberal Feminism.* Boston: Northeastern University Press, 1986.

Ellsberg, Robert, ed. *Dorothy Day: Selected Writings.* Maryknoll, NY: Orbis, 1992.

Eltzbacher, Paul. *Anarchism: Exponents of the Anarchist Philosophy.* New York: Libertarian Book Club, 1960.

Engel, Barbara Alpern, and Clifford N. Rosenthal, eds. and trans. *Five Sisters: Women Against the Tsar.* New York: Knopf, 1975.

Esenwein, George R. *Anarchist Ideology and the Working-Class Movement in Spain, 1868–1898.* Berkeley: University of California Press, 1989.

Ettinger, Elzbieta. *Rosa Luxemburg: A Life.* Boston: Beacon Press, 1986.

Evanoff, Richard. "Social Ecology: Basic Principles, Future Prospects—An Interview with Murray Bookchin," *Japan Environment Monitor,* 1996, on the internet <http://www.yin.or.jp/user/rdavis/bookchin.html>.

Falk, Candace Serena. *Love, Anarchy, and Emma Goldman.* New Brunswick: Rutgers University Press, 1990.

Farber, David. *Chicago '68.* Chicago: University of Chicago Press, 1988.

Felix, David. *Protest: Sacco-Vanzetti and the Intellectuals.* Bloomington: Indiana University Press, 1965.

Fellman, Michael. *The Unbounded Frame.* Westport, CT: Greenwood Press, 1973.

Ferm, Alexis, and Joseph J. Cohen. *The Modern School of Stelton.* Stelton, NJ: Modern School Association of New Jersey, 1925.

Fernandez, Frank. *Cuba—the Anarchists and Liberty.* London: ASP, 1989.

Fetherling, Dale. *Mother Jones: The Miners' Angel.* Carbondale: Southern Illinois University Press, 1974.

Fischer, Louis. *Gandhi: His Life and Message for the World.* New York: Signet Key Book, 1954.

Fisher, Louis. *The Life of Mahatma Gandhi.* New York: Harper and Brothers 1950.

Fishman, William J. *East End Jewish Radicals, 1875–1914.* London: Duckworth, 1975.

Flynn, Elizabeth Gurley. "Memories of the IWW," Web edition of transcript by Eugene W. Plawiuk, on the internet <http://www.geocities.com/CapitolHill/5202/rebelgirl.html>.

———. *The Rebel Girl: An Autobiography; My First Life, 1906–1926.* Originally published by Masses and Mainstream as *I Speak My Own Piece: Autobiography of "The Rebel Girl."* Reprint New York: International Publishers, 1973.

Foner, Philip Sheldon. *The Case of Joe Hill.* New York: International Publishers, 1965.

Foner, Phillip Sheldon, ed. *The Letters of Joe Hill.* New York: Oak Publishers, 1965.

———. *The Autobiographies of the Haymarket Martyrs.* Atlantic Highlands, NJ: Humanities Press, 1969.

———. *Mother Jones Speaks: Collected Writings and Speeches.* New York: Monad Press, 1983.

Forman, James D. *Anarchism: Political Innocence or Social Violence?* New York: Dell, 1976.

Fourier, Charles. *The Utopian Vision of Charles Fourier.* Edited and translated by Jonathan Beecher and Richard Bienvenu. Boston: Beacon Press, 1971.

Frankfurter, Felix. *The Case of Sacco and Vanzetti: A Critical Analysis for Lawyers and Laymen.* Boston: Little, Brown, 1927.

Fraser, Ronald. *Blood of Spain: An Oral History of the Spanish Civil War.* New York: Pantheon Books, 1979, 1986.

Gabriel, Mary. *Notorious Victoria: The Life of Victoria Woodhull, Uncensored.* Chapel Hill: Algonquin Books, 1998.

Gallagher, Dorothy. *All the Right Enemies: The Life and Murder of Carlo Tresca.* New Brunswick, NJ: Rutgers University Press, 1988.

Gambs, John S. *The Decline of the IWW.* New York: Columbia University Press, 1932.

Gandhi, Mohandas K., Mahadev Desai, trans. *An Autobiography: The Story of My Experiments with Truth.* Boston: Beacon Press, 1957.

Ganz, Marie. *Rebels—Into Anarchy and Out Again.* New York: Dodd, Mead, and Co., 1920.

Gay, Kathlyn. *Communes and Cults.* New York: Twenty-First Century Books/Holt, 1997.

Gay, Kathlyn, and Martin K. Gay. *Heroes of Conscience.* Santa Barbara, CA: ABC-CLIO, 1996.

George, John. *Nazis, Communists, Klansmen, and Others on the Fringe: Political Extremism in America.* Buffalo, NY: Prometheus Books, 1992.

Gibson, W. *Paris During the Commune.* Brooklyn: M. S. G. House, 1974.

Ginger, Ray. *The Bending Cross: A Biography of Eugene Victor Debs.* New Brunswick, NJ: Rutgers University Press, 1949.

Godwin, William. *The Anarchist Writings of William Godwin.* Edited by Peter Marshall. London: Freedom Press, 1986.

Godwin, William, and Mary Wollstonecraft. *Letters of William Godwin and Mary Wollstonecraft.* Lawrence: University of Kansas Press, 1966.

Goldman, Emma. *My Disillusionment in Russia.* Garden City, NY: Doubleday, Page, and Co., 1923.

———. *Anarchism and Other Essays.* 1910. Reprint New York: Dover, 1969.

———. *Living My Life,* 2 vols. New York: Knopf, 1933. Reprint New York: Dover, 1970.

Goldman, Emma, and Alexander Berkman. *Letters from Exile of Emma Goldman and Alexander Berkman.* Edited by Richard and Anna Maria Drinnon. New York: Schocken Books,
1983.

Goldsmith, Barbara. *Other Powers: The Age of Suffrage, Spiritualism, and the Scandalous Victoria Woodhull.* New York: Knopf, 1998.

Goodman, Paul. *Growing Up Absurd.* New York: Random House, 1960.

———. *The Community of Scholars.* New York: Random House, 1962.

———. *Drawing the Line: Political Essays by Paul Goodman.* Edited by Taylor Stoehr. New York: Free Life Editions, 1977.

Goodway, David, ed. *For Anarchism: History, Theory, and Practice.* London and New York: Routledge, 1989.

Goss, Miriam. *The World of George Orwell.* New York: Simon and Schuster, 1971.

Graur, Mina. *An Anarchist "Rabbi": The Life and Teachings of Rudolf Rocker.* New York: St. Martin's Press, 1997.

Green, Martin. *Gandhi: Voice of a New Age Revolution.* New York: Continuum, 1993.

Green, Martin, ed. *Gandhi in India: In His Own Words.* London: University Press of New England, 1987.

Greenbaum, Susan. *Afro-Cubans in Ybor City: A Centennial History.* Tampa: University of South Florida, 1986.

Greene, William Bradford. *Equality.* West Brookfield, MA: by the author, 1849.

———. *Mutual Banking.* West Brookfield, MA: by the author, 1850.

Gross, Miriam, ed. *The World of George Orwell.* New York: Simon and Schuster, 1971.

Gurin, Daniel. *Anarchism: From Theory to Practice.* New York: Monthly Review Press, 1970.

Harper, Clifford. *Anarchy: A Graphic Guide.* London: Camden Press, 1987.

Harris, Richard. *Death of a Revolutionary: Che Guevara's Last Mission.* New York: W. W. Norton, 1970.

Hart, John M. *Anarchism and the Mexican Working Class, 1860–1931.* Austin: University of Texas Press, 1978.

Hawxhurst, Joan C. *Mother Jones: Labor Crusader.* Austin, TX: Steck-Vaughn Company, 1994.

Heider, Ulrike. *Anarchism: Left, Right, and Green.* San Francisco: City Lights Books, 1994.

Helmer, Diana Star. *Women Suffragists.* New York: Facts on File, 1998.

Hine, Robert V. *Community on the American Frontier: Separate but Not Alone.* Norman: University of Oklahoma Press, 1980.

Hodges, Donald Clark. *Mexican Anarchism After the Revolution.* Austin: University of Texas Press, 1995.

Hoffman, Robert, ed. and trans. *Anarchism.* New York: Atherton Press, 1970.

Holloway, Mark. *Heavens on Earth: Utopian Communities in America, 1680–1880.* New York: Dover, 1966.

Horne, Alistair. *The Fall of Paris: The Siege and the Commune 1870–1871.* New York: Viking Penguin reprint 1981.

Horowitz, Irving L., ed. *The Anarchists.* New York: Dell, 1964.

Howe, Irving, comp. *Twenty-five Years of Dissent: An American Tradition.* New York: Methuen, 1979.

Hoyt, Edwin P. *The Palmer Raids, 1919–1920: An Attempt to Suppress Dissent.* New York: Seabury Press, 1969.

Hunter, Robert. *Violence and the Labor Movement.* 1914. Reprint New York: Arno Press and *New York Times,* 1969.

Huxley, Aldous. *Brave New World.* New York and London: Harper, 1946.

———. *Brave New World Revisited.* New York: Harper and Row, 1958.

Hyams, Edward. *Pierre-Joseph Proudhon: His Revolutionary Life, Mind, and Works.* New York: Taplinger Publishing, 1979.

Ilgenfritz, Elizabeth. *Anne Hutchinson.* New York: Chelsea House, 1991.

Intelligence Report, Issue 90, Montgomery, AL: Southern Poverty Law Center, Spring 1998.

Jacker, Corinne. *The Black Flag of Anarchy; Antistatism in the United States.* New York: Charles Scribner's Sons, 1968.

Jackson, J. Hampden. *Marx, Proudhon, and European Socialism.* New York: Collier Books, 1962.

James, Daniel. *Che Guevara: A Biography.* New York: Stein and Day, 1970.

James, Edward T., ed. *Notable American Women,* 3 vols. Cambridge: Harvard University Press, 1971.

Jerome, Judson. *Families of Eden: Communes and the New Anarchism.* New York: Seabury Press, 1974.

Jezer, Marty. *Abbie Hoffman: American Rebel.* New Brunswick, NJ: Rutgers University Press, 1992.

Joll, James. *The Anarchists.* Boston: Little, Brown, 1964.

Kaplan, Temma. *Anarchists of Andalusia, 1868–1903.* Princeton: Princeton University Press, 1977.

Kedward, Roderick. *The Anarchists: The Men Who Shocked an Era.* New York: American Heritage Press, 1971.

Keefer, Tom. "Marxism Vs. Anarchism," *New Socialist,* March 1996.

Kelly, Florence Finch. *Flowing Stream.* New York: E. P. Dutton, 1939.

Kendall, Walter. *The Revolutionary Movement in Britain, 1900—1921.* London: Weidenfeld and Nicolson, 1969.

Kern, Robert W. *Red Years/Black Years: A Political History of Spanish Anarchism, 1910–1937.* Philadelphia: Institute for the Study of Human Issues, 1978.

Kornbluh, Joyce L., ed. *Rebel Voices: An IWW Anthology.* Ann Arbor: University of Michigan Press, 1964.

———. *Rebel Voices: An IWW Anthology.* Expanded ed., Chicago: Charles H. Kerr, 1988.

Krimerman, Leonard I., and Lewis Parry, eds. *Patterns of Anarchy.* New York: Doubleday, 1966.

Kropotkin, Peter. *Memoirs of a Revolutionist.* Boston: Houghton Mifflin, 1889, 1905.

———. *Selected Writings on Anarchism and Revolution.* Edited by Martin A. Miller. Cambridge: MIT Press, 1970.

———. *The Conquest of Bread.* London: Chapman and Hall, 1906. Reprint New York: New York University Press, 1972.

———. *The Essential Kropotkin.* Edited by Emile Capouya and Keitha Tompkins. New York: Liveright, 1975.

———. *Fields, Factories, and Workshops.* Edited by Colin Ward. New York: Harper and Row, 1975.

Leech, Margaret. *In the Days of McKinley.* New York: Harper and Brothers, 1959.

Lehning, Arthur, ed. *Michael Bakunin: Selected Writings.* New York: Grove, 1975.

Leighten, Patricia Dee. *Re-ordering the Universe: Picasso and Anarchism, 1897–1914.* Princeton: Princeton University Press, 1989.

LeWarne, Charles Pierce. *Utopias on Puget Sound, 1885–1915.* Seattle: University of Washington Press, 1975.

Lockwood, George B. *The New Harmony Movement.* New York: D. Appleton, 1905.

Lockwood, Lee. "Still Radical After All These Years." *Mother Jones,* September/October 1993.

Long, Priscilla. *Mother Jones: Woman Organizer.* Boston: South End Press, 1976.

Lum, Dyer Daniel. *The Great Trial of the Chicago Anarchists.* Reprint of the 1886 ed., New York: Arno Press, 1969.

MacEoin, Gary. "Sanctuary Movement Lives on in New Interest, Commitment." *National Catholic Reporter,* April 3, 1998.

Machan, Tibor R., ed. *The Libertarian Reader.* Totowa, NJ: Rowman and Littlefield, 1982.

MacKinnon, Catherine A. *Toward a Feminist Theory of the State.* Cambridge: Harvard University Press, 1989.

MacLachlan, Colin M. *Anarchism and the Mexican Revolution: The Political Trials of Ricardo Flores Magón in the United States.* Berkeley: University of California Press, 1991.

Marsh, Margaret S. *Anarchist Women, 1870–1920.* Philadelphia: Temple University Press, 1981.

Marshall, Peter. *William Godwin.* New Haven: Yale University Press, 1984.

———. *Demanding the Impossible: A History of Anarchism.* London: HarperCollins, 1992.

Marshall, Peter, ed. *The Anarchist Writings of William Godwin.* London: Freedom Press, 1986.

Martin, James J. *Men Against the State.* Colorado Springs: Ralph Myles, 1970.

Masters, Anthony. *Bakunin, The Father of Anarchism.* New York: Saturday Review Press, 1974.

May, Eric Charles. "19 Arrested Protesting Gulf Action." *The Washington Post,* December 31, 1990.

McElroy, Wendy, ed. *Freedom, Feminism, and the State: An Overview of Individualist Feminism.* Washington, D.C.: Cato Institute, 1982.

McLean, George N. *The Rise and Fall of Anarchy in America.* New York: Haskell House, 1972.

McNulty, Timothy. "Jail Time Still Doesn't Deter Philip Berrigan." *Chicago Tribune,* June 20, 1994, Tempo Section.

Meltzer, Albert. *The Anarchists in London, 1935–1955.* Sanday, Orkney: Cienfuegos Press, 1976.

———. *The Anarcho-Quiz Book.* Black Flag, organ of the Anarchist Black Cross, 1976.

Meltzer, Milton. *Bread—and Roses: The Struggle of American Labor, 1865–1915.* New York: Knopf, 1967.

Miller, James. *"Democracy Is in the Streets": From Port Huron to the Siege of Chicago.* New York: Simon and Schuster, 1987.

Miller, Martin A. *Kropotkin.* Chicago: University of Chicago Press, 1976.

Mintz, Jerome R. *The Anarchists of Casas Viejas.* Chicago: University of Chicago Press, 1982.

Morton, Marian. *Emma Goldman and the American Left: "Nowhere at Home."* New York: Twayne, 1992.

Murray, Charles A. *What It Means to Be a Libertarian: A Personal Interpretation.* New York: Broadway Books, 1997.

Nehring, Neil. *Flowers in the Dustbin: Culture, Anarchy, and Postwar England.* Ann Arbor: University of Michigan Press, 1993.

Neill, A. S. *Summerhill: A Radical Approach to Child Rearing.* New York: Hart, 1960.

Nelson, Bruce C. *Beyond the Martyrs: A Social History of Chicago's Anarchists, 1870–1900.* New Brunswick, NJ: Rutgers University Press, 1988.

Newell, Peter. *The Forgotten Heroes: Makhno and Durruti.* London: Freedom Press, 1969.

Nisbet, Robert. *The Social Philosophers: Community and Conflict in Western Thought.* New York: T. Y. Crowell, 1973.

Nomad, Max. *Apostles of Revolution.* New York: Collier Books, 1961.

———. *Rebels and Renegades.* Freeport, NY: Books for Libraries Press, 1932, 1968.

Nordhoff, Charles. *The Communistic Societies of the United States: From Personal Observations.* New York: Dover Publications, 1966. Orig. publ. by Harper and Brothers, 1875.

Nozick, Robert. *Anarchy, State, and Utopia.* New York: Basic Books, 1974.

Nursey-Bray, Paul F., ed., with Jim Jose and Robyn Williams. *Anarchist Thinkers and Thought: An Annotated Bibliography.* New York: Greenwood Press, 1992.

O'Connor, Richard. *The German Americans: An Informal History.* Boston: Little, Brown, 1968.

Orwell, George. *Homage to Catalonia.* New York: Harcourt, Brace, 1952.

Osugi Sakae. *The Autobiography of Osugi Sakae.* Translated by Byron K. Marshall. Berkeley: University of California Press, 1992.

Palij, Michael. *The Anarchism of Nestor Makhno, 1918–1921: An Aspect of the Ukranian Revolution.* Seattle: University of Washington Press, 1976.

Parisi, Peter. *Artist of the Actual: Essays on Paul Goodman.* Metuchen, NJ, and London: Scarecrow Press, 1986.

Parsons, Albert Richard. *Anarchism: Its Philosophy and Scientific Basis, as Defined by Some of Its Apostles.* Chicago: Mrs. A. R. Parsons, Publisher, 1887. Reprint Westport, CT: Greenwood Press, 1970.

Parton, Mary Field, ed. *The Autobiography of Mother Jones.* Chicago: Charles H. Kerr, 1925, reprint 1972.

Paz, Abel, and Nancy Macdonald, trans. *Durruti: The People Armed.* Montreal: Black Rose Books, 1976.

Peck, James. *The Chomsky Reader.* New York: Pantheon Books, 1987.

Perlin, Terry M., ed. *Contemporary Anarchism.* New Brunswick, NJ: Transaction Books, 1979.

Pernicone, Nunzio. *Italian Anarchism, 1864–1892.* Princeton: Princeton University Press, 1993.

Plotkin, I. L. *Anarchism in Japan: A Study of The Great Treason Affair, 1910–1911.* Lewiston, NY: E. Mellen Press, 1990.

Polner, Murray. *Disarmed and Dangerous: The Radical Lives and Times of Daniel and Philip Berrigan.* Boulder: Westview Press, 1997.

Poole, David, comp. *Land and Liberty: Anarchist Influences in the Mexican Revolution.* Montreal: Black Rose Books, 1977.

Preston, William, Jr. *Aliens and Dissenters: Federal Suppression of Radicals, 1903–1933.* 2d ed. Urbana and Chicago: University of Illinois Press, 1994.

Proudhon, Pierre-Joseph. *Selected Writings of Pierre-Joseph Proudhon.* Edited by Stewart Edwards. Garden City, NY: Anchor Books, 1969.

Puente, Isaac. *Libertarian Communism.* Sydney, Australia: Monty Miller Press, 1985.

Pyziur, Eugene. *The Doctrine of Anarchism of Michael A. Bakunin.* Milwaukee: Marquette University Press, 1955.

Randall, Willard Sterne. *Thomas Jefferson: A Life.* New York: HarperCollins, 1993.

Raskin, Jonah. *For the Hell of It: The Life and Times*

of Abbie Hoffman. Berkeley: University of California Press, 1996.

Read, Herbert Edward, Sir. *Anarchy and Order: Essays in Politics.* Boston: Beacon Press, 1971.

Reed, James. *From Private Vice to Public Virtue: The Birth Control Movement and American Society Since 1830.* New York: Basic Books, 1978.

Reichert, William O. *Partisans of Freedom: A Study in American Anarchism.* Bowling Green, Ohio: Bowling Green University Popular Press, 1976.

Renshaw, Patrick. *The Wobblies: The Story of Syndicalism in the United States.* Garden City, NY: Anchor Books, 1967.

Reuters. "Activists Dump Dye in White House Fountain." *Los Angeles Times,* December 31, 1990.

Riazanov, David, and Joshua Kunitz, trans. *Karl Marx and Frederick Engels: An Introduction to Their Lives and Work.* New York: Monthly Review Press, 1973. Originally published in 1927.

Rice, Jon F. "Lucy Parsons: Chicago Revolutionary," *People's Tribune,* electronic edition, February 13, 1995.

Richards, Vernon. *Lessons of the Spanish Revolution, 1936–1939.* Enlarged ed. London: Freedom Press, 1972.

Riley, Thomas. "New England Anarchism in Germany." *New England Quarterly,* March 1945.

Ritter, Alan. *Anarchism: A Theoretical Analysis.* Cambridge: Cambridge University Press, 1980.

Roberts, John Morris. *History of the World.* New York and Oxford: Oxford University Press, 1993.

Robertson, Priscilla. *The Revolutions of 1848: A Social History.* Princeton: Princeton University Press, 1952.

Rocker, Rudolf. *Nationalism and Culture.* Los Angeles: Rocker Publications Committee, 1937.

———. *Pioneers of American Freedom.* Los Angeles: Rocker Publications Committee, 1949.

———. *The London Years.* London: Robert Anscombe, 1956.

———. *Anarchism and Anarcho-Syndicalism.* London: Freedom Press, 1988. Originally published as *Anarchosyndicalism* by Martin Secker and Warburg Ltd., 1938.

Rodriguez, Felix I. *Shadow Warrior.* New York: Simon and Schuster, 1989.

———. BBC documentary, "Executive Action," 1992.

Roediger, Dave, and Franklin Rosemont, eds. *Haymarket Scrapbook.* Chicago: Charles H. Kerr, 1986.

Rojo, Ricardo. *My Friend Che.* The Dial Press, 1968.

Rolland, Romain. *Mahatma Gandhi: The Man Who Became One with the Universal Being.* New York: The Century Co., 1924.

Roussopoulos, Dimitrios I., ed. *The Anarchist Papers 2.* Montreal and New York: Black Rose Books, 1989.

Runkle, Gerald. *Anarchism, Old and New.* New York: Delacorte Press, 1972.

Ryan, Henry Butterfield. *The Fall of Guevara.* New York: Oxford University Press, 1997.

Sachs, Emanie. *"The Terrible Siren": Victoria Woodhull, 1838–1927.* New York: Harper (1928).

Salerno, Salvatore. *Red November, Black November: Culture and Community in the Industrial Workers of the World.* Albany: State University of New York Press, 1989.

Scalapino, Robert A., and George T. Yu. *The Chinese Anarchist Movement.* Berkeley: Center for Chinese Studies, University of California, 1961. Reprint Westport, CT: Greenwood Press, 1980.

Schaack, Michael J. *Anarchy and Anarchists.* Chicago: J. J. Schulte, 1889. Reprint New York: Arno Press, 1977.

Schuster, Eunice M. *Native American Anarchism: A Study of Left-Wing American Individualism.* Northampton, MA: Smith College, 1932. Reprint New York: AMS Press, 1970.

Scrivener, Michael Henry. *Radical Shelley: The Philosophical Anarchism and Utopian Thought of Percy Bysshe Shelley.* Princeton: Princeton University Press, 1982.

Scudder, Horace E., ed. *The Complete Poetical Works of Percy Bysshe Shelley.* Boston and New York: Houghton Mifflin, 1901.

Shatz, Marshall S., ed. *The Essential Works of Anarchism.* New York: Bantam Books, 1971.

Shelden, Michael. *Orwell: The Authorized Biography.* New York: HarperCollins, 1991.

Shepherd, Naomi. *A Price Below Rubies: Jewish Women As Rebels and Radicals.* Cambridge: Harvard University Press, 1993.

Shotton, John. *No Master High or Low: Libertarian Education and Schooling, 1890–1990.* Bristol: Libertarian Education, 1993.

Shulman, Alix Kates. *To the Barricades: The Anarchist Life of Emma Goldman.* New York: Crowell, 1971.

Shulman, Alix Kates, ed. *Red Emma Speaks: Selected Writings and Speeches by Emma Goldman.* New York: Random House, 1972.

Also published as *Red Emma Speaks: An Emma Goldman Reader.* New York: Schocken Books, 1983.

Silverman, Henry J., ed. *American Radical Thought: The Libertarian Tradition.* Lexington, MA: D. C. Heath, 1970.

Smith, Gary. "Peace Warriors." *Washington Post Magazine,* June 5, 1988.

Smith, Gibbs M. *Joe Hill.* Salt Lake City: University of Utah Press, 1969.

Solomon, Martha. *Emma Goldman.* Boston: Twayne, Macmillan, 1987.

Sonn, Richard D. *Anarchism and Cultural Politics in Fin de Siècle France.* Lincoln: University of Nebraska Press, 1989.

———. *Anarchism.* New York: Twayne/ Macmillan, 1992.

Sperber, Jonathan. *The European Revolutions, 1848–1851.* New York: Cambridge University Press, 1994.

Spooner, Lysander. *The Unconstitutionality of Slavery,* 2d ed. Boston: B. Marsh, 1860. Reprint New York: Franklin, 1965.

———. *Natural Law or the Science of Justice.* Boston: by the author, 1870. On the internet at <http://www.mind-trek.com/treatise/ls-nl.htm>.

———. *The Collected Works of Lysander Spooner.* Biography and introduction by Charles Shively. Weston, MA: M and S Press, 1971.

St. Clair, William. *The Godwins and the Shelleys: A Biography of a Family.* Baltimore: Johns Hopkins University Press, 1989.

Stansky, Peter, and William Abrahams. *The Unknown Orwell.* New York: Knopf, 1972.

Steffy, Joan Marie. *The Cuban Immigrants of Tampa, Florida, 1886–1898.* Tampa: Unpubl. Thesis, University of South Florida, 1974.

Stern, Kenneth S. *A Force Upon the Plain: The American Militia Movement and the Politics of Hate.* New York: Simon and Schuster, 1996.

Stoehr, Taylor, ed. *Crazy Hope and Finite Experience: Final Essays of Paul Goodman.* San Francisco: Jossey-Bass, 1994.

Straub, Deborah Gillan, ed. *Contemporary Heroes and Heroines, Book II.* Detroit: Gale Research, 1992.

Suskind, Richard. *By Bullet, Bomb, and Dagger: The Story of Anarchism.* New York: Macmillan, 1971.

Taylor, Michael. *Anarchy and Cooperation.* London and New York: Wiley, 1976.

———. *Community, Anarchy, and Liberty.* Cambridge: Cambridge University Press, 1982.

Thompson, Fred W., and Patrick Murfin. *The IWW: Its First Seventy Years 1905–1975.* Chicago: Industrial Workers of the World, 1976.

Thoreau, Henry David. *Walden or, Life in the Woods and On the Duty of Civil Disobedience.* New York: New American Library, 1960.

Tierney, Kevin. *Darrow: A Biography.* New York: Thomas Y. Crowell, 1979.

Tindall, George Brown. *America: A Narrative History, vol. 2,* 2d ed. New York: W. W. Norton, 1988.

Tucille, Jerome. *Radical Libertarianism: A New Political Alternative.* New York: Harper and Row, 1970.

Tucker, Benjamin R. *Instead of a Book: By a Man Too Busy to Write One.* New York: Benjamin R. Tucker, 1897. Reprint New York: Haskell House, 1969.

Underhill, Lois Beach. *The Woman Who Ran for President: The Many Lives of Victoria Woodhull.* Bridgehampton, NY, and Lanham, MD: Bridge Works (1995).

van Creveld, Martin, ed. *The Encyclopedia of Revolutions and Revolutionaries: From Anarchism to Zhou Enlai.* New York: Facts on File, 1996.

Varias, Alexander. *Paris and the Anarchists: Aesthetes and Subversives During the Fin de Siècle.* New York: St. Martin's Press, 1996.

Veysey, Laurence. *The Communal Experience: Anarchist and Mystical Counter-Cultures in America.* New York: Harper and Row, 1973.

———. *The Communal Experience: Anarchist and Mystical Communities in Twentieth-Century America.* Chicago: University of Chicago Press, 1978.

Vincent, Steven K. *Between Marxism and Anarchism: Benoit Malon and French Reformist Socialism.* Berkeley: University of California Press, 1992.

Wackerman, Daniel T. "Mind's Eye.," (Interview) *America,* March 18, 1995.

Walter, Nicolas. *About Anarchism.* London: Freedom Press, 1969.

Werstein, Irving. *Pie in the Sky, an American Struggle: The Wobblies and Their Times.* New York: Delacorte, 1969.

Wexler, Alice. *Emma Goldman: An Intimate Life.* New York: Pantheon, 1984.

———. *Emma Goldman in Exile: From the Russian Revolution to the Spanish Civil War.* Boston: Beacon Press, 1989.

Whitman, Alden, ed. *American Reformers.* New York: H. W. Wilson, 1985.

Widmer, Kingsley. *Paul Goodman.* Boston: Twayne Publishers, 1980.

Williams, Roger L. *The French Revolution of 1870–1871.* New York: W. W. Norton, 1969.

Williams, Selma R. *Divine Rebel: The Life of Anne Marbury Hutchinson.* New York: Holt, Rinehart, and Winston, 1981.

Woodcock, George. *Anarchy or Chaos.* London: Freedom Press, 1944.

———. *Anarchism: A History of Libertarian Ideas and Movements.* Cleveland: World Publishing Company, 1962. Reprint New York: New American Library, 1974.

———. *Dawn and the Darkest Hour: A Study of Aldous Huxley.* New York: Viking Press, 1972.

———. *William Godwin: A Biographical Study.* Montreal and New York: Black Rose Books, 1989.

Woodcock, George, and Ivan Avakumovic. *The Anarchist Prince: A Biographical Study of Peter Kropotkin.* London: T.V. Boardman, 1950.

Woodcock, George, ed. *The Anarchist Reader.* Hassocks, England: Harvester Press; Atlantic Highlands, NJ: Humanities Press, 1977.

Yellen, Samuel. *American Labor Struggles.* New York: Harcourt, Brace, 1936.

Young, William, and David E. Kaiser. *Postmortem: New Evidence in the Case of Sacco and Vanzetti.* Amherst: University of Massachusetts Press, 1985.

Zarrow, Peter. *Anarchism and Chinese Political Culture.* New York: Columbia University Press, 1990.

Index